Do It Yourself

Visual Basic™ for Windows™

Second Edition

Do It Yourself

Visual Basic™
for Windows™
Second Edition

William J. Orvis

PUBLISHING

A Division of Prentice Hall Computer Publishing
11711 North College, Carmel, Indiana 46032 USA

To Julie, who fought off the kids, took care of Cub Scouts, bussed kids to school, coached soccer, represented GATE, bussed kids from school, secretaried PTA, doctored the animals, bussed kids to school, doctored Dad's animals, bussed kids from school, and even managed to do the laundry once in a while. Thank You.

International Standard Book Number: 0-672-30259-4
Library of Congress Catalog No.: 92-062394

94 93   8 7 6 5 4 3

Interpretation of the printing code: the rightmost double-digit number is the year of the book's printing; the rightmost single-digit number, the number of the book's printing. For example, a printing code of 92-1 shows that the first printing of the book occurred in1992.

Composed in ITC Garamond and MCPdigital typefaces by Prentice Hall Computer Publishing

Screen reproductions in this book were created by the means of the program Collage Plus from Inner Media, Inc., Hollis, NH.

Printed in the United States of America

Publisher
Richard K. Swadley

Acquisitions Manager
Jordan Gold

**Acquisitions and
Development Editor**
Greg Croy

Editors
Fran Hatton
Becky Freeman
Michael Cunningham

Technical Editor
Gary Entsminger

Editorial Assistant
Rosemarie Graham

**Director of Production
and Manufacturing**
Jeff Valler

Production Manager
Corinne Walls

Imprint Manager
Matthew Morrill

Production Analyst
Mary Beth Wakefield

Book Designer
Michele Laseau

**Proofreading/Indexing
Coordinator**
Joelynn Gifford

Cover Art
Dan Armstrong

Graphic Image Specialists
Jerry Ellis
Dennis Sheehan
Sue VandeWalle

Production
Katy Bodenmiller, Christine Cook,
Dennis Hager, Carla Hall-Batton,
Howard Jones, John Kane,
Sean Medlock, Angela Pozdol,
Linda Quigley, Michelle Self,
Greg Simsic, Angie Trzepacz,
Alyssa Yesh

Index
Suzanne Snyder

About the Author

William Orvis is an electronic engineer at the University of California's Lawrence Livermore National Laboratory, where he is involved in the large scale numerical modeling of solid state devices, the development of micron-sized vacuum microelectronic devices, and computer security research. (He describes himself as being a computer virus smasher.) Orvis received both B.S. and M.S. Degrees in Physics and Astronomy at the University of Denver in Colorado. He is the author of : *Do It Yourself Visual Basic for MS-DOS* (Sams Publishing, 1992), *ABC's of GW-BASIC* (Sybex 1990), *Excel Instant Reference* (Sybex 1989), *1-2-3 for Scientists and Engineers* (Sybex 1987, 2nd ed. 1991), and *Electrical Overstress Protection for Electronic Devices*, (Noyes Data Corporation, 1986). His books have been translated into Japanese, Italian, and Greek. He also has written for *Computers in Physics*, and *IEEE Circuits and Devices* magazines.

Overview

Contents

Part II: Opening Up Visual Basic

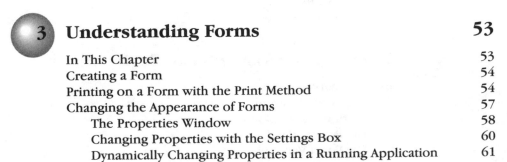

3 Understanding Forms   **53**

4 Using Strings — 75

5 Using Numbers and Control Structures — 97

Part III: A Comprehensive Example

15 Creating an Application   377

16 Mouse Events and Responding to Commands   417

Acknowledgments

I want to thank Greg Croy, Joe Wikert, and Jennifer Flynn from Sams Publishing who kept the pressure on to get this work done, and of course, all of the others at Sams who got this book from manuscript to print. Without them, you wouldn't be looking at anything now. I also want to thank Danny and Tien at Today Computers in Plestanton, California, for all the help straightening out some new hardware. A special thanks to Gary Entsminger who created the comprehensive example in Part III. Without his help, I wouldn't have gotten this done on time.

I want to thank BJ, Skye, and Sierra for not being too upset as I shut myself away for a second time to learn all the new features in Version 2 of Visual Basic; we start on your projects tomorrow. Well, maybe the day after tomorrow. I need some sleep first. Even Shane gets thanked this time, for not helping too much. Lastly, I want to thank Julie for keeping everything else going, and holding the house together while I worked on this book.

Trademark Acknowledgments

Sams Publishing has made every attempt to supply trademark information about company names, products, and services mentioned in this book. Trademarks indicated below were derived from various sources. Sams Publishing cannot attest to the accuracy of this information.

Microsoft BASIC is a registered trademark of Microsoft Corporation.

IBM is a registered trademark of International Business Machines Corporation.

Pac-Man is a registered trademark licensed to Atari by Namco-America, Inc.

Microsoft, MS-DOS, GW-BASIC, BASICA, and Excel are registered trademarks of Microsoft Corporation

QuickBASIC, Visual Basic, and Windows are trademarks of Microsoft Corporation

OS/2 is a registered trademark licensed to Microsoft Corporation

Apple and Macintosh are registered trademarks of Apple Computer, Inc.

Preface to the Second Edition

Visual Basic has come a long way in the last year, with many new features and improvements, including a toolbar to speed access to common commands, more uniformity among properties, and the capability to do larger applications. Also exciting is the release of Visual Basic for MS-DOS, which makes it relatively easy to port an application between the DOS and Windows environments.

I started beta testing the software about two months ago, and originally figured that revising this book for the second edition would not take too long. However, the more I got into the project, the more new features and capabilities I found, and consequently the less sleep I got trying to get it done by the publisher's deadline. Well, I didn't miss the deadline by too much, and I think you will appreciate the extra time we spent putting this together.

Who knows what Microsoft will come up with next year. (Visual Basic for Cray would be nice.)

William J. Orvis
Livermore, California

Introduction

Microsoft Visual Basic is a considerable branch in the development of BASIC computer languages—and all computer languages. Computer languages and the programs they create are essentially text files. The program is text, the results are text, and most of the output is text. Even on the Macintosh, where the Graphical User Interface (GUI) is a well-defined art, programs created with the BASIC interpreters and compilers are still text files that write or draw on a window rather than the whole screen. With Windows, as with the Macintosh operating system, you can create GUI applications, but the process is long and painful. Mountains of code must be written to create and draw windows on the screen, draw buttons and other controls on the windows, and track the keyboard and mouse.

Visual Basic, on the other hand, includes the GUI interface from the beginning. You start with a window (called a form), draw buttons or controls on it, and Visual Basic generates the code to create them on the screen and track the interactions of the mouse and keyboard with them. In fact, you never see any of that code; it is all handled in the background by Visual Basic. When something happens to a form or control (an event), Visual Basic passes control of a program to you, the programmer. For example, if you press a button by clicking it with the mouse, you don't have to worry about determining whether the button has been pressed or writing code to show the button being pressed. You just write the code that tells the computer what to do after the button is pressed.

In the past, up to 90 percent of the code written for a large application dealt with the user interface, with only 10 percent going to the meat of the application. So switching to a programming environment that handles most of the user interface for me (I still have to create the interface and draw it) results in a major change in my program development time. Now, in minutes, I can create a professional-looking Windows application, complete with windowed interface, buttons, check boxes and graphics windows. Rather than spending my time figuring out how to make the user interface work, I spend it making the meat of the program work, and work efficiently.

If you have programmed before, I think you will find this an exhilarating experience. If you have never programmed before, may you never have to find out what it's like not to have a Visual Basic-like environment.

In This Book

This book teaches the novice programmer the elements of the Visual Basic environment, the BASIC language, programming conventions and methods, and the development of a Graphical User Interface (GUI). Using the different GUI controls as a vehicle, this book guides the reader through the conventional BASIC language and the Visual Basic enhancements. With each control, I develop a significant programming example both to show off the control and to provide the user with a useful application. I hope that as you develop each application, you learn how to modify it to suit your particular needs. Throughout this particular book, I inserted sidebars called FYI-Ideas (set off with a light-bulb icon) to point you toward more advanced versions of the applications.

Many books develop simple trivial examples to demonstrate programming and the language. These examples are fine for demonstrating a piece of the language, but they don't show how larger applications work, and they aren't useful later on. The example programs used in this book are not only vehicles for learning the language, but are meant to be usable additions to your programming library. Some of them are slightly longer than you might be used to seeing in a book on a programming language. However, I think the increased functionality of the programs is well worth it.

Part I is an introduction to Windows, Windows programming, and Visual Basic programming. This part explains how to use the Windows environment and the basics of Windows programming. The Visual Basic programming environment is then examined, along with an overview of the program development process.

Part II is a tutorial on Visual Basic programming. In Part II, each Visual Basic object introduced in Part I is examined in more detail. Visual Basic objects are the forms, buttons, and text boxes that make up the visual interface of a Visual Basic program. In addition, as the part progresses through the objects, the BASIC programming language (which ties all these objects together), is also developed.

Part III is a comprehensive example. It will take you through the initial design of application, its user interface, and its data structures, as well as through development of the actual code modules to the final compiled application. This part will give you a complete overview of application developments.

Part IV is an Appendix to Visual Basic, containing a description of the run-time Library, a table of the ASCII (ANSI) character codes, and a table of the keycodes. The ASCII character codes are the standard encoding used to store strings of characters in a BASIC program, and the keycodes are used to identify the specific keys on the keyboard.

Who Can Use this Book?

This book is for the novice computer programmer who wants to learn Visual Basic programming in the Windows environment, and for the advanced or not-so-advanced computer user who wants to learn programming. It's also for the programmer who wants to learn about programming in the Windows environment, without the mass of code needed in other languages that tends to obscure an understanding of the environment. Advanced programmers will probably find this book too slow for them, but if they glance at the language syntax in each chapter and work through the examples, they will get a useful understanding of the language, and of programming in the Windows environment.

The direction of this book is toward the home and small business computer user, though large business and technical computer users will have no problem applying the techniques to their work. The problems are all somewhat generic in their application, so they can readily be adapted to a particular situation. I often indicate extensions to a problem, and point the reader in the direction needed to achieve them.

What You Must Know

You must be familiar with using Windows and Windows methods. I don't expect you to be an expert, but you must at least be able to launch Windows, launch a program under Windows, maximize and minimize windows, and switch between applications. If you have never used Windows before, play with it for an hour or two. Run a word processor or a spreadsheet program and move the windows around, resize them, and try the commands and controls. The Windows package contains lots of good information and examples to help you learn it quickly.

What You Must Have

Visual Basic Version 2.0 requires some specific hardware and software. You must have a computer with at least a 286 processor and one megabyte (1M) of memory. To efficiently use Windows, 2M of memory or more is better, and considering the current price of memory, I think you will find it well worth the cost. You need a graphics monitor and card such as the CGA, EGA, VGA, 8514, Hercules, or compatible. I wouldn't recommend anything less than an EGA system in order to use the full capabilities of Windows or Visual Basic. You need a hard disk drive with approximately 18M free for the complete Visual Basic Professional package. The standard version requires about 6M for the complete package. You can get away with about 3.5M if you leave out everything but the Visual Basic Program and its libraries. You also need a mouse. I know the Windows documentation says you don't need a mouse, and perhaps you can operate everything without one, but get a mouse anyway. Using Windows without a mouse is like driving a boat without a rudder. You probably can make the boat turn with a lot of hard work, but a rudder makes things much simpler and smoother. The same goes for a mouse and Windows.

For software, you need DOS 3.1 or later and Windows 3.0 or later. If Windows isn't installed on your machine, you must install it first, before trying to install Visual Basic. Follow the directions in the Windows package, and maybe you will get lucky the first time. Windows sometimes needs some experimentation before it works properly. After Windows is installed and running, install Visual Basic. Installing Visual Basic is easy after installing Windows.

Visual Basic 1.0 users should upgrade to Version 2.0 if you can. The improvements are worth it. Most of this book is applicable to Version 1.0 of Visual Basic. The main differences are locations of the commands on the menus and the Properties window. If you look a little, you will find the Version 1.0 commands specified in the instructions.

I made the mistake of upgrading my hardware and installing Windows at the same time, and it took a while to get all the right drivers and memory managers in place and working together. Then I ran into an incompatibility between my disk manager software and Windows. It turned out that I needed to change only a simple software switch, but it took a while to find it. Much thanks to Danny and Tien at Today Computers in Plesanton, California, who helped me straighten everything out.

What Conventions Do You Use?

As I develop the language elements, I often resort to syntax statements to describe the syntax of that element. In Part III of this book, every function, statement, and method includes a syntax statement. A syntax statement is an expression of the grammar of the computer language, showing where the commas go and how the words are spelled. The format of a syntax statement is as follows.

- Words and symbols that must be typed exactly as they are shown in the syntax statement are in `monospace bold`.

- Placeholders for variable names or constant values are in *monospace italic*, and, where appropriate, are followed by the variable type suffix characters. The variable type suffix characters indicate the type of variable or number that is expected at this location. The types are, % (Integer), & (Long integer), ! (Single precision floating point), # (Double precision floating point), @ (Currency), and $ (String). These types will be explained in more detail later.

- Alternate entries (where you must make a choice) are separated with vertical bars (|) and surrounded by braces ({ }).

- Repeated clauses are followed by an ellipsis (...).

- Optional entries are surrounded by square brackets([ ]).

For example,

```
On [Local] Error {GoTo line|Resume Next|GoTo 0}
```

In the example, the key words **On**, **Local**, **Error**, **GoTo**, **Resume**, and **Next** must be typed exactly as shown so they are in monospace bold. The words **On** and **Error** are required, but [**Local**] is optional, so it is surrounded by square brackets. At the end of the statement are three clauses from which you must select one, so they are surrounded with braces and separated by vertical bars. The word *line* is a placeholder for a variable or a constant value so it is in monospace italic.

A second example is

```
MsgBox(msg$[,type%[,title$]])
```

In this example, the keyword **MsgBox**, the two parentheses, and the two commas must be typed exactly as shown, so they are bold. The first argument, *msg$*, is a placeholder for a string. The argument *type%* is a placeholder for an integer, and *title$* is a placeholder for another string. The first argument is required, but the second two are optional. The bracket-within-bracket arrangement indicates that if the third argument, *title$,* is used, the second argument, *type%,* must also be included.

Outside of the syntax statements, the following conventions are used to highlight different items.

- Words, such as the code in programming examples, that the reader must type exactly as they are written, are in `monospace bold`.

- The access keys ("hot" keys) for keyboard access to menu items and buttons are underlined on the computer but are bold in the text of this book (the **File** menu, for example).

- Some keyboards have Return keys and others have Enter. I use Enter in this text, but these keys are interchangeable, so use the one on your keyboard whenever I use Enter.

- Visual Basic keywords, variable names, methods, procedures, functions, events, properties, and objects are in computer font, such as `End`, `Open`, `MsgBox`, and `Form1`.

- Visual Basic buttons, such as **View Code**, **Insert**, and **OK** are in **bold**.

- In the step-by-step programming examples, Visual Basic's drawing tools are used to create the various buttons and boxes that make up the visual interface of the example. Whenever a drawing tool is needed to complete a step described in this book, an icon representing the particular tool appears next to the step.

 For example, the icon for a picture box is at the beginning of this paragraph. Use these icons to insure that you are using the correct tool. The Toolbox window is described in Chapter 2, "Learning the Visual Basic Environment."

- The length of a line in Visual Basic is occasionally longer than can be printed in the book. Visual Basic statements cannot be arbitrarily split into two lines because the program will not continue working. Therefore, when a line must be split in this book, it is prefaced with the character ➡. Note that when you type a line followed by one that is started with this character, the two lines must be joined for the program to work. For example, in the following procedure, the first and second lines must be typed as a single line in a Visual Basic program or you receive a syntax error.

```
Sub LeftArrow_MouseDown (Button As Integer,
  Shift As Integer, X As Single, Y As Single)
➡LeftArrow.BackColor = BLACK
End Sub
```

Where You Can Find the Examples

If you don't feel like typing all the examples in this book, they are available on disk directly from the author for $20. In addition to the examples from this book, the disk includes some simple applications and pieces of test code for the advanced methods not covered in this book, such as Dynamic Data Exchange (DDE) and Dynamic Link Libraries (DLL). To get the disk, use the coupon at the end of this book. Note that Prentice Hall Computer Publishing is not involved in the sale of this disk and makes no warranty for it.

Boxed Notes

Occasionally, a piece of information or advice does not fit within the current tutorial. Notes of this type are separated from the rest of the text of the chapter in a boxed note, as shown here.

This is an example of a boxed note.

Programming tips and shortcuts also are separated from the examples in a tip, as shown here.

Holding down the Ctrl, Alt, Shift, and CapsLock keys with the right hand while pressing Shift, Enter, and Backspace with the left hand is guaranteed to get you strange looks.

Tips and notes that warn of problems or possibly unwanted results are inserted as cautions.

If you try the last tip, you may look dumb.

Finally, all the examples represent fairly basic applications that can be expanded and modified to show a lot more functionality. In these cases, I describe some of the possible changes that can be made and briefly point you in the right direction to make those changes in an FYI-Idea box.

Wow!! I just had a great idea and I want to share it with you!!

Where Are You Going?

You are going on a wonderful trip where you create your own worlds, travel among friends or enemies, win battles, and become the master of your computer. You are going to teach this machine who is boss and make it politely carry out your wishes.

Part I

Visual Basic Basics

Windows Programming

Early versions of high-level computer languages, such as BASIC and FORTRAN, were largely text oriented. The program was a text file typed on cards or at a Teletype, and the results were printed on a line printer or Teletype. With the help of special libraries and graphical output devices such as plotters and film recorders, they could do graphics, but the graphics were not real-time. They usually arrived on a roll of microfilm an hour or two after the program had finished running.

With the advent of glass-fronted terminals (terminals with the output on a CRT rather than on paper), programmers started drawing graphics on the terminals. However, the graphics were still a part of the output, they only got to you faster than microfilm.

The Graphical User Interface (GUI) actually started at the Xerox Palo Alto Research Center (Xerox PARC), where engineers developed a graphical interface complete with icons and a mouse. Unfortunately, that project was not a commercial success and largely disappeared. On the other hand, a visit to Xerox PARC by Steve Jobs, one of the founders of Apple

Computers, provided the inspiration for the Macintosh's GUI. Because of the popularity of the Macintosh interface, Microsoft developed Windows, and Microsoft and IBM developed OS/2 for the PC and PC-compatible computers.

One of the basic tenets of the modern operating systems is the use of reusable blocks of code, and the even more modern concept of a code object. An *object* is an abstraction of the world of subroutines and code to the real world of physical things. Objects consist of such things as windows, buttons, and menus, and are much more than reusable blocks of code. An object is a combination of the data that comprises the object and the code that manipulates that data. For example, a button consists of the drawing of the button on the screen, several parameters describing where and how large to make the button, and the code that draws the button on the screen and initiates the action of the button when it is pressed.

Much of a modern operating system comprises large libraries of these reusable objects, the use of which significantly reduces the amount of time needed to develop a new application. When you want a button on your application, you no longer have to spend several days coding it from scratch; instead, you spend a few minutes attaching a button object to your program and passing it the information about where and how big you want the button. The button object actually draws the button on the screen and changes the image of the button to simulate a pressed button.

In This Chapter

This chapter gives you some background on Windows, and the Object-Oriented Programming (OOP) methods used in Visual Basic. This is not a detailed discussion of Windows' methods or Object-Oriented Programming, but a brief overview of these two topics. This chapter covers

- Using Windows.
- The Windows Environment.
- Object-Oriented Programming.
- Object-Oriented Programming with Visual Basic.

Using Windows

A window in Windows 3.0 and later versions contains several distinct parts—see Figure 1.1. Along the top is a Title bar. The title in the center of the Title bar can be several different things. The usual choices are the name of the running application or the file name of the document the application is working on. On the right side of the window are two buttons. The left button is the **Minimize** button. The right one is the **Maximize/Restore** button, which is a **Maximize** button when a window is normal size, and a **Restore** button when a window is maximized. A **Maximize** button has a single vertical arrow on it and a **Restore** button has a vertical double arrow on it.

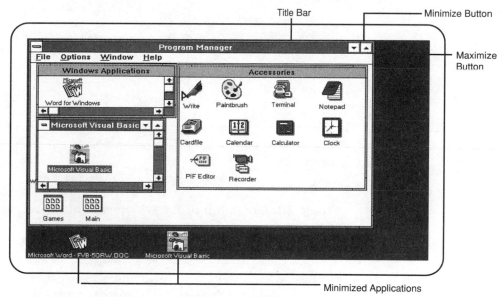

Figure 1.1. *A program window of normal size.*

On the left side of the Title bar is the **Control** button that opens the Control menu, as shown in Figure 1.2. To open the Control menu, click the button with the mouse, or press Alt-spacebar (for a program window), or Alt-hyphen (for a document Window). You can also press Alt and use the left and right arrow keys to move the focus to the button, then press Enter.

The Control menu contains the Restore, Move, Size, Minimize, Maximize, and Close commands. Program windows also have the Switch To command on the Control menu. The primary use of these commands is for running windows without a mouse. To select a command without a mouse, press the underlined letter (the hot key) or move the focus with the arrow keys and press Enter when the command is selected. To select a command with the mouse, click the command. Table 1.1 describes the operation of the buttons on the title bar and the commands on the Control menu.

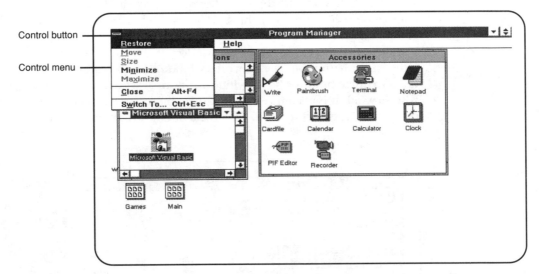

Figure 1.2. *A maximized program window with the Control menu open.*

Table 1.1. Operation of the Windows controls on the Control menu.

Command	Function
Restore	Returns a maximized or minimized window to its initial size. To restore a maximized window with the mouse, click the **Restore** button, double-click the Title bar, or click the **Restore** command on the Control menu. To restore a minimized application, double-click the minimized application's icon.

Command	Function
Move	Moves the window with the arrow keys. Press Enter when you have the window where you want it. To move the window with the mouse, place the mouse pointer on the Title bar, press down on the left mouse button, and drag the window to its destination.
Size	Resizes the window with the arrow keys. To resize the window using the mouse, place it on the border of the window (pointer should change to double-ended arrow), then press the left mouse button and drag the border to the new position.
Mi**n**imize	Reduces the window to an icon, such as those along the bottom of Figure 1.1. To minimize the application with the mouse, click the **Minimize** button.
Ma**x**imize	Expands the window to fill the screen, such as in Figure 1.2. To maximize the window with the mouse, click the **Maximize** button, or double-click the Title bar.
Close	Closes the window; this action ends the application if the window is an application window. To close the window with the mouse, double-click the button that opens the Command menu.
Switch To	Brings up a list so you can switch to another running application. To change applications with the mouse, click the applications window. You also can cycle through a list of the open applications by pressing Alt, Tab, or Esc.

The Windows Environment

The Windows environment maintains the visual interface of a Windows program. It also keeps track of which code is running, and what resources that code needs. As it is currently implemented, Windows is a shell over the DOS operating system. Windows also provides a large library of functions to make developing a Windows program much simpler. All the functions to create and manage windows are available in the system, so a programmer does not have to develop these functions on his or her own. These libraries not only make programming easier, but make programs more consistent with each other so you have less to learn in order to use a new program.

A Shell Over DOS

The Windows environment is a shell over the DOS operating system that provides the control and capability to run multiple applications in a graphical, "windowed," user interface. A shell is a program that forms an interface between DOS and the user. It accepts user commands, and issues the respective DOS commands. In Windows, multiple applications can run simultaneously, with each given one or more windows on the screen to draw on and a piece of memory to run in. The Windows operating system manages the visual interface, allocates the memory to different programs, records which program is running, and provides access to the disk drives.

Memory and Screen Management

Each running application appears in one or more windows on the screen, with the active application's windows in front. Applications also can have document windows within their program windows that contain documents. Each application must stay in its assigned window and block of memory, otherwise bad things can happen. In a 286 machine, any application that uses memory outside of its assigned area causes problems by destroying the other application in the area it used. In 386 and later machines with Windows running in 386 enhanced mode, the hardware prevents an application from moving out of its assigned area by not allowing any memory accesses outside of that area.

Because not all computers are 386 machines, the Windows programmer must ensure that his or her code does not access memory outside of its assigned memory blocks. The operating system does take care of assigning and managing those blocks, however.

Multitasking

In addition to managing memory, the Windows operating system manages task-switching between multiple running applications. In most cases, the application in the foreground is using most the CPU time; however, the system and other applications can also run in the background when the foreground application isn't busy. The Multitasking method used in Windows is not preemptive, meaning it does not interrupt a running application to run another but depends on the benevolence of the running application to yield time to the system. If a Windows application does not occasionally yield the CPU to the system, background jobs won't run, and the system won't update windows or handle the peripheral devices such as the printer.

The Windows programmer must ensure that his or her program regularly yields control to the system. The system then takes care of its tasks, and passes control to one of the programs running in the background. When the background program passes control back to the system, the system then activates the foreground job again.

Libraries of Windows Functions

The Windows operating system contains a large library of functions, available for any application to use. There are functions to create the visual environment such as windows and menus, functions to manage memory, functions to communicate with other applications, functions to communicate with system resources such as the printer and the disk drives, and general functions to facilitate drawing pictures.

These functions are stored in Dynamic Link Libraries (DLLs), which are accessible by any running program. They are called Dynamic Link Libraries because they don't have to be attached to a program to be used but are dynamically linked to it as needed at run time. All these functions significantly reduce the amount of coding a programmer must do, by providing most of the standard functions in a ready-to-use format.

Device Independence

One of the biggest headaches found when creating an application on a DOS machine is the large number of different peripheral devices that you, the programmer, must be prepared to handle. It's not uncommon for an application program to come with a hundred device drivers to handle all the different types of monitors and printers that could possibly be attached to a system. With Windows, the operating system communicates with all the devices and provides a standard interface for all programs to use. Thus, a Windows programmer no longer has to worry about what monitor or printer is attached to a system; she or he simply prints on the assigned window or to the standard printer.

Language Types

There are basically two different types of languages available on a computer, Interpreted and Compiled. The difference between these two is how a program is executed, not in the physical structure of the language. When a code is first written, it resides in a file in text form. An interpreter reads each line of that code, converts the line into machine language commands and then executes them. The machine language commands are the numeric codes that the CPU understands. When the code for one line has run, the interpreter moves to the next line, and converts and executes it. The benefits of an interpreted language are almost immediate execution of a code after a change, modification of a running application, and simplified error detection and correction.

A compiler, on the other hand, first converts a whole program into machine language codes then stores those codes in a file. That file is now an executable program that can be run directly without further interpretation. The benefits of a compiled code are increased speed over an interpreted code, and stand-alone execution. A compiled code runs faster because the lines of code are already in machine language form and don't have to be reinterpreted each time they are executed. The increase in speed can be a factor of 100 or more over interpreted codes. An interpreted code must have the interpreter in memory as well as the code. After compilation, the compiler is no longer needed and the code can run by itself.

Visual Basic is both an interpreter and a compiler. The interpreter is used to speed code development, and the compiler is used to increase the speed of the code after development is complete.

Object-Oriented Programming

Object-oriented programming is the current development in programming methodology. This method bundles code and data into somewhat autonomous objects. The idea is that when you create an object to do something, you no longer have to know how it works, you simply pass it messages. That way, an object created in one program can be reused easily in another.

Objects

With the introduction of Visual Basic, Microsoft has made a large advance in the field of Object-Oriented Programming (OOP). Not only does Visual Basic have objects, but the objects are real, touchable things like buttons and boxes. Other object-oriented languages create objects with an object command of some sort that defines a block of code and data as an object. You are then supposed to imagine that object as a "thing" with features you can use. Visual Basic makes it easier by making the object a visible thing rather than a coding abstraction.

The main object in a Visual Basic program is the form. A form is a window that you build an application on. On the Form you attach Controls, such as command buttons, option buttons, check boxes, text boxes, labels, and scroll bars. Each of these is a Visual Basic object. To attach an object to a form, you draw it with the mouse. The whole visual interface of a Visual Basic program is drawn rather than coded.

Events

Objects communicate with each other, with the system, and with the program using events. Events are actions that an object might want to respond to. When the mouse is moved and a mouse button is clicked, the system keeps track of where the mouse pointer is and what object was under it when it was clicked. If the object was a button, the system sends a `Click` event to the button object. The button object visually simulates a pressed button and passes a `button_click` event to the program. If the programmer writes a procedure to handle `button_click` events, that procedure gets control and carries out its function. When that function is complete, control passes back to the system to wait for the next event.

As a programmer, you have the option to respond to numerous events passed to you by the objects that make up your program. These events include things like clicking or double-clicking an object, or pressing a key while the object has the focus. Chapter 17, "Events," in Part III of this book lists all the events you can respond to. To respond to an event, you create an event procedure with the name

```
object_event
```

which is then executed whenever the object passes on that event.

Objects don't pass all events to the program; many events are handled by the object or by the Windows operating system. For example, if you drag the edge of a window, you can change its size. Resizing the window is handled by the operating system; you, the programmer, don't have to do anything, though you will be passed a `Resize` event by the window (called a form in Visual Basic), to inform you that a change has taken place.

Methods

Objects are not simply bundled code blocks, but a bundling of data and the code that manipulates it. Every object contains code to manipulate its own data, known as methods. To invoke a method, type the object name, a dot, then the method name. Following the method name are any arguments the method needs. For example,

```
Form!PrintForm
```

This is a statement executing the Form's `PrintForm` method. The `PrintForm` method prints the contents of a Form (a Visual Basic window) on the printer. Another example follows.

```
Form!Print "Good Morning"
```

Here, `Print` is another method contained in the Form object that prints on a Form. In this case, it prints the text `"Good Morning"` on the Form.

Properties

The data contained in an object is stored in its properties. Properties not only contain the data stored in an object, such as the text to be printed in the `Printer` object, but also the object's dimensions, color, and numeric codes that specify its capabilities. For example, go back to the form object, which has a property called `BorderStyle`. Setting the `BorderStyle` property to `1 - Fixed Single` prevents a form from being resized by dragging its borders. Changing `BorderStyle` to `2 - Sizable`, makes it possible to change the size of the object by dragging its borders. Chapter 16, "Properties," in Part III of this book lists all the properties of the different objects.

Inheritance

Inheritance is the property of OOP where an object inherits the methods of the objects from which it is made. When you draw a label on a form, the form inherits the label's properties. For example, the `Caption` property of a label contains the text printed on the label. If the label is named `Label1` (all objects have names), and it is drawn on `Form1`, then `Form1` inherits the `Caption` property, which is accessed as follows.

```
Form1!Label1.Caption
```

All the properties of objects drawn on a form are accessed in this way.

Forms also inherit the methods of the objects, so when a form has a Picture box drawn on it, the form inherits the Picture box's `Print` method. The form can now print on a Picture box.

Visual Basic, the Next Step

Visual Basic represents the next step in Object-Oriented Programming. In Visual Basic, not only is code and data encapsulated, it even looks like the object it represents. In most object-oriented languages, you access a button object and tell it its location and size with lines of code. Only after you run your program can you actually see what it looks like. In Visual Basic, button objects look like buttons rather than lines of code. No longer do you have to imagine what it will look like, you draw it on a form with a button drawing tool. Check boxes, Option buttons, and all the standard Windows objects look like the object they represent.

What You Have Learned

This chapter presented a brief overview of the Windows environment and the use of Object-Oriented Programming in Visual Basic. The intent here is to give you a feeling for the methods and procedures discussed in this book. For more information on Windows methods, see the Microsoft Windows User's Guide included in your Windows package. For more information on programming with Visual Basic, read on; an adventure begins.

Learning the Visual Basic Environment

Visual Basic is more than a programming language—it's a complete environment for developing Windows applications. This environment includes a program editor to create and modify the code you write, an interpreter to execute an application within the environment, a compiler to turn an application into stand-alone code that runs in the Windows environment, and a debugger to determine why an application does not work. Visual basic is unique in that only a few lines of code are needed to create a complete, working Windows application. In most programming languages, it takes a hundred or so lines of code simply to open a window, let alone create anything with it.

In This Chapter

In this chapter, you learn the application and operation of all the different commands and windows of the Visual Basic environment. The purpose of this chapter is to give you the flavors of the Visual Basic environment, and teach you how to develop programs in that environment. If you are concerned when you find that many of the descriptions are superficial, don't be; the next few chapters cover the individual parts more completely. For now, get a feel for the overall structure of Visual Basic and how the windows and commands work together to make a program. Specifically, this chapter shows you how to

- Use the Visual Basic windows.

- Use the menu commands.

- Use tools from the Tool window to create controls.

- Create a Windows application.

- Save and retrieve an application.

- Compile an application.

Starting Visual Basic

Like most Windows applications, Visual Basic is extremely simple to start. First, find the Visual Basic icon in one of the Program Manager's Group windows. When you install Visual Basic with the Setup program, it usually places the icon in a special Microsoft Visual Basic Group window by itself. When you find the icon, simply double-click it. Visual Basic opens to the environment shown in Figure 2.1. Visual Basic 1.0 users will see a different screen. The main difference is the properties bar is replaced with a tool bar, and the properties are now in a properties window.

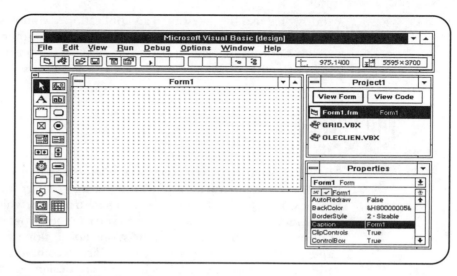

Figure 2.1. *The Visual Basic screen at startup.*

Negotiating the Windows

The first things you see when Visual Basic opens are four windows: the Form window (Form1), the Project window (Project1), the Properties window, and on the left side, the Toolbox window. Along the top, just below the Menu bar, is the Toolbar. Three other windows are opened as you need them: the Code window, the Color Palette window, and the Menu Design window. You can access hidden or closed windows from either the Windows menu on the menu bar or from the Project window. Two other windows, Debug and Procedures, can be opened only when a running program has been stopped with a Stop statement or a Break command.

The Project Window

The Project window is home for the Visual Basic application. The names of all the files and modules that comprise an application reside in the Project

window. It's also the gateway to an application's windows. By selecting a Form or module in the Project window and pressing either the **View Form** or **View Code** button, you can bring the selected Form or Code window to the front so that you can edit it.

The Form Window

The Form window, or Form, lies to the left of the Project window in Figure 2.1. It is the foundation of your application's user interface. All your buttons, Text boxes, and Lists are attached to a Form, which becomes the application window that you see when you run your program. The simplest application usually consists of at least one Form, although an application can contain as many Forms as are necessary to complete the application. Although all Forms are visible when you are designing your application, Forms can be made visible or invisible by your program. Consequently, only the Forms that have to be seen are visible on-screen when your application runs.

The Toolbox Window

The Toolbox window contains all the objects that can be placed on a Form. An object is a programming abstraction relating a physical object and the code attached to it. That is, an object is something that has physical presence on the screen, or at least corresponds to a physical presence in a computer application, such as a Timer. The following list of icons shows all the objects on the Toolbox window that are included with Visual Basic. The last five are new in Version 2.0.

With the professional version of Visual Basic, you can create custom controls that can be added to the Toolbox window and used like built-in controls. Custom controls also are available from third party programming.

 Picture box—Displays a picture.

 Label—Displays text Labels that the user cannot edit.

 Text box—Displays or inputs text that the user can edit.

Frame—Provides a visual frame for combining controls.

Command button—A button that causes the application to take a particular action.

Check box—A button for setting nonexclusive options.

Option button—A button for setting mutually exclusive options.

Combo box—A combined Text box and List box.

List box—A box containing a list of items.

Horizontal Scroll bar—An input device for setting a value visually with a horizontal scale.

Vertical Scroll bar—An input device for setting a value visually with a vertical scale.

Timer—An alarm clock that causes an event to take place at a certain time.

Drive List box—A List box that contains all the disk drives available.

Directory List box—A List box that contains all the subdirectories in the current directory.

File List box—A List box that contains all the files in the current directory.

Shape—For drawing circles, squares, rectangles, and ellipses on a form.

Line—For drawing lines on a form.

Image—Simpler version of a Picture box.

Grid—Spreadsheet like row/column grid of values.

OLE Client—For imbedding an OLE object in a program.

To attach an object, select it on the Toolbox window by clicking it with the mouse. Move the cursor to where you want the object's upper-left corner to be positioned. Hold down the left mouse button, move the mouse pointer to the lower-right corner of the object, and release the mouse button.

To reshape an object, select it and place the pointer on one of the black selection rectangles that surround the object. Press the left mouse button, and drag the rectangle until the object is the desired shape.

To move an object, select it by clicking it with the mouse, then hold down the left mouse button and drag the object to the desired location. Go ahead and create a few controls on Form1 and experiment with them a little. You can't hurt anything by doing so.

The Properties Window

The Properties window (Figure 2.2) is a feature unique to Visual Basic. All the forms and controls have properties such as color, size, and location. With the Properties window, you select a property and change its value. The Properties window consists of two text boxes and the Property list. The upper text box is the Object box, and contains the name of the object whose properties are to be set. Initially, the Object box contains the name of the currently selected control. Clicking the arrow on its left displays a list of all the controls on the current form. The second text box is the Settings box, which works with the Property list to set the properties of the selected object. The Property list contains the name of each property and its current value. Clicking a value inserts it into the Settings box so that you can change it.

Figure 2.2. *The Properties window for a form.*

For example, start Visual Basic (if it isn't running) and click Form1. Figure 2.2 shows the Properties window with the form's Caption property selected. The caption of a form is the title in the title bar at the top of the form. When a property is selected, its current value is displayed in the Settings box. If a property has a fixed set of allowed values, you can click the arrow on the right side of the Settings box which displays a list of allowed values for you to choose. Also, double clicking a value in the Property list cycles you through the list of allowed values. In Figure 2.2, the value of the Caption property is Form1. Because this property is a title, it can have any value you desire, but that value must be typed in the Settings box.

Select FontName from the Property list and click the arrow to the right of the Settings box. You see a list like the one in Figure 2.3, which shows all the Fonts available on your system. Your list might be different, depending on the fonts you have installed.

Figure 2.3. *Using the Settings box.*

To change the font used for printed text, simply select the new font from the list and click the box with the check mark in it (the box that falls to the left of the Settings box). The box containing an X is a cancel box. If clicked, it returns the Property to its original value.

The properties listed in the Properties window are only those properties that can be set at design time, that is, when you are writing your program. Forms and controls also have other properties that can only be set at runtime by your program. A Visual Basic program can set or change most of the properties at runtime. This topic is discussed in greater detail in Chapter 3, "Understanding Forms."

In Version 1 of Visual Basic, the properties are set in the Properties bar instead of the Properties window. The Properties bar replaces the toolbar and has two edit boxes, the Property list and the Setting box. Except for the location, these edit boxes are similar to the Setting box and Properties list in Version 2 and later.

The Code Window

Associated with each Form is a Code window, shown in Figure 2.4, that contains the BASIC code for the Form and for all the objects attached to it. You access the Code window from the Project window by selecting the Form and pressing the **View Code** button. You also can access the Code window by double-clicking the interior of the Form or any control on the Form or by executing the Code command on the View menu. Actual BASIC code resides in the Code windows of a Visual Basic program. Code windows are attached also to modules (discussed later), which are places to store code not associated with any specific Form or Code control.

The two drop-down menus at the top of the window in Figure 2.4 are for creating a code template to use with the Form. On the left, the Object menu lists all the objects (buttons, Text boxes, and so on) attached to the Form, including the Form itself. On the right, the Procedure menu lists all the events (mouse click, keystroke, and so forth) associated with the currently selected object. When you select an Object and an Event, Visual Basic automatically inserts the correct procedure header and footer in the Code window. You could type the header and footer in the window, but by using the menus you ensure that the format and spelling are correct.

The Color Palette Window

The Color Palette window, which is shown in Figure 2.5, is used to select colors visually. The Color Palette window normally is not visible, so you must activate it with the Color Palette command in the Window menu.

Colors and patterns are defined in Visual Basic with large, unintuitive hexadecimal numbers (base 16). The Color Palette window makes selecting a color much more straightforward.

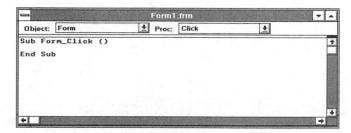

Figure 2.4. *A Visual Basic Code window.*

The Color Palette window changes the colors of the front-most Form, or the colors of the active object on the front-most Form. The Color Palette window is activated also by the Settings box on the Properties window when a color property is being set.

The two squares on the left side of the Color Palette window control where your color selection is applied. If you click the small inner square, your next color selection becomes the foreground color. The foreground of a window is usually any text or objects drawn on the Form. If you click the large, outer square, the next color selection becomes the background color of the selected object. Experiment with the Color Palette window all you want. Select Form1 or one of the controls you placed on Form1. Then select the Color Palette window and change the colors. Any foreground or background change immediately appears on that Form or object.

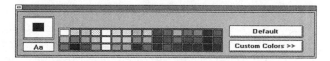

Figure 2.5. *The Color Palette window.*

The Menu Design Window

The Menu Design window is hidden also. Activate it by clicking the **Menu** Design command on the **Windows** menu. The Menu Design window

attaches one or more menus to the front-most Form, as shown in Figure 2.6. You can experiment with the Menu Design window if you want, but it's not as simple to figure out as the Color Palette window. You will learn about it in more detail in Chapter 7, "Using Custom Menus."

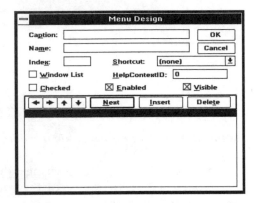

Figure 2.6. *A Menu Design window.*

The Debug Window

The Debug window appears only when an application is running, or paused by encountering a stop statement or breakpoint, or by having the Break command executed. The Debug window is a two-paned window as shown in Figure 2.7. The upper pane displays the current values of watch variables, and the lower pane is the immediate pane. Watch variables are variables and formulas whose value you want to track while debugging a program. The immediate pane receives debugging messages from a running program sent by printing to the Debug object. You also can use this command to execute one-line BASIC commands and statements.

```
Debug Window [DBOOKG.BAS]
66 [DBOOKM1.BAS:FillMonth] RecNo: 306
66 [DBOOKM1.BAS:FillMonth] theDay: 1
66 [DBOOKM1.BAS:FillMonth] Index: 35
```

Figure 2.7. *The Debug window.*

The Procedures Window

Like the Debug window, the Procedures window is only active when a program is running or paused in break mode. The Procedures window provides a shortcut to any procedure in a program, and is used to quickly move to a procedure to make changes or set breakpoints. As you can see in Figure 2.8, the top of the window lists all the forms and modules in a program, and the bottom lists all the procedures in the currently selected module. Click a procedure, click OK, and the Code window for that procedure is displayed.

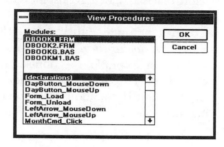

Figure 2.8. *The Procedures window.*

Understanding Modules

Forms and modules are similar because they are both objects that have code attached to them. However, Forms are visible objects that contain control objects and interact with the user. Modules are invisible objects used for storing procedures not attached to a Form or control. Although you can store unattached procedures on a Form, it is a good programming practice to "modularize" a code by placing the unattached procedures in a module, especially if you have several of them.

Procedures on modules are available for use by all other modules and Forms, whereas procedures on a Form are available only to the other procedures on the same Form. For example, a procedure that clears all printed text from a Form could be attached to the Form it clears, but a procedure to convert text strings into binary numbers would go into a Module where it could be used by any other procedure. Note that these locations are not absolute; they depend on your particular application.

Unattached procedures stored in a module or Form are reusable. If several parts of your program have to execute identical procedures, you can store one copy of each procedure in a module and access it time and time again. This not only saves space, but it also makes maintaining your code easier because you only have to make corrections to the one copy in the module.

At the beginning of every module or form is the general or declarations section. The declarations section is where module level variables are defined. Module level variables are available throughout a form or module. It is also the place where global variable's definitions and declarations are placed. Global variables are variables that are available throughout a module. A *definition* is a name that is assigned a constant value. For example, the name Red is usually defined as &H0000FF, the Hex code for Red color. The name Red can then be used in a program rather than &H0000FF, making the program more readable. A *declaration* defines the type of value that can be stored in a variable. For example, the phrase Index As Integer in a Dim or Global statement declares the variable Index as the numeric type Integer. More on definitions and declarations in Chapter 4, "Using Strings and Text Boxes," and Chapter 5, "Using Numbers and Control Structures."

Global definitions and declarations are available everywhere in your application. The file CONSTANT.TXT has a large list of useful definitions that you can load into the declarations section of a form or module and use in your application.

In Version 1 of Visual Basic, all global definitions and declarations must appear in the Global module. Also, only definitions and declarations may appear in the Global module.

Using the Menus

Visual Basic uses eight menus: File, Edit, View, Run, Debug, Options, Window, and Help. If you have used other Windows applications, you probably are familiar with the File, Edit, Window, and Help menus.

File, Edit, Window, and Help are available in some form on most Windows applications. The View menu contains commands for working with Code windows. As you might expect, the **R**un menu contains commands for running an application. The **D**ebug menu contains the commands for debugging.

The File Menu

As with most Visual Basic applications, the File menu (see Figure 2.9) is used to open and close files. The first command is New Project, which clears the screen of all old Forms and modules and creates a new Form and project window. If you haven't saved the old project, Visual Basic gives you one last chance to do so before deleting the project.

File	
New Project	
Open Project...	
Sa**v**e Project	
Sav**e** Project As...	
New **F**orm	
New MD**I** Form	
New **M**odule	
A**d**d File...	Ctrl+D
Remove File	
Save File	Ctrl+S
Save File **A**s...	Ctrl+A
Load Text...	
Save **T**ext...	
Print...	Ctrl+P
Ma**k**e EXE File...	
E**x**it	

Figure 2.9. *The File menu.*

Visual Basic programs actually are stored in several files that are brought together in the Project window. The contents of the Project window are stored in a .MAK file. Forms are stored in .FRM files, including any code attached to the Form or its controls. Modules are stored in .BAS files.

If you are familiar with other languages and operating systems such as UNIX, you will notice that the .MAK files are similar in function to makefiles. A makefile contains all the information necessary to recreate a compiled program. When a program is compiled, the Make program examines the makefile to determine what files to compile and combine to create the final application. Visual Basic uses a similar process in that the Project file contains the names of all the files that are necessary to recreate an application.

You use the Open Project, Save Project, and Save Project As commands to open or save all the files in a project. When you open a project, you only have to open the .MAK file. Loading the .MAK file automatically opens the rest of the .FRM and .BAS files that make up the project. The Save Project As command allows you to save the current Project file (the .MAK file) with a new name or in a different directory.

To change the name of every file in a project, or to save them in a different directory, select each file in the Project window, then use the Save File As command on the File menu. Once all the files are saved, use the Save Project As command to save the project description shown in the Project window.

The New Form, New MDI Form, and New Module commands add either a new blank Form, a new blank MDI Form, or a new blank module to the list of files in the Project window. An MDI form is the parent form for a multiple Document Interface program. The Add File command adds a Form or module file existing on disk to the current Project window. The Save File and Save File As commands copy a current Form or module to a disk file. Thus, you can share useful pieces of code between different programs by simply attaching previously written Forms and modules.

The Remove File command deletes a Form or module from the Project window and removes the Form or module from your application. Note that Remove File removes a Form or module only from the current project. It does not delete the file from the disk. You must use the File Manager to do that.

The Load Text and Save Text commands either load the contents of a text file into the Code window or save the contents of the Code window in a text file. You can create or edit text files with most word processing programs, although they have to be saved in the word processing applications as plain text files, without any formatting information. The Print command lets you print the contents of the active Form or module.

The Make .EXE File command compiles the current project into a stand-alone, executable Windows application. Once compiled, a program is independent of the Visual Basic program and only requires the VBRUN200.DLL (VBRUN100.DLL for Version 1.0 programs) run-time library file in order to run. Your Windows directory is a good place to store the run-time library file.

The last command on the File menu is the Exit command, which quits the Visual Basic application. As with the New Project command, you have another chance to save the current project before Visual Basic quits.

The Edit Menu

The Edit menu, shown in Figure 2.10, is standard among Windows applications. It contains the Undo, Cut, Copy, and Paste commands. In addition, the Visual Basic Edit menu contains commands to search and replace text, and to control the order of objects drawn on a form.

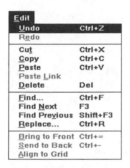

Figure 2.10. The Edit menu.

The Undo command, as its name suggests, undoes or reverses your previous change. Because Undo applies only to the last change you made, execute it immediately if you have to reverse some action; otherwise you won't be able to do so. Redo reverses the effect of Undo.

The Cut, Copy, and Paste commands move data between the clipboard and your Visual Basic project. After you copy something to the clipboard, you can save it, paste it to another location in your project, or paste it to a completely different application (such as a word processor).

To cut or copy data, select it with the cursor and execute the Cut or Copy command. The Copy command places a copy of the selected text or object on the clipboard without deleting it from its original location. The Cut command removes the selected text or object from its original location and places it on the clipboard. The Paste command inserts the contents of the clipboard at the cursor if it is text, or on the current Form if it's a control. The Paste Link command also pastes the contents of the clipboard to the current project. In addition, it establishes a link between Visual Basic and the source application from which the data was copied (assuming that application supports a link). Once linked, every data change made in the source application also is made to the linked application. The Delete command erases the currently selected control or text.

The Find, Find Next, and Find Previous commands locate specific strings of text in the Code window. First, use the Find command first to set the string to be located. Then use the Find Next and Find Previous commands to find the next and previous locations of that string. To find and replace a string, use the Replace command.

The last three commands on the Edit menu control the ordering of objects drawn on the current Form and grid snap. When grid snap is on (when the Align to Grid box is checked), new controls drawn on a Form are automatically aligned to the grid. Edit menu; menus: Edit;.

The View Menu

The menu shown in Figure 2.11 contains the commands for manipulating the View window. The first command, Code, opens the View window associated with the currently selected object. You can open a View window also with the **View Code** button in the Project window, or by simply double-clicking the object.

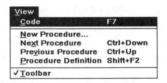

Figure 2.11. The View menu.

The New Procedure command creates a new function or subroutine template on the active Code window. If the procedure is going to be attached to a control, use the Object drop-down menu at the top of the Code window instead of the New Procedure command. The Next Procedure and Previous Procedure commands move forward and backward through the different procedures stored on a Form. The Procedure Definition command opens the code window for the selected procedure. The Toolbar command controls the display of the Toolbar.

The Run Menu

The **Run** menu, shown in Figure 2.12, contains the commands for running, stopping, and debugging a project. The **Start** and **End** commands start and stop the current program. When a program is running, the **Start** command changes into **Break**, which pauses a running program so that you can examine the variables and make minor changes if necessary. The Ctrl-Break keyboard command has the same effect. When a program is paused, **Break** changes into **Continue**. Use the **Continue** or **Restart** commands to resume execution after executing a **Break**. The **Continue** command continues execution from where it was stopped. The **Restart** command starts everything over as if you executed End and then Start.

Figure 2.12. *The Run menu.*

The Debug Menu

The Debug menu, shown in Figure 2.13, contains the controls for debugging code. The Add Watch command creates a *watch variable* in the Debug window. A watch variable displays the current value of the selected variable and can be set to trigger a break if the value goes outside a defined range. The Instant Watch command displays the current value of a variable while a program is in break mode. The Edit Watch command is used to change existing watch variables. The Calls command displays the current *active call chain*. The active call chain is the list of procedures in a paused application that have not yet run to completion. Anytime a procedure calls another procedure, and that other procedure has not returned, the first procedure is in the active call chain. When a procedure completes its function and returns to its calling procedure, it is removed from the active call chain.

You use the Single Step and Procedure Step commands to step through a program that has been stopped with a Break command, a Stop statement, or a breakpoint set with a Toggle Breakpoint command. The

Single Step command steps through every statement in a program, whereas the Procedure Step command single-steps only in the current procedure. If the current procedure calls another procedure, that procedure is executed in its entirety before the program halts at the next statement in the current procedure. That is, stepping occurs only in the current procedure and not in any external procedures.

```
Debug
Add Watch...
Instant Watch...        Shift+F9
Edit Watch...           Ctrl+W
Calls...                Ctrl+L
Single Step             F8
Procedure Step          Shift+F8
Toggle Breakpoint       F9
Clear All Breakpoints
Set Next Statement
Show Next Statement
```

Figure 2.13. The Debug menu.

The Set Next Statement command changes the execution order of a program that has been paused with the Break command or a Stop statement or a breakpoint. Normally, when you use the Continue command or one of the Step commands, Visual Basic executes the next executable statement. The Set Next Statement command is used to start execution at a different statement. In a paused program, place the cursor in the place in the statement where you want execution to continue, then execute the Set Next Statement command.

When you execute Continue or one of the Step commands, execution continues at that statement. Use it to run the same piece of code repeatedly to see the effect of changes. You can use the Show Next Statement command to display the next statement to be executed, without actually executing it.

If you know approximately where a code is having problems, insert either a Stop statement or a breakpoint directly before the problem code. You insert and remove breakpoints with the Toggle Breakpoint command. When the execution of a code reaches a breakpoint, it halts execution and pauses as if you had executed the Break command. The Clear All Breakpoints command is used to remove all breakpoints that were inserted with the Toggle Breakpoint command. Breakpoints also disappear when you close a Project. You must edit the program to remove the Stop statements.

The Options Menu

The Options menu, shown in Figure 2.14, is used to set environment variables for both the program and the programming environment. The Environment command opens a dialog box for setting the current colors, the grid spacing for automatic alignment of controls on a form, Tab stop placement, syntax checking, and so forth. The Project command sets the startup form, the Help file to use, and any command line arguments for the current project. The startup form is the first form loaded and executed in a project. The default startup form is the first form defined.

Figure 2.14. The Options menu.

The Window Menu

The Window menu, shown in Figure 2.15, activates the different windows listed in the menu. In a windowed environment, it is easy to "lose" a window behind other windows. Executing any of the Window menu commands brings the window to the screen if it already is open, or opens it if it is not yet open. The windows that can be opened are the Color Palette window, the Debug window, the Menu Design window, the Procedures window, the Project window, the Properties window, and the Toolbox window.

Window	
Color Palette	
Debug	Ctrl+B
Menu Design	Ctrl+M
Procedures	F2
Project	
Properties	F4
Toolbox	

Figure 2.15. The Window menu.

The Help Menu

The Help menu, shown in Figure 2.16, contains the standard help commands: Contents, Search, Product Support, Introducing Microsoft Visual Basic, Learning Microsoft Visual Basic, and About Microsoft Visual Basic. The Contents command opens the table of contents for the online help. The Search command opens a search menu for searching the help file for specific words and phrases. The Product Support command displays directions for getting support. The Introducing Microsoft Visual Basic and Learning Microsoft Visual Basic commands start the online tutorials, and the About Microsoft Visual Basic gives the current version, copyright notice, licensing information, serial number, windows mode, and memory available for Visual Basic.

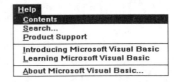

Figure 2.16. *The Help menu.*

Understanding the Toolbar

The Visual Basic toolbar is shown in Figure 2.17. The toolbar replaces the properties bar of Visual Basic Version 1.0, which is now in the Properties window. The Toolbar speeds development by making the commonly used commands available at the press of a button. Executing a tool on the Toolbar is the same as executing the equivalent command on a menu, just more convenient. The icons on the toolbar stand for the following commands.

 New Form—Add a new form to the current project.

 New Module—Add a new module to the current project.

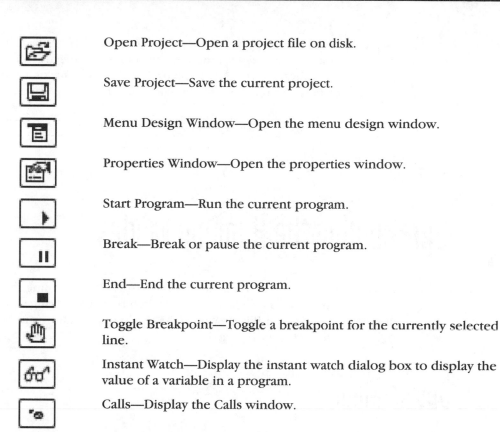

Open Project—Open a project file on disk.

Save Project—Save the current project.

Menu Design Window—Open the menu design window.

Properties Window—Open the properties window.

Start Program—Run the current program.

Break—Break or pause the current program.

End—End the current program.

Toggle Breakpoint—Toggle a breakpoint for the currently selected line.

Instant Watch—Display the instant watch dialog box to display the value of a variable in a program.

Calls—Display the Calls window.

Single Step—Execute one step in the current program.

Procedure Step—Execute one step in the current program. If the current statement calls another procedure, execute all the code in that procedure in one step.

On the right side of the Toolbar (see Figure 2.17) are two text boxes, each containing two numbers. These boxes display the values of the Height, Width, Top, and Left properties of the selected object. The leftmost two numbers are the height and width of the selected object. The rightmost two numbers are the x,y coordinates of the upper-left corner of the object with respect to the origin of the enclosing object. For forms, the origin is the upper-left corner of the screen. For controls on forms, the origin is the upper-left corner of the user area of the form. The user area of a form is the area within a form's borders, and below its title bar. For controls on frames

or picture boxes, the origin is the upper-left corner of the frame or picture box. The units used are determined by the enclosing object. For forms on the screen, it is always *twips* (1/1440 inch). For objects on forms, the default is twips, but that can be changed by changing the form's ScaleMode property.

Figure 2.17. *The Toolbar.*

Understanding the Running Modes

Before I go on, a short discussion of the Visual Basic running modes of operation; modes is necessary. As you switch between editing a program and running it, Visual Basic switches its mode of operation and behaves differently toward user interaction.

Design Mode

When you first start Visual Basic, it is in Design mode, which is where you create your application. Everything you have done so far has been in Design mode. In Design mode, you can

> Create files
> Open projects
> Close projects
> Save projects
> Copy code
> Cut code
> Paste code
> Compile code
> Run code

In short, you can make just about any changes you want to your project.

Interpreted Running Mode

When you select the Start command from the Run menu, the Visual Basic interpreter takes over and begins running your program. First, all the Form and Project windows you used to create your application are closed. Next, the interpreter displays the first Form that you have defined or that you have designated the startup form with the **Program** command on the **Options** menu. Then the interpreter executes your program one line at a time. The interpreter also opens the Debug window.

The interpreter reads a line of code, *converts* (interprets or compiles) it into microprocessor commands (*machine codes*), and executes those commands. Machine codes are numbers that your microprocessor interprets as commands to do something. Because the microprocessor commands are not saved, each time a line of code is executed it must be interpreted again. A benefit of this process is that you can make a change and run your program immediately without having to compile it. Unfortunately, the program runs more slowly than a compiled code because each statement must be interpreted before it can be executed.

While your program is running, you cannot make changes to your code, open project files, or save project files. For the most part, the only commands available (other than those you defined in your program) are those on the **Run** menu: **End, Break, Restart**. When you execute Break, Visual Basic pauses your program in a semi-Design mode state. You can edit the code in this state, then restart it from where it stopped. Visual Basic goes back to Design mode if you execute the End command, or if your code finishes executing.

Compiled Running Mode

Compiled mode isn't actually a Visual Basic mode, although it is a different state of operation for your program. When you compile a program, Visual Basic reads the statements in your program, interprets them, converts them into microprocessor commands, and stores the commands in an .EXE file (an executable program file). The increase in speed originates at this point. Because all your code already has been interpreted and converted into microprocessor commands, the statements do not have to be interpreted each time they are executed, which saves a step.

When you execute the .EXE file, your processor reads and executes the microprocessor commands independently of Visual Basic. (Well, the execution is *almost* totally independent. The VBRUN200.DLL Visual Basic run-time library must be accessible by your program.) At this point, the only commands available are those that you built into your program.

Building a First Program

Now that you have a basic idea of how the Visual Basic environment works, you can go through the steps to build a program. This program doesn't do much; however, when you create it, you use many of the commands and procedures discussed in this chapter. It also uses some language elements that have not been discussed so far. Don't worry about the new language elements now. You learn about them in more detail later in this book.

The Good Morning Program

The Good Morning program, MYONE.EXE, displays a window with two Text boxes and two buttons. You type your name in one box. Good Morning appears in the second box, followed by the name you typed in the first box. Also, Good Morning changes to Good Afternoon or Good Evening, depending on the time of day. MYONE.EXE isn't an exciting program, but it does exercise many of the options in Visual Basic. As you make your changes, use Figure 2.18 as a guide.

1. Start Visual Basic or execute the New Project command on the File menu to get new Project and Form windows.

   First change the caption of the Form1 Form window. The Caption property is the name displayed at the top of the Form. The current caption is Form1. That's not terribly informative, so change it to My First Program.

2. Click the Form to select it. The Properties windows should show the Caption property. If not, select Caption from the Properties list.

3. In the Settings box, select the text Form1 and type **My First Program** in its place. Press Enter or click the Check box to make the change in the Caption property.

Now that you have a blank Form, put the Controls and Text boxes on it.

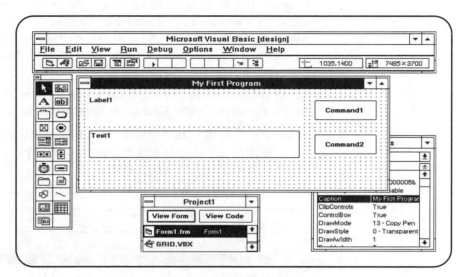

Figure 2.18. The My First Program *Form layout.*

4. In the Toolbox window, select the Label tool (the icon shown in the outside margin) and draw a Label on the Form. Make the Label about 3/4 of an inch tall and 5 inches wide.

The two boxes on the right side of the Properties bar contain the location of the upper-left corner of the selected object and the current width and height measured in *twips*. A twip is 1/1440 of an inch and 5 by 3 inches is 7200 by 1080 twips.

5. In the Toolbox window, select the Text box icon (the icon shown in the outside margin) and draw a Text box of about the same size as the Label. Place it directly below the Label.

6. In the Toolbox window, select the Command button tool (the icon shown in the outside margin) and draw a button to the right of the Label. Select the Command button tool again and draw a second button below the first.

The next step is to change the properties of the boxes and buttons you just drew on the Form. Change the `Caption` properties of the buttons to reflect their use. Change the `CtrlName` properties to make your program more readable. The `Caption` property of a button is the text displayed on top of the button. The `Caption` property of a Label is the text displayed in the Label. The `CtrlName` property is the name that the object is referred to in the code.

7. Select the first button (marked **Command1**) and change its `Caption` property to `OK`. Change its `Name` property to `OKButton`.

8. Select the second button (marked **Command2**) and change its `Caption` property to `Exit` and its `Name` property to `ExitButton`. Your Form now should look like Figure 2.19.

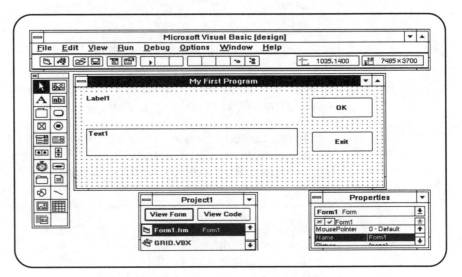

Figure 2.19. *The* `My First Program` *Form (edited).*

The next step is to attach code to the different objects on the screen. Attach code to the **Exit** button first. When the **Exit** button is pressed you want the code to end. When you open the Code window, it already has a template in it for the selected object and for the most probable event. To change either of these, select the object and event from the Object and Procedure List boxes at the top of the Code window.

9. Double-click the **Exit** button to open the Code window associated with it. The code template already should be set for the ExitButton object and the Click event. If not, select ExitButton from the Object list and Click from the Proc list. The Code window now should show the header and footer for an ExitButton_Click event. That is, the code in this Procedure is executed whenever you click the button marked **Exit**. Type a Stop or End statement between the procedure header and footer. Your Code window now should look like Figure 2.20.

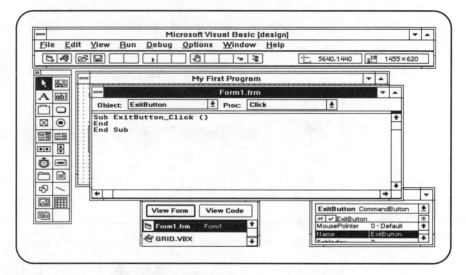

Figure 2.20. *The* ExitButton_Click *procedure.*

When the program starts up, you want the contents of the Label and the List box to have some initial values. You could set these values at design time, as you did for the Caption properties of the Command buttons, or you could do it in code that is executed when the application starts. A good place to put startup code is in the Form_Load procedure, which is executed when the Form is loaded (right before it is displayed).

In the Label, put the instructions to the user, such as

Please type your name below.

To access the Caption property of the Label1 Label, combine the CtrlName (Label1) and the property (Caption) separated with a period (Label1.Caption). All properties are accessed in this way.

The visible text in a Text box is contained in the Text property rather than in the Caption property, as it is with the Label and Command buttons. You want the Text box to be blank, so set its Text property to the empty string.

10. In the Object list, select Form. The Code window changes to the Form window. In the Proc list, select the Load event. Type the following code between the `Form1_Load` header and footer:

```
Label1.Caption = "Please type your name below."
Text1.Text = ""
```

Your Code window now should look like Figure 2.21.

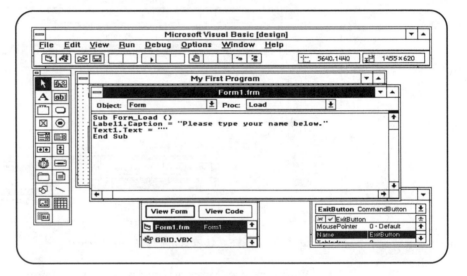

Figure 2.21. *The* `Form1_Load` *procedure.*

The code that does all the work in this program is attached to the OK button. When that button is pressed, you want the code to check the time of day to see if it is morning, afternoon or evening. Then the code should combine the text Good Morning, Good Afternoon, or Good Evening with what the user typed in the Text box, displaying the result in the Label.

11. Select OKButton from the Object list. Select Click from the Proc list. Type the following code between the OKButton_Click header and footer (notice the space after the text "Good Morning", "Good Afternoon", and "Good Evening"):

```
If Val(Time$) > 0 And Val(Time$) < 12 Then
   Label1.Caption = "Good Morning " + Text1.Text
ElseIf Val(Time$) >= 12 And Val(Time$) < 18 Then
   Label1.Caption = "Good Afternoon " + Text1.Text
Else
   Label1.Caption = "Good Evening " + Text1.Text
End If
```

Your Code window now should look like Figure 2.22. The `Time$` function gets the time of day. It returns a string of text that contains the current time. The format of that string is "hh: mm: ss," in which hh is the hour, mm is the minute, and ss is the second. Applying the `Val()` function to this string returns the first number in the string, which is the current hour (on a 24-hour clock).

To test the hour to see what time it is, use the `If Then Else` statement. The first `If` statement checks to see if the time is between 0 and 12 (Midnight and Noon). If it is, the next statement is executed, which combines the text "Good Morning" with the contents of the Text box (`Text1.Text`). The result is assigned to the Caption of the Label (`Label1.Caption`). If the time isn't between 0 and 12, the `ElseIf` statement checks to see if it is between 12 and 18 (Noon and 6 p.m.). If it is, `Good Afternoon` is used rather than `Good Morning`. If the time isn't between 0 and 12 or 12 and 18, the statement following the Else statement is executed, which uses `Good Evening` rather than `Good Morning` or `Good Afternoon`.

Actually, you can have fun with this program by making changes to it. You can add more `ElseIf` statements between the `If` statement and the `EndIf` statement to test for different ranges in the time and to print an appropriate message. For example, you could test for the range 9 a.m. to 10 a.m. and display a rude comment about being late. Or you could test for 6 p.m. to 7 p.m. and display `Go Home, it's dinner time`. When you complete this chapter, come back to this point and experiment a little.

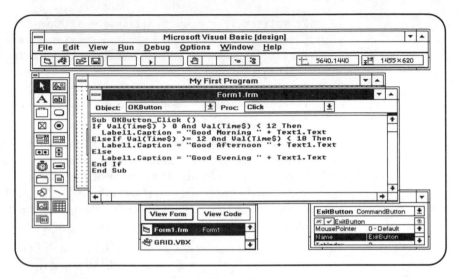

Figure 2.22. *The* `OKButton_Click` *procedure.*

Running Your Program

Your running program is ready to be run in interpreted mode, so select **S**tart from the **R**un menu or click the Run button on the Toolbar. If you made no typing errors, your screen looks like Figure 2.23. Your Form window waits for you to use it.

Type your name in the Text box and click the **OK** button to see your message appear in the Label, as in Figure 2.24. If you made a typing mistake somewhere, Visual Basic probably will give you a syntax error and show you the offending statement. Fix it, and try to run your program again.

You may have noticed the Immediate window hanging around the Form window. The Immediate window appears whenever a program is being run in interpreted mode, its primary use to debug programs—see Chapter 13, "Debugging," for more information.

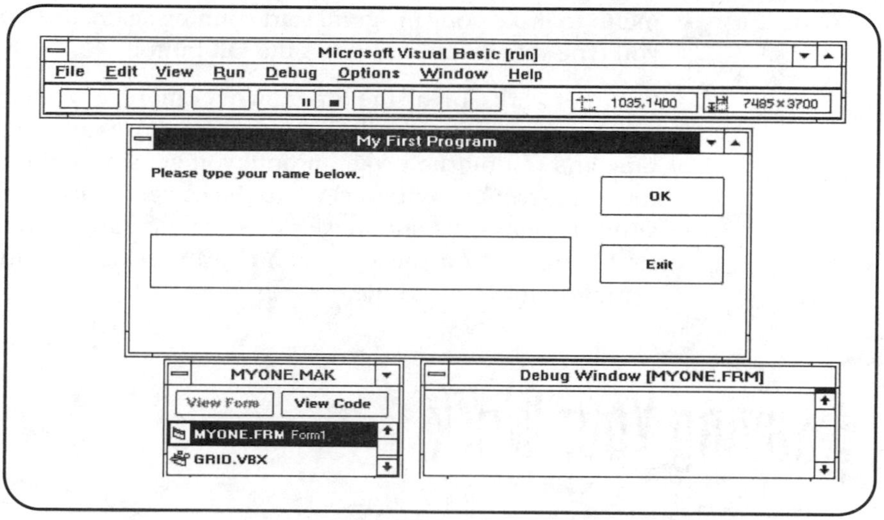

Figure 2.23. *The* My First Program *after startup.*

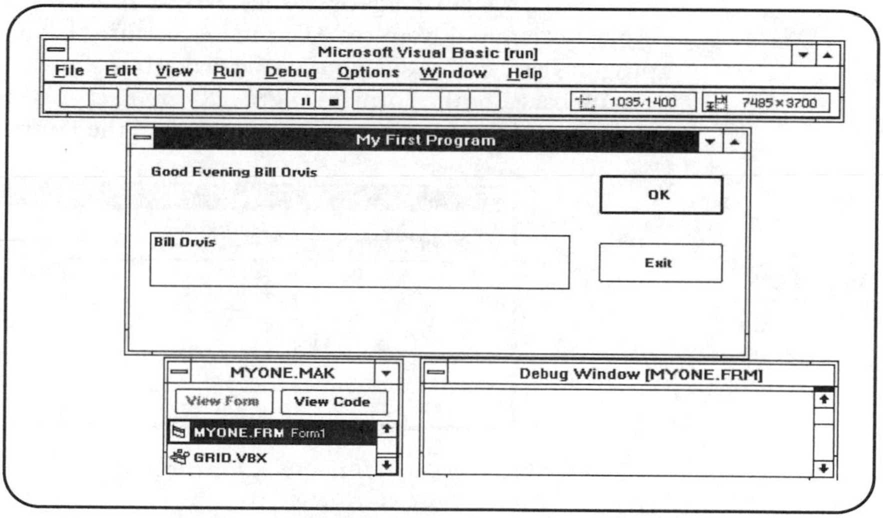

Figure 2.24. *The* My First Program *after pressing the* **OK** *button.*

To test your code for different times of day, run the code and execute the **Break** command in the **Run** menu. Open the Immediate window, type **time$="9:00"**, and press Enter. This sequence changes the setting of your system clock to 9 a.m. Also, you could type **print time$** and press Enter to see what the current time is. Select the **C**ontinue command under the **Run**

menu to make your program start running again. See what it prints when you type your name and press the **OK** button.

If it works, break the program once more, change the system clock to a different time, and run the program again. You can continue changing the time and testing the program until you are satisfied that it works. Don't forget to reset the system clock to the correct time when you are done. If your program runs but doesn't do what it is supposed to do, execute the **End** command on the **R**un menu and check your code and properties settings until you find the error.

Saving Your Work

Now that you have a running code, you should save it. When you work on longer programs, save them frequently so you don't risk losing all your work if your system hangs or crashes. To save your program, select the Save Project command from the **F**ile menu. Because this is the first time this program has been saved, you see the dialog box shown in Figure 2.25. The default name for the Form is FORM1.FRM, but I changed it to MYONE.FRM and selected the VB directory. Click **OK**, and the Form is saved.

Figure 2.25. *The save dialog box for the Form.*

Next, the dialog box in Figure 2.26 appears for you to save the Project file. Again, I changed the default name from PROJECT1.MAK to MYONE.MAK and clicked **OK**. If your code has more Forms or modules, a dialog box appears for each one. The second time you save your work, these dialog boxes won't appear. Visual Basic knows where to store your work, and what names to use. To save your code in a different directory, or with a different name, use the Save Project **As** and the Save File As commands in the File menu. If you change the file names, don't change the .MAK or .FRM extensions to the file names.

Figure 2.26. *The save dialog box for the Project.*

Retrieving Your Work

Retrieving your work is easier than saving it. You have to retrieve only the project file; all the other files are retrieved automatically. Right now, your program is still in memory. Delete it with the New Project command in the File menu. Select the **Open** Project dialog from the File menu and a file open dialog box appears. Set the directory by double-clicking the disk letters and directory names until you get into the directory that contains the MYONE.MAK file. Click the MYONE.MAK file and click the **OK** button. Your program is loaded back into memory.

Compiling Your Program

The last step is to compile your program into a stand-alone application. With your program in memory, select the Make .EXE File command from the File menu. The dialog box shown in Figure 2.27 appears for you to select the directory and name for your application. As you can see in the

figure, the VB directory is on the d: drive. When you click **OK**, your program is compiled and stored on disk. Note that the library file, VBRUN200.DLL, included with Visual Basic must be accessible by the running program.

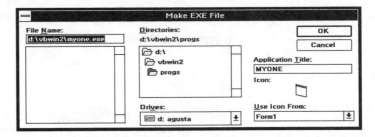

Figure 2.27. *The Make .EXE File dialog box.*

To run your program, switch to the File Manager, open the VB directory, and double-click MYONE.EXE. Alternatively, open the Microsoft Visual Basic Group window under the Program Manager and the VB directory under the File Manager. Drag the icon of the MYONE.EXE application from the directory window to the Group window. This installs MYONE.EXE in the Microsoft Visual Basic Group (see Figure 2.28). You then can close the File Manager and execute MYONE by double-clicking its icon in the Group window.

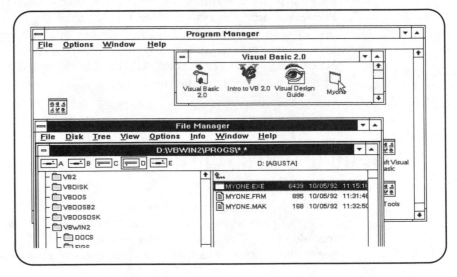

Figure 2.28. *Copying your program to a File Group window.*

This completes all the steps necessary to create and compile a Visual Basic program. If you want, go back now and try to change some of the properties of the Form, buttons, and Text boxes. Try changing the font with the `FontName` property, or the size of the text with the `FontSize` property. Or you could experiment with the colors of the Form and controls with the `ForeColor` and `BackColor` properties. Go ahead and experiment with the code. Have some fun with it.

> The Iconwrks example program is used to create custom icons, and is included with Visual Basic (see Plate II). Use it to create a custom icon for your first program. Once you have the icon stored in a file, attach it to the program using the **P**roperties command on the **F**ile menu of the Program compiling programs; programs: compiling; Manager or attach the icon to the Icon property of a Form.

What You Have Learned

In this chapter, you examined the Visual Basic environment and its capabilities, including the commands, menus, controls, and windows. You also built your first windows application, performing all the steps from designing it to compiling it into a stand-alone application. Specifically, you examined

- The Project window.
- The Form window.
- The Toolbox window.
- The Code window.
- The Color Palette window.
- The Menu Design window.
- The Debug window.
- The Procedures window.

● The File window.

● The Edit menu.

● The View menu.

● The Run menu.

● The Debug window.

● The Options window.

● The Windows menu.

● The Help menu.

● The Toolbar.

● The running modes of operation.

● Creating and running a first application.

● Compiling an application.

● Saving and retrieving a program.

Part II

Opening Up
Visual Basic

Understanding Forms

In This Chapter

This chapter discusses Forms. Pay close attention to Forms, because they are the foundation of most Visual Basic programs. This chapter shows you how to

- Create a Form.
- Change the appearance of a Form.
- Print on a Form.
- Print to a printer.
- Draw objects on a Form.
- Create custom printed Forms.
- Print a Form to a printer.

Creating a Form

Forms are the visual background for all the controls and boxes that make up an application. When you first create a Form, it appears as a standard, blank Windows window. It has a title bar showing its name, and draggable borders to change its size and shape. The Form also has a Control menu in the upper-left corner and **Maximize** and **Minimize** buttons in the upper-right corner.

A Form is like an adjustable drawing board on which you draw objects (such as buttons and labels) to form the visual interface of a project. Everything you want to see when your application is running is attached to a Form. In addition to being the place where the visual parts of objects are attached, Forms also contain objects attached to the Form. Nearly every project has at least one Form attached to it. Although you can create projects with a visual interface without using Forms, it is much more difficult.

You can attach as many Forms to a project as you want to create your application. I suspect there is a limit to the number of Forms you can attach to a single project; however, I haven't run into it yet. To avoid cluttering the screen, you can hide Forms that are not being used and make them visible when you want them.

The first Form in a project is created automatically when you open Visual Basic or execute the **New Project** command on the **File** menu. If the Form is hidden by other windows, bring it to the front by clicking a corner, or select it from the list on the Project window and press the **View Form** button. To add Forms to a project, execute the New Form command on the **File** menu. A new Form appears on the Project window and the screen.

Printing on a Form with the Print Method

In addition to drawing buttons and boxes on a Form, you can print on a Form using the `Print` method. Text printed on a Form starts in the upper-left corner and continues down the Form with each successive `Print` statement.

Printing on a Form in this manner is similar to printing on the screen in other versions of BASIC, with one important difference: A Form does not scroll when your printed text goes off the screen. It simply disappears off the bottom as your application continues printing. If you continue printing off the bottom of the Form, an overflow error results after approximately 100 lines. To print onto a scrollable window, add the new text to the Text property of the Text box. You also can print on the Immediate Pane of the Debug window when a program is running, by using the Debug object with the Print method. See Chapter 13, "Debugging and Error Trapping," for more details.

The Print method prints text on Forms, on picture boxes, to the printer, and on the Immediate Pane of the Debug window. Its syntax is

```
[Object.]Print [Expression][{;¦,}]
```

in which Object is the name of the object to print on and Expression is the text you want printed. Use the ! separator if the object is a form. Ending the method with a comma, a semicolon, or nothing controls where the cursor is left after Expression is printed. The cursor position determines where printing starts the next time you execute Print. Appending nothing to the end of a Print method causes the insertion point to move down one line and left to the margin. A comma moves the insertion point to the next print field (every 14 spaces). A semicolon leaves the insertion point at the end of Expression. For example, print a few lines on a Form.

1. Start with a new project by opening Visual Basic. If Visual Basic is already open, execute the **New Project** command on the **File** menu.

2. Select Form1 and open its Code window by double-clicking the Form, by clicking the **View Code** button on the Project window, or by selecting the View Code command in the Code menu.

3. The Click event should be selected. If not, select it from the Procedure list.

4. Add one line of code to the procedure template so it reads

```
Sub Form_Click ()
Print "Hello"
End Sub
```

5. Execute the **Start** command on the **R**un menu, press the Start button, or press F5. A blank Form appears.

6. Click the Form to execute the procedure. "Hello" is printed on the Form, as shown in Figure 3.1.

Figure 3.1. Printing a single line on a Form.

7. Click several times on the Form. "Hello" is repeated as shown in Figure 3.2. If you continue to click the Form, the text eventually runs off the bottom.

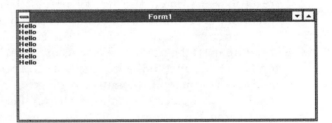

Figure 3.2. Printing several lines on a Form.

8. Execute the **End** command on the **R**un menu or press the End button to quit the program and go back to Design mode.

Try printing other text on the Form. Also try placing a comma or semicolon after the expression and see what happens.

Don't delete this program yet, because you use it again later to examine some of a Form's properties.

Changing the Appearance of Forms

The appearance of a Form (its size, shape, color, text style, and so forth) is controlled by its properties. In addition, properties control how a Form reacts to certain events, such as the redrawing of a Form's contents when it's uncovered. Three different classes of properties are associated with objects: those that can be changed only at design time, those that can be changed only at run time, and those that can be changed at any time. The majority of a Form's properties can be changed at any time. Most design-time-only properties are readable at run time, even though they can't be changed. Table 3.1 lists some of the more commonly used properties of a Form. See Chapter 15, "Command Reference," for a complete list.

Table 3.1. Commonly used properties of a Form.

Run-time and Design-time Properties

Property	Description
BackColor	The background color
Caption	The title displayed at the top of the Form
FontBold	Make the next text printed on the Form bold (True or False)
FontItalic	Make the next text printed on the Form italic (True or False)
FontName	The name of the font used for text printed on the Form
FontSize	Set the point size of the next text printed on the Form
FontUnderline	Underline the next text printed on the Form (True or False)
ForeColor	The foreground color
Height	The height of the Form (in twips—one-twentieth of a point)

continues

Table 3.1. continued

Run-time and Design-time Properties

Property	Description
Left	The distance from the left side of the Form to the left side of the screen (in twips)
Top	The distance from the top of the Form to the top of the screen (in twips)
Visible	Is the Form visible at run time? (True or False)
Width	The width of the Form (in twips)

Design-time-only Properties

BorderStyle	The thickness of the Form's border
ControlBox	Does the Form have a Control box? (True or False)
FormName	The name used internally for the Form in the Code window
MaxButton	Does the Form have a **Maximize** button? (True or False)
MinButton	Does the Form have a **Minimize** button? (True or False)

The Properties Window

To change a Form's properties at design time, select the Form and change its properties with the Properties Window. The Properties Window contains a list box and two drop-down list boxes. The first List box on the left is the properties list. It contains all properties that can be changed at design time, and their current settings. It does not contain any properties that can be changed *only* at run time. Above the properties list is the Settings box, which contains the value of the current setting for the selected property displayed in Figure 3.3.

Figure 3.3. *The Properties bar with the properties list dropped down.*

Above the properties list is the Objects box. The Objects box displays the object whose properties are being changed. To select a different object, click the arrow on the right side of the Objects box. This drops down a list of all the objects in the project. Click the object you want to change.

Four numbers in two groups of two appear on the right side of the Toolbar. The two numbers on the left show the location of the upper-left corner of the currently selected object. The position is measured down and to the right of the upper-left corner of the screen if the object is a Form. The position is measured down and to the right of the upper-left corner of the drawing area of the Form if the object is on the Form. The drawing area of a Form is everything below the title bar. The right pair of numbers displays the width and height of the current object.

By default, both the location and the size of an object are measured in twips (which, as you recall from Chapter 2, "Learning the Visual Basic Environment," are equal to 1/1440 of an inch). Although the twip might seem to be an odd unit of measure, it is 1/20 of a *point*, which is a printer's unit of measure. Most older versions of BASIC use pixels; pixels as the unit of measure on the screen. A pixel is the smallest point that can be drawn on a screen; however, the size of a pixel is dependent on the video adapter and monitor used. Thus, an object with its size defined in pixels is different sizes on different monitors. An object with its size defined in twips is the same size on any monitor. The scale used can be changed to inches, centimeters, millimeters, or to some user-defined unit using the Scale Mode property– see Chapter 12, "Drawing with Visual Basic."

Changing Properties with the Settings Box

To change the appearance of a Form (or any object on a Form), you must change the value of its properties. At design time, the values of properties are changed in two ways. For properties such as size and location, moving the Form and dragging its borders automatically changes the Top, Left, Width, and Height properties. Other properties are changed using the Settings box. Note that the size and location also can be changed with the Settings Settings box.

To use the Settings box on the Properties Window, first select the Form that has properties you want to change. Then select the property you want to change from the Properties list. At this point, the current value of the property is displayed in the Settings box. To change a property, type a new value in the Settings box. Some properties have a fixed list of possible values (for example, True or False). If this is the case, the Settings box becomes a List box. You change the property by pulling down the list of settings (click the down arrow on the right side of the Settings box). Then select the value from the list of settings. Double clicking the property in the properties list cycles the list of property values, one at a time. For color properties, the down arrow changes into an ellipsis (...). Clicking the ellipsis displays the Color Palette window. When you select a color in the Color Palette window, the numeric code for that color is inserted in the Settings box.

You can return to the earlier example and change some properties.

1. You should be in Design mode. If you aren't, execute the **End** command on the **Run** menu. If you made any changes in the procedure you created in the earlier example, remove them before continuing.

2. Select Form1. Then select the FontSize property on the Properties bar.

3. Pull down the Settings list. Select the largest point size available. I chose 24 points; however, your sizes might be different from mine, depending on which fonts you have installed on your system, what kind of printer you have, and the video adapter you have.

4. Run the program and click the Form a few times. It should look like Figure 3.4.

5. Quit the program with the **End** command on the **Run** menu.

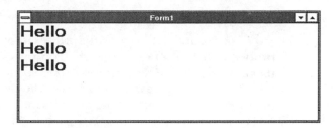

Figure 3.4. Printing on a Form with the FontSize *property set to 24 points.*

Try changing some of the other properties of the Form (such as ForeColor or BackColor), or some of the text attributes (such as FontUnderline and FontName), and run the example again. Don't be afraid to experiment with the properties or code. Although the manual might tell you what will happen, it could be ambiguous or wrong. The only way to see exactly what a property or code segment does is to try it.

Dynamically Changing Properties in a Running Application

You can change properties in a running application with a statement of the following format:

```
[object.{!¦.}]property = value
```

in which object is the name of the object having the property to be changed (the Form name in this case), property is the name of the property, and value is a new value for that property. If the object is a form, use the ! seperator, otherwise use ..If object is omitted, the attached form is assumed to be the value. If the construction [object.]property is used on the right side of a formula rather than on the left side, it returns the current value of that property. For example, the following code changes the foreground color to &HFF, where &HFF is the hexadecimal number for red.

```
ForeColor = &HFF&
```

For example, add a line to the print example to turn the `FontStrikethru` property on and off each time the Form is clicked. The `FontStrikethru` property can be either `True` or `False`, so use the `Not` function, which switches `True` to `False` or `False` to `True`. The value of `Form1.FontStrikethru` on the right side of the formula provides the old value of the property. The `Not` function reverses the property's value. The equals sign assigns the new value back to `Form1.FontStrikethru` on the left side of the formula.

1. Continue with the preceding example. You should be in Design mode. If you aren't, execute the **End** command on the **Run** menu. If you have made any changes in the procedure that was created in the earlier example, remove them before continuing.

2. Change the code in the `Form_Click` procedure so it reads

```
Sub Form_Click ()
Form1.FontStrikethru = Not Form1.FontStrikethru
Print "Hello"
End Sub
```

3. Run the program and click the Form a few times. It should look like Figure 3.5.

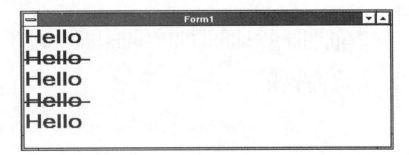

Figure 3.5. *Setting properties with code.*

Printing to the Printer

In addition to printing on Forms, you can print to the printer by using `Printer` as the object in the `Print` method. For example, change the Form-printing example so it prints to the printer rather than on the Form.

1. In Design mode, select the Form, open its Code window, and select the Click process.

2. Change the object in the Print method to the Printer object so that the procedure reads

```
Sub Form_Click ()
Form1.FontStrikethru = Not Form1.FontStrikethru
Printer.Print "Hello"
End Sub
```

3. Run the program and click the Form.

   The program doesn't seem to be doing anything. However, if you check on the desktop of your Windows environment, the Print Manager has appeared. The Print Manager actually is storing the text to be printed to the printer until you either quit the application or issue the Printer.EndDoc method.

4. End the program.

   The Print Manager now sends the text to the printer. The Print Manager prints one Hello to the printer for every time you clicked the Form. But what's this? The font has changed back to the small 12-point size, and FontStrikethru doesn't seem to be working. The problem is that the second line of the procedure still refers to the Form and not the Printer object. Also, at design time you cannot set any of the printer properties. You must set them with code, so go back and change the Form1_Click procedure.

5. Open the code window and select the Click procedure. Change the object to Printer where you change the FontStrikethru property. Add a line to set the name of the printed font. Then add another line to change the font's point size. The procedure now should read

```
Sub Form_Click ()
Printer.FontName = "Tms Rmn"
Printer.FontSize = 24
Printer.FontStrikethru = Not Printer.FontStrikethru
Printer.Print "Hello"
End Sub
```

6. Run the program and click the Form a few times. Then end the program. This time the printed output looks much like the printing in Figure 3.5.

Unlike other versions of BASIC, Visual Basic has no `LPRINT` statement. The `LPRINT` statement is replaced with the `Printer.Print` method; however, the text is not printed until you quit the program or execute the `Printer.EndDoc` method. Also, you cannot insert a `Printer.EndDoc` statement after every `Printer.Print` statement, because `Printer.EndDoc` also issues a page feed after the last printed text.

Printing on a Text Box

Often you have to print a list of items on the screen, and you want them to be in a scrollable box. Word processors and telecommunication programs are examples of programs that have to write on scrollable lists. Do this by adding text to the Text property of a large `Text` box.

First you need a large Text box on a Form. Clear any text already on the box, and set the `Multiline` property to `True`. If `Multiline` is `False`, only one line of text is printed on the Text box. Turn on the Vertical Scroll bar with the `ScrollVertical` property.

1. Clear the old project by executing the **New Project** command on the **File** menu (save the old project first if you want to keep it and name it whatever you want to).

2. Select the Text box tool in the Toolbox window, and draw a List box that is nearly as large as the interior part of the Form. Leave a little space at the top so a small amount of the Form is showing to click.

3. With the Text box selected, double click the `Multiline` property in the Properties list changing its value to `True` in the Settings box.

4. Select the Text property and delete the contents of the Settings box. This clears the text inside the window.

5. Select the `ScrollBars` property and set it to `2-Vertical`.

In the `Form_Click` procedure, append the new text to the text currently in the Text box. Also append a carriage return and a line feed.

6. Open the Code window. Select the Form object and the Click procedure. Then insert a line to add the text Hello to the contents of the Text box. The procedure should look like the following:

```
Sub Form_Click ()
Text1.Text = Text1.Text + "Hello" + Chr$(13) + Chr$(10)
End Sub
```

7. Run the program and click several times on the Form where it isn't covered by the Text box. Your Form now looks like Figure 3.6.

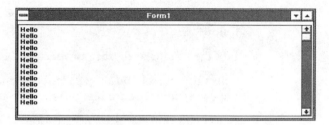

Figure 3.6. *Printing in a Text box.*

Drawing Your User Interface

Forms are most commonly used as backgrounds for the user interface to your application. As you did in Chapter 2, "Learning the Visual Basic Environment," you draw the different controls and boxes on your Form to create the interface you want. The Toolbox window is the source of the drawing tools for creating your interface. All the tools work in the same manner.

- Select a tool in the Toolbox window.

- Move to where you want the upper-left corner of your object.

- Hold down the left mouse button (or the right button if you are left-handed and have used the Windows Setup program or the Control Panel to switch the buttons).

- Drag down to the lower-right corner of your object, and release the mouse button. The object appears where you drew it. Its location, height, and width appear on the right side of the Properties bar.

Some objects, such as the Timer, have a fixed size. No matter how large you draw them, they always appear the same size. Other objects (such as the Label box and the Text box) are the size you drew them. If an object you've drawn is the wrong size or in the wrong location, you can adjust it.

- To move an object, select it and do one of the following:

  Edit the object's `Top` and `Left` properties.

  Place the cursor on the object, and hold down the left mouse button. Drag the object to its new location, and release the button.

- To change the size of an existing object, you can do one of the following:

  Edit the `Height` and `Width` properties.

  Select the object and drag one of the small black squares that appear around it until it is the shape you want.

Editing an object's size and location properties also is useful when grid snap is turned on and you want a size or location that isn't on a grid point. When grid snap is turned on, the screen is covered with an array of equally spaced points. When you move or size an object, the mouse pointer jumps from one grid point to the next, skipping the points in between. You could turn grid snap off by unchecking the `Align to Grid` check box in the Environment Options dialog box on the Options menu. Then you could move or resize the object, and then turn on grid snap again. Or you could simply edit the object's properties.

You can move or change the properties of multiple objects at the same time by selecting all the objects you want to change and changing the property in the Properties window. The new value of the property is applied to all the selected objects that have that property. To select multiple objects, click the first object, then hold down Shift while selecting the others. For objects on a form, you can drag a selection box around the objects, and any object that the selection box touches is selected. For objects on a picture box, hold down Shift while dragging the selection box to prevent the picture box from becoming part of the selection.

Creating a Custom Form

In business situations, you often have to either fill out or create a form. You can buy a form-generation program, or you simply can use Visual Basic to create an on-line form you can fill out on the screen. The form's contents are either printed or stored on a disk for use by another program.

A few evenings ago, my wife ran up to me and said she was out of vaccination certificates (she's a veterinarian). She had just vaccinated a dog (Jessie) we were giving away in the morning, and she needed a blank certificate. Her suppliers take a week or two to get forms to her; however, she needed a form right away so the new owners would have the correct paperwork when they picked up Jessie.

Using Visual Basic, I created the following vaccination certificate as a stand-alone application. You run the application, fill in the form, and press a button to print it. Creating the custom form took only about an hour. Of course, to be able to legally sign it takes about eight years of college and a license, so don't try to use this form for your own pets (unless you are a veterinarian too).

The first step is to design the form. Sketch the different fields and labels you want so you have a rough idea where they go. The ordering of the fields is not terribly important.

Something else to consider at this time is the tab ordering of the Text boxes. When you are filling out the Form, you can press Tab to move from object to object. The order in which the objects are selected is determined by the order in which they are drawn on the Form. However, that ordering can be changed by changing the `TabIndex` property. The `TabIndex` property, which is incremented each time a new object is drawn on a Form, determines the tab order. If you change the value of the `TabIndex` property of an object, it moves to that position in the tab order. All the `TabIndex` properties of the other objects on the Form are adjusted to make room for it. In this example, you want to tab from one Text box to the next. So you need to put all the Text boxes on the Form first.

I give you the exact positions and sizes of all the objects on this Form so you can create a Form identical to the one in Figure 3.7. Alternatively, you can look at the figure and draw the objects to make your Form similar to mine. It might not be identical, but you will see how to create a custom Form.

1. Start with a blank Form by either starting Visual Basic or executing the New Project command on the File menu.

2. Enlarge the Form until it is 8475 twips wide by 4500 twips high.

3. Select the Frame tool and draw a frame that is about the same size as the Form. Set the following properties of the frame:

Top = **-80**   Left = **5**
Width = **8340**   Height = **4060**
Caption = " "

4. Table 3.2 lists 13 Text boxes and their properties. Look at Figure 3.7 and draw the boxes first. Then adjust their properties to match those in the table. Set the Text property for each Text box to a blank.

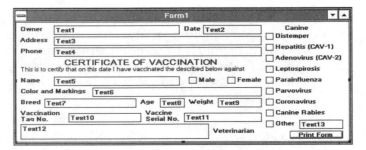

Figure 3*.7. *The vaccination Form in progress.

It's easiest to draw all the boxes on the Form first in roughly the right location and size. Then you select one property and adjust it on all the boxes, rather than setting all the properties for a single box before going on to the next. If multiple objects need the same value for a property, select all the objects by holding down Shift while clicking the objects, or surround them with a selection rectangle and change the property in the Properties window. The change is applied to all the selected objects. If each object gets a different value for the property, then select the first box and select the property to be adjusted. Change the property and press Enter to accept the change. Then press Tab to move to the next box. Using this procedure, you can go down the list of boxes, then change to the next property and do it again. Continue this process for all the properties that have to be adjusted.

Table 3.2. Text box properties for the custom Form.

CtlName	Left	Top	Width	Height
Text1	960	220	3135	300
Text2	4680	220	1455	300
Text3	960	580	5175	300
Text4	960	940	5175	300
Text5	960	1900	3135	300
Text6	1920	2260	4215	300
Text7	720	2620	2295	300
Text8	3600	2620	615	300
Text9	5040	2620	1095	300
Text10	1320	3100	1815	300
Text11	4200	3100	1935	300
Text12	120	3460	4695	500
Text13	7080	3340	1095	300

5. There are 15 Labels on the Form. Using Figure 3.7 and Table 3.3, attach them to the Form.

Table 3.3. Label box properties of the custom Form.

CtlName	Left	Top	Width	Height	Caption
Label1	120	220	735	260	Owner
Label2	4200	220	495	260	Date
Label3	120	580	855	260	Address
Label4	120	940	855	260	Phone
Label5	120	1300	6015	260	CERTIFICATE OF VACCINATION *(see note)

Table 3.3. continued

CtlName	Left	Top	Width	Height	Caption
Label6	120	1540	6135	260	This is to certify that on this date I have vaccinated the described below against **(see note)
Label7	120	1900	615	260	Name
Label8	120	2260	1815	260	Color and Markings
Label9	120	2620	615	260	Breed
Label10	3120	2620	495	260	Age
Label11	4320	2620	735	260	Weight
Label12	120	2980	1095	380	Vaccination Tag No.
Label13	3240	2980	975	380	Vaccine Serial No.
Label14	4920	3580	1215	260	Veterinarian
Label15	6720	200	975	260	Canine

Notes: * For Label5, set these additional properties: FontSize = 12,

```
Alignment = 2 - Center.
```
** For Label6, set this additional property: FontBold = False.

 6. Place 11 Check boxes on the Form using Figure 3.7 and Table 3.4 as guides. Draw the smallest box that shows the entire check box.

Table 3.4. Check-box properties of the custom Form.

CtlName	Left	Top	Width	Heigth	Caption
Check1	4320	1920	735	260	Male
Check2	5280	1920	975	260	Female
Check3	6240	480	2055	260	Distemper

CtlName	Left	Top	Width	Heigth	Caption
Check4	6240	840	2055	260	Hepatitis (CAV-1)
Check5	6240	1200	2055	260	Adenovirus (CAV-2)
Check6	6240	1540	2055	260	Leptospirosis
Check7	6240	1900	2055	260	Parainfluenza
Check8	6240	2260	2055	260	Parvovirus
Check9	6240	2620	2055	260	Coronavirus
Check10	6240	2980	2055	260	Canine Rabies
Check11	6240	3360	2855	260	Other

7. Using the Command button tool, insert a button on the lower-right corner of the Form. Give the button the following properties:

Left = **6840** Top = **3700** Width = **1335** Height = **260**

Caption = **Print Form** CtlName = **PrintIt**

Your Form should now look like Figure 3.8. All that remains is to add some code to automatically fill in the current date and to print the Form when the user presses the Command button.

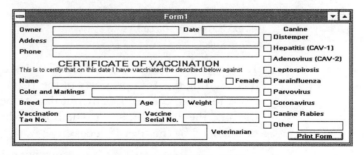

***Figure 3.8.** The user interface for the vaccination certificate custom Form.*

The PrintForm Method

Rather than having to draw the contents of the Form on the `Printer` object, you can use a special method. The `Print.Form` method prints a Form to the printer as it appears on the screen. The format of this method is

```
[Form.]PrintForm
```

If you leave out the Form argument, it prints the current Form.

1. Open the code window for the Form and select the `PrintIt` object and the `Click` procedure. Insert code into the procedure template until it appears as the following:

   ```
   Sub PrintIt_Click ()
   PrintIt.Visible = 0
   PrintForm
   PrintIt.Visible = -1
   End Sub
   ```

   Setting the `PrintIt.Visible` property of the Command button to 0 (`False`) makes the button disappear before printing the Form with the `PrintForm` method. After the Form is printed, setting `PrintIt.Visible` equal to -1 (`True`) makes the button visible again.

2. Select the Form object and the `Load` procedure, and insert the following code:

   ```
   Sub Form_Load ()
   Text2.Text = Date$
   End Sub
   ```

   The `date$` function always returns a string containing the current date. Setting the Text property of the `Text2` Text box with the `DATE$` function causes the current date to be inserted in the box at the time the Form is loaded. The box is editable, so the date can be changed by the user if necessary.

3. Save the program with the name VETFRM (in files VETFRM.FRM and VETFRM.MAK).

4. Run the program with the **Start** command on the **Run** menu, the start button, or F5.

   If you were a veterinarian, you would type the dog owner's name and a description of the dog. You also would click the check boxes to select the vaccines you gave to the dog. When the form is filled out, click the **Print It** button. The form is printed to the printer.

If everything works correctly, you now can compile the custom form into an .EXE file that can be given to anyone who needs to create the form.

> In addition to printing the form, the data could be written to a file that could be read by a database program to keep a record of what animal has received what vaccinations—see Chapter 9, "Using Sequential Files"—and print a bill for the patient's owner. I'm sure you can imagine many other uses for custom forms developed in this way.

To print on a preprinted form takes much trial and error. To do so, create a custom form that has the text box fields in the same place as the fields on the preprinted form. In the `PrintIt_Click` procedure, make all the field descriptions invisible (the Label boxes in this example) during printing, in the same manner as was done with the **Print It** button. Then fill out the form with dummy text and print it. If it doesn't fit the preprinted form, move things around and print it again. Continue this trial-and-error procedure until you are satisfied with the result.

What You Have Learned

In this chapter you learned about forms, which are the foundation of most Visual Basic programs.

- You created new forms with the **New Project** and **New form** commands.

- You printed text on a form and to the printer using the `Print` method.

- You changed the appearance of a form and the text printed on it by changing its properties both in Design mode and dynamically in a running program.

- You created a custom form-filling program.

- You printed the contents of a form to the printer using the `PrintForm` method.

Using Strings

The primary method of communication with Visual Basic objects and with the user of a Visual Basic program are strings of text. While numbers are used internally for calculations, indices, and counters, they must be converted to strings before they can be displayed in a text box or label. Thus, manipulating strings and converting numbers to strings are important aspects of any Visual Basic program.

In This Chapter

Most of what you've read so far in this book has dealt with strings of text. List boxes and labels display text on the screen. Many object properties are defined as strings of text. This chapter formally defines strings and string formulas and expands on the details of using strings in programs. This chapter shows you how to

- Define variables and determine their scope.

- Define strings.

- Create string formulas.

- Manipulate strings with string functions.

- Create an envelope-addressing program.

The Variable

Before discussing strings and string formulas, you have to consider the concept of variables and their scope because variables are where you store information in a computer program. Later, you will learn about strings and how to manipulate them.

A *variable* is a descriptive name used to store information and the results of calculations. Actually, the information is stored in the computer's memory, and the variable name points to that location. Whenever a variable name is used in a program, it is replaced by the contents of that memory location. A variable name is an abstraction that makes computer programs more readable. For example, `Label1.Caption` is a string variable that names the location of the string of text used for the caption of `Label1`. If I used an address such as `9FC80` for that location rather than the variable name, no one, including me, would have any idea what the program was doing. Using variable names makes reading a computer program understandable.

A variable name can contain up to 40 characters, including letters, numbers, and the underscore (_). The first character of a variable name must be a letter, and you cannot use a reserved word such as `Print` as a variable. However, a reserved word can be contained within a variable name, as in the variable `PrintIt`. Although you are allowed 40 characters for a variable name, I recommend that you not use that many characters. Use enough characters to make it obvious what the variable is, but not so many that you spend all day typing 40-character variable names. A good rule of thumb is to imagine that you must give your program to someone else (your mother, for example), and she must be able to read your program and understand what it is doing. When you come back to your program in a year or so, the odds are good that you still will understand it.

The Scope of Variables

The scope of a variable is a description of where in a program the variable can be accessed—see Figure 4.1. The variables associated with the properties of objects, such as `Label1.FontName`, are predefined and available to any code attached to the Form containing that object. User variables (those that you define for your own use) are defined either by using them in a procedure, or with the `Dim` or `Global` in the module statements.

At the highest level any variable defined in the Global module is available anywhere in a program. To define variables in the Global module, use the Global statement as

```
G1lobal MyName As String
```

which defines `MyName` as a global string variable.

At the highest level are the global definitions defined with the Global statement as follows,

```
Global MyName As String
```

which defines the variable `MyName` as a global string variable. Global variables can't be defined in a form's declaration statement. Global variables are defined in the declarations section of any module and are available in every procedure of every form or module in a program, unless a procedure defines a new variable with the same name. If a procedure defines a local variable with the same name as a global variable, the local variable overrides the global variable.

In Version 1 of Visual Basic, all global definitions had to reside in the Global module. In Version 2 of Visual Basic, that restriction is relaxed and global definitions may appear in the declarations section of any module. Be careful with global variables, because of their global nature, you can change them in some procedure without realizing it. In Visual Basic for DOS, global definitions are created with identical COMMON SHARED statements placed in every form or module that you want to have access to the variables. If you plan to create Windows and DOS versions of a program, try to keep the global definitions all in one place.

4

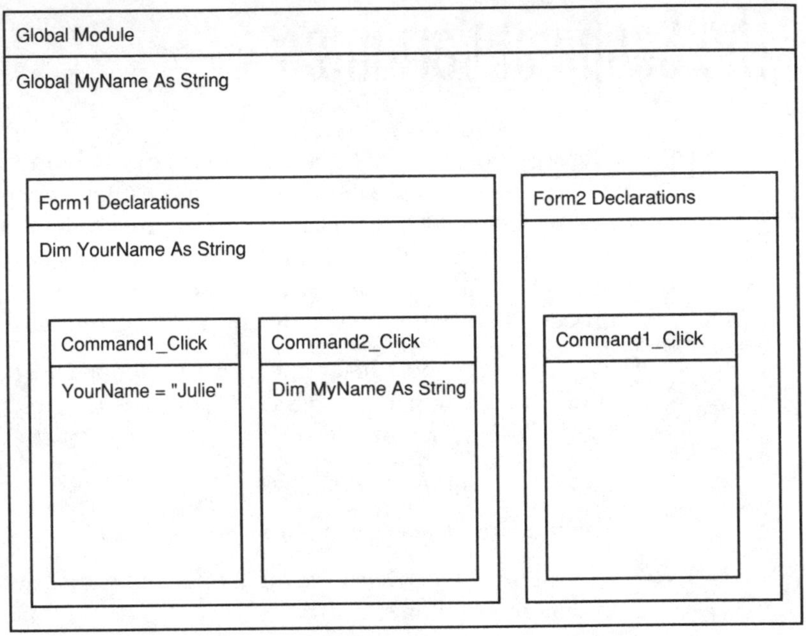

```
Global Module

Global MyName As String


    Form1 Declarations                              Form2 Declarations

    Dim YourName As String


        Command1_Click      Command2_Click              Command1_Click

        YourName = "Julie"  Dim MyName As String
```

Figure 4.1. The scope of a variable.

On the next level below global definitions are variables defined in the `declarations` sections of forms or modules. Variables defined there are available in any procedure in that particular Form or module, but not in any other Form or module. In other words, they are defined only in the Form or module in which they are defined with the `Dim` statement. Variables are defined in the `declarations` section of a form or module, which has exactly the same format as a `Global` statement. Here, `YourName` is defined as a string variable:

```
Dim YourName As String
```

At the lowest level are the local variables that are defined or used in an individual procedure. Local variables are available only in the procedure in which they are used or defined, and nowhere else. When the procedure ends, the local variables go away, and their old values are unavailable the next time the procedure is called. To make local variables survive the ending of a procedure, define them in the procedure with the Static statement. Variables defined with the Static statement persist until the next time the procedure is called. The Static statement also has exactly the same syntax as the Global statement. The following code defines OurName as a static string variable.

```
Static OurName As String
```

The declaration of a local variable always overrides the global declaration of a variable with the same name (see Figure 4.1, in which MyName is defined globally in the Global module but also is defined as a local variable in Command2_Click). The global variable and the local variable are two different variables. Changing one has no effect on the other. The variable YourName also is defined globally in Form1 and used in Command1_Click. However, because YourName is not defined in Command1_Click, the global variable and the local variable are the same. Changing one changes the other.

The Variable Scope Example

Try experimenting with the scope of variables, using an example set up like Figure 4.1. Create a form and a module. Define MyName as a global variable and Click Form1 in Command2_Click.

1. Start with a new project. Create a module with the New **Module** command on the **File** menu.

2. Draw two Command buttons on Form1.

3. Select Module in the Project window and type **Global MyName as String** in the declarations section.

4. Execute the New Procedure command on the View menu to create a SUB procedure name Procedure1 in the module.

5. Select Form1 in the Project Window and press the **View Code** button.

6. Select the Form_Click procedure for Form1 and type

```
Sub Form_Click()
Print "Form:"; MyName
End Sub
```

7. Select the Form_Load procedure and type

```
Sub Form_Load()
MyName = _Bill_
End Sub
```

8. Select the Command2_Click procedure and type

```
Sub Command2_Click()
Dim MyName As String
```

```
Print "Command 2:"; MyName
Procedure1
End Sub
```

9. Select the `Command1_Click` procedure and type

```
Sub Command1_Click ()
Print MyName
End Sub
```

10. Select `Module1`. Open its Code window, select the `Procedure1_Click` procedure, and type

```
Sub Procedure1()
Form1. Print "Procedure 1:"; MyName
End Sub
```

Now by clicking the buttons or the Form, you see the value of the variable. You first work with `MyName`, which is defined globally and given a value in `Form_Load` on `Form1`.

11. Run the program and click first on `Form1`, then on `Command1`, and finally on `Command2`. The value of `MyName` is known at the Form level in `Command1_Click` and in `Procedure1` from `Command2_Click` because it is a global variable (Figure 4.2a).

12. The global value of `MyName` is not printed from `Command2_Click`. It is not available there because `MyName` is a local variable in that procedure and is currently an empty, or null, string.

13. End the program. Open `Command2_Click` on `Form1` and change it to

```
Sub Command2_Click()
Dim MyName As String
MyName = "Shane"
Print "Command2:"; MyName
Procedure1
EndSub
```

14. Run the program again, pressing all the buttons.

Notice that `MyName` has the value `Shane` only in the **Command2_Click** procedure. The value reverts to `Bill` everywhere else (see Figure 4.2b). Thus, the global definition persists everywhere but in the procedure `Command2_Click`, in which the local variable definition overrides the global definition.

a.   b.

Figure 4.2. *The two versions of the Variable Scope program after clicking the form and both buttons.*

Experiment with this code. Try defining MyName in different places to see what happens. Rather than defining it in the Global module, for example, define it in the declarations section of Form1 (use a Dim statement rather than a Global one); or define it in the Form_Load procedure.

Strings and String Formulas

Now that you have a feel for variables and their scope, you can begin examining strings and string variables.

Defining Strings

The definition of a string is a sequence of text characters. Although most *strings* consist of printable characters, they also can contain any of the non-printing control characters such as the carriage return and line feed. A string also can be the null or empty string, which has a length of zero and doesn't contain any characters. All the Text boxes in the Vaccination Certificate program initially contain null strings.

A second type of string is a *substring*. A substring is an ordinary string that is contained in another string. In other words, it is a piece of another, longer string.

Characters actually are stored in the computer's memory and on disk as *ASCII* codes. (ASCII stands for American Standard Code for Information Interchange.) The standard set of ASCII codes ranges from 0 to 127 and includes all the standard typewriter symbols—see Appendix B, "ASCII\ANSI Code Chart." Codes from 128 through 255 are the extended character set. The extended character set contains many symbols, foreign characters, and Greek letters. The first 32 ASCII characters are *control characters*. Control characters are used to control data flow in communication programs, and line and page control on printers or the screen. The control codes you use regularly are backspace (8), tab (9), line feed (10), form feed (12), and carriage return (13).

There are two functions for converting between characters and ASCII codes, Asc() and Chr$(). You might wonder why you would want to use the codes at all when you can use the more readable characters. A simple example is inserting end-of-line characters (carriage return and line feed) within a string in a program. If you try to type a carriage return in a program, the program editor moves you down to the next line in the program rather than inserting that character in the string you were typing. (It probably will give you a syntax error, too.) To insert a carriage return in a string, you must create one with the function Chr$(13) and add it to your string. You will do this a little later in this chapter. The syntaxes of the Asc() and Chr$() functions are

```
Asc(string$)
Chr$(code)
```

Here, *string$* is a string. Asc() returns the ASCII code of its first character, and *code* is an ASCII code. Chr$() returns the character that the code represents as a one-character string.

Declaring String Variables

There are several ways to declare a string variable. As I mentioned previously, all the string variables in the properties of objects are predefined, so they do not have to be defined explicitly before they are used. User variables can be used without being defined; however, it is a much better programming practice to declare everything first in the appropriate procedure or declarations section. Doing so ensures that if you use the name of a global variable as a local variable, the two variables are kept separate. Another way to define a string variable is to append a $ to it. For example,

```
MyName$
```

also is a string variable. Notice that it is the same variable as the string variable `MyName` defined previously with the `Dim` statement. That is, the `$` is not included as part of the variable name.

Using String Formulas

After you define a variable, you have to create a string and store it in the variable. Assigning a value to a string is done with an Assignment statement. The syntax of an Assignment statement is

```
Variable = Formula
```

In this case, Variable is a string variable, and Formula is a string formula or constant. The equal sign makes this an Assignment statement. When it is executed, the formula on the right is evaluated, and the string result is assigned to the variable on the left. You have used Assignment statements in this book to change the values of the properties of objects.

A string formula consists of a combination of quoted strings of text and string functions linked with the *concatenation* operator (+). Concatenation is the act of combining two short strings into a long string by placing the strings end to end. For example, the formula

```
Name = "Bill " + "Orvis"
```

combines the strings `"Bill "` and `"Orvis"` into the longer string `"Bill Orvis"` and assigns the result to the string variable `MyName`. As another example,

```
Dim MyName As String, YourName As String
MyName = "Bill"
YourName = "Julie"
OurName$ = MyName + " Loves " + YourName
```

combines the two string variables with the string `" Loves "` to create the string `"Bill Loves Julie"`, which is assigned to the string variable `OurName$`. Here `MyName` and `YourName` are defined as string variables with a `Dim` statement. `OurName$` is defined as a string variable because it has the `$` suffix.

Strings Displayed in Labels and Text Boxes

After you have created a string, you have to display it. Printing it on a form is an adequate way to display the string; however, in this age of dialog boxes and windows, inserting the string in a label or text box is more modern. Both labels and text boxes dynamically display text on the screen. The difference between them is that the user can edit the text in a text box, but cannot edit the text in a label.

Setting the Text with the Properties Bar

The simplest way to display text in a label or text box is to use the Properties window at design time. For a label, select the Caption property and type the text into the Settings box. For a text box, find the `Text` property and again type the text into the Settings box. Although it is simple to do, setting the text in a box using the Properties window is good only for static text (text that won't change) or to set an initial string for a Text or Caption property that is changed later by the program.

Setting the Text with a Formula

To dynamically change the text in a box, use Assignment statements in your program. The Assignment statement to change a property of an object has the following format:

```
object.property = formula
```

in which the formula must evaluate to a value consistent with the property being changed. The construct `object.property` is treated like any other variable that is defined at the Form level and refers to the contents of the property of the object. For text properties such as `Text` and `Caption`, `formula` must evaluate to a string of text.

The LOVES Program

Take the preceding example and turn it into the LOVES program.

1. Open a new project and draw two text boxes.

2. Add one label on the form, as shown in Figure 4.3.

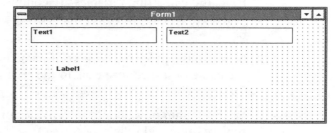

Figure 4.3. Layout for the LOVES application.

3. Select the Text properties of the two text boxes and set them to the null string.

4. Select the Caption property of the label and set it to the null string.

5. Open the Code window and select the (general) object and the (declarations) procedure. Then type

```
Dim MyName As String, YourName As String
```

This statement makes MyName and YourName module level definitions available anywhere in the form. Thus, they are available to any procedure on the form that wants to use them.

6. Select the Text1_Change procedure and type

```
Sub Text1_Change ()
MyName = Text1.Text
End Sub
```

This step stores the value of the Text property of the Text1 box in the string variable MyName.

7. Select the Text2_Change procedure and type

```
Sub Text2_Change ()
YourName = Text2.Text
End Sub
```

4

This step does the same for the `Text` property of the `Text2` box.

8. Select the `Form_Click` procedure and type

```
Sub Form_Click ()
Label1.Caption = MyName + " Loves " + YourName
End Sub
```

Here, the two string variables are combined with the string `" Loves "` and are stored in the `Caption` property of the `Label1` box.

9. Now run the program. Type your name in the first text box. Type the name of someone special in the second box, and click the form.

Your program now should look like Figure 4.4 (your names replace mine and Julie's, of course).

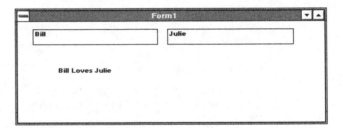

Figure 4.4. The running LOVES application.

10. End the program by selecting **End** from the **R**un menu and save it as LOVES1 (LOVES1.MAK and LOVES1.FRM).

Try this program again, but without the declarations in the (declara-tions) procedure. The program won't work because the `Form_Click` procedure won't know the value of `MyName` or `YourName`. `MyName` and `YourName` now are local to the procedures that contain them.

Changing the Text Attributes

The text attributes in the label and text boxes are set in exactly the same manner as the text attributes of a form. You change them either at design time with the Properties bar or at run time with assignment statements. To set the properties at run-time,

1. Select the label and change the following properties:

```
Label1.Alignment = 2 - Centered
Label1.FontName = Script
Label1.FontSize = 24
```

2. Run the program again. It now looks like Figure 4.5.

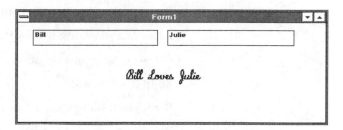

Figure 4.5. *The LOVES program with changed* Text *properties in the* Label *box.*

3. End the program and save it as LOVES2 (LOVES2.MAK and LOVES2.FRM).

The Manipulation of Strings

As you might expect, you can do more to strings than simply concatenate them. Visual Basic has a set of functions that deal exclusively with strings. The set includes functions to locate substrings, and others to extract a substring from a string. Table 4.1 contains a complete list of the string functions available in Visual Basic. See Chapter 15, "Command Reference," for descriptions of the individual functions.

Table 4.1. String functions.

Function	Description
Asc()	Converts a character to an ASCII code.
Chr$()	Converts an ASCII code to a character.
Format$()	Converts a number to a string with a specific format.
InStr()	Locates a substring in a string.
LCase$()	Converts a string to all lowercase.
Left$()	Extracts the left side of a string.
Len()	Determines the length of a string.
LSet()	Left-justifies a string.
LTrim$()	Removes leading spaces from a string.
Mid$()	Extracts a substring from a string.
Right$()	Extracts the right side of a string.
RSet()	Right-justifies a string.
RTrim$()	Removes trailing spaces from a string.
Space$()	Returns a string of spaces.
String$()	Returns a string of a specific character.
StrComp()	Compares two strings.
Trim$()	Removes leading and trailing spaces.
UCase$()	Converts a string to all uppercase.

If your program has to deal with a string typed by the user or sent by another program, the first thing you usually do is test it to see whether it is the one you expected to receive. You can calculate its length with the Len() function, or search for a specific substring with InStr(). If the Len() function returns a length of 0, the string is empty, a situation that your program must be able to deal with. The InStr() function searches for a specific substring within another string and returns the character location of the start of that substring. If it doesn't find the substring, it returns a zero. The syntaxes of the Len() and InStr() functions are

```
Len(string$)
InStr([start-position,]string$,substring$)
```

After you have found a substring, you might want to extract it, or some other substring. Do this with the Mid$(), Left$(), and Right$() functions. The Mid$() function extracts any substring within a string. The Left$() and Right$() functions are special cases of Mid$() that extract some number of characters from the left or right side of a string. The syntaxes of these functions are

```
Mid$(string$,start-character[,length])
Left$(string$,length)
Right$(string$,length)
```

Here, *string$* is the string from which to extract a substring, start-character is the number of the first character to include in the substring, counting from the first character in *string$*, and length is the length of the substring to extract from *string$*. In Mid$(), if you omit the length argument, the entire right side of the string is extracted.

Mid$() also can be written as a statement (on the left side of a formula rather than on the right) that replaces a substring in a string with another string of equal length. That syntax is

```
Mid$(string$,start-character[,length]) = substring$
```

Here, the substring in *string$* that starts at start-character and is *n*length long is replaced with length characters from *substring$*. If length is omitted, all *substring$* is used. In both cases, the resulting length of string$ is the same length as the original *string$*.

The Envelope Addresser Program (Version 1)

The LOVES application is cute, but you can make something more useful. Often when you write a letter, you have to type an envelope to go with it. Here is a program that prints addresses on envelopes. The program has a built-in return address. It accepts the address that is to be typed in a Text box. When your address is ready, click the Form to print the address.

1. Start with a new project and a single form.

2. Draw a text box on Form1 that is large enough to hold an address. Reduce the size of the form by dragging its borders until it looks like Figure 4.6. Set the property Multiline = True so the text box can contain more than one line of text. Set the Text property to null.

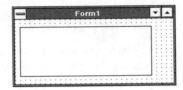

Figure 4.6. `Form1` *setup for the Envelope Addresser.*

3. Create a second Form with the New **F**orm command. Drag its borders until it looks like Figure 4.7.

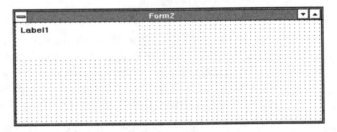

Figure 4.7. `Form2` *setup for the Envelope Addresser.*

4. Draw a label in the upper-left corner for the return address. Set the property `FontSize = 10`.

5. Select `Form2`. Set `FontSize = 10` and `AutoRedraw = True`.

The `FontSize` property increases the size of the text printed on the form to 10 points. `AutoRedraw` must be turned on so the form remembers text that is printed on it. Otherwise, when it is printed to the printer, only the text in the labels and text boxes is printed. `AutoRedraw` also makes it possible to cover a form with another form, uncover it, and still have the text appear.

> `AutoRedraw` is needed only for forms and picture boxes, because text boxes and labels already store the text printed on them in one of their properties.

6. Select `Form1` and open its Code window. Select the `Form_Load` procedure and type

```
Sub Form_Load ()
Form2.Show
End Sub
```

This procedure is executed when Form1 loads. It loads Form2 and makes it visible.

7. Select the Text1_Change procedure and type

```
Sub Text1_Change ()
TheLine = Text1.Text
End Sub
```

This procedure extracts the text from the text box as it is typed and stores it in the string variable TheLine. The Change event causes this procedure to be executed every time the user types a character into the text box. To pass the value of TheLine from Form1 to Form2 where it is printed, define it in a module.

8. Execute the new Module comand on the File menu. Open the declarations section and type

```
Global TheLine As String
```

9. Select Form2 and open its Code window. Select the (declarations) section and type

```
Dim eol$
```

The string eol$ is a constant that is needed in two routines on Form2. By defining it in the (declarations) section of Form2, you have to define its value only once. You can't give it a value here with the Const declaration because you can't type a carriage return and a line feed into a string. Such functions as Chrs$(13) are not allowed in the (declarations) section.

10. Select the Form_Load procedure and type the following text. Substitute your own return address for the one I use here.

```
Sub Form_Load ()
     eol$ = Chr$(13) + Chr$(10)
Label1.Caption = "William J. Orvis" + eol$
Label1.Caption = Label1.Caption + "123 Some St." + eol$
Label1.Caption = Label1.Caption + "Anywhere, CA  91234"
End Sub
```

This routine inserts the return address into the label. This must be done with code because you can't type a return in a label. The

routine first defines eol$, the end-of-line string, as a carriage return (Chr$(13)) and a line feed (Chr$(10)). Next, it combines the text of the return address into a single string with the end-of-line separating each line. This string is stored in the Caption property of the Label1 label.

11. Select the Form_Click procedure and type

```
Sub Form_Click ()
start = 1
Form2.Cls
Print eol$ + eol$ + eol$ + eol$ + eol$ + eol$ + eol$ + eol$
Print Space$(80); Mid$(TheLine, start, InStr(start, TheLine,
➥eol$) - start)
start = InStr(start, TheLine, eol$) + 2
Print Space$(80); Mid$(TheLine, start, InStr(start, TheLine,
➥eol$) - start)
start = InStr(start, TheLine, eol$) + 2
Print Space$(80); Right$(TheLine, Len(TheLine) - start + 1
Form2.PrintForm
Form1.Show
End Sub
```

This procedure uses eol$, which was given a value in the Form_Load procedure and passed to this routine through the form's declarations section. It then initializes the variable start, clears the Form, and prints eight new-line characters on the Form. The next Print statement uses the Space$() function to print 80 blank spaces. It then uses the Mid$() function to extract the name line of the address from TheLine. TheLine was passed to Form2 from Form1 through the Global statement in the module. You get the length of string to extract by using the InStr() function to look for the first end-of-line after character number start. Next, the procedure changes the value of start to point to the beginning of the next line (the first character after the two-character end-of-line). The address is extracted and printed in the same way. Then the city and state are extracted with the Right$() function. Finally, this procedure prints the form to the printer (on your envelope) and then redisplays Form1 so you can address a second envelope.

One limitation of this procedure is that it must receive a three-line address. It does not make allowances for addresses with two lines, four lines, or any other number of lines but three. The book will discuss putting protections in programs later.

12. Save the program as ADDR1 (ADDR11.FRM, ADDR12.FRM, ADDR1.BAS and ADDR1.MAK).

13. Run the program. Type the address for your letter in the text box on Form1. When you are ready, insert an envelope in your printer (or leave the paper in it if you just want to experiment), and click Form2.

    Your address and return address now should be printed on the envelope.

The Use of an InputBox$

In the envelope-addressing program, you created a small form to use when inputting the address to be printed on the envelope. In effect, you created what is called an *Input box*. The InputBox$ function performs a similar function, although you can input only one line of text at a time. The syntax of the function is

```
InputBox$(prompt$,[title$[,default$[,xpos%,ypos%]]])
```

Here, *xpos%* and *ypos%* are the location of the top-left corner of the Input box, *default$* is a default string of text placed in the box, *title$* is a string to be used as the title of the box, and *prompt$* is a string of text describing what you are supposed to do with the box. When you execute this function, it presents the user with an Input box with the specified prompts and titles, and with **OK** and **Cancel** buttons. When you click **OK**, what you typed in the box is returned by the function.

The Envelope Addresser (Version 2)

Modify the envelope addresser to use an InputBox$ to get the address.

1. Open the ADDR1.MAK project file. Save it as ADDR2.MAK so you won't accidently overwrite the previous version of this program.

2. Select Form1 and delete it with the **R**emove File command on the **File** menu.

3. Select Form2 and open the Code window to the Form_Click procedure. Change the procedure to

```
Sub Form_Click ()
Form2.Cls
Print eol$ + eol$ + eol$ + eol$ + eol$ + eol$ + eol$ + eol$
Print Space$(80); InputBox$("Name", "Mailing Address")
Print Space$(80); InputBox$("Address" , "Mailing Address")
Print Space$(80); InputBox$("City and State" , "Mailing
➥Address")
Form2.PrintForm
End Sub
```

Here, you first replace the Mid$() function with an InputBox$ with the string Name as the prompt and the string Mailing Address as the box title—see Figure 4.8. What the user types is printed immediately on Form2. The second and third lines of the address are done the same way. Then the Form is printed.

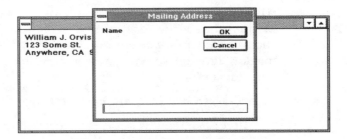

Figure 4.8. The first Input box requesting the name.

4. Save the Form as ADDR2.FRM by selecting it and executing the Save File **As** command on the File menu. Save the project again as ADDR2.MAK.

5. Run the program. A dialog box appears and asks you to select the start-up routine. Select Form2 and click **OK**. Form1 is the default start-up Form, and because it was deleted, you have to tell Visual Basic which Form or procedure to use. This happens only the first time you run the program; the next time you run it, Visual Basic can recall the Form used for start up.

6. Click the Form. The Input box shown in Figure 4.7 appears. Type the name and press Enter.

7. After pressing Enter, another similar Input box appears. Type the address in the Input box.

8. After pressing Enter, a third similar Input box appears. Type the city and state and press Enter.

   At this point, Form2 is filled out and printed to the printer.

The Use of a MsgBox

If you simply want to send a message to the user rather than requesting input from him, you can use the MsgBox function. The syntax of the MsgBox function is

```
MsgBox(msg$[,type[,title$]])
```

in which *msg$* is the message to be shown, *type* is a number indicating the number and type of buttons on the box (see Chapter 15, "Command Reference," for a complete list), and *title$* is a string title for the box. If you omit type, a simple message box with a single **OK** button is used. Add this to the envelope addresser program so the program pauses before printing. As a result, the user has time to insert the envelope in the printer.

1. Select Form2 and open the Code window to the Form_Click procedure. Change the procedure to

```
Sub Form_Click ()
Form2.Cls
Print eol$ + eol$ + eol$ + eol$ + eol$ + eol$ + eol$ + eol$
Print Space$(80); InputBox$("Name", "Mailing Address")
Print Space$(80); InputBox$("Address", "Mailing Address")
Print Space$(80); InputBox$("City and State", "Mailing
➥Address")   Print
MsgBox ("Insert an envelope in the printer and click OK")
Form2.PrintForm
End Sub
```

   The extra Print statement in line 8 is needed to overcome what seems to be a bug in Visual Basic. Without it, the third line of the address does not print.

2. Run the program again. After entering the city and state, the message box in Figure 4.9 appears.

4

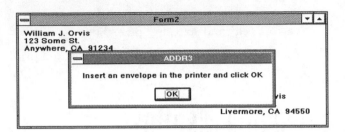

Figure 4.9. Using a message box for a pause in the Envelope Addresser.

3. End the program. Save the Form as ADDR2B.FRM, the module as ADDR2B.BAS, and the project as ADDR2B.MAK.

What You Have Learned

Now you know all about strings and string functions. As you have seen, strings are important in Visual Basic because all communication with the user is done with them. Keyboard input starts as a string, which is then turned into numbers and commands. Output to the screen or printer can start as numbers but must be converted to strings to be printed. In this chapter you

- Defined variables as storage locations for information.
- Examined the scope of variables.
- Defined strings and string variables.
- Created string formulas.
- Manipulated strings using the string functions.
- Used Input and Message boxes.
- Created an envelope addresser.

Using Numbers and Control Structures

In most computer language books, numeric variables are discussed first and strings are mentioned almost as an afterthought. In Visual Basic, strings are discussed prior to the numeric types in a chapter of their own because they play such an important part in the user interface. Now that you know all about strings, it's time to look at numeric values and control structures.

In This Chapter

This chapter describes numeric variables and control structures. Numeric variables are variables that contain a number rather than a string of characters as a binary value. Although you can only display or store strings, you can perform real numeric operations with numeric variables. In

addition, control structures make it possible to examine the value of a variable and alter the order of execution of a program based on that value. In this chapter you learn to

- Compare the different numeric types.

- Examine integers.

- Examine floating-point numbers.

- Examine currency format.

- Define numeric variables.

- Create formulas using numeric variables.

- Examine array variables.

- Examine control arrays.

- Create logical formulas.

- Control program flow with loops and logical variables.

The Numeric Types of Visual Basic

There are seven different data types in Visual Basic. The five numeric types (Integer, Long, Single, Double, Currency), the String type, and the Variant type. I discussed the String data type in the previous chapter. Integer and Long data types are used for storing whole numbers (numbers with no fractional parts). Single and Double data types are used for storing real numbers (numbers with fractional parts). Currency is a special data type designed to do calculations with decimal numbers rather than binary numbers. This data type is used to eliminate the round-off errors caused by converting binary numbers to decimal notation. The Variant data type is the default for all variables that are not explicitly declared. The variant type stores whatever data type is assigned to it in an assignment statement.

In general, a numeric Variant data type is stored in the data type assigned to it. For example, if you assign an Integer to a Variant data type, subsequent operations treat the Variant data type as if it were an Integer. However, if you perform an arithmetic operation on a Variant data type which contains an Integer, a Long, or a Single, and the result exceeds the normal range for the data type, the result is automatically promoted within the Variant to the next larger data type. For example, an Integer is promoted to a Long, and Longs and Singles are promoted to Doubles.

Table 5.1 lists the numeric types available in Visual Basic and describes their properties.

Table 5.1. Data types in Visual Basic.

Type	Suffix Character	Memory Usage	Range	Description
Integer	%	2 bytes	–32,768 to 32,767	Two-byte integer.
Long	&	4 bytes	–2,147, 483,648 to 2,147,483,647	Four-byte integer.
Single	!	4 bytes	–3.37E–38 to 3.37E+38	Single-precision floating-point number. This is the default for unspecified variables.
Double	#	8 bytes	–1.67D–308 to 1.67D+308	Double-precision floating-point number.
Currency	@	8 bytes	–9.22E+14 to 9.22E14	Fixed-point number with two digits after the decimal. Math is done in decimal to eliminate round-off errors when converting from binary to decimal.

continues

5

Table 5.1. continued

Type	Suffix Character	Memory Usage	Range	Description
String	$	1 byte + 1 byte per character		String of characters.
Variant		variable		The variant data type. It stores whatever variable type is assigned to it.

Integers

The Integer and Long data types represent whole numbers only. They cannot be used to represent fractions. As a result, they take less storage space than floating-point numbers. Mathematical operations that involve Integers and Long types are much faster than those involving floating-point numbers. Use Integers when you know you do not have a fractional number. Use Long integers when you have to store values larger than those allowed by the Integer data type.

You might wonder why the limits in Table 5.1 are such odd numbers. Why should a type have a limit of 32,767 rather than a nice round number like 33,000? The fact is they *are* nice round numbers—in binary. The Integer data type is stored in two bytes (16 bits) of memory. The first bit is used as the sign bit (+ or –), and the rest represent the number in binary notation. The largest number that a sequence of n bits can represent is 2n, which in this case is 215 = 32,767.

Floating-Point Numbers

Single- and Double-precision floating-point numbers are used to represent real numbers (numbers with fractional parts). The Single-precision floating-point number is the default numeric type for variables that are not defined with the suffix characters, or with `Global`, `Dim`, or `Static` statements. Single-precision numbers have about 7-digit precision, whereas Double-precision numbers have about 15-digit precision. The precision of a data type is its ability to store a certain number of digits. If you try to store a number with more digits than the precision allows, the extra digits are lost.

On input and output, large floating-point numbers are expressed in `E` or `D` format as

```
1.94E+04 = 19,400.
9.2279E-28 = 0.00000000000000000000000000092279
0.3141592653589793D+01 = 3.141592653589793
```

in which `E` represents the Single-precision floating-point, `D` is the Double-precision floating-point, and the numbers following the `E` or `D` are the powers of 10 used to multiply the number on the left.

Currency

The `Currency` numeric type is a fixed-point type used to calculate money values. In most cases, calculations are done in binary. The result is converted to decimal when it is printed or displayed on the screen. In the conversion process, round-off errors are caused often by the fact that there are decimal numbers that cannot be represented exactly in binary. As a result, you often get results like 0.99999 rather than 1.00. In many cases, this is no problem. However, if you are dealing with money, you usually want the results to be exact to the penny. A number like 0.99999 is not acceptable when 1.00 is expected. The Currency numeric type takes care of this by doing calculations in decimal rather than in binary, albeit decimal calculations are much slower than binary calculations. Currency type numbers have about 14-digit precision.

5

Variant

The Variant data type is new in Version 2 of Visual Basic, and is the default data type for all variables that are not explicitly declared with suffix characters, or in Dim, Global, or Static statements. The Variant type is different from other data types because this type can store whatever data type is passed to it. To find out what data type is stored in a Variant type variable, use the VarType function. The VarType function returns one of the following codes.

Code	Data type
0	Empty—uninitialized
1	Null—initialized but contains no data.
2	Integer
3	Long
4	Single
5	Double
6	Currency
7	Date
8	String

Remember that the Variant data type must determine what type of value is being passed to it instead of just storing a known data type. This checking slows any program that makes significant use of variant types. Whenever possible, use explicit types. Do use the Variant type when a variable might contain a date.

Defining Numeric Variables

Numeric variables are defined in exactly the same manner as the String data type. Moreover, all the arguments about the range of a variable apply equally to numeric types.

```
Global Width As Single
Dim Account As Currency
Dim RoadLen As Double, Counter As Integer
```

In addition, you can use the variable prefix characters listed in Table 5.1 to define the type of any local variable or to override the type of a Global variable.

One defining statement you have not looked at so far is the Const statement. The `Const` statement is used anywhere you want to give a constant a name. This is different than defining a variable and assigning it a name, because once the variable is defined, the value of a constant cannot be changed. The syntax of the `Const` statement is

```
[Global] Const variable = value [,variable = value ...]
```

Here, the `Global` prefix defines a global constant; `variable` is the name of the constant, and `value` is its value. `Value` can consist of simple numbers, other constants, and all the operators except those for exponentiation and concatenation. Value cannot include any functions. The numeric type of `variable` is determined either by the value assigned to it, or by the placement of a variable suffix character on it. Strings also can be constants. However, as mentioned previously, they cannot be concatenated, and you cannot use the `Chr$()` function to insert carriage returns or line feeds in your constant string. For example,

```
Global Const RED = &HFF&
```

defines the constant, RED, as the hexadecimal value for the red color. The constant then is used in the different procedures of the program rather than the hexadecimal value, making the procedures more readable.

Using Arrays

An array isn't actually a different numeric type. It is an indexed group of variables of the same type that can be referenced as a single object. An array variable must be defined with a `Global` or `Dim` statement, with the following syntax:

```
Dim ArrayName([lower To] upper[,[lower To] upper])[ As type]
```

Here, each set of `lower` and `upper` is a dimension of the array, with `lower` as the lower limit of the index and `upper` as the upper limit. If you leave

out the lower limit, its default value is 0. The range of array limits is the same as the range of the integer data type (–32,768 to –32,767). The maximum number of dimensions for a single array is 60. For example,

```
Dim TaxRate(5)
Dim CostTable(2,5 To 8)
```

The first example defines `TaxRate` as a one-dimensional array variable with five elements. Each element is accessed by placing an index within the parentheses. The value of the index then identifies the array element to be used. For example, the elements of `TaxRate` are

```
TaxRate(0)

TaxRate(1)

TaxRate(2)

TaxRate(3)

TaxRate(4)

TaxRate(5)
```

The second example, `CostTable (2,5 to 8)`, defines a two-dimensional, three-cell-by-three-cell array named `CostTable`. A two-dimensional array is like the two-dimensional grid of cells in a spreadsheet. The first number is the row index, and the second is the column. The array elements are accessed as

```
CostTable(0,5) CostTable(0,6)     CostTable(0,7)
CostTable(1,5) CostTable(1,6)     CostTable(1,7)
CostTable(2,5) CostTable(2,6)     CostTable(2,7)
```

You can imagine a three-dimensional array as a cube of cells with a row, column, and depth index. Higher-dimensional arrays such as this are a little difficult to imagine, but they are occasionally useful.

Arrays are used for storing large blocks of data. For example, imagine you are working on your super stock estimator, which needs the average daily value of a stock over several months. You don't want to create a program with several hundred variables to hold all these values (`Day1`, `Day2`, `Day3`, ...). Instead, create a single array variable to hold them, such as `Day(Index1)`. Then the value of `Index1` selects the value of the stock for any specific day.

You can use this process for three different stocks as well; just create a two-dimensional array with three elements in one direction and a few hundred in the other. For example, Day(1 To 300, 1 To 3), with the values retrieved with Day(Index1,Index2). (Index1 selects the day and Index2 selects the stock.) Assume you want to store the high and low values as well as the average. Add another dimension to the array when you define it, Day(1 To 300, 1 To 3, 1 To 3), then access the elements with Day(Index1,Index2,Index3), where Index1 selects the day, Index2 selects the stock and Index3 selects high, low, or average.

Inputting Numbers

In Chapter 4, "Using Strings and Text Boxes," you saw how to input strings of text from the user. But what about inputting numbers? You get numbers from the user in exactly the same way you get strings. In fact, you input the number as a string, using the methods from the previous chapter, and then convert it into a number. Conversion of strings into numbers is performed with the Val() function, which has the syntax

```
Val(string$)
```

Here, string$ is any string representation of a number. The string can have leading white space (spaces, tabs, and line feeds). However, it cannot have leading nonnumeric characters. The function converts the numeric characters into numbers. The function continues until it encounters a character it cannot convert, then it stops. For example,

```
Val("    456abs") = 456
Val("456 789") = 456
Val("a345") = 0
Val(" 0 ") = 0
```

As you can see by the previous two examples, you must be careful what strings you give to the Val() function. A string with a mistyped leading character—in this example, it's a—causes the result to be 0, even when the rest of the string contains a number. No error is generated if the function can't find a number in a string.

Displaying Numbers

Again, numbers are displayed in the same manner as strings. They are converted to a string first. Then the string is either printed or displayed in a Label or Text box. The simplest routine for converting numbers to text is the Str$() function. The Str$() function takes a number as an argument and converts it into a string. The format of the string is the simplest format that can display the full precision of the number. If you want the number formatted in a specific format, use the Format$() function. The syntaxes of these functions are

```
Str$(number)
Format$(number[,format-string$])
```

in which number is the value to be converted to a string, and format-string$ is a formatting string that controls how the string is converted. In the

formatting string, place zeros or pound signs (0 or #) where you want the digits of the number to go. Insert commas and the decimal point where you want them. If you use the pound signs, the space in the output string of the Format$() function is reserved for a number. If you use zeros rather than pound signs, leading and trailing zeros are included at those positions, if needed. Specific formatting strings also exist for dates and times. See Chapter 15, "Command Reference," for a complete list. You can insert +, -, $, (,), and spaces in the string; those characters are included in the output, where they were placed in the formatting string. To insert any other characters in the output, they have to be surrounded by double quotation marks (use Chr$(34), not "). For example,

```
ANumber = 1234.567
Str$(ANumber) = " 1234.567"
Format$(ANumber,"#####.") = "1235."
Format$(ANumber,Chr$(34)+"Balance = "+Chr$(34)+"$00000.00"=
➥"Balance = $01234.57"
Format$(ANumber,"##.##") = "1234.57"
ANumber2 = 0.123
Format$(ANumber2,"##.#####") = ".123"
Format$(ANumber2,"00.#####") = "00.123"
```

Users of other versions of BASIC should recognize the formatting capabilities of the PRINT USING statement contained in the Format$() function.

Calculating Mathematical Formulas

Mathematical formulas in Visual Basic look much like the equivalent algebraic formula for the same calculation. In other words, they are Assignment statements like those discussed for strings, with a numerical variable on the left and a formula that evaluates to a numeric result on the right. Visual Basic has a complete set of operators and mathematical functions to use when constructing a mathematical formula.

Arithmetic Operators

The arithmetic operators available in Visual Basic are listed in Table 5.2. They include the standard set of addition, subtraction, multiplication, division, and powers (such as 10^4), as well as modulus arithmetic and integer division. The precedence of the operators tells you which operation is done first in an expression involving more than one operator.

Table 5.2. The Visual Basic arithmetic operators and precedences.

Operator	Operation	Precedence
^	Power	1
−	Negation (unary operation)	2
*	Multiplication	3
/	Division	3
\	Integer division	4

continues

Table 5.2. continued

Operator	Operation	Precedence
Mod	Modulus	5
+	Addition	6
–	Subtraction	6

Addition, subtraction, multiplication, and powers operate as you would expect, in the algebraic sense. The modulus operator is defined as the remainder of an integer division. First, the operands are rounded to integers. Then the modulus operation is performed. For example, if you had 6.9 Mod 2, 6.9 would be rounded to 7 and then divided by 2. The remainder (the Mod) would be 1. The integer division operator also rounds the operands to integers, performs a normal division operation, and then truncates the result to an integer. For example, if you had instead specified 6.9\2, 6.9 again would be rounded to 7, then divided by 2. The answer would be 2. Table 5.3 shows more examples.

Table 5.3. Modulus and integer division.

Modulus Division	Integer Division
5 Mod 3 = 2	5\3 = 1
–5 Mod 3 = –2	–5\3 = –1
5.8 Mod 3 = 0	5.8\3 = 2

As you can see, the modulus and integer division operators perform a complementary set of operations. The modulus operator is most often used to unwind cyclical events, such as the actual angle between two lines when it is specified as a number greater than 360 degrees. It also can be used to determine the day of the week (or the year) when the number of days between now and then is greater than a week (or a year). For example, to find the day of the week 138 days from now you could use

```
138 Mod 7 = 5
```

If today is a Monday, 138 days from now would be Monday plus five days, or Saturday.

Relational Operators

The relational operators shown in Table 5.4 compare two values and return a logical result. If the relationship between the two values is the same as the one expressed by the operator, the expression returns True (–1) otherwise, it returns False (0). All the relational operators have the same precedence, so use parentheses to ensure that the correct comparisons are done.

Table 5.4. The Visual Basic relational operators.

Operator	Operation
=	Equals
>	Greater than
<	Less than
<>	Not equal to
<=	Less than or equal to
>>=	Greater than or equal to

Logical Operators

The logical operators shown in Table 5.5 apply a logical operation to one or two logical values, and return a logical value. In addition, if they are applied to numeric values rather than logical values, the operation is performed bit by bit to each bit in the numeric values. All the Logical operators have the same precedence, so use parentheses to ensure the operations are performed in the order you want. Along with the logical operators are two logical values, True (–1) and False (0). These values can be used directly in a program. The logical operators are explained later in this chapter.

5

Table 5.5. The Visual Basic logical operators.

Operator	Operation
Not	Negation
And	Logical and
Or	Logical or
Xor	Logical exclusive or
Eqv	Logical equivalence
Imp	Logical implies

Precedence of the Operators

As stated before, the precedence of the operators tells you which operation is done first in an expression involving more than one operator. When the computer has a choice between two operations, the operation with the highest precedence is performed first. When two operations have the same precedence, they are evaluated left to right. Parentheses always override the precedence of operators, so use them to control the order of calculation. If you are unsure what the order is in a situation, use parentheses to make the formula calculate in the order in which you want it to be calculated. Inserting unnecessary parentheses won't hurt anything, and they assure you the calculations are being done in the order you want. Some examples are

```
A * B^C + D
A*B + C
A*(B + C)
```

In the first example, the power, B^C, is done first. Then this result is multiplied by A and added to D. In the second example, the multiplication, A*B, is done first. Then the result is added to C. The third example reverses the order of the second by using parentheses: The addition, (B + C), is done first. Then the result is multiplied by A.

Numeric Functions

The numeric functions consist of arithmetic functions, trigonometric functions, and logarithms. Table 5.6 lists the numeric functions available in Visual Basic.

Table 5.6. The numeric functions in Visual Basic.

Arithmetic Functions

Function	Result
Abs()	Absolute value
CCur()	Convert to Currency

Arithmetic Functions

Function	Result
CInt()	Convert to Integer
CDbl()	Convert to Double
CLng()	Convert to Long
CSng()	Convert to Single
CVar()	Convert to Variant
Fix()	Truncate to an integer
Int()	Round to an integer
Randomize()	Initialize the random number generator
Rnd()	Generate a random number
Sgn()	The sign of the argument
Sqr()	Square root

continues

5

Table 5.6. continued

Trigonometric Functions

Function	Result
Sin()	Sine
Cos()	Cosine
Tan()	Tangent
Atn()	Arctangent

Logarithmic Functions

Function	Result
Exp()	Exponential
Log()	Natural

There are four functions for converting a floating-point number to an integer: CInt(), CLng(), Fix(), and Int(). The first two, CInt() and CLng(), force the result to be an Integer or Long type by rounding the floating-point number to an integer. For example, CInt(6.8) would equal the integer 7. Fix() forms an integer by truncating the fractional part of the floating-point number. Int() returns the largest integer that is less than or equal to the argument. For example,

```
CInt(4.7) = 5    CLng(4.7) = 5    Fix(4.7) = 4    Int(4.7) = 4
CInt(4.3) = 4    CLng(4.3) = 4    Fix(4.3) = 4    Int(4.3) = 4
CInt(-4.7) = -5  CLng(-4.7) = -5  Fix(-4.7) = -4  Int(-4.7) = -5
CInt(-4.3) = -4  CLng(-4.3) = -4  Fix(-4.3) = -4  Int(-4.3) = -5
```

The Randomize() and Rnd() functions initialize and return random numbers. The numbers are not truly random, but they are generated by a pseudo-random function. The Randomize function is normally executed inside a program to initialize the seed of the random number generator. By setting the seed (starting number) of that generator, you can either repeat a set of random numbers or give the generator a random starting place. If you execute Randomize with no argument, the random number generator gets a random starting point using the Timer function. If you use a numeric argument with Randomize, the generator uses it as the seed, and Rnd(1) returns the same set of numbers every time. A new random number is generated every time the Rnd() function is executed with a positive argument.

The available trigonometric functions are sine, cosine, tangent, and arctangent. The rest of the common trigonometric and hyperbolic functions can be calculated using the built-in functions and the well-known rules of trigonometry.

The logarithmic functions available in Visual Basic calculate the natural logarithm (base e = 2.71828) and the exponential (power of e). To calculate the common logarithm (base 10), use

```
Log10(x) = Log(x)/Log(10)
```

Type Conversion

Because five different numeric types are available in Visual Basic (Integer, Long, Single, Double, and Currency), some type of conversion has to take place when you create a formula that contains different types. Before a calculation takes place, Visual Basic converts all the values on the right side of the formula into the most precise Form before performing the actual calculations. For example, if a formula combines Single-precision floating-point numbers and integer numbers, Visual Basic converts everything to Single-precision floating-point before performing the calculation. After the result is calculated, it is converted to the type of the variable on the left side of the formula.

The Self-Paced Learning Program (Version 1)

My son is learning mathematics and needs to practice for his weekly tests. The following program automatically creates a test for him to practice.

1. Start with a new project.

2. Draw five labels (615 x 500 twips) on Form1, as shown in Figure 5.1.

3. Draw five text boxes (615 x 260 twips).

113

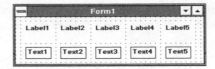

Figure 5.1. The initial form layout of the Self-Paced Learning program.

4. For each text box set the following. Note that `""` stands for the empty or null string; therefore, delete the contents of the `Text` property.

    ```
    BorderStyle = 0 - None
    FontName = Courier
    Text = ""
    ```

5. For each Label set

    ```
    FontName = Courier
    ```

    In these previous two steps, the font is Courier, a monospaced font (in which all characters are the same width). The numbers in the top row are then lined up with those in the bottom row.

6. Draw five lines, each with a width of 615 twips to create the five horizontal lines between the labels and the text boxes, as shown in Figure 5.2.

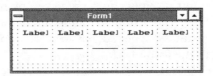

Figure 5.2. Modified form layout for the Self-Paced Learning program.

7. Open the code window for the form. Select the `declarations` section and type

    ```
    Dim Probs(2, 5) As Single
    ```

    This line defines the array `Probs`, which has three rows and six columns as a Single-precision array. The array is to hold the two numbers per addition problem. I define it here so the numbers are available for other routines to use. In the following step, don't forget you can use the **Copy** and **Paste** commands on the **Edit** menu to make multiple copies of a line, then go back and edit the difference.

114

8. Select the Load event and type

```
Sub Form_Load ()
Rem Initialize the random number generator
Randomize
Rem Define the end-of-line character
eol$ = Chr$(13) + Chr$(10)
Rem Fill the probs array with 2 sets of 5 values
Rem between 0 and 100
Probs(1, 1) = Int(Rnd(1) * 100)     'line 8
Probs(1, 2) = Int(Rnd(1) * 100)
Probs(1, 3) = Int(Rnd(1) * 100)
Probs(1, 4) = Int(Rnd(1) * 100)
Probs(1, 5) = Int(Rnd(1) * 100)
Probs(2, 1) = Int(Rnd(1) * 100)
Probs(2, 2) = Int(Rnd(1) * 100)
Probs(2, 3) = Int(Rnd(1) * 100)
Probs(2, 4) = Int(Rnd(1) * 100)
Probs(2, 5) = Int(Rnd(1) * 100)     'line 17
Rem Insert the random numbers into the labels
Label1.Caption = Format$(Probs(1, 1), " 00") + eol$ +
➡Format$(Probs(2, 1), "+00")
Label2.Caption = Format$(Probs(1, 2), " 00") + eol$ +
➡Format$(Probs(2, 1), "+00")
Label3.Caption = Format$(Probs(1, 3), " 00") + eol$ +
➡Format$(Probs(2, 1), "+00")
Label4.Caption = Format$(Probs(1, 4), " 00") + eol$ +
➡Format$(Probs(2, 1), "+00")
Label5.Caption = Format$(Probs(1, 5), " 00") + eol$ +
➡Format$(Probs(2, 1), "+00")
End Sub
```

The second line of code contains a Rem or remark statement used to store remarks about what your code is doing. Visual Basic ignores anything following the Rem keyword at the beginning of a line or a single quotation mark anywhere in a line. I use remarks of this type to mark lines of code as I describe them.

Be liberal with remark statements in your code. They won't slow anything down much, and they immensely improve the comprehension of your code. If you are one of those people who can remember every word you have ever written and why you wrote it, and your code is never going to be read by anyone else, you can forget about including remark statements. However, if you are like me, you should use many remark statements so you don't forget what you have done and why.

Line 3 initializes the random number generator. Line 5 creates an end-of-line string as you have done before. Lines 8 through 17 fill the array Probs() with random numbers between 0 and 100. The Rnd(1) function generates random numbers between 0 and 1. Multiplying by 100 extends the range of the numbers from 0 to 100. Randomize utilizes the random number generator and should be called at least once in a program that uses random numbers.

Lines 19 through 23 insert the numbers into the five labels. First the numbers are converted to strings with the Format$() function. Then those strings are combined with an end-of-line character and stored in the Caption property of the labels.

There is a bug in the first version of Visual Basic that should be fixed in the next version. The # placeholder does not hold a place as it is supposed to. Even if you use two #s in the format statement, numbers less than 10 won't line up correctly with numbers greater than 10. Using the "00" format instead is a simple way to work around the bug. This format prints 01 through 09 for the numbers 1 through 9. Another option is to right-justify the text in the Label using the Alignment property.

9. Run the program. A Form like Figure 5.3 appears on the screen (your numbers will be different). Type the first answer. Then press Tab to go to the next problem.

   My son now can take this math test by typing his answers in the Text boxes below the problems. Maybe he will think this is another computer game and will spend hours practicing his math problems.

10. Save the project as MATH1 (MATH1.FRM and MATH1.MAK).

```
Form1
 65    26    64    28    69
+41   +60   +42   +45   +85
___   ___   ___   ___   ___
```

Figure 5.3. Running the Self-Paced Learning program (Version 1).

This test was purposefully made into a five-problem test so it would be less confusing to explain. You can increase the number of problems to 10 or 20 easily by increasing the number of labels and text boxes, enlarging the `Probs()` array, and filling in the extra elements. Now you can exercise a young mind.

Using Loops and Control Arrays

If you look closely at the code in step 7, you notice two blocks of nearly identical statements. You shouldn't have to write the same statement repeatedly when the only difference is the value of an index. Loops are a good way to shorten the length of a program (and the amount of typing you have to do) by repeatedly executing a single block of statements rather than having multiple copies of that block.

There are three types of loops in Visual Basic: `For/Next`, `While/Wend`, and `Do/Loop`. The `For/Next` loop is a counted loop, which executes a block of statements a fixed number of times. I use this type of loop most often. The `While/Wend` loop executes a block of statements until some condition is no longer satisfied. The `Do/Loop` loop executes a block of statements as long as a condition is satisfied or until one condition becomes satisfied. The syntaxes of the loops are

```
For counter = start To end [Step stepsize]
    block of statements
[Exit For]
    block of statements
Next [counter[,counter]]

While condition
    block of statements
Wend

Do [{While|Until} condition]
    block of statements
[Exit Do]
    block of statements
```

```
Loop

Do
    block of statements
[Exit Do]
    block of statements
Loop [{While|Until} condition]
```

Here, counter is a variable used to count the number of times the For/Next loop is iterated, start is the beginning value of the counter, end is the stopping value of the counter, and stepsize is the increment given to the counter at each step. If the Step phase is omitted, step 1 is assumed. For the While/Wend and Do/Loop loops, condition is a numeric formula that results in the value True (–1) or False (0). The While and Until keywords determine how the condition is used. While continues executing the block until condition becomes False. Until continues executing the block as long as condition is False. With the Exit For and Exit Do statements, you can terminate a loop prematurely and go on to the next statement after the Next or Loop statement.

The Self-Paced Learning Program (Version 2)

A For/Next loop is made for the code in the Self-Paced Learning program, because you want things done exactly two times in five places. The data used in the program is stored in an array so individual elements are accessible with an index value. To use a loop here, you also have to be able to access the Text properties of five Text boxes using an index. Do this by combining the Text boxes into a control array. A control array is one or more controls with the same name. Individual controls in the control array are accessed with an index, like an array variable is.

A control array is created by giving all the controls (Text boxes in this case) the same CtlName and then setting the Index property to 1, 2, 3, and so on, to identify the individual control.

1. Select the Label1 box and set Index = 1.

2. Select the Label2 through Label5 label boxes, and set CtlName = Label1. The Index property is incremented automatically when you add a control to a control array.

3. Open the Code window for the form. Select the Load event and change the code to

118

```
Sub Form_Load ()
Rem Initialize the random number generator
Randomize
Rem Define the end-of-line
eol$ = Chr$(13) + Chr$(10)
Rem Fill the probs array with 2 sets of 5 values
Rem between 0 and 100
For I = 1 To 2        'line 8
  For J = 1 To 5
    Probs(I, J) = Int(Rnd(1) * 100)
  Next J              'line 11
Next I
Rem Insert the random numbers into the labels
For J = 1 To 5        'line 14
  Label1(J).Caption = Format$(Probs(1, J), " 00") + eol$ +
➥Format$(Probs(2, J), "+00")
Next J
End Sub
```

4. Save the code as MATH2 (MATH2.FRM and MATH2.MAK), then run it. The results should be similar to those in Figure 5.3, but with different numbers.

> When saving a modified project with a new name, be sure to save the Forms and modules first with the File Save As command on the File menu, then save the Project with the Save Project As command. If you save the project first, it is saved with the Form and module names of the previous version. To save a project with a new name:
>
> 1. Select a Form or module.
>
> 2. Use **File**, Save **As** with a new name.
>
> 3. Continue this process until you have saved all the Form and modules.
>
> 4. Execute **File**, Sav**e** Project As to save the project with a new name.

As you can see, this is much simpler than the code in step 7, but it performs exactly the same functions. In lines 8 and 9, I start two nested

119

For/Next loops that surround line 10. They are called *nested loops* because the loop for the counter J is within the loop for counter I. When line 8 is executed, I is set to 1. In line 9, J is set to 1. In line 10, Probs(1,1) is loaded. When the execution reaches line 11, the bottom of the J loop, it jumps back up to line 9, where J is set to 2, and lines 10 and 11 are executed again. This continues until J equals 5, at which point the J loop is finished. Execution moves to line 12. Line 12 is the bottom of the I loop, so execution jumps back up to line 8, where I is set to 2. Line 9 is executed again, starting up the J loop again to go through five more iterations. At this point, both the I loop and the J loop are done, so execution moves to line 14, where another J loop is started to load the Caption properties of the Label boxes. The five labels now are a control array named Label1(). Inserting an integer between the parentheses selects the particular label to access.

Something else you should notice in this piece of code is the use of indentation. The indentation is purely for visual delineation of the blocks of code associated with the For/Next loops. It has no effect on the actual execution of the code, although it does make the code much more readable. Everything between the For I =... and the Next I statements is indented two spaces, which makes it easy to see the block iterated by that loop. The statements between the For J =... and the Next J statements are indented an additional two spaces. Again, the use of indentation has no effect on the operation of the code, but it greatly improves the readability.

Creating Logical Formulas

Logical formulas (or *conditionals*) are formulas that have a numerical result of –1 (True) or 0 (False). They are created by relating two formulas with one of the relational operators from Table 5.5. If the two formulas fit the relation specified by the operator, the value of the formula is True. Otherwise it is False. For example,

```
(3 > 5) = 0 (False)
(3 + 1 = 4) = -1 (True)
A = 4: B = 5: (A <= B) = -1 (True)
```

Logical formulas are the *conditions* used to determine when to terminate the Do/Loop and While/Wend loops discussed previously. They are the arguments also of the If Then Else branching statements I discuss in a few moments. Logical formulas are how you make a decision in a program to control what is done.

The logical operators (listed in Table 5.5) have two functions. They are most commonly used to connect two or more logical formulas into a more complicated logical formula. Second, they perform bitwise operations on one or two numbers. A bitwise operation on one number is applied to every bit in that number as if each bit were a separate entity. Bitwise operations are used only for specialized applications that must access the individual bits in a computer word. For example, if you want to know whether the fourth bit in an integer is null or 1, create a mask with only that bit set to 1, then And it with the integer. If the result is null, the bit is null; otherwise the bit is 1.

Table 5.7 is a *truth table* for the logical operators. A truth table shows the result for all combinations of True and False inputs. The Not operator switches True to False and False to True. The And operator returns True only when both operands are true. The Or operator returns True when either of the operands is true. Xor is the Exclusive Or operator, which returns True when either of the operands is true, but not both. Eqv is the equivalence operator, which returns True whenever both operands are the same. Imp is the implies operator, which always returns True, except when the first operand is true and the second is false. For example,

```
<C2>(3 > 2) And (5 <= 7) = True
<C1>(2 = 2) Xor (5 > 3) = False
```

The logical operators all have the same precedence, so you must use parentheses to control the order of evaluation. Otherwise, you might not get the results you expect. For example, the only difference in the following statements is the placement of parentheses; however, each statement gives a different result.

```
False And True Or True = True
(False And True) Or True = True
False And (True Or True) = False
```

Table 5.7. Truth table of the logical operators T = True (–1), F = False (0).

A	B	Not A	A And B	A Or B	A Xor B	A Eqv B	A Imp B
T	T	F	T	T	F	T	T
T	F	F	F	T	T	F	F
F	T	T	F	T	T	F	T
F	F	T	F	F	F	T	T

Branching—Controlling Program Flow

The programs created in this book so far are relatively linear in function. Every step in the program is executed in order from the first to the last. *Branching* is the capability to change the order in which statements are executed. The simplest branch is the unconditional GoTo. The GoTo statement has the syntax

```
GoTo label
```

in which label is a line label or number. In older versions of BASIC, all lines in a program had to be numbered. Visual Basic supports this numbering but does not require it. More modern programming languages use line labels on only those lines that need special access. A label consists of an alphabetic name that follows the same rules as a variable name and ends with a colon. When a GoTo statement is executed, execution branches immediately to the statement following the label. Although the GoTo statement is extremely powerful, it is better programming practice to use structured branches such as the loops or If Then Else statements whenever possible. A program with many GoTo statements rapidly becomes unmanageable.

A conditional branch uses a logical formula to decide which block of code to execute. The most heavily used conditional branch statement is the If Then Else statement, which examines a condition and branches accordingly. The If Then Else statement has two forms: a simple, one-line Form, and the block If statement. The syntax of the simple If statement is

```
If condition Then iftrue [Else iffalse]
```

Here, condition is a logical formula that results in a True (–1) or False (0) value, and iftrue and iffalse are statements that are executed if condition is True or False. Iftrue and iffalse are Visual Basic statements, such as Assignment or GoTo statements.

The preferred form of the If Then Else statement is the block form. It is preferred because the statements comprising the Then and Else clauses are within the If Then Else block, making it simpler to see what is going on. The syntax of the block If statement is

```
If condition1 Then
   block of statements
[ElseIf condition2 Then]
   block of statements
```

```
[Else]
   block of statements
End If
```

Here, if condition1 is True, the block of statements between the If and ElseIf statements is executed, and control passes to the statement after the End If statement. If condition1 is False, control passes to the first ElseIf statement where condition2 is tested. If it is True, the statements between the ElseIf statement and the Else statement are executed. There can be multiple ElseIf statements to test for different conditions. Visual Basic tests each one in turn until it finds one with a True condition. If none of the conditions is True, control passes to the Else statement, and the block of statements between the Else and End If statements is executed.

The Self-Paced Learning Program (Version 3)

Something that's missing from the Self-Paced Learning program is a test of the answers. The computer easily can calculate the correct answer for the math problems and compare them to the numbers my son types. In addition, it keeps track of the number of correct and incorrect answers and produces a percentage score at the end of the test.

1. Start with version 2 of the Self-Paced Learning program.

2. Select Text1 on Form1 and set Index = 1 to start a control array.

3. Select Text2 through Text5 and set CtlName = Text1 to create the rest of the control array.

4. Enlarge the Form as shown in Figure 5.4. Add a label (2655 x 260 twips), and set

   Caption = " **Wrong   Right   Score**"

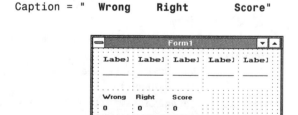

Figure 5.4. *Layout for the Self-Paced Learning program (Version 3).*

5. Below the word Wrong, place a label (615 x 260 twips), and set

```
CtlName = NumWrong
Caption = ""
```

6. Below the word Right, place a label (615 x 260 twips), and set

```
CtlName = NumRight
Caption = ""
```

7. Below the word Score, place a label (615 x 260 twips), and set

```
CtlName = Score
Caption = ""
```

8. Open the (declarations) section and change it to

```
Const NumProbs = 5
Dim Probs(2, NumProbs) As Single, Answer(NumProbs) As Single
Dim GotIt(NumProbs) As Integer
Const Red = &HFF
```

I have added some arrays and defined two constants in the (declarations) section. NumProbs is the number of problems on the Form. I could use the number 5 in the program, but using the variable name makes the code more readable. Using the variable also makes it simpler to expand the program to more problems. Red is defined as the hexadecimal string that produces the color red. To get it, I selected the ForeColor property of a box, opened the Color Palette window, selected red, and copied the value out of the Settings box. The &H at the beginning of the number specifies that the following characters are a hexadecimal (base 16) value.

9. Select the Form_Load event. Change it to read

```
Sub Form_Load ()
Rem Initialize the random number generator
Randomize
Rem Define the end-of-line character
eol$ = Chr$(13) + Chr$(10)
Rem Fill the probs array with 2 sets of 5 values
Rem between 0 and 100
For I = 1 To 2
  For J = 1 To NumProbs
    Probs(I, J) = Int(Rnd(1) * 100)
  Next J
Next I
Rem Insert the random numbers into the labels and
```

```
Rem calculate the answers
For J = 1 To NumProbs
  Label1(J).Caption = Format$(Probs(1, J), " 00") + eol$ +
➦Format$(Probs(2, J), "+00")
  Answer(J) = Probs(1, J) + Probs(2, J)        'added line
Next J
End Sub
```

Here I have added one line (marked **added line**) near the end of the procedure, to calculate the answers for each of the displayed problems.

10. Select the Text1_KeyPress event, and type

```
Sub Text1_KeyPress (Index As Integer, KeyAscii As Integer)
Rem Test for a return, if not, go on
If KeyAscii <> 13 Then GoTo SkipIt      'line 3

Rem Block one
Rem test for right or wrong answer when CR is pressed
If Text1(Index).text = "" Then          'line 7
  Rem No value typed, do nothing
  GoTo SkipIt
ElseIf Val(Text1(Index).text) = Answer(Index) Then
  Rem solution correct
  GotIt(Index) = True
Else                                    'line 13
  Rem solution wrong
  GotIt(Index) = False
End If

Rem Block 2
Rem When the last problem is done, score the test.
If Index = NumProbs Then                'line 20
  Rem Calculate scores
  NRight = 0
  NWrong = 0
  For I = 1 To NumProbs
    If GotIt(I) = True Then
      NRight = NRight + 1
      Text1(I).FontStrikethru = False
    Else
      NWrong = NWrong + 1
      Text1(I).FontStrikethru = True
```

```
        Text1(I).Forecolor = Red
      End If
    Next I
    NumRight.Caption = Str$(NRight)        'line 34
    NumWrong.Caption = Str$(NWrong)
    Score.Caption = Format$(NRight / (NumProbs), "##%")
  Else
    Text1(Index + 1).SetFocus              'line 38
  End If

SkipIt:
End Sub
```

The `Text1_Keypress` event automatically is passed two values, `Index` and `KeyAscii`. `Index` is the value of the `Index` property of the control in the control array that had the event. `KeyAscii` is the ASCII code of the key that was pressed. The user types the answer in a Text box and presses Enter. When Enter is pressed, the code checks the answer and moves the *focus* to the next problem. When the last problem is done, the program counts the right and wrong answers, calculates the score, and displays the results.

The *Focus*, in Visual Basic and in Windows programs in general, refers to the control or form that is currently active. The control or form currently with the focus receives any events generated by the keyboard or mouse. Thus, if a command button is active, pressing Enter activates the Command button; if a text box has the focus, anything you type appears in that text box. To move the focus to a different object on a form, press the Tab key. To move the focus to the menu bar, press the Alt key, then use the arrow keys to move from menu item to menu item. Press Esc to move back to the form. To move the focus with code, use the `SetFocus` method. The syntax of `SetFocus` is

```
object.SetFocus
```

where `object` is the name of the Form or control you want to move the focus to.

In line 3, the value of `KeyAscii` is tested to see whether Enter (13) was pressed. If not, the code jumps to `SkipIt` and returns control to the text box. If Enter was pressed, the procedure executes block 1.

Block 1 is a block `If` statement that checks for three different situations. First, in line 7, it checks for no value in the text box, which occurs if the user presses Enter without typing anything. If that happened, the GoTo statement in line 10 jumps to SkipIt, ignoring the improper Return. Next, it compares what the user typed with the value in the array Answers() to see whether the user got it right. If he did, the array GotIt() is set to True for that problem. If the user has answered wrong, the code jumps to line 13, which changes GotIt() to False.

Block 2 of the code checks now to see whether this is the last problem. If not, the focus is moved to the next problem in line 38. The code starting in line 22 counts the number of correct answers and the number of incorrect answers. It does this by first zeroing the counters NRight and NWrong.

It then loops over each problem and, using another block If statement, adds one to either NRight or NWrong. Then it turns on the Strikethru property and changes the Forecolor to red for any incorrect answers. Starting in line 33, the code inserts the number of right and wrong answers in the labels at the bottom of the form and calculates the percent score. The fraction correct is calculated and converted to text using the Format$() function and the percent field specifier. The percent field specifier automatically multiplies the value it is converting by 100.

11. Save the program as MATH3 (MATH3.FRM and MATH3.MAK), run it, and try to answer a few problems. Your results should look like Figure 5.5 (with different numbers, of course). I purposely answered the second problem incorrectly to demonstrate what happens when the user misses a question.

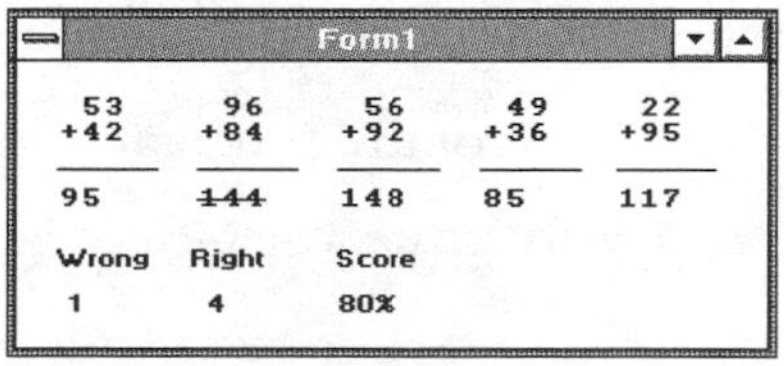

Figure 5.5. *Running Version 3 of the Self-Paced Learning program.*

Although this is a simple, five-problem math test, you easily could make it include more problems by increasing the sizes of the arrays and adding more labels to the Form.

For a challenge, try changing the logic so the user gets more than one try per problem. Also, you could make the program tell the user whether the answer is correct as soon as it is typed. There are many variations, depending on what you want to do. A structure like this can be adapted to other forms of self-paced teaching, such as multiple-choice problems.

What You Have Learned

This chapter has been devoted to defining and using numeric data types. In addition, you have controlled program flow with loops and logical branches. You have learned

- About the different numeric types.
- About the capabilities of integers, floating-point numbers, and Currency type numbers.
- How to define numeric variables.
- How to create formulas using numeric variables.
- About array variables.
- About control arrays.
- About logical formulas.
- How to control program flow with loops and logical variables.
- How to create a Self-Paced Learning program.

Using Controls

In This Chapter

Everything placed on a form is a control. Even the labels and text boxes are controls, because they not only display text, they also initiate actions when they are changed or clicked. This chapter investigates the more traditional controls: buttons, check boxes, and scroll bars. More complex controls (such as menus) are discussed in later chapters; it's easier to learn the simplest control methods first. This chapter shows you the use of

- Command buttons
- Option buttons
- Check boxes
- Scroll bars

Using a Command Button to Initiate an Action

A command button is a standard push button, which you push or click to make something happen. You can also double click it, or press a key while it has the focus to initiate an action. A command button is created in exactly the same manner as any other control: select the command button tool from the Toolbox window, and draw the button on a form.

The Advanced Annuity Calculator

Creating an annuity calculator, with buttons to select the calculation to perform, is a good exercise in using command buttons. I realize that almost every book on programming calculates annuities as an example, and I'm going to do it, too. Although annuities are calculated using well-known but nasty little formulas, they are immensely useful in many home and business situations.

An annuity calculator enables you to deal with accounts that have periodic deposits or withdrawals, and that grow or deplete at a specific interest rate. You can calculate what you owe the bank every month when you finance a house or car. Annuities also tell you how fast an investment grows in an interest-bearing account, or how much money you must put into an account now, to have some specific amount later.

The Advanced Annuity Calculator has five text boxes and five command buttons to calculate the interest rate, payment, number of periods, present value, and future value. It uses cash flow conventions to determine the sign of the dollar values—that is, cash received is positive and cash paid out is negative. Whether a transaction is paid in or out depends on your point of view. If you are the bank, a car payment is positive; if you are the car buyer, the payment is negative. Be sure to pick your point of reference before using the calculator.

To calculate one of these five values, you must solve one of two equations for that value. The first (Equation 6.1) is used for all calculations in which IRate, the interest rate, is nonzero. The second (Equation 6.2) is used whenever IRate is zero.

$$PVal\ (1+IRate\ )^{NPer} +Pmt\left(\frac{(1+IRate\ )^{NPer}-1}{IRate}\right)+FVal\ =0$$

Equation 6.1. *Used if* PVal *is not equal to zero.*

$$PVal + Pmt * NPer + FVal = 0$$

Equation 6.2. *Used if* `Pval` *is equal to zero.*

Here, `IRate` is the fractional interest rate per period (the fraction, not the percent), `NPer` is the number of payment periods, `Pmt` is the periodic payment, `PVal` is the present value—that is, the amount of money in the account now—and `FVal` is the future value, or the amount of money in the account at some future time. If you are dealing with a savings account in a bank, then the payment rate is probably zero, the present value is your initial deposit, and the future value is what you will have after several years. If you are calculating a car loan, then the present value is what you owe, and you want the future value to be zero, indicating you have paid off the loan.

To create this calculator, you need five sets of formulas: solutions of the two annuity equations (6.1 and 6.2) for each of the values. The results of solving these two equations are one pair of equations for each value but the rate, and a transcendental equation for the rate. A transcendental equation is one for which an analytical solution does not exist. To solve it, use the iterative numerical method known as successive approximations.

First, draw the user interface for the problem. The interface has five text boxes for inputting or outputting numerical results, and five command buttons to determine which value to calculate. Follow these initial steps:

1. Open a new project.

2. Select the form and adjust its size to 3885 by 2680 twips. Set its `Caption` property to `Advanced Annuity Calculator`.

3. Draw five text boxes on the form as shown in Figure 6.1. The top three are 1095 by 380 twips; the bottom two are 1575 by 380 twips.

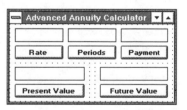

Figure 6.1. *Layout of the form in the Advanced Annuity Calculator.*

4. Selecting the text boxes from left to right, top to bottom, set the Text properties to blank, and the CtrlName properties to: Rate, Per, Pay, PV, and FV.

5. Below the five text boxes, draw five command buttons the same size as the text boxes.

6. For the five command buttons, set the Caption properties to: Rate, Periods, Payment, Present Value, and Future Value. Set the CtrlName properties to: RateButton, PerButton, PayButton, PVButton, and FVButton.

Now that the interface is drawn, define some module level variables in the form so they can be passed between procedures on the form. Here, five variables are defined to hold the numeric results. IRate is the interest rate, and is defined as a single precision floating point number. NPer is the number of periods, and is defined as an integer. Pmt, FVal, and PVal are the payment, present value, and future value, defined as double precision floating point numbers. Double precision is needed here so large numbers, like the mortgaged amount on a home, can be calculated accurately. The Currency type does not work here, it appears that the intermediate values calculated in some of the formulas cause numeric overflow errors.

7. Open the code window for the form, select the declarations procedure, and type

```
Dim IRate As Single, NPer As Integer, Pmt As Double
Dim FVal As Double, PVal As Double
```

Whenever a number is typed into one of the text boxes, extract it, convert it to a number, and store it in the appropriate variable.

8. Open the code windows, one at a time, for the five text boxes, and type the following Change procedures.

```
Sub Rate_Change ()
IRate = Val(Rate.Text)
End Sub

Sub PV_Change ()
PVal = Val(PV.Text)
End Sub

Sub Per_Change ()
NPer = Val(Per.Text)
End Sub
```

```
Sub Pay_Change ()
Pmt = Val(Pay.Text)
End Sub

Sub FV_Change ()
FVal = Val(FV.Text)
End Sub
```

Now, if you solve the annuity equations for the number of periods, you get the following two equations (Equations 6.3 and 6.4). These equations are calculated whenever the `PerButton` command button is pressed.

$$NPer = \frac{Log\left(\dfrac{Pmt - FVal * IRate}{Pmt + PVal * IRate}\right)}{Log(1 + IRate)}$$

Equation 6.3. *Used if* `NPer` *is not equal to zero.*

$$NPer = \frac{-(FVal + PVal)}{Pmt}$$

Equation 6.4. *Used if* `NPer` *is equal to zero.*

9. Open the code window for the `PerButton` command button and type

```
Sub PerButton_Click ()
If IRate <> 0 Then
  NPer = Log((Pmt - FVal * IRate) / (Pmt + PVal * IRate))
  ➥/ Log(1 + IRate)
Else
  NPer = -(FVal + PVal) / Pmt
End If
Per.Text = Str$(NPer)
End Sub
```

This procedure uses a block `If` statement to select the equation to calculate, according to whether `IRate` is zero or not. If `IRate` isn't zero, the formula in line 3 is calculated; otherwise, the formula in line 5 is calculated.

After the value of NPer is calculated, it is converted to text in line 7 and stored in the Text property of the Per text box. The Payment, Present Value, and Future Value buttons follow in the same way.

The formulas (Equation 6.5 and 6.6) for the payment are

$$Pmt = \frac{IRate\ (PVal\ (1+IRate\ )^{NPer} +FVal\ )}{1-(1+IRate\ )^{NPer}}$$

Equation 6.5. *Used if* Pmt *is not equal to zero.*

$$Pmt = \frac{-(FVal\ +PVal\ )}{NPer}$$

Equation 6.6. *Used if* Pmt *is equal to zero.*

10. Open the code window for the PayButton procedure, and type

```
Sub PayButton_Click ()
If IRate <> 0 Then
  Pmt = IRate * (PVal * (1 + IRate) ^ NPer + FVal)
  ➥/ (1 - (1 + IRate) ^ NPer)
Else
  Pmt = -(FVal + PVal) / NPer
End If
Pay.Text = Format$(Pmt, "####.00")
End Sub
```

This is largely the same as the PerButton_Click procedure, except the conversion of the number Pmt into a string of text is accomplished with a Format&() function.

Don't use dollar signs or commas in the formatting strings. Although they do make the numbers more readable, the Val() function is not able to convert the text strings back into numbers correctly. This is because the Val() function stops converting characters into numbers when it reaches a non-numeric character such as a dollar sign or comma.

Replace the `Val()` function in these procedures with code that can convert a numeric text string containing dollar signs and commas into a numeric value, then use dollar signs and commas in the `Format$()` function. Hint: Use the string functions to remove the dollar signs and commas, then use the `Val()` function to convert the string into a number.

Do the same for the `PVButton`, and the `FVButton`. The equations (Equations 6.7-6.10) for the present value and future value are

$$PVal = \frac{-FVal - Pmt \left(\dfrac{(1+IRate)^{NPer} - 1}{IRate} \right)}{(1+IRate)^{NPer}}$$

Equation 6.7. *Used if* Pval *is not equal to zero.*

$$PVal = -FVal - * NPer$$

Equation 6.8. *Used if* Pval *is equal to zero.*

$$FVal = -PVal (1+IRate)^{NPer} - Pmt \left(\frac{(1+IRate)^{NPer} - 1}{IRate} \right)$$

Equation 6.9. *Used if* Fval *is not equal to zero.*

$$FVal = -PVal - Pmt * NPer$$

Equation 6.10. *Used if* Fval *is equal to zero.*

11. Open the code window for the `PVButton_Click` procedure and type

```
Sub PVButton_Click ()
If IRate <> 0 Then
  PVal = -(FVal + Pmt * ((1 + IRate) ^ NPer - 1)
  ➥/ IRate) / ((1 + IRate) ^ NPer)
Else
  PVal = -FVal - Pmt * NPer
End If
PV.Text = Format$(PVal, "######.00")
End Sub
```

12. Open the code window for the FVButton_Click procedure and type

```
Sub FVButton_Click ()
If IRate <> 0 Then
  FVal = -PVal * ((1 + IRate) ^ NPer)
    - Pmt * ((1 + IRate) ^ NPer - 1) / IRate
➡Else
  FVal = -PVal - Pmt * NPer
End If
FV.Text = Format$(FVal, "######.00")
End Sub
```

When you try to solve the annuity equations for the interest rate, you can't get an analytic solution. To solve this equation numerically, use a method known as successive approximations. "The Method of successive approximations" might sound exotic and complicated, but it is actually quite simple. You do a series of calculations (approximations) to bring the two sides of the equation as close in value as possible (convergence).

The equation is first solved so IRate is on the left side of the equal sign, and a function of IRate is on the right. Because there is more than one way to do this, the results may diverge (grow further apart) as you iterate, if you choose the wrong approach. The simplest way to determine whether you have solved the equation correctly is to try it and see if it converges to a solution. If it doesn't, try solving the equation (for example Equation 6.11 or 6.12) a different way.

$$IRate = \frac{Pmt \, (1 - (1 + IRate)^{NPer})}{PVal \, (1 + IRate)^{NPer} + FVal}$$

Equation 6.11. *Used if* Pmt *is not equal to zero.*

$$IRate = -1 + \left(-\frac{FVal}{PVal}\right)^{\frac{1}{NPer}}$$

Equation 6.12. *Used if* Pmt *is equal to zero.*

Next, guess a value of IRate, insert it in the right side of the equation, and calculate a new approximation. Insert this new approximation on the right to produce yet another approximation to IRate. Continue this iteration until the value of IRate inserted on the right converges with the value calculated by that insertion. Actually, you could iterate forever without getting identical values, so make them the same within some tolerance (0.001 in this case).

13. Open the `RateButton_Click()` procedure and type

```
Sub RateButton_Click ()
Dim Denom As Double
If Pmt <> 0 Then
  Rem Give IRate an initial guess
  IRate = .5
  IRateOld = 0
  counter = 0
  Rem Use the method of successive approximations
  Rem to solve for the value of IRate
  Rem Test for convergence and loop again if IRate isn't
  Rem converged.
  Do While Abs((IRate - IRateOld) / IRate) > .001    'line 12
    counter = counter + 1
    Rem Quit if it didn't converge after 200 iterations
    If counter > 200 Then
      MsgBox "Problem didn't converge after 200 iterations", 0
      Exit Do
    End If
    IRateOld = IRate      'line 19
    Denom = PVal * (1 + IRateOld) ^ NPer + FVal
    If Denom = 0 Then
      Rem Go here if Denom is zero.
      IRate = 0
      MsgBox "The interest rate is undefined (divide by zero)", 0
      Exit Do
    Else
      Rem Use this equation if Pmt and Denom are not 0
      IRate = Pmt * (1 - (1 + IRateOld) ^ NPer) / Denom
    End If
  Loop
Else
  Rem Use this equation if Pmt is 0.
  IRate = -1 + (-FVal / PVal) ^ (1 / NPer)      'line 32
End If
Rate.Text = Format$(IRate, "0.0000 ")
End Sub
```

In this procedure, the first statement defines `Denom`, a double precision floating point variable. Next, a block `If` statement tests `Pmt` to see if it
is zero. If it is, the alternate formula in line 33 is used to calculate the rate.

137

If `Pmt` is not zero, the next four lines select the initial guess for `IRate` and also initialize the variables `IRateOld` and `Counter`. `IRateOld` holds the value inserted in the formula, and `IRate` holds the new value calculated from the formula. `Counter` counts the number of times the loop is iterated so you can cancel the calculation if it isn't converging.

Line 12 starts a `Do` loop, which then ends with the `Loop` statement in line 30. The loop terminates when `IRateOld` and the calculated value `IRate` differ by only a tenth of a percent. The next six lines increment `Counter` and test it to see whether it is greater than the 200 iteration limit. If the calculation reaches 200 iterations, it probably isn't going to converge, so the procedure displays a Message box informing you of that fact.

In line 19, `IRateOld` is set equal to the previously calculated value of `IRate`.

In line 20, the denominator of the function is calculated. In line 21, a block `If` statement tests the value of the denominator to see whether it is zero. If it were zero, and you used it anyway, the program would crash. Testing the denominator prevents this problem; the program puts up a Message box if the denominator is zero. If it's not zero, the new value of `IRate` is calculated in line 28.

14. Save the project as ANUT (ANUT.MAK and ANUT.FRM).

15. Run the program, and type **0.01** (1%) in the rate box, **36** in the Periods box, **10000** in the Present Value box, and **0** in the Future Value box. This represents a loan, typical of one for a new car ($10,000 for three years at 12% a year).

16. Press the **Payment** button to calculate the payment of $–322.14. Your Advanced Annuity Calculator should now look like Figure 6.2.

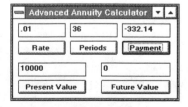

Figure 6.2. Advanced Annuity Calculator after calculating the payment required on a $10,000 loan at 12% per year.

Notice the $10,000 is positive, because you receive it from the bank, and the payment of $–322.14 is negative because you pay it to the bank. Note also, that because you have not tested for every possible invalid value, such as a negative interest rate, or both PVal and FVal as zero, this program can still crash. If that happens, just rerun the program with different values, or insert more protection (If statements) in the RateButton procedure to check for invalid data.

See if you can make this program uncrashable by testing the inputs for inconsistent or out-of-range data before calculating a value. Each command button will have its own set of invalid values. Look at the denominators of the fractions in the formulas to see what combinations of values make them zero. These sets of values are invalid, and should not be allowed in the input. Check also for large values that cause overflow errors.

To calculate any other quantity, insert values in the boxes for all but the one you want to calculate, then press the button to calculate that value. For example, you can find out what interest rate you must have so $10,000 grows to $20,000 in five years. Type **60** in the Periods box (five years x 12 months/year), **0** in the Payment box, **10000** in the Present Value box (positive because the bank is receiving the money), **-20000** in the Future Value box (negative because the bank is giving you back the money in the future), and press the **Rate** button. The program would now look like Figure 6.3, with the value 0.0116 in the rate box, which represents 13.92% per year (0.0116 x 12 months x 100%).

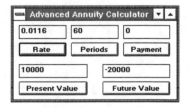

Figure 6.3. *The Advanced Annuity Calculator after calculating the interest rate necessary for $10,000 to increase to $20,000 in five years.*

Using Option Buttons to Select an Option

Option buttons are used in groups, which are defined by placing the option buttons on a form, frame, or picture window. All the option buttons placed directly on a single form, frame, or picture window constitute one group. Option buttons are often called "radio buttons" because they operate much like the station-changing buttons on a car radio. Only one option button in a group can be pressed at any one time, and pressing one button releases the previously pressed button.

To add option buttons to an application, first draw a frame with the frame tool, then draw the option buttons within the frame. Option buttons have the property Value, which is True (–1) if the button is pressed or False (0) if it is released.

The Self-Paced Learning Program (Version 4)

To demonstrate the use of option buttons, add some to the Self-Paced Learning Program developed in Chapter 5, "Using Numbers." Version 3 of the program creates an addition test. This new version gives you the choice of addition, subtraction, multiplication, or division, selected with a group of four Option buttons.

1. Open the MATH3 program (MATH3.MAK), and save it as MATH4 (MATH4.MAK, and MATH4.FRM) so you don't accidentally overwrite the previous version.

2. Using the frame tool, draw a frame (1575 by 860 twips) to the right of the Score text box as shown in Figure 6.4.

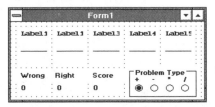

Figure 6.4. *Layout for Version 4 of the Self-Paced Learning program.*

3. Draw four option buttons (255 by 260 twips), from left, along the bottom of the frame.

4. Draw four labels (255 by 260 twips) above the four option buttons.

5. Select each label and set the `Caption` properties to +, -, *, and /.

6. Select the first option button on the left, and set the property, `Value = True`.

7. Select the frame and set the `Caption` property to `Problem Type`.

This completes the changes to the user interface. Now change the `Form_Load` procedure to check the option buttons when it sets up the problems. You also have to add `Click` procedures to the option buttons to run the `Form_Load` procedure whenever one of the buttons is pressed.

8. Open the code window, select the declarations section, and add the definition for black color, as shown.

```
Const NumProbs = 5
Dim Probs(2, NumProbs) As Single, Answer(NumProbs) As Single
Dim GotIt(NumProbs) As Integer
Const True = -1
Const False = 0
Const Red = &HFF
Const Black = &H0
```

9. Select the `Form_Load` procedure, and change it to the following. The changes are in the last block.

```
Sub Form_Load ()
Rem Initialize the random number generator
Randomize
Rem Define the end-of-line character
eol$ = Chr$(13) + Chr$(10)
Rem Fill the probs array with 2 sets of 5 values
Rem between 0 and 100
For I = 1 To 2
  For J = 1 To NumProbs
    Probs(I, J) = Int(Rnd(1) * 100)
  Next J
Next I
Rem Insert the random numbers into the labels and
Rem calculate the answers
For J = 1 To NumProbs
  If Option1.Value = True Then      'line 16
```

continues

```
        Label1(J).Caption = Format$(Probs(1, J), " 00")
    ➡+ eol$ + Format$(Probs(2, J), "+00")
        Answer(J) = Probs(1, J) + Probs(2, J)
      ElseIf Option2.Value = True Then
        Label1(J).Caption = Format$(Probs(1, J), " 00")
    ➡+ eol$ + Format$(Probs(2, J), "-00")
        Answer(J) = Probs(1, J) - Probs(2, J)
      ElseIf Option3.Value = True Then
        Label1(J).Caption = Format$(Probs(1, J), " 00")
    ➡+ eol$ + Format$(Probs(2, J), "*00")
        Answer(J) = Probs(1, J) * Probs(2, J)
      ElseIf Option4.Value = True Then
        Label1(J).Caption = Format$(Probs(1, J), " 00")
    ➡+ eol$ + Format$(Probs(2, J), "\/00")
        Answer(J) = Probs(1, J) / Probs(2, J)
      End If
      Text1(J).text = ""        'line 29
      Text1(J).FontStrikethru = False
      Text1(J).ForeColor = Black
    Next J
    NumRight.Caption = ""
    NumWrong.Caption = ""
    Score.Caption = ""
    End Sub
```

The changes start in line 16, with a block `If` statement. Each block of the block `If` statement checks the `Value` property of one of the option buttons, to find the one that is pressed. The contents of each block are nearly the same; the first line (line 17, for example) inserts the numbers in the label, along with the symbol for the type of operation (+, -, *, /). Each block inserts a different symbol. The second statement in each block (line 18, for example) calculates the correct answer for the problem using the operator selected with the option button.

The second `Format$()` function in line 26 must have a division operator (/), but a slash used in a formatting string is a date separation operator. To insert a formatting operator as a literal symbol rather than the operator, precede it with a backslash (\). The pair of characters \/ produces a single / in the printed string. The multiplication operator in line 23 has the same problem.

Line 29 removes any old answers left from a previous test, and lines 30 and 31 reset the `FontStrikeThru` and `ForeColor` properties that were previously set for wrong answers. Lines 31, 32, and 33 remove any old scores. You also must move the focus back to the first text box, but this is not the place to do it. The first time the `Form_Load` routine is called, the form has not been loaded yet, so there is no text box to move the focus to. The routine would fail if you tried to move the focus to it. The next step takes care of that problem.

10. Select the `Option1_Click` procedure and type

```
Sub Option1_Click ()
Form_Load
Text1(1).SetFocus
End Sub
```

Here I introduce a new piece of the BASIC language, procedure calling. Up to now, all the procedures have been called by the system. When you click a control, the system calls the `Click` procedure; if a text box is changed, the system runs the `Changed` procedure. Not only can the system call a procedure, but any procedure can call any other procedure in its scope. To call a procedure, simply type its name in your code. When the called procedure completes, execution returns to the procedure that called it and begins at the statement after the calling statement.

The rules of scope for procedures are the same as they are for variables. Any procedure on a form is accessible by any other procedure on the same form, and any procedure in a module is available to any procedure in the application. Chapter 8, "Writing Custom Procedures," discusses procedures in more detail.

In the `Option1_Click` procedure, the second line calls the `Form_Load` procedure and runs it. When it is complete, control returns to the third line, which moves the focus to the first text box. The other three `Option` procedures work the same way.

11. Select the `Option2_Click` procedure and type

```
Sub Option2_Click ()
Form_Load
Text1(1).SetFocus
End Sub
```

12. Select the `Option3_Click` procedure and type

```
Sub Option3_Click ()
Form_Load
Text1(1).SetFocus
End Sub
```

13. Select the `Option4_Click` procedure and type

```
Sub Option4_Click ()
Form_Load
Text1(1).SetFocus
End Sub
```

14. Save the project, then run it.

You now can change the test type by pressing one of the option buttons. Notice how pressing one button releases whichever one was previously pressed.

The subtraction test can have large numbers subtracted from small ones with a negative result. Add code to reverse the top and bottom numbers in the subtraction test when that is the case. Negative numbers are too advanced for most children.

Using a Check Box to Set an Option

Unlike option buttons, check boxes are independent of each other, and more than one can be checked at the same time. Otherwise, they behave much like option buttons. When a check box is checked, its `Value` property is 1; if it's unchecked, the value is zero. The `Value` property also can be 2 if the check box is grayed (disabled). You draw check boxes in almost the same way you draw option buttons, except they do not have to be on a frame because they are independent of each other. However, you can put them on a frame if you want to visually group them.

The Envelope Addresser (Version 3)

As an example, add the following options to the envelope addresser.

- Optional return address.

- Bold or plain text.

- Large or small type.

Follow these steps to add the options to Version 1 of the envelope addresser to include the options.

1. Open the ADDR1.MAK project file and then save it as ADDR3.MAK so you won't accidently overwrite the previous version of this program. Save the two forms as ADDR31.FRM and ADDR32.FRM, and the module as ADDR3.BAS.

2. Select Form1 and enlarge it to 3900 by 3540 twips.

3. Using the check box tool, draw three check boxes on the form as shown in Figure 6.5.

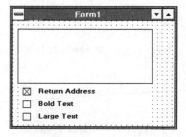

Figure 6.5. *Setup of* Form1 *for Version 3 of the Envelope Addresser.*

4. Change the Caption properties of the three check boxes to

```
Check1.Caption = Return Address
Check2.Caption = Bold Text
Check3.Caption = Large Text
```

Because most people want a return address, make it the default.

5. Select the first check box and change its Value property to
   1 - Checked.

6. Select Form2 and add a label box Label2 (3375 by 1220 twips) as shown in Figure 6.6.

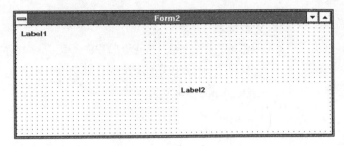

Figure 6.6. *Setup of* Form2 *for Version 3 of the Envelope Addresser.*

This completes the changes to the interface. Now make some adjustments to the code so it reacts to changes in the check boxes.

7. Select Form1, open the code window for the Check1_Click procedure, and type

```
Sub Check1_Click ()
RetAddr = Check1.Value
End Sub
```

8. Select the Check2_Click procedure and type

```
Sub Check2_Click ()
BoldFace = Check2.Value
End Sub
```

9. Select the Check3_Click procedure and type

```
Sub Check3_Click ()
LargeType = Check3.Value
End Sub
```

10. Open the module, and insert references to these three options so they are passed to the procedures on Form2. Also, define the values Checked, and Unchecked.

```
Global TheLine As String
Global RetAddr As Integer, BoldFace As Integer
Global LargeType As Integer
Global Const Checked = 1, Unchecked = 0
```

In the original version of the envelope addresser, the return address is printed on the form by the Form_Load procedure. This has to be moved to the Form_Click procedure so you can use logical statements to decide to print it or not.

146

11. Select Form2 and cut the three lines, which define the return address, from the Form_Load procedure (saving them for the Form_Click procedure) using the Cut command on the Edit menu. Add the default values of the check boxes to the Form_Load procedure, which should now read

```
Sub Form_Load ()
eol$ = Chr&(13) + Chr$(10)
RetAddr = Checked
BoldFace = Unchecked
LargeType = Unchecked
End Sub
```

12. Change the Form_Click procedure to read as follows. First, paste text from the Form_Load procedure into the Form_Click procedure using the **Paste** command on the Edit menu.

```
Sub Form_Click ()
If BoldFace = Checked Then
  Label1.FontBold = True
  Label2.FontBold = True
Else
  Label1.FontBold = False
  Label2.FontBold = False
End If
If LargeType = Checked Then
  Label1.FontSize = 12
  Label2.FontSize = 12
Else
  Label1.FontSize = 10
  Label2.FontSize = 10
End If
If RetAddr = Checked Then
  Label1.Caption = "William J. Orvis" + eol$
  Label1.Caption = Label1.Caption + "123 Some St." + eol$
  Label1.Caption = Label1.Caption + "Anywhere, CA  91234"
Else
  Label1.Caption = ""
End If
Label2.Caption = TheLine          'line 23
Form2.PrintForm
Form1.Show
End Sub
```

Notice there are three independent block If statements. They are independent because each check box is independent of the others. The first block If statement in lines 2 through 8 checks whether the Bold Text check box is checked, and changes the FontBold property of both labels to True or False. The second block in lines 9 through 15 does the same for the FontSize property of the two label boxes. The third If block in lines 16 through 22 checks the value of the Return Address check box, and if it is true, inserts the return address into the Caption property of the Label1 box. If it isn't True, it blanks the Caption property. In line 23, the value of the address is placed in the Caption property of the second label, and in line 24, the form is printed. Line 25 redisplays Form1 so you can print a second envelope.

13. Save the project and run the program. Type the address for the envelope in the text box on Form1; select the options you want and then click Form2 to print the envelope.

Using Scroll Bars to Set a Value

Scroll bars are used to select a numeric value in some range. Because of their more familiar use to control windows, you might not have thought of scroll bars as a way to set a value. However, a scroll bar returns a number that indicates the relative location of the thumb (the white square that slides along the Scroll bar). When you move the thumb up and down (or left and right) the number stored in the Value property of the scroll bar changes accordingly.

It is up to the attached program to convert changes in that number to movement of a window. Also, there is no reason that a scroll bar can only control windows. In any program where an integer has to be selected from a range, a scroll bar can be used. It also can be used like a gauge with the program changing the Value property, which makes the thumb move along some scale. There are two properties that control the range of the number returned in the Value property, as listed.

Min - The minimum value of the scroll bar when the thumb is at the left of a horizontal scroll bar or at the top of a vertical one.

Max - The maximum value of the scroll bar when the thumb is at the bottom or right.

Changing the `Value` property by a program causes the thumb to move, and moving the thumb with the mouse changes `Value`. Thus, a scroll bar can be used either as an indicator, or as an input device.

The Self-Paced Learning program currently uses numbers between 0 and 100 to create the math problems. My son has been complaining that the numbers in the multiplication test are too big for him, so I added a pair of horizontal scroll bars to the program to enter the maximum range for the first (top) and second (bottom) numbers. This way, he can start with small numbers and, as he grows more proficient, he can increase the size of the numbers.

The Self-Paced Learning Program (Version 5)

Make the upper limits of the numbers used in the math test adjustable with two horizontal scroll bars.

1. Open Version 4 of the Self-Paced Learning Program (MATH4.MAK) and save it as Version 5 (MATH5.MAK and MATH5.FRM).

2. Select `Form1` and increase its size to 4635 by 3520 twips.

3. Add two horizontal Scroll bars (3135 by 260 twips).

4. Add two Labels (735 by 260 twips) as shown in Figure 6.7. Change the `CtlName` property of the upper label to `TopRange` and change the lower label to `BottomRange`.

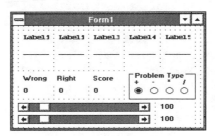

Figure 6.7. *Setup for Version 5 of the Self-Paced Learning program.*

5. Select the Scroll bars and set their properties.

```
Max = 1000
Min = 0
Value = 100
LargeChange = 10
```

The LargeChange property controls how large a change you get when you click the gray area of a scroll bar above or below the thumb. Setting the Value property sets the initial, or default, position of the thumb.

6. Select the two new labels and set the Caption properties to 100.

7. Open the HScroll1_Change code window and type

```
Sub HScroll1_Change ()
TopRange.Caption = Str$(HScroll1.Value)
End Sub
```

8. Select the HScroll2_Change code window and type

```
Sub HScroll2_Change ()
BottomRange.Caption = Str$(HScroll2.Value)
End Sub
```

These two routines set the values in the two labels whenever you move the thumb on the scroll bar.

9. Select the Form_Load procedure and change it as follows.

```
Sub Form_Load ()
Rem Initialize the random number generator
Randomize
Rem Define the end-of-line character
eol$ = Chr$(13) + Chr$(10)
Rem Fill the probs array with 2 sets of 5 values
For J = 1 To NumProbs        'line 7
    Probs(1, J) = Int(Rnd(1) * HScroll1.Value)
    Probs(2, J) = Int(Rnd(1) * HScroll2.Value)
Next J                  'line 10
Rem Insert the random numbers into the labels and
Rem calculate the answers
For J = 1 To NumProbs
  If Option1.Value = True Then
    Label1(J).Caption = Format$(Probs(1, J), " 00")
    ➥+ eol$ + Format$(Probs(2, J), "+00")
    Answer(J) = Probs(1, J) + Probs(2, J)
  ElseIf Option2.Value = True Then
    Label1(J).Caption = Format$(Probs(1, J), " 00")
    ➥+ eol$ + Format$(Probs(2, J), "-00")
    Answer(J) = Probs(1, J) - Probs(2, J)
```

```
        ElseIf Option3.Value = True Then
          Label1(J).Caption = Format$(Probs(1, J), " 00")
          ➥+ eol$ + Format$(Probs(2, J), "\*00")
          Answer(J) = Probs(1, J) * Probs(2, J)
        ElseIf Option4.Value = True Then
          Label1(J).Caption = Format$(Probs(1, J), " 00")
          ➥+ eol$ + Format$(Probs(2, J), "\/00")
          Answer(J) = Probs(1, J) / Probs(2, J)
        End If
        Text1(J).Text = ""
        Text1(J).FontStrikethru = False
        Text1(J).ForeColor = Black
      Next J
      NumRight.Caption = ""
      NumWrong.Caption = ""
      Score.Caption = ""
      End Sub
```

The only changes in this routine are in lines 7 through 10, where the multipliers of the RND() functions are changed to the values from the two scroll bars. This version differs from Version 4 of this program in that the outer Loop is replaced with two equations, one for the upper values and one for the lower values.

10. Save the project, then run it. Change the lower scroll bar until the value reads 10, then press the multiplication option button. A test similar to Figure 6.8 appears.

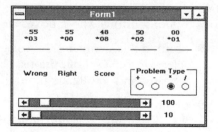

Figure 6.8. *A multiplication test with numbers between 0 and 100 for the upper values and numbers between 0 and 10 for the lower values.*

Create a math test with more problems, such as the test shown in plate IV of the inside back cover.

Custom Controls

In addition to the built-in controls, Visual Basic can use *custom controls.* Custom controls are contained in .VBX files. These files are added to a project in the same manner as a form or module. When a custom control file is added to a project, the controls icon is added to the toolbox window so that you can draw the custom control on a form. Two custom controls are included with the Standard Edition of Visual Basic (more are in the Professional Edition), the grid, and the OLEClient. The grid control is a two-dimensional grid of cells, much like a spreadsheet. Using these properties any cell in the grid can be accessed and filled with text or a picture. In addition, a user can select a cell or a range of cells and type into them.

The OLEClient control creates a window for an object from an application that supports Object Linking and Embedding to be placed. Object Linking and Embedding is discussed in more detail in Chapter 14, "Advanced Language Features."

What You Have Learned

This chapter has examined the more traditional controls: command buttons, option buttons, check boxes, and scroll bars. In this chapter you

- Learned that command buttons initiate actions; option buttons select one of a set of options; check boxes enable individual options, and scroll bars input integer values.

- Created an Advanced Annuity Calculator, two versions of a Self-Paced Learning Program, and a version of the Envelope Addresser.

- Studied more complicated logical statements, remote procedures, and the method of successive approximations for solving transcendental equations.

Using Custom Menus

Rather than pressing buttons and checking boxes, you can control programs conveniently with pull-down menus. When you select a menu command it executes a procedure, and that procedure can set options or carry out complex calculations.

In This Chapter

Menus are attached to forms using the Menu Design window, then procedures are written and attached to the commands on the menu. This chapter shows you how to

- Construct menus with the Menu Design window.
- Attach procedures to menus.
- Create the standard File and Edit menus.

- Access the Clipboard with the Edit menu.

- Implement the Undo command.

Using the Menu Design Window

In contrast to controls you draw on a Form, menus are created in a Menu Design window, as shown in Figure 7.1. The top half of the window is used to set the properties of the currently selected menu item, and the bottom half lists all the menus and menu items on a Form. A menu item is any of the menu names or commands that show on a menu. The buttons along the center of the window insert and move menu items.

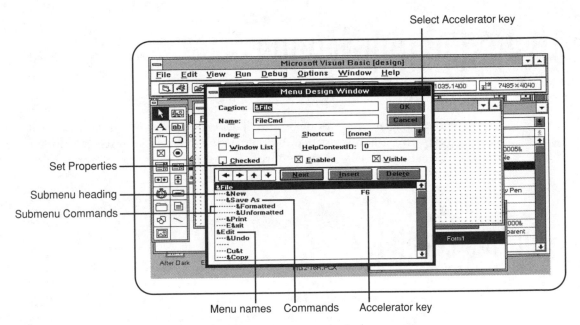

Figure 7.1. The Menu Design window.

The left-hand items in the list at the bottom of the window in Figure 7.1 are the menu names that appear on a form's menu bar. In this figure, File and Edit are the two menus defined for this form. Menu commands and submenu headings are indented below the menu names. Here, New, Print, and Exit are menu commands under the File menu, and Undo, Cut, Copy, and **Paste** (**Paste** is scrolled off the bottom of the window) are menu commands under the Edit menu. Submenu headings have additional menu items indented below them. When a submenu heading is selected, the submenu drops to the left or right of the submenu heading. Save As is a submenu heading under the File menu with Formatted and Unformatted as the submenu commands. Figure 7.2 shows the menus defined in the Menu Design window in Figure 7.1, including the Save As submenu.

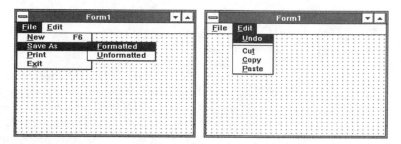

Figure *7.2. The File menu with the Save As submenu open and the Edit menu.*

Although there can be five levels of submenus in a Visual Basic program, try not to go beyond one or two. Too many levels causes your program to become confusing and the menus become difficult to select—see Figure 7.3, for example.

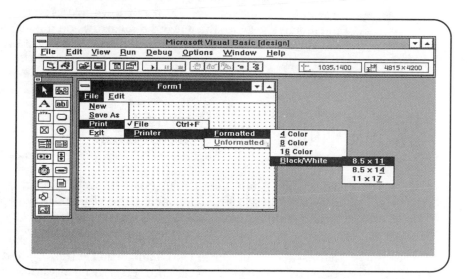

Figure *7.3. Multiple levels of submenus can be confusing.*

A separator bar also can appear on a menu. For example, in Figure 7.2 there is a separator bar on the **Edit** menu between the **Undo** and **Cut** commands. Separator bars are for purely visual separation of commands on a menu and are created by typing a hyphen as the Caption of a menu item. Separator bars also must have control names, even though they are never selected or executed.

Editing Menu Items

To create a menu, open the form you want to attach a menu to, and open the Menu Design window above it. Type a menu name in the Caption box, and it appears in the bottom window. Type a control name, which must be a legal variable name, in the Name box. You must supply a control name for each menu item (including separator bars, as mentioned earlier), even if you do not intend to attach code to the menu item.

Click the **Next** button and type another Caption and Name. If this is a menu command or submenu name, click the right arrow to indent it. Continue typing Captions and Names until you have inserted all the menu items for all your menus in the window. To edit a menu item, select it and change the names in the Caption and Name boxes. To move a menu item up or down in the list, use the up and down arrows on the window. Change the indent level with the left and right arrows on the window. The **Delete** button deletes the selected menu item, and the **Insert** button inserts a new item at the selection point by moving all those below it down one line.

Setting Menu Item Properties

Three main properties of menu items are set with check boxes in the Menu Design window: **Checked**, **Enabled**, and **Visible**. These properties not only are set at design time, but are adjustable at run time.

The Checked check box places a check mark to the left of the item's name—see the File **Print** File command in Figure 7.3—and sets the Checked property to True. The Checked property is used most often to show whether the option accessed by the menu item is enabled. You can write code so that selecting a menu item sets the check mark and enables the option, and selecting it again disables the option and removes the check mark. This is done by changing the value of the Checked property. Note that you cannot check a menu name or submenu head.

The Enabled property determines whether a menu item is executable. Disabled menu items are grayed on the menu and cannot be selected—see the **File Print Printer** Unformatted command in Figure 7.3. You should disable menu items for commands and options that are currently unavailable. If you disable a menu name, the whole menu is disabled.

The Visible property is another way to control access to menu items. When the visible box is not checked or the Visible property is False, the menu item and all its submenus disappear from the menu bar. By having several menus, with some visible and others not, you can make different menus, or different versions of the same menu, available at different times during the execution of your program. Making a menu name invisible makes the whole menu invisible.

Two more properties of menu items can be set only at design time: Shortcut keys and Access keys. *Shortcut keys* are command or function keys that access a menu command directly from the keyboard without pulling down the menu. Shortcut keys are created by selecting them from the **Shortcut** box on the Menu Design window. As a reminder, the selected key or key combination appears on the menu to the right of the command name. For example, in Figure 7.2, if you pressed F6, the **File New** command would be executed, or, in Figure 7.3, if you pressed Ctrl-F, the **File Print** File command would be executed.

Access keys allow you to select menus and menu items without using the mouse. The Access key for any menu item is underlined in the item's name. (In this book, access keys are shown in bold.) When a program is running, the Menu bar is activated by pressing the Alt key, then a menu is pulled down by pressing its Access key. When a menu is open, menu items are selected with the up and down arrow keys, or by pressing the Access key for the item you want.

The Access key for a menu item is selected when you type the Caption property. Place an ampersand (&) before the letter you want to use (as shown for the File menu in Figure 7.1); it appears underlined in the menu—see the **File** menu in Figure 7.2. You don't have to use the first letter in a file item's name as the Access key, although it is a good idea for frequently used items. You can place the ampersand anywhere in the file

item's name, and the letter following the ampersand becomes the Access key. Be careful what letters you select for access keys, because if two menus or two items on the same menu have the same key, only the first item is selectable.

The `Index` property is used when creating a control array of menu commands. A control array of menu commands are menu commands that share the same `Name` property and event procedures but not necessarily the same `Caption`. An element of a control array is identified by it's `Index` property, which you can set here in the Menu Design window in the Index box. Menu command control arrays are also menu commands added by an executing application. Menu commands are added to a menu at runtime with the `Load` statement and removed with the `Unload` statement. Each new menu item becomes the next element of a control array and gets the next Index number.

The **Window List** check box is for Multiple Document Interface (MDI) programs, and specifies if the menu is to contain the names of all the open documents. This check box is used to implement the **Window** menu seen in many applications. A **Window** menu enables you to bring a specific window to the front. You learn more on MDI programs in Chapter 14, "Advanced Language Features."

The **HelpContextD** box is used to select a help context, for context sensitive help with this menu item. The help file is identified with the `HelpFile` property of the form. The particular page in the help file to display (the context) is selected by a number placed in the **HelpcontextD** dialog box.

Attaching Code to a Menu

Code is attached to a menu command in the same way you attach it to the other controls. To open a Code window attached to a menu item, you can either open the Code window for a Form, then select the `Name` of the menu item, or select the menu command directly on the Form. Menu items respond to only one event, the `Click` event, which corresponds to selection of the command from its menu. The menu names also respond to the Click event, and any code placed in that procedure is executed before the menu drops down.

Creating the Standard Menus

Most Windows applications contain a minimum of two menus, the **File** menu and the **Edit** menu. The File menu starts and stops the application, and opens, closes, and prints documents. The **Edit** menu contains the standard editing commands, **Undo**, **Cut**, **Copy**, and **Paste**.

If you plan to open and close files, or you want to edit your application, it's important to make the commands operate in the standard way so other users do not have to learn new methods. For example, you might have invented the best method for editing text, but if your application does not have a working **Edit** menu with the standard **Cut**, **Copy**, and **Paste** commands, your frustrated users will be thinking unkind things about you. If, however, they can use your code without having to learn anything new, they might not notice—but they will not be calling you to complain, either.

If you plan to have your application share data through the Clipboard with other Windows applications, you must have the **Edit** menu, and the appropriate code to acccss the Clipboard. The Clipboard is a special area in Windows available to all running applications. When you cut or copy data in an application, a copy of the current selection is placed on the Clipboard. When you paste data, the contents of the Clipboard is inserted at the insertion point, or replaces the current selection.

Creating the File Menu

A standard **File** menu contains the **New**, **Open**, **Close**, **Save**, Save **As**, **Print**, and **Exit** commands, or some similar set with the same functions. In a particular program, one or more of these commands might be missing, or there might be additional commands. The **File** menu in Visual Basic is a good example; it contains commands for opening, saving and deleting Forms and projects, creating new Forms and projects, printing, and ending the program.

The Envelope Addresser Program (Version 4)

The Envelope Addresser Program is currently designed to print an envelope when you click the Form. The only ways to end the program are to end it in Visual Basic or to close the window. Both these commands could be placed on a menu. This example also shows you how to add a **Print** Options submenu, move the options originally set on Form1 to that menu, delete Form1, and type the address directly on Form2.

1. Open Version 3 of the Envelope Addresser ADDR3.MAK, and save it as ADDR4.MAK.

2. Select Form1 and delete it with the **File Remove** File command.

3. Select Form2 and save it as ADDR42.FRM. Select the module and save it as ADDR4.BAS.

   Because the start-up Form has been deleted, redefine it in the Project dialog box called from the **Options** menu. Select Startup Form in the dialog box and change its value to Form2.

4. Under the **Run** menu, execute the Application command, select Startup and select Form2.

   To type the address directly on Form2, you need a text box on Form2 because you cannot type on a label. Also, it would be nice to have an outline around the text box so you can see where you are typing, but that goes away when the form is printed. However, the Outline property cannot be changed at run time, only at design time. To solve this difficulty, draw two text boxes, one with an outline and one without, and one visible and the other invisible. When you type the visible, outlined box, the text is sent to the invisible, unoutlined box. At print time, switch the visible box for the invisible box to get the address without an outline.

5. Select Label2 on Form2 and delete it.

6. Draw a text box 3375 by 1220 twips where Label2 used to be. Change its properties to:

```
Name = PrintBox
Text = ""
BorderStyle = 0 - None
Multiline = True
```

7. On top of the first text box, draw a second text box exactly the same size. Change the text box properties to:

```
Name = EditBox
Caption = ""
BorderStyle = 1 - Fixed Single
Multiline = True
```

Now, attach the menu to Form2. It has a **New** command to clear the Form, a **Print** command to print it, a Print **Options** menu to allow changes in any of the options, and an **Exit** command to end the program.

8. Open the Menu Design window, and type the following table of values, listed in Table 7.1, and shown in Figure 7.4. Use the arrow button to indent the menus and press Done when you are finished.

Table 7.1. Menu definitions for the Address program 4.

Caption	Name	# of indents
&File	FileMenu	0
&New	NewCmd	1
-	SepBar1	1
&Print	PrintCmd	1
Print &Options	OptionMenu	1
&Return Address	RetAddrCmd	2
&Bold Text	BoldTextCmd	2
&Large Text	LargeTextCmd	2
-	SepBar2	1
E&xit	ExitCmd	1

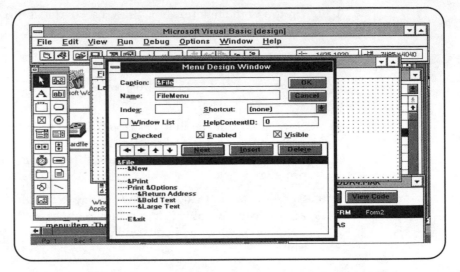

Figure 7.4. *Menu Design window for Version 4 of the Envelope Addresser.*

This completes the interface. Now change the code. Much of the code can be copied from the old version of the program into the new one, or retyped as you please. First, change the global definitions. Actually, TheLine does not have to be defined here, because you are no longer passing it from one Form to another. It also could be defined in the declarations section of Form2. However, because it is already here, leave it alone.

9. Open the declarations section of the module and change it to read:

```
Global TheLine As String
```

10. The declarations section of Form2 is not changed and should still read:

```
Dim eol$
```

11. Open the Form_Load procedure and change it to the following. Pieces of this were copied from the old Form_Click procedure.

```
Sub Form_Load ()
eol$ = Chr$(13) + Chr$(10)
Rem set initial values
RetAddrCmd.Checked = True
BoldTextCmd.Checked = False
```

```
LargeTextCmd.Checked = False
Rem Insert return address
Label1.FontBold = False
Label1.FontSize = 10
Label1.Caption = "William J. Orvis" + eol$
Label1.Caption = Label1.Caption + "123 Some St." + eol$
Label1.Caption = Label1.Caption + "Anywhere, CA  91234"
EditBox.FontBold = False
PrintBox.FontBold = False
EditBox.FontSize = 10
PrintBox.FontSize = 10
EditBox.Text = ""
End Sub
```

Line 2 of this procedure defines the eol$ (end-of-line) character. Lines 3 through 6 set the initial values of the options. Lines 7 to the end carry out the initial options, such as inserting the return address, turning off bold, and setting the size of the text.

The next procedure is executed whenever the Return Address menu command is executed. The procedure toggles the return address option on or off each time the menu command is executed. Much of this also can be copied from the Form_Load procedure.

12. Open the RetAddrCmd_Click procedure and type

```
Sub RetAddrCmd_Click ()
Rem Reverse the check mark
RetAddrCmd.Checked = Not RetAddrCmd.Checked
If RetAddrCmd.Checked = True Then
            Label1.Caption = "William J. Orvis" + eol$
            Label1.Caption = Label1.Caption + "123 Some
St." + eol$
            Label1.Caption = Label1.Caption + "Anywhere,
CA  91234"
        Else
            Label1.Caption = ""
        End If
        End Sub
```

Line 3 uses the NOT operator to change the Checked property of the Return Address command. The NOT operator changes True to False or False to True. Lines 4 through the end of this procedure are a

block `If` statement that checks the state of the check mark, and if it is `True`, inserts the return address in the `Label1` Label. If it's `False`, it blanks the contents of the Label. The next procedure performs a similar function for the **Bold Text** command.

13. Open the `BoldTextCmd_Click` procedure and type

```
Sub BoldTextCmd_Click ()
Rem Reverse the check mark
BoldTextCmd.Checked = Not BoldTextCmd.Checked
If BoldTextCmd.Checked = True Then
     Label1.FontBold = True
     EditBox.FontBold = True
     PrintBox.FontBold = True
Else
     Label1.FontBold = False
     EditBox.FontBold = False
     PrintBox.FontBold = False
End If
End Sub
```

Again, line 3 switches the state of the check on the **Bold Text** menu command, and the block `If` statement changes the `FontBold` property in the `Label1` label and the `EditBox` and `PrintBox` text boxes.

The next procedure does exactly the same thing for the **Large Text** menu command. First, it switches the state of the check mark, then it changes the property in the three boxes.

14. Open the `LargeTextCmd_Click` procedure and type

```
Sub LargeTextCmd_Click ()
Rem Reverse the check mark
LargeTextCmd.Checked = Not LargeTextCmd.Checked
If LargeTextCmd.Checked = True Then
     Label1.FontSize = 12
     EditBox.FontSize = 12
     PrintBox.FontSize = 12
Else
     Label1.FontSize = 10
     EditBox.FontSize = 10
     PrintBox.FontSize = 10
End If
End Sub
```

The EditBox_Change procedure makes sure that whenever the EditBox is changed, the invisible PrintBox also is changed. This way, when the form is printed, the PrintBox contains the correct text.

15. Open the EditBox_Change procedure and type

```
Sub EditBox_Change ()
PrintBox.Text = EditBox.Text
End Sub
```

16. Open the PrintCmd_Click procedure and type

```
Sub PrintCmd_Click ()
Rem switch between the edit box with the border and
Rem the edit box without the border for printing
EditBox.Visible = False
PrintBox.Visible = True
Form2.PrintForm
Rem Switch back to the edit box
PrintBox.Visible = False
EditBox.Visible = True
End Sub
```

The **Print** menu command executes the PrintCmd procedure, as shown previously. It first makes EditBox invisible and PrintBox visible to eliminate the bounding box surrounding the address. The bounding box makes it easier to type the address, but you don't want it to be printed on the envelope. Next, the procedure prints the form using the PrintForm method, and then turns the bounding box back on.

The next two procedures are relatively simple. The **New** menu command calls the Form_Load procedure again to reset everything as it was at the beginning, and the **Exit** menu command executes the End statement to end the program.

17. Open the NewCmd_Click procedure and type

```
Sub NewCmd_Click ()
Form_Load
End Sub
```

18. Open the ExitCmd_Click procedure and type

```
Sub ExitCmd_Click ()
End
End Sub
```

165

19. Select the Form_Click procedure and delete it by selecting its contents and pressing Delete. We no longer need this procedure because all its functions have been moved to other procedures.

20. Save the project and run it. The Form looks like Figure 7.5.

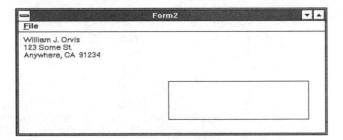

Figure 7.5. *Startup of version 4 of the Envelope Addresser.*

21. Type an address in the EditBox, and select any options from the Print Options submenu as shown in Figure 7.6.

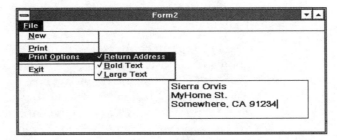

Figure 7.6. *Changing options in version 4 of the Envelope Addresser.*

22. Print an envelope by selecting **P**rint from the File menu. To print another envelope, either edit the old address or clear the form with the **N**ew command and type a new address. Then print again.

Creating the Edit Menu

The next standard menu is the Edit menu, which is used to transfer text and graphics between the Clipboard and a running application. The standard Edit menu commands are Undo, Cut, Copy, and Paste. Like the File menu, the Edit menu can have more or fewer commands, depending on the application.

Of all the commands, the Undo command is the most difficult to program. Undo returns the program to the state it had just before the last command was executed, or editing was done. Thus, any procedure that makes a change you want to be able to Undo must save the original state, and signal the Undo command that something can be undone. Unfortunately, I cannot give you much help here, because what you do or don't want to undo depends on your particular application. Take editing, for example. Because you don't want Undo just to undo the last character typed, you must select certain events to mark the beginning of a piece of editing that can be undone. Standard editing actions include deleting one or more characters, or executing a menu command.

The Cut, Copy and Paste commands transfer data between the application and the Clipboard. Because the Clipboard is a part of the system, all Windows applications have access to material placed on it. Text is transferred between a program and the Clipboard using the Clipboard object, and the GetText and SetText methods. Other methods exist for transferring pictures and other data to the Clipboard.

The GetText and SetText methods transfer text between the Clipboard and a Visual Basic program. The GetText method works like a function and returns any text stored on the Clipboard. SetText does just the opposite and places text on the Clipboard, replacing any text already there. The syntax of these methods are

```
Clipboard.GetText([type])
Clipboard.SetText String$, type
```

Where *type* is a constant that indicates the type of data to get or put on the Clipboard. If *type* is omitted, the default type is text. *String$* is a string containing the text to be placed on the Clipboard.

Three text box properties are needed to correctly perform the Cut, Copy, and Paste functions: SelLength, SelStart, and SelText. The SelLength property is a Long integer that contains the number of characters selected in the text box. The SelStart property is also a Long integer that contains the location of the first selected character, or the insertion point if no characters are selected. The SelText property is a string that contains the selected text. The SelText property has a unique characteristic: if you change it, the selected text in the text box is replaced with the changed text. Thus, the Cut, Copy, and Paste commands can be implemented by simply copying or changing the SelText property.

This characteristic makes it very easy to implement the Cut, Copy, and Paste commands. To Copy the selected text, simply copy the contents of `SelText` to the Clipboard. To Cut the selected text, copy it first with the Copy command and then set `SelText` equal to the null string, deleting the selected text. To implement the Paste command, equate `SelText` to the `GetText` method, which replaces the currently selected text with the contents of the Clipboard.

The Envelope Addresser Program (Version 5)

When you write a letter using a word processor program, you usually have typed the address already. Rather than typing it again in the Envelope Addresser program, add an Edit menu to that program so you can paste the address into it after copying the address onto the Clipboard in the word processor. Additionally, implement the Undo command on the Edit menu. To implement the Undo command, you have to decide what is "undoable." In this case, any Cut or Paste is "undoable," and any sequence of Backspaces or Deletes is "undoable."

1. Open version 4 of the envelope addresser ADDR4.MAK, and save it as version 5, ADDR5.MAK, ADDR52.FRM, and ADDR5.BAS.

   First, add the Edit menu to `Form2`.

2. Open `Form2`, open the Menu Design window, and add the following menu, using the values shown in Table 7.2. Don't remove the File menu in the process, but add this to the end, as shown in Figure 7.7.

Table 7.2. Menu definitions for Version 5 of the Envelope Addresser program.

Caption	Name	# of indents
&Edit	EditMenu	0
&Undo	UndoCmd	1
-	SepBar3	1
Cu&t	CutCmd	1
&Copy	CopyCmd	1
&Paste	PasteCmd	1

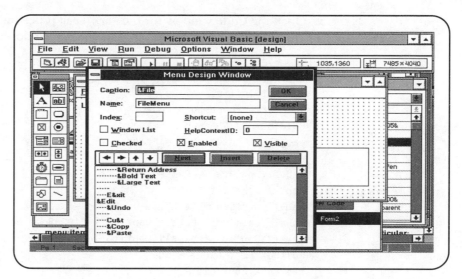

Figure 7.7. *Menu Design window showing the added Edit menu.*

The Undo procedure has to watch for the Backspace and Delete keys to determine when to start saving editing changes, so put constant definitions of the key codes for those two keys in the global module.

Key codes are numeric codes for the different keys on the keyboard (see Appendix B). You can either type them into your program, or copy them from the file CONSTANT.TXT where they are stored as global constants. To copy them into a program, open the CONSTANT.TXT file as if it were a Form with the Add File command on the File menu. Next, scroll through the Code window until you find the definitions you want, then use the Copy command on the Edit menu to copy them onto the Clipboard. Select the module, open its Code window, and paste the definitions using the Paste command on the Edit menu. After you have pasted all the definitions you need, remove the CONSTANT.TXT file from the project by selecting it and executing the Remove File command on the File menu.

3. Open the code window of the module and add the two key definitions at the end so it reads:

```
Global TheLine As String
Global Const KEY_BACK = &H8, KEY_DELETE = &H2E
```

4. In the declarations section of Form2, define the three variables to store the state of the system for the Undo command.

```
Dim eol$
Dim UndoText As String, UndoLength As Long, UndoStart As Long
```

169

5. Open the Code window for the `Form_Load` procedure and add the three statements at the end to initialize the Undo variables.

```
Sub Form_Load ()
eol$ = Chr$(13) + Chr$(10)
Rem set initial values
RetAddrCmd.Checked = True
BoldTextCmd.Checked = False
LargeTextCmd.Checked = False
Rem Insert return address
Label1.FontBold = False
Label1.FontSize = 10
Label1.Caption = "William J. Orvis" + eol$
Label1.Caption = Label1.Caption + "123 Some St." + eol$
Label1.Caption = Label1.Caption + "Anywhere, CA  91234"
EditBox.FontBold = False
PrintBox.FontBold = False
EditBox.FontSize = 10
PrintBox.FontSize = 10
EditBox.Text = ""
UndoText = ""
UndoStart = 0
UndoLength = 0
End Sub
```

The `CopyCmd_Click` procedure implements the Copy command. The selected data in `EditBox` is copied to the Clipboard. The selected text is accessed with the `SelText` property and passed to the Clipboard using the `SetText` method.

6. Select the `CopyCmd_Click` procedure and type

```
Sub CopyCmd_Click ()
Clipboard.SetText EditBox.SelText
End Sub
```

The next three procedures save the state of the system for the Undo command. In the `CutCmd_Click` and the `PasteCmd_Click` procedures, the contents of `EditBox` are saved before the command is carried out. Also saved are the `SelStart` and `SelLength` properties; this way, the cursor position and the selection size also can be restored. The third procedure, `EditBox_KeyDown`, intercepts keypresses being sent to `EditBox`, and saves the contents of `EditBox` whenever one or more Backspaces or Deletes are pressed.

The `CutCmd_Click` procedure implements the **Cut** command. After the data is saved for the Undo command, the selected data in `EditBox` is copied to the Clipboard as in the `CopyCmd_Click` procedure. The selected text is then deleted in line 9 by equating `SelText` to a null string.

7. Open the `CutCmd_Click` procedure and type

```
Sub CutCmd_Click ()
Rem Save state for undo
UndoText = EditBox.Text
UndoStart = EditBox.SelStart
UndoLength = EditBox.SelLength
Rem Cut the selected text out of the Text box
Rem and put it on the Clipboard
Clipboard.SetText EditBox.SelText
EditBox.SelText = ""
End Sub
```

The `PasteCmd_Click` procedure implements the **Paste** command. Lines 2 through 5 save the data for the Undo command. Line 8 then replaces the selected text with the contents of the Clipboard.

8. Select the `PasteCmd_Click` procedure and type

```
Sub PasteCmd_Click ()
Rem Save state for undo                        line 2
UndoText = EditBox.Text
UndoStart = EditBox.SelStart
UndoLength = EditBox.SelLength
Rem Replace the selected text with the contents
Rem of the Clipboard
EditBox.SelText = Clipboard.GetText()     line 8
End Sub
```

9. Open the `EditBox_KeyDown` procedure and type

```
Sub EditBox_KeyDown (KeyCode As Integer, Shift As Integer)
Static Flag As Integer
If KeyCode = KEY_BACK Or KeyCode = KEY_DELETE Then
     If Flag = False Then
          Flag = True
          UndoText = EditBox.Text
```

```
            UndoStart = EditBox.SelStart
            UndoLength = EditBox.SelLength
        End If
    Else
        Flag = False
    End If
End Sub
```

The `EditBox_KeyDown` procedure watches for `KeyDown` events directed at `EditBox`. This procedure captures those events before they are sent to `EditBox`. The key pressed is stored in the variable `KeyCode`, and `Shift` contains the state of the `Ctrl`, `Shift`, and `Alt` keys. The value of `KeyCode` and `Shift` must not be changed if you want the typed characters to eventually reach `EditBox`. The second statement defines the variable `Flag` as a `Static` variable. Normally, all the local variables in the `EditBox_KeyDown` procedure disappear as soon as the procedure ends. In this case, you want the variable `Flag` to stay around. `Flag` is initially `False`, but is set to `True` the first time Backspace or Delete is pressed. Note that the initial value of all numeric values is null, and all strings are the null string.

The next statement tests the key pressed to see whether it is the Backspace or the Delete key. If it isn't either of these, the block `If` statement sets `Flag` to `False` and ends. If a Backspace or Delete key is pressed, the `If` statement starting in line 4 is executed, testing the value of `Flag`. If `Flag` is `False`, this is the first Backspace or Delete pressed, and it is time to save the contents of `EditBox` and to set `Flag` to `True`. If `Flag` is `True`, this is one of several Backspaces or Deletes pressed in a row, and you don't have to do anything.

10. Open the `UndoCmd_Click` code window and type

```
Sub UndoCmd_Click ()
Rem Restore the state
EditBox.Text = UndoText
EditBox.SelStart = UndoStart
EditBox.SelLength = UndoLength
End Sub
```

This procedure actually performs the Undo command, and restores the contents of `EditBox`, the location of the cursor, and the characters selected.

11. Save the project, and run it. Try typing some text in EditBox, then select, **Cut**, and **Paste** it to a different place. Try the **Undo** command. Try copying an address in your favorite word processing program, switch to the Envelope Addresser, then paste the address into EditBox.

> Add a menu command to select one of two or three return addresses. Add another menu command to open a dialog box so you can input the return address. Add a menu to select one of several, frequently used, built-in addresses, and place the address in the text box.

When you execute the **Cut** command, the selected text should disappear, and the cursor should be located at the point where the text was removed. When the **Paste** command is executed, the selected text is replaced by the contents of the Clipboard. If no text is selected, the Clipboard contents are inserted at the insertion point. The cursor should be located at the end of the pasted text. The **Copy** command should make no apparent change to the text or the location of the insertion point. After a **Cut** or **Paste** command, the **Undo** command should return EditBox to the same state as before the **Cut** or **Paste** command, including the location of the cursor and the text selected. After typing some changes, **Undo** returns the EditBox to its state when the last **Cut** or **Paste** command was executed, or to the state when the last Backspace or Delete was pressed.

What You Have Learned

A common way of controlling Windows programs is with menus, and this chapter has investigated how you create and use them. Rather than pressing buttons and checking boxes, menus are used to set options and execute commands. Menus are created using the Menu Design window, which attaches them to the top form. Procedures are attached to menu commands in exactly the same way as other controls, by inserting code in the Code window for that command. Specifically, you learned to

● Construct menus with the Menu Design window.

● Set the Checked, Enabled, and Visible properties.

● Attach Shortcut and Access keys to menu items.

● Attach procedures to menu commands.

● Create the standard **File** and **Edit** menus.

● Access the Clipboard with **Cut**, **Copy**, and **Paste**.

● Implement the **Undo** command in the Envelope Addresser
Program.

Writing Custom Procedures

The code in this book, until now, has been written in procedures that are attached to controls and forms. These procedures are actually event-procedures, because they are executed when some specific event (such as a control being clicked) occurs to the control or form it is attached to. In a couple of instances, you also executed an event-procedure directly by placing its name in another procedure. Now it's time to look at the creation and use of procedures.

In This Chapter

This chapter investigates `Function` and `Sub` procedures, two types of procedures that differ only slightly from the event-procedures used so far in this book. Specifically, you learn how to

● Use `Sub` procedures.

- Use user-defined functions.

- Pass arguments to procedures.

- Use list boxes.

You also will create the Automatic Check Register program, a program that records checks and deposits and automatically maintains the account balance.

What are Procedures?

A *procedure* is a self-contained block of code that performs a specific task. The more specific the task, the easier the procedure is to write and maintain. Procedures enable you to group a block of statements together, give them a name, and use the name to execute the specified code. Procedures are the building blocks of a computer program.

When writing a program in Visual Basic, you naturally break it into procedures as you attach code to the different controls and forms. These event-procedures break a program into tasks that are performed when each event occurs. Although these procedures are automatically created by Visual Basic, any other procedures must be created by the programmer.

You might wonder, "Why bother with procedures?" You know what you want your code to do, so why separate it with artificial barriers? In the early days of computing, that's exactly the philosophy people followed. Memory was expensive, so programmers spent much of their time writing the most compact code possible. This compact code became known as "spaghetti code," because, unfortunately, the point of execution would jump all over the place with apparently random intent. Maintaining this code was only barely possible if you were the original programmer, and modifying it was usually impossible. It was generally faster to write a new program than to try to decipher someone else's program. Procedures were available, but were used only to reuse common blocks of code.

As restrictions on memory usage have rapidly diminished, program design has focused more on maintainability than on size. Modern programming practice encourages the use of procedures to not only reuse blocks of code, but to functionally organize a program. Procedure use has increasingly modularized codes, making codes more readable, and much easier to maintain or modify.

Procedures isolate not only the code associated with a task, but the data. All variables used in a single procedure, and not defined at a higher level (in the declarations section of a form, or globally in a module), are available only in that procedure. A variable of the same name in another procedure is unaffected by changes in the first variable. As discussed before, these are local variables.

Communication with a procedure is by way of global variables defined at a higher level, and through variables passed to a procedure via its arguments.

Creating Sub Procedures

All the event-procedures attached to controls are Sub procedures. A Sub procedure or subroutine begins with the keyword Sub and the procedure name, followed by an optional argument list in parentheses. Procedures that deal only with global variables do not have an argument list, but must still have the parentheses.

The argument list consists of the names of the local variables that receive the values sent to the Sub procedure by the calling routine, plus any needed type declarations (As Integer, for example). All Sub procedures end with an End Sub statement. The syntax of the Sub statement, which is the heading of the Sub procedure, is

```
[Static] [private] Sub subname [(arguments)]
End Sub
```

where subname is the name of the Sub procedure, and arguments is the argument list. The Static option makes all the variables defined in the Sub procedure persist from one call of the Sub procedure to the next. Normally, when a procedure ends, all of its local variables go away. The Static option, however, causes the local variables to be stored until the procedure is called again.

The Private option makes procedures in a module available only to other procedures in the same module. Normally, the procedures in a

module are available throughout an application. The Private option hides a procedure from other modules and forms. Use this option to prevent problems when you have procedures with the same name in two or more different modules. This does not apply to procedures in a form that already are private.

For example, a subroutine to calculate the sum of two numbers and return the value in a third could be written as follows:

```
Sub AddEmUp (NumOne As Single, NumTwo As Single, TheSum As Single)
TheSum = NumOne + NumTwo
End Sub
```

Now, this procedure is so simple you would probably never write it yourself, but it does illustrate all the parts of a Sub procedure. The first line declares the procedure name and arguments, with each argument getting an explicit type declaration. The second line adds the first two arguments together and stores that value in the third, which is passed back to the calling routine in the argument list. You also could pass the value back in one of the first two arguments.

To execute or call a procedure from some other procedure, type its name followed by the arguments you want sent to the procedure. In contrast to the argument list in the heading of the Sub procedure, the argument list in the calling statement is not surrounded by parentheses. However, each argument in the calling statement corresponds, one for one, with the arguments in the procedure heading. If an argument is passing a value back to the calling procedure, a variable must be used to receive it; otherwise you could use constant values. For example, to call the AddEmUp procedure from the Form_Click procedure, type

```
Sub Form_Click ()
A = 185
B = 723
AddEmUp A, B, C
Form1.Print A, B, C
AddEmUp 5, 7, ANumber
Form1.Print ANumber
End Sub
```

The first line defines the Form_Click event-procedure. The second and third lines load the variables A and B with the values 185 and 723. The fourth line calls the procedure AddEmUp with A, B, and C as the arguments. Note that there are no parentheses around the arguments as there are in the definition of AddEmUp. The fifth line prints the values of the three arguments after control returns from AddEmUp. The sixth line calls the procedure again, this time with constant values, rather than variables, as two of the arguments. The third argument still must be a variable, because it receives the result of the Sub procedure's calculation. When this procedure is run, it produces this text on the Form:

```
185             723             908
12
```

To write a procedure on a form in Visual Basic, move to the general object of a form, and execute the New Procedure command on the **Code** menu. Alternately, type the first line of the procedure. As soon as you press Enter, Visual Basic creates a template for the new procedure under the general object, including the End Sub statement. To find the procedure, select the general object, and locate the procedure in the Proc. list box. Do the same to create a Sub procedure in any module.

User-Defined Functions

8

In addition to Sub procedures, you also can create Function procedures. A Function procedure is similar to such built-in functions as Sin() or Mid$(). A Function procedure, like a Sub procedure, can modify its arguments and execute BASIC statements. In addition, it returns a value stored in the function's name. The syntax of a function statement is

```
[Static] [Private] Function funcname [(arguments)] [As type]
End Function
```

Here, *funcname* is the name of the function, and *arguments* are the names of the local variables that receive the arguments from the calling procedure. Because a Function procedure returns a value in the function name, that name must have a type like any other variable. To set the type of the function name, either declare it globally with a Global or Dim statement, use a type declaration suffix on the name, or include the *As type* clause in the function statement. The Static option makes the Local variables persist from one calling of the function to the next. The private option makes a procedure available only within the module where it is defined.

Before the end of the Function procedure, an assignment statement must assign a value to a variable with the same name as the function, to be

returned by it when the End Function statement is reached. For example, the following function returns the sum of its two arguments.

```
Function AddEmUpFunc (VarOne As Single, VarTwo As Single) As
Single
AddEmUpFunc = VarOne + VarTwo
End Function
```

Again, this function is overly simple, but it demonstrates the syntax of the Function statement. A function need not be this simple; it can contain many statements, including calls to other Function and Sub procedures. The first line defines the function name, its data type, and the types of the arguments it expects. The second line calculates the sum of the two arguments and assigns that value to the function name. The third line ends the procedure.

The calling syntax of a function is somewhat different than that of a Sub procedure, due to the value returned. A Function procedure is called in exactly the same way as any of the built-in functions. For example, this function might be called, in lines 4 and 6 of the Form_Click procedure, as

```
Sub Form_Click ()
A = 185
B = 723
C = AddEmUpFunc(A, B)
Form1.Print A, B, C
Form1.Print AddEmUpFunc(5, 7)
End Sub
```

This procedure gives exactly the same results as the one that used the AddEmUp Sub procedure. Note that only two arguments are passed to the function, and the third is returned as the function name. The value assigned to C could just as easily have been returned as an argument in the Sub procedure. Note in the sixth line that the value returned by the function isn't assigned to a variable, but is passed directly to the Print method as one of its arguments.

Passing Arguments to Procedures

There are two ways to pass an argument to a Sub or Function procedure: as an address, or as a value. The default is to pass arguments to a procedure by address. An address is the location of the variable in memory. By passing the address as an argument, the procedure that was called operates on the same variable as the one that called it, even though it might have a different name in the called procedure.

If you don't want the procedure you are calling to have access to the original variable, pass it as a value, using the `ByVal` keyword in front of the variable name when it is declared in the first line of the procedure. An alternate approach is to surround the argument with parentheses in the calling statement. When a variable is passed as a value, a copy of the original variable is made, and that copy is passed to the procedure. Because the procedure is no longer operating on the original variable, any changes it makes to the copy are not reflected in the original.

Formulas used as arguments of procedures are always passed as values, even though the default is by address. The values of properties cannot be passed by address. They must either be passed by value, or assigned to another variable first, then passed to the procedure. Be careful of passing array variables by value, because the whole array must be duplicated to do so.

This example demonstrates calling by value and by address:

```
Sub Form_Click ()
A = 1
B = 2
C = 3
D = 4
PassTest A, B
Form1.Print A, B
PassTest (C), D
Form1.Print C, D
End Sub

Sub PassTest (One As Single, ByVal Two As Single)
Form1.Print One, Two
One = 10
Two = 20
End Sub
```

When this program is run, and the form clicked, the following values are printed:

```
1          2
10         2
3          4
3          4
```

Lines 2 through 5 of the `Form_Click` procedure initialize the four variables A, B, C, and D, as 1, 2, 3, and 4. In line 6, the `PassTest` `Sub` procedure is called, and is passed A and B as arguments. In the `PassTest` procedure, the first line specifies that the second argument is passed by value and the first is by address. The second line then prints the two variables `One` and `Two`, which have been passed the values 1 and 2. In lines 3 and 4, the `PassTest` procedure changes the values of the arguments to 10 and 20, and then ends in line 5.

In line 7 of the `Form_Click` procedure, the current values of A and B are printed. Because the first argument is passed by address, the new value of 10 is passed back from the variable `One` in the `PassTest` procedure to the variable A in the `Form_Click` procedure. The second argument was passed by value, so the new value of 20 for variable `Two` is not passed back to the variable B.

In line 8, the variables C and D are passed to the `PassTest` procedure. As before, the value of the second variable, D, is passed by value, and is unchanged by the procedure. This time, however, the parentheses around C pass the first argument by value as well, so neither variable is changed outside the `PassTest` procedure.

Displaying and Selecting With Lists

Two new controls are list boxes and combo boxes. A list box holds a list of strings the user can choose from. A combo box combines a list box with a text box, so users also can type a value not on the list.

There are three types of combo boxes, selected with the `Style` property. Figure 8.1 shows a list box and the three types of combo boxes.

The drop-down combo box in Visual Basic looks different from those in other Windows applications. The drop-down combo box has a space between it and the down arrow button that causes the list to drop down. Everywhere else, there is no space.

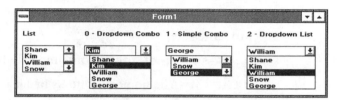

Figure 8.1. *A list box and three types of combo boxes.*

A list box contains a list of values, and the user can select only one value from the list. A combo box combines a list and a text box, and offers more options. A Style 0 combo box is a *Drop-down Combo* box, with a text box at the top and a list box that drops down when the small down arrow on the right is pressed. If a list item is selected in the list part of the Combo box, it is placed in the text part of the combo box where it can be edited. Style 1 is a *Simple Combo* box, which also has a text box at the top and a list box below it. The only difference between a Style 0 and Style 1 combo box is that the list does not drop down in the Style 1 Combo box, but is permanently displayed. A Style 2 combo box is a *drop down List* box, which is actually a list box rather than a combo box because the box at the top only displays the currently selected item, and cannot be edited.

Use list and drop down list boxes when you have a specific list of values for users to choose from, and don't want users to be able to type their own values. Use the simple and drop down combo boxes when you have a list of possible values for users to select, but users also can type their own values. The drop-down versions of these boxes also save space on a form.

Although all these boxes respond to the Click event when an item is selected, it is better to let the user select an item, then use a button to signify acceptance of that item. This is especially true if the action performed is irreversible, such as the deletion of a file. You could then add a DoubleClick

event on the list or combo box that also executes the button's event-procedure. That way, a user can click an item in the list and press the button to accept it, or double click it to get the same effect.

Combo and list boxes have some special properties and methods for dealing with them. The important methods are

AddItem—Adds an item to a list.
RemoveItem—Removes an item from a list.

The properties are

List—An array of strings, containing all the items in the list.

ListCount—The number of items in a list.

ListIndex—The index of the currently selected item.

Sorted—An indicator of whether the list is sorted or displayed as input.

All of the text box properties, such as SelLength, SelStart, SelText, and Text, also apply to the text box part of the combo boxes. You cannot insert values in the list part of these boxes at design time, but must insert them at run time using the AddItem method. The syntax of the AddItem method is

```
[form.] control.AddItem item$ [,index%]
```

where *form* is the name of the form the *control* is attached to, control is the Name of the list or combo box, and *item$* is a string to insert into the list. (The *form* variable defaults to the form containing the statement if the variable is omitted.) The optional *index%* argument controls where the item is inserted in the list. If *index%* is omitted, the new item is inserted at the bottom of the list, unless the Sorted property is True, in which case the item is inserted into its alphabetical location.

As you might expect, the RemoveItem method performs the opposite function of the AddItem method. The syntax is

```
[form.]control.RemoveItem index%
```

Items in a list are indexed from the top, starting with index number 0. The second item is index number 1, the third is 2, and so on. The ListCount property contains the number of items currently in the list, and the ListIndex property contains the index number of the currently selected item. To see the contents of the currently selected item, use the List property with ListIndex as the argument in the following manner:

```
Item$ = [form.] control.List([form.]control.ListIndex)
```

As you can see, the List property is an array of strings, and you are selecting the current one using the ListIndex property. The Text property also contains the currently selected item when the item is selected, but can be changed afterwards by the user.

The Automated Check Register Program

The Automated Check Register program is an automated check register stored in the computer. It automatically inserts the next check number and date, has a combo box containing several common entries for the description field, and automatically maintains the account balance. The register is stored in a list box, and selecting an item in that list brings it into the text boxes for editing.

First, draw the user interface:

1. Open a new project, and save it as CKREG (CKREG.MAK and CKREG1.FRM).

2. Open Form1, adjust its size to 8625 by 3320 twips, and set the following properties:

```
Caption = Check Register
ControlBox = False
MaxButton = False
BorderStyle = 3 - Fixed Double
```

3. Draw five labels on the Form, as shown in Figure 8.2, and type the properties, as shown in the following table.

	Label1	*Label2*	*Label3*	*Label4*	*Label5*
Caption =	Number	Date	Description of Transaction	Amount	Balance
Height =	260	260	260	260	260
Width =	900	1215	2775	1455	1455
Top =	120	120	120	120	120
Left =	120	960	2160	5280	6840

Draw a row of text, label, and combo boxes to use as input boxes for an entry into the check register, as shown in Figure 8.2. The three text boxes are for the check number, the date, and the amount of the check or deposit, all of which are editable quantities. The combo box is for the description of the transaction, and has a list of standard transactions, plus an editable

box to insert a transaction not on the list. The label is for the balance, which cannot be edited because it depends on the previous balance and the current entry applying to Automated Check Register Program.

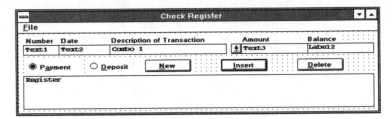

Figure 8.2. *Layout of the Form for the Check Register program.*

4. Draw a text box on the form to hold the check number, and set its properties.

```
Name = CkNumBox
Height = 380
Width = 855
Top = 360
Left = 120
FontName = Courier
FontSize = 10
```

5. Draw another text box on the form to hold the date, and set its properties.

```
Name = DateBox
Height = 380
Width = 1215
Top = 360
Left = 960
FontName = Courier
FontSize = 10
```

6. Draw a third text box on the form to hold the amount, and set its properties.

```
Name = AmountBox
Height = 380
Width = 1575
Top = 360
```

```
Left = 5280
FontName = Courier
FontSize = 10
```

7. Draw a label on the form to hold the balance, and set its properties.

```
Name = BalanceBox
Height = 380
Width = 1575
Top = 360
Left = 6840
FontName = Courier
FontSize = 10
```

8. Draw a combo box on the form to hold the description of the transaction, and set its properties.

```
Name = DescBox
Height = 380
Width = 3135
Top = 360
Left = 2160
Style = 0 - Dropdown Combo
FontName = Courier
FontSize = 10
```

The font name and size is changed to 10 point Courier in all these boxes, because the data is going to be stored in strings in the following list box, and you want the strings to line up. Use Courier because it's a monospace font; if you use a proportionally spaced font, the data won't line up.

9. Draw a list box on the form and type its properties.

```
Name = Register
Height = 1100
Width = 8295
Top = 1320
Left = 120
FontName = Courier
FontSize = 10
```

Next, attach two option buttons to select whether the current entry is a payment or deposit, then three command buttons to control insertion and deletion of new records. (Your screen will look like Figure 8.2.) The

New button sets up the entry boxes for a new entry, setting the current date, check number and balance. The **Insert** button inserts the data currently in the text boxes into the check record, either at the end for a new entry, or to replace an entry selected for corrections. The **Delete** button deletes the selected entry from the check record.

Note the ampersand (&) in the Caption properties of the controls for these buttons. That marks the following letter in their names as an Access key for the controls, just as it did for the menu commands in Chapter 7, "Using Custom Menus." A control with an Access key can be selected by pressing **Alt** and the Access key. Note also that the **Insert** button has the Default property set to True. Only one control on a form can have its Default property set, and that control is clicked if the Enter key is pressed, assuming the focus is not on another command button.

10. Draw an option button on the form and set its properties.

```
Name = Debit
Caption = &Payment
Height = 380
Width = 1215
Top = 840
Left = 240
Value = True
```

11. Draw a second option button on the form and set its properties.

```
Name = Credit
Caption = &Deposit
Height = 380
Width = 1215
Top = 840
Left = 1680
Value = False
```

12. Draw a command button on the form and set its properties.

```
Name = NewCmd
Caption = &New
Height = 380
Width = 1095
Top = 840
Left = 3000
```

13. Draw a second command button on the form and set its properties.

```
Name = InsertCmd
Caption = &Insert
Height = 380
Width = 1575
Top = 840
Left = 4440
Default = True
```

14. Draw a third command button on the form and set its properties.

```
Name = DeleteCmd
Caption = &Delete
Height = 380
Width = 1095
Top = 840
Left = 6600
```

Change the tab order of the controls so pressing the Tab key moves the focus to the object that you most likely will want to access next.

15. Select the NewCmd command button, and change its TabIndex property to 0. Select the rest of the controls on the form, in order, and set the TabIndex property according to Table 8.1.

Table 8.1. TabIndex values for the Check Register program.

Name	*TabIndex*
NewCmd	0
Register	1
DescBox	2
AmountBox	3
Debit	4
Credit	5
InsertCmd	6
CkNumBox	7
DateBox	8
DeleteCmd	9

16. Open the menu design window and create a **File** menu according to Table 8.2.

Table 8.2. File menu setup for the Check Register program.

Caption	Name	# of indents
&File	FileMenu	0
&Print	PrintCmd	1
-	SepBar1	1
E&xit	ExitCmd	1

This completes the visual interface, which should now look like Figure 8.2. The next step is to add code to these controls. First declare some variables at the Form level to hold the check number (CkNum), and current balance (Balance). NewFlag is a flag that indicates whether this is a new record being inserted into the check record, or an old record being edited. InitialBalance is the starting balance for the program.

17. Open the declarations section of Form1, and type

```
Dim CkNum As Integer, Balance As Double, NewFlag As Integer
Dim InitialBalance As Double
```

The Form_Load procedure initializes the variables and sets up the program. The procedure inserts the initial balance into the register, as if it were a deposit. I chose a starting number of 1000 for the checks in line 3 and an initial balance of $980 in line 4. Lines 6 through 14 load values in the DescBox list box. Because a list box cannot be loaded at design time, it must be loaded by the running code. Lines 16 through 21 load the initial values in the text boxes, then the routine Box2List is called in line 22. The Box2List routine takes the data from all the text boxes, stores it in a string, and returns that string to the argument Entry$. In line 23, the AddItem method inserts Entry$ into the Register list box.

You don't want users to be inserting data or changing the entry type until they have either initialized a new record with the **New** button, or selected a list item from the Register for editing, so the rest of this procedure disables the **Insert** and **Delete** buttons and the **Debit** and **Credit** option buttons. Once you have pressed New or have selected a record, the buttons are enabled again.

18. Open the Form_Load procedure and type

```
Sub Form_Load ()
InitialBalance = 980      'Set the initial values
CkNum = 1000
Balance = InitialBalance
'Insert some items in the Description list
DescBox.AddItem "Shane's Grocery"
DescBox.AddItem "Sierra Bank and Trust"
DescBox.AddItem "Skye's Sewing Shop"
DescBox.AddItem "Today Computers"
DescBox.AddItem "Julie's Day-care"
DescBox.AddItem "B.J.'s Consulting"
DescBox.AddItem "Orvis Cattle Co."
DescBox.AddItem "Pay"
DescBox.AddItem "Royalty Payment"
'Insert the initial balance in the register as a deposit
line 15
CkNumBox.Text = ""
DateBox.Text = "01-01-1992"
DescBox.Text = "Starting Balance"
Credit.Value = True
AmountBox.Text = "       980.00"
BalanceBox.Caption = "       980.00"
Box2List Entry$     'Store the data in the string Entry
Register.AddItem Entry$     'Store the new item in the Register
'Disable the Insert and Delete Buttons
InsertCmd.Enabled = False
DeleteCmd.Enabled = False
'Disable the Payment/Deposit options
Debit.Enabled = False
Credit.Enabled = False
End Sub
```

The **New** command button sets up the text boxes for a new entry. First, in lines 2 and 3, the **Debit** and **Credit** option buttons are enabled. In lines 5 through 11, the default values for a check are entered into the text boxes. In line 13, the NewFlag is set to indicate that this is a new entry. A new record has now been initialized, so enable the **Insert** Command button in line 14 so the record can be stored, then disable the **Delete** button. The most logical thing for the user to do next is to select the description, so move the focus to the Description box in line 16.

19. Open the `NewCmd_Click` procedure and type

```
Sub NewCmd_Click ()
Debit.Enabled = True
Credit.Enabled = True
'Set default values for a new check
Debit.Value = True
CkNumBox.Text = Str$(CkNum)
DateBox.Text = Date$
DescBox.Text = ""
AmountBox.Text = ""
Balance = GetBalance(Register.ListCount - 1)
BalanceBox.Caption = Format$(Balance, "0.00")
'Set the new flag and enable the Insert command
NewFlag = True
InsertCmd.Enabled = True
DeleteCmd.Enabled = False
DescBox.SetFocus
End Sub
```

After pressing the **New** button, you might want to insert a deposit rather than a check. Clicking the **Deposit** button executes the `Credit_Click` procedure, which changes the entry to a deposit, and deletes the check number. Clicking the **Payment** button executes the `Debit_click` procedure, changes the entry back to a check record, and inserts the check number back into the check number text box. Both procedures end by calling the `AmountBox_Change` procedure to update the balance.

20. Open the `Credit_Click` and `Debit_Click` procedures and type

```
Sub Credit_Click ()
CkNumBox.Text = ""
AmountBox_Change
End Sub
Sub Debit_Click ()
CkNumBox.Text = Str$(CkNum)
AmountBox_Change
End Sub
```

After you have completed filling the text boxes for a record, press the **Insert** button. The procedure attached to this button first calls the `Box2List` procedure to copy the data from the text boxes and return it in the string `Entry$`. In line 3, a block `If` statement breaks the routine into two different parts, one for a new record, and one for a changed record. If the record is a new one, it is added to the `Register` list box with the `AddItem` method in line 4. Then, if the entry was for a check (Debit.Value = True), it adds one to the variable CkNum to advance the check number, and updates the current balance. It then disables the **Insert** and **Delete** buttons so you can't insert or delete a record until you either press New or select a record in the Register list box.

If the entry was for a changed record rather than for a new one, the block of code starting in line 14 is executed. Instead of using the AddItem method to add a new entry, this statement uses the List property of the Register list box to replace the existing entry with the edited one in the string Entry$.

The List property is an array of strings containing the items in the list, and the ListIndex property contains the currently selected one. Because an entry has been changed, the current balance in the replaced entry and all those following it might not be correct, so the FixBalance procedure is called in line 15 to recalculate the balance for all the entries in the Register. Then the Register_Click procedure is called to read the corrected data back into the text boxes. The last few lines of the routine disable the option buttons and move the focus to the **New** command button.

21. Open the InsertCmd_Click procedure and type

```
Sub InsertCmd_Click ()
Box2List  Entry$    'copy the data into the string Entry
If NewFlag = True Then
  Register.AddItem Entry$
  If Debit.Value = True Then
    CkNum = CkNum + 1
  End If
  Balance = GetBalance(Register.ListCount - 1)
  Rem If you wanted to print checks from this program
  Rem you would call a check printing routine here.
  InsertCmd.Enabled = False
  DeleteCmd.Enabled = False
Else
  Register.List(Register.ListIndex) = Entry$
  FixBalance       'Recalculate the Balance field
  Register_Click
End If
Debit.Enabled = False
Credit.Enabled = False
NewCmd.SetFocus
End Sub
```

The `Register_Click` procedure is executed whenever an item in the `Register` list box is clicked. It first sets the flag `NewFlag` to `False`, indicating this is an old record rather than a new one. Then, in lines 4 and 5, it extracts the selected record into the string variable `Entry$`, and calls the `List2Box` `Sub` procedure to put the values in the text boxes. In line 6, it uses the `GetBalance` `Function` procedure to get the current balance from the record just before the selected one (`Register.ListIndex - 1`). It finally enables the **Insert** and **Delete** buttons.

22. Open the `Register_Click` procedure and type

```
Sub Register_Click ()
NewFlag = False
'Get the entry from the Register and put it in the Text boxes
Entry$ = Register.Text
List2Box Entry$
Balance = GetBalance(Register.ListIndex - 1)
'Turn on the Insert and Delete commands
InsertCmd.Enabled = True
DeleteCmd.Enabled = True
End Sub
```

The `DeleteCmd_Click` procedure is executed when the **Delete** button is pressed. It first checks to ensure that the selected list item is not the first list item that contains the starting balance. If it isn't, the procedure deletes the selected item with the `RemoveItem` method. Because removing an item will probably make the current balance incorrect, the procedure calls the `FixBalance` `Sub` procedure to recalculate it. Finally, the procedure disables the **Delete** and **Insert** buttons.

23. Open the `DeleteCmd_Click` procedure and type

```
Sub DeleteCmd_Click ()
If Register.ListIndex > 0 Then
Register.RemoveItem Register.ListIndex
FixBalance
End If
DeleteCmd.Enabled = False
InsertCmd.Enabled = False
End Sub
```

The `PrintCmd_Click` procedure is executed whenever the **Print** command is selected from the File menu. The procedure starts a `For`/`Next` loop counting over the number of items in the List box (0 to `ListCount-1`.). The integer variable I% is the loop counter for the For/Next loop, and is used to select the list item in line 30. It then uses the Print method to print the list item. At the end, it executes the EndDoc method to tell the printer it is done, and to begin printing.

24. Open the PrintCmd_Click procedure and type

```
Sub PrintCmd_Click ()
For i% = 0 To Register.ListCount - 1
  Printer.Print Register.List(i%)
Next i%
Printer.EndDoc
End Sub
```

25. Open the ExitCmd_Click and Form_Unload procedures and type

```
Sub ExitCmd_Click ()
End
End Sub
Sub Form_Unload()
End
End Sub
```

The ExitCmd_Click procedure is executed when the Exit command is selected from the File menu. It simply executes an End statement to end the program. The Form_Unload procedure also contains an End statement. You can end the program by closing the form using the Close command on the control menu, or double-clicking the control menu. The AmountBox_Change procedure is executed whenever you type a number into the Amount Text box. It checks to see whether this is a deposit or a payment, and recalculates the value in the BalanceBox label accordingly. As a result, the value in the Balance box changes dynamically as you type a deposit or withdrawal.

26. Open the AmountBox_Change procedure and type

```
Sub AmountBox_Change ()
If Debit.Value = True Then
➥BalanceBox.Caption = Format$(Balance
    - Val(AmountBox.Text), "0.00")
Else
➥BalanceBox.Caption = Format$(Balance
    + Val(AmountBox.Text), "0.00")
```

```
End If
End Sub
```

This completes the event-procedures; now the user-defined procedures are discussed. As you type these procedures, be sure to select the correct type—Function or Sub—otherwise the program does not work. The first user-defined procedure is Box2List, which copies the data from the text boxes and returns it in a string variable so it can be stored in the list box. The data is stored in the string variable, according to Table 8.3.

Table 8.3. Breakdown of the TheString$ variable.

Contents	Starting Character	Length
Check number	1	6
Date	8	10
Description	19	25
Debit or Credit	45	1
Amount	47	14
Balance	62	14

The procedure first initializes the value of TheString$ as a string of 81 spaces. In line 3, the Mid$ statement is used to insert the check number in the first six character positions. Line 4 puts the date in 10 character positions starting at position number 8. Line 5 inserts the description in 25 characters, starting at position number 19. Lines 6 through 10 insert a D or C at character position 45, depending on whether this is a payment or deposit. Next are two dollar amounts. Although all the items so far have been left justified into the string locations, dollar amounts look better if they are right justified. To right justify the variables, create a temporary variable, Temp$, containing 14 blanks. Use the RSet method to right justify the dollar amounts into the temporary variable, then insert the temporary variable into TheString$. Lines 11 through 13 insert the amount of the debit or credit starting at position 47, and lines 14 through 16 insert the balance starting in position 62.

27. Select the general section of the form and create a template for the Box2List Sub procedure. Either use the **New Procedure** command on the **View** menu, or type Sub Box2List at the bottom of the declarations section, open the procedure and type

```
Sub Box2List (TheString$)
TheString$= Space$(81)
Mid$(TheString$ , 1, 6) = CkNumBox.Text
Mid$(TheString$, 8, 10) = DateBox.Text
Mid$(TheString$, 19, 25) = DescBox.Text
If Debit.Value = True Then
   Mid$(TheString$, 45) = "D"
Else
   Mid$(TheString$, 45) = "C"
End If
Temp$ = Space$(14)
RSet Temp$ = Format$(Val(AmountBox.Text), "0.00")
Mid$(TheString$, 47, 14) = Temp$
Temp$ = Space$(14)
RSet Temp$ = BalanceBox.Caption
Mid$(TheString$, 62, 14) = Temp$
End Sub
```

The List2Box Sub procedure reverses the process of the Box2List procedure. Substrings are extracted from TheString$ using the Mid$() function and stored in the text boxes.

28. Create a template for the List2Box Sub procedure, and type

```
Sub List2Box (TheString$)
CkNumBox.Text = Mid$(TheString$, 1, 6)
DateBox.Text = Mid$(TheString$, 8, 10)
DescBox.Text = Mid$(TheString$, 19, 25)
If Mid$(TheString$, 45, 1) = "D" Then
   Debit.Value = True
Else
   Credit.Value = True
End If
Debit.Enabled = False
Credit.Enabled = False
AmountBox.Text = LTrim$ (Mid$(TheString$, 47, 14))
BalanceBox.Caption = LTrim$ (Mid$(TheString$, 62, 14))
End Sub
```

The FixBalance Sub procedure loops over all the list items in Register, and calculates and updates the running balance. The balance is calculated in line 5 using the GetBalance() Function procedure to get the previous balance, and the GetChange() Function procedure to get the current debit or credit. It updates the balance with the PutBalance Sub procedure.

29. Create a template for the FixBalance Sub procedure, and type

```
Sub FixBalance ()
Rem Fix the balance column after an adjustment
If Register.ListCount > 0 Then
  For i% = 0 To Register.ListCount - 1
    Balance = GetBalance(i% - 1) + GetChange(i%)
    PutBalance i%, Balance
  Next i%
End If
End Sub
```

The GetChange() procedure returns the debit or credit amount from the record indicated by its argument. Because this procedure returns a single value, make it a Function procedure. This procedure first checks to be sure the argument index is valid, then uses it to select a list item in Register and store it in Entry$. It extracts the amount from Entry$ in line 6, and stores it in a temporary double precision variable, temp#. It then tests to see whether this is a debit or credit, and accordingly returns a positive or negative value in GetChange.

30. Create a template for the GetChange() Function procedure, and type

```
Function GetChange (index As Integer) As Double
If index
< 0 Then
  GetChange = 0
Else
  Entry$ = Register.List(index)
  Temp# = Val(Mid$(Entry$, 47, 14))
  If Mid$(Entry$, 45, 1) = "D" Then
    GetChange = -Temp#
  Else
    GetChange = Temp#
  End If
End If
End Function
```

The GetBalance() and PutBalance() procedures either get or change the balance in the list item selected with the index. GetBalance is a Function procedure because it returns a single value, and you want to use it like a function. GetBalance() first checks for an out-of-range index. It then extracts the list item into the string Entry$, then extracts the numeric value of the balance and returns it in `GetBalance`. `PutBalance()` does just the opposite; it also checks the index, then it extracts the list item into `Entry$` in line 3. It then replaces the value in the list item with the new value in lines 4 through 6, then stores the list item back into the list in line 7.

31. Create a template for the `GetBalance()` Function procedure, and type

```
Function GetBalance (index As Integer) As Double
If index
< 0 Then
  GetBalance = InitialBalance
Else
  Entry$ = Register.List(index)
  GetBalance = Val(Mid$(Entry$, 62, 14))
End If
End Function
```

32. Create a template for the `PutBalance()` Sub procedure, and type

```
Sub PutBalance (index As Integer, bal As Double)
If index > 0 Then
    Entry$ = Register.List(index)
  Temp$ = Space$(14)
  RSet Temp$ = Format$(bal, "0.00")
  Mid$(Entry$, 62) = Temp$
  Register.List(index) = Entry$
End If
End Sub
```

33. Save the procedure and run it. Click the **New** button, then click the down arrow on the right side of the drop down combo box. Your screen should look like Figure 8.3.

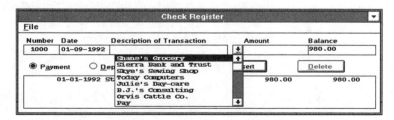

Figure 8.3. *The Automated Check Register program with the description list pulled down.*

199

Select Shane's Grocery as the description, type **50** as the amount, and press Enter, or click the **Insert** button. The check register should now look like Figure 8.4.

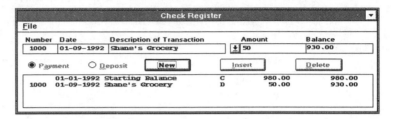

Figure 8.4. *The Automated Check Register program with the first entry inserted.*

34. Type several more entries, both payments and deposits. The check register should look something like Figure 8.5.

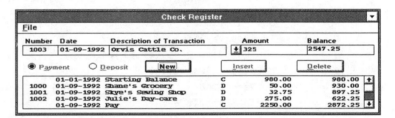

Figure 8.5. *The Automated Check Register program with several entries.*

35. Select an entry from the Register list box, and note how it is extracted into the text boxes at the top of the form, as shown in Figure 8.6. Try changing the amount and click **Insert** to carry out the change and update the balance. Try deleting an entry by selecting it and pressing the **Delete** button. Try printing with the **Print** command on the **File** menu.

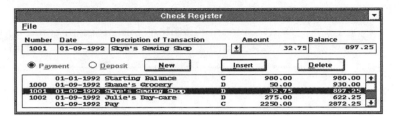

Figure 8.6. *The Automated Check Register program with a list item selected.*

This check register program lacks a command to insert new records within the record rather than at the end. However, that would be a relatively easy command to add. Just follow the logic of the `Insert` command, but insert the record using an index with the `AddItem` method.

Because you have already typed all the names and numbers, you could add a command to read the `Register` and to print your checks for you. You would have to tell the routine which check to start with and to skip any deposits. In addition, you could create a similar command that reads deposits and prints deposit slips.

Right now, the program also lacks a way to save all the entries after they have been entered, so don't spend a week typing all your checks into this program—you will be upset when you exit the program and everything disappears. Saving the lists is covered in Chapter 9, "Using Sequential Files."

With some modification, this program could be used as a general-purpose journal, which forms the beginning of an accounting system.

What You Have Learned

This chapter examined how to create procedures to modularize a program and reuse code. There are two types of procedures: Sub procedures and Function procedures. They are quite similar, except the Function procedures return a value stored in the functions name. The chapter also looked at list and combo boxes for inputting and storing lists of data. You have explored the details of

- Sub procedures.
- Function procedures.
- Arguments passed to procedures as values or addresses.
- List boxes.
- An Automated Check Register program.

Using Sequential Files

Until now, you have saved programs in disk files with the save commands on Visual Basic's File menu, but you haven't saved the data within your programs. Saving data is essential; in the last chapter, for example, the Check Register program you developed is useless if you can't save the data in the register. So now it's time to look at the different ways to use disk files to save and retrieve data.

In This Chapter

There are three types of disk files in Visual Basic: sequential, random access, and binary. Binary disk files are used for advanced applications that require access to the raw bytes of a data file, and are beyond the scope of this book.

Random access files are discussed in Chapter 10, "Using Random Access Files." This chapter discusses:

- Creating and opening sequential files.

- Reading and writing data to sequential files.

- Creating file access dialog boxes.

Storing Data In Disk Files

The three types of data files used in Visual Basic are sequential, random access, and binary. Sequential files are text files, read or written sequentially (from the beginning to the end) as a linear sequence of variable-length lines of text, with a line-feed carriage return at the end of each line. They are text files that can be listed on the screen or printer with the DOS TYPE or PRINT commands, or can be opened with any word processor. Numbers are stored as a sequence of digits, much as you would type them on the screen. Because they are linear, they can either be read or written, but not both simultaneously. That is, you cannot be reading part of a file at the same time you are writing another part, although you can be reading two different parts at the same time.

Random access files, as the name implies, are not accessed in linear fashion. They are accessed in fixed-length blocks, known as records, in any order.

The third file type, binary, is actually similar to random access, except that it is read and written byte by byte rather than record by record, and no special significance is placed on the value of any byte (such as the carriage return line-feed pair). I won't discuss any more details of binary files here.

Opening and Closing Sequential Files

Sequential files and, in fact, all files, are created or opened with the Open statement. The syntax of the Open statement is

```
Open name$ [For mode] [Access access] [lock] As [#]filenumber%
[Len = rlen%]
```

Here, *name$* is a string variable, or quoted string containing the name of the file to open, and the path, if it isn't in the default directory. The path, in Windows as in DOS, is the list of disk names and directories you must traverse to reach a file. For example, let's say that the absolute path to the file FILE.TXT is

```
D:\DIR1\DIR2\DIR3\FILE.TXT
```

where D is the disk letter, DIR1, DIR2, and DIR3 are the directories you must traverse, and FILE.TXT is the file name and extension of the file. In this case, the file FILE.TXT is in directory DIR3, which is in directory DIR2, of directory DIR1, in the root directory of disk D. A path can also be relative to the current default directory. For example, if DIR2 is the current default directory, then the path

```
DIR3\FILE.TXT
```

points to the same file. The default directory is changed by several commands and programs, so you can't always depend on it to be a specific directory. In any program, it's much safer to use absolute paths because they always point to a specific file.

The *mode* of the file is either Append, Binary, Input, Output, or Random. The access argument controls the file access type, and is either Read, Write, or Read Write. The lock argument has the value Lock Read, or Lock Write, and controls access to a file by other processes. The filenumber% is a unique number that identifies the open file to all the other file access commands. The rlen% argument is the record length, in bytes, to use with random access files.

For sequential files, the acceptable modes are Input, Output, or Append. When a file is opened For Input, the file already must exist, and you can only read data from it. When a file is opened For Output, it is opened if it exists, or created if it does not, and you can only write data to it. When an existing file is opened For Output, writing starts at the first record, overwriting any old data in the file. The Append mode is a variation of Output. When the file is opened, writing starts at the end, preserving the old data.

The *access* and *lock* arguments apply to networked environments, where multiple users may have access to the same file. The access argument controls what access you want for the file, in case someone else already has it open, and the lock argument controls what access to the file you are willing to allow others if you are the first to open the file. These are unneeded in a single-user situation.

205

The *filenumber* argument must be included with every Open state-ment, and used with every command that accesses the file. Because you might have more than one file open at any one time, this number uniquely identifies each file. Usually, the first file you open is file number 1, the second is 2, and so forth. If you close a file, you can reuse its file number. If you know how many files you have open, you can assign a constant for the file number. However, if you don't know how many files your program has open, such as when you are using a word processor that has multiple files open simultaneously, use the FreeFile function to give you the next available file number. For example,

```
InputFileNum% = FreeFile
Open "MYFILE.TXT" For Input As # InputFileNum%
```

This opens the file named MYFILE.TXT as a sequential file for reading only. The file number is selected with the FreeFile function, so use the variable InputFileNum% whenever the file is accessed. If this is the only file that is accessed by a program, you could simply use the file number 1 to open the file and, as the following example shows, use the file number 1 with every file access command.

```
Open "MYFILE.TXT" For Input As #1
```

When you are done with a file, close it with the Close statement. The Close statement empties all Visual Basic's file buffers and gives the informa-tion to the system for writing to the disk. The Close statement also releases the file numbers for reuse with other files. The syntax is

```
Close [[#]filenumber%] [,[#]filenumber%]...
```

where filenumber% is the file number used when the file was opened. To close all open files, use the Close statement without the file numbers.

File systems don't write bytes to open disk files as you send them, but collect the bytes in file buffers. A file buffer is simply a place in memory where the information is stored until it is written to disk. When a buffer is full, it is written to disk all at once. This is why you must close files before removing a disk. If you don't do so, the file might not be there in its entirety.

Writing Sequential Files

Data is written to sequential files using the Print # and Write # statements in the same way that data is printed on the screen or on the printer. The Print # statement writes data to disk files in exactly the same way that the Print method writes data on the screen. The printed data is converted to text, and the text is sent to the disk file. All the formatting conventions discussed previously apply here as well. The format of the Print # statement is

```
Print # filenumber%, expressionlist [{;¦,}]
```

where filenumber% is the file number used when the file was opened, and expressionlist% is a comma- or semicolon-separated list of expressions to be printed. Expressions that evaluate to strings are printed as is; expressions that evaluate to numbers are converted to strings before being sent to the file. If expressions are separated by commas, the point of printing moves to the next tab stop (one every 14 spaces) before printing the next item. If the expressions are separated by semicolons, the next item is printed immediately following the last. Normally, a carriage-return line feed pair is inserted at the end of every Print # statement, unless it ends in a semicolon or comma. For example, the fragment

```
A = 5.3
Print #1, "The length = ";A
```

would print (write)

```
The length = 5.3
```

in file number 1.

The second way to send data to a disk file is with the Write # statement. The Write # statement works much the same as the Print # statement, except that commas are inserted between printed expressions, and strings are surrounded by quotations. Data written with a Write # statement is easier to read back into a program than that written with Print #. Thus, the Print # statement is used mostly for creating files that are eventually read or printed on a printer, and Write # is used for data that is going to be read back into a BASIC program. For example, the fragment

9

```
A1 = 5.355
B1 = 4.788
Print #1, "The values, are: ", A1, B1, " units"
Write #1, "The values, are: ", A1, B1, " units"
```

would produce the following code in a disk file.

```
The values, are:              5.355          4.788            units
"The values, are: ",5.355,4.788," units"
```

Reading Sequential Files

After you have written data to a sequential file, you might want to read it back into a program. Actually, any text file can be read by Visual Basic as a sequential file. To read a sequential file, use the `Input #` and `Line Input #` statements, and the `Input$()` function.

The Input # statement

The `Input #` statement reads data from a disk file into its arguments. The syntax is

Input # filenumber% , expressionlist

where `filenumber` is the number that opened the file, and `expressionlist` is a list of Visual Basic variables that receive data that is read from the file.

When reading a file, leading spaces are always ignored. For a number, the first nonblank character is assumed to be the start of the number, and the first blank, comma, or the end of the line terminates it. For a string, the first nonblank character starts the string, and a comma or the end of the line terminates it. If the string is quoted, everything between the quotations is included in the string, including commas. Thus, data written with the `Write #` statement is more accurately read than data written with `Print #`. For example, reading the disk file you previously created with the `Print #` and `Write #` statements, with the code fragment

```
Input #1, A$, B, C, D$
Input #1, E$, F, G, H$
```

would store the following data in the variables:

```
A$ = "The values"
B = 0
C = 5.355
D$ = "4.788          units"
E$ = "The values, are: "
F = 5.355
G = 4.788
H$ = " units"
```

Note how the first Input # statement stopped reading the string into A$ at the first comma, so that the first numeric input, B, sees text rather than a number and gets a value of zero. Then the second numeric input, C, reads the first number, and the remaining number and string end up in D$.

The Line Input # Statement

The Line Input # statement inputs one line of text into a single string variable. It reads everything in a line up to a carriage return, including leading spaces, trailing spaces, commas, and quotation marks. The syntax is

```
Line Input # filenumber%,string$
```

where filenumber% is the file number used in the Open statement, and string$ is a string variable. For example, if you redo the previous example with Line Input # statements, as such,

```
Line Input #1, A$
Line Input #1, B$
```

the variables contain exactly what is in the file.

```
A$ = The values, are:         5.355        4.788          units
B$ = "The values, are: ",5.355,4.788," units"
```

The Line Input # statement is typically used to input text files for a word processor or similar program, or in a program where you are going to use the string functions, such as Mid$(), to extract portions of a line.

The Input$() Function

The last input method for sequential files is the Input$() function. The Input$() function is used to input every byte in a file, including line terminators. The Input # and Line Input # statements skip carriage returns and line feeds, but the Input$() function reads every byte in a file and returns a string. The syntax is

```
Input$(numbytes%[#]filenumber%)
```

where numbytes% is the number of bytes to return and filenumber% is the file number used in the Open statement. For example, again using the same input file as the preceding one,

```
A$ = Input$(5,#1)
```

The string variable, A$, contains

```
A$ = The v
```

The EOF() Function

An auxilary function used with sequential files is the EOF() function. It returns True if you have reached the end-of-file. If you attempt to read past the end-of-file, your program generates an error, so use the EOF() function to test a file before reading from it, if you don't know where the end-of-file is. The syntax of the function is

```
Flag% = EOF(filenumber%)
```

where filenumber% is the file number used in the Open statement. In the following example, EOF(1) is tested, and if it is False (0), another record is needed.

```
False = 0
If Not EOF(1) = False Then Input#1, A$
```

Creating File Access Dialog Boxes

Most Windows programs that access files selected by the user do so with a file access dialog box. A file access dialog box is a form that lets you select the drive, directory (folder) and file from a list, rather than typing a file name. A file access dialog box is created using three special list controls: the drive, directory, and file list boxes. A drive list box contains a drop-down list of all the drives on your machine. Selecting a drive from the list puts the drive letter in the list's Path property.

A directory list box contains a list of the directories on the current drive. Selecting a directory from the list places the path to that directory in the box's Path attribute. A file list box displays a list of the files in the directory in its Path property. Clicking a file places the file's name in the box's FileName property.

An Open Dialog Box

Combining these three lists and some code on a form creates a file access dialog box. The three lists aren't connected in any way, so changing the drive in the drive list box doesn't change the directory list box. You need some simple pieces of code to connect the three box types.

Changing the drive in the drive list box creates a Click event on that box and changes the Path property. In the Click event code window, change the Path property of the directory list box to equal the new Path in the drive list box. Clicking a directory in the directory list box also creates a Click event and changes the Path variable, so insert a formula to change the Path property of the file list box to that in the directory list box. Add a button to combine the FileName and Path properties, and you have an Open dialog box. Add a text box to insert a new file name, and you have a Save dialog box.

The Check Register Program (Version 2)

This new version of the Check Register program is actually a continuation of the example started in Chapter 8, "Writing Custom Procedures," because without a save capability, the Check Register program isn't much use. In this chapter, you will add **Open**, **Save**, and **Save As** commands to the **File** menu,

211

and attach two new forms containing an Open dialog box and a Save As dialog box. The rest of the program remains largely unchanged.

1. Open the Check Register program, and display Form1.

2. Open the Menu Design window and add **O**pen, **S**ave, and Save **A**s commands to the File menu according to Table 9.1.

Table 9.1. Menu design for the check register program, version 2.

Caption	CtlName	# of indents
&File	FileMenu	0
&Open	OpenCmd	1
&Save	SaveCmd	1
Save &As	SaveAsCmd	1
-	SepBar2	1
&Print	PrintCmd	1
-	SepBar1	1
E&xit	ExitCmd	1

The following three procedures are attached to the three new commands on the File menu. Their only function is to pass control to the file access dialog boxes. Note the constant AsModal following the Show method in each procedure. It's defined as the number 1 in the Global module and it makes the dialog boxes *modal*. When a form is modal, you can't select any other forms until you have edited or viewed the modal form and closed it. Also, any code following the Code method for a modal form isn't executed until the form is hidden or unloaded. If a form isn't modal, you can move to other forms by clicking them. The SaveCmd_Click procedure tests the global variable FileName to see whether it is blank. If it's not blank, a file already is attached to this program, so the procedure calls the SaveIt Sub procedure to save the contents of the Register list box. If FileName is blank, the data hasn't been saved yet, and the procedure calls the SaveDialog form to attach a file.

3. Open the OpenCmd_Click procedure and type

```
Sub OpenCmd_Click ()
OpenDialog.Show AsModal
End Sub
```

4. Open the SaveCmd_Click procedure and type

```
Sub SaveCmd_Click ()
If FileName <> "" Then
  SaveIt
Else
  SaveDialog.Show AsModal
End If
End Sub
```

5. Open the SaveAsCmd_Click procedure and type

```
Sub SaveAsCmd_Click ()
SaveDialog.Show AsModal
End Sub
```

Move all the declarations and definitions to the Global module, so they are available to these Forms.

6. Create a module with the New Module command on the File menu. Name the file CKREGM.BAS. Open the declarations section of Form1 and cut everything there. Open the module and paste it all. Change Dim to Global and add Global before each constant declaration. Add the definition for the FileName variable and modal constant. It should now read

```
Global Const AsModal = 1
Global CkNum As Integer, Balance As Double, NewFlag As Integer
Global InitialBalance As Double
Global FileName As String
```

7. Add two new forms to this project with the New Form command on the File menu. Save them as CKREG2.FRM and CKREG3.FRM. Select the first one and change its properties as follows:

```
Caption = Open
Height = 2640
Width = 4845
ControlBox = False
Name = OpenDialog
MaxButton = False
MinButton = False
```

8. Draw a file list box on the form with these properties

```
Top = 120
Left = 120
Height = 1820
Width = 1575
Pattern = *.*
```

The Pattern property controls what files are listed in the box. Using *.* (wild card) lists all the files in the directory.

Because the Pattern property controls which files are visible in the file list box, you might want to allow the user to change that property. The simplest way to do this is to add a text box and have its Change procedure set the Pattern property of the file list box. You also can select a standard pattern with a set of option buttons, or select from a menu. A third option is to have a text box display the currently selected file in the file list box, and if you type something that isn't a file name, use it to set the pattern property.

9. Draw a directory list box on the form with these properties

```
Top = 600
Left = 1800
Height = 1340
Width = 1335
```

10. Draw a drive list box on the form with these properties

```
Top = 120
Left = 1800
Width = 1335
```

11. Draw a command button on the form with these properties

```
Caption = OK
Name = OKCmd
Top = 120
Left = 3360
Height = 380
Width = 1215
Default = True
```

12. Draw another command button on the form with these properties. (The form should now look like figure 9.1.)

```
Caption = Cancel
Name = CancelCmd
Top = 600
Left = 3360
Height = 380
Width = 1215
```

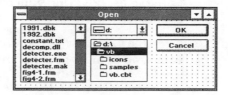

Figure 9.1. *Layout of the Open dialog box.*

13. Open the Drive1_Change procedure and type the following. This links the directory shown in the directory list to changes in the drive from the drive list.

```
Sub Drive1_Change ()
Dir1.Path = Drive1.Drive
End Sub
```

14. Open the Dir1_Change procedure and type the following. This links the File list to the directory selected in the directory list.

```
Sub Dir1_Change ()
File1.Path = Dir1.Path
End Sub
```

15. Open the OKCmd_Click procedure and type

```
Sub OKCmd_Click ()
If File1.FileName = "" Then
  MsgBox "Please select a file first."
  Exit Sub
End If
FileName = File1.Path + "\" + File1.FileName    'line 6
ClearIt
ReadIt
OpenDialog.Hide
End Sub
```

When the **OK** button is clicked, this procedure first checks the FileName property of the file list box to see whether a file has been selected. If not, it displays a message box asking you to select a file name first, then executes the Exit Sub statement to exit this Sub procedure. If a file name has been selected, line 6 combines the Path property with a backslash and the file name to produce a complete path to the selected file. Next, the ClearIt procedure is called to clear the contents of the Register list box on Form1. Then the ReadIt procedure is called to read the contents of the selected file into the Register list box. Line 9 then hides the Open dialog box, passing control back to Form1.

16. Open the CancelCmd_Click procedure and type the following. This command changes nothing, and returns control to Form1.

```
Sub CancelCmd_Click ()
OpenDialog.Hide
End Sub
```

17. Open the File1_DblClick procedure and type the following. This procedure makes double-clicking a file name in the file list box the same as clicking the file and pressing the **OK** button.

```
Sub File1_DblClick ()
OKCmd_Click
End Sub
```

A Save As Dialog Box

This completes the Open dialog box. Next, create the Save As dialog box, which is nearly identical to the

Open dialog box, but adds a text box for the new file name.

1. Select the third form saved as REG3.FRM. Change its properties to

```
Caption = Save As
Height = 2640
Width = 4845
ControlBox = False
Name = SaveDialog
MaxButton = False
MinButton = False
```

2. Draw a file list box on the form with these properties

```
Top = 600
Left = 120
Height = 1460
Width = 1575
Pattern = *.*
```

3. Draw a directory list box on the form with these properties

```
Top = 600
Left = 1800
Height = 1460
Width = 1335
```

4. Draw a drive list box on the form with these properties

```
Top = 120
Left = 1800
Width = 1335
```

5. Draw a command button on the form with these properties

```
Caption = OK
Name = OKCmd
Top = 120
Left = 3360
Height = 380
Width = 1215
Default = True
```

6. Draw another command button on the form with these properties

```
Caption = Cancel
Name = CancelCmd
Top = 600
Left = 3360
Height = 380
Width = 1215
```

7. Draw a text box with these properties (the form should now look like Figure 9.2.)

```
Name = FName
Top = 120
Left =120
Height = 380
Width = 1575
Text = ""
```

217

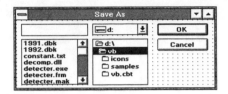

Figure 9.2. Layout of the Save As dialog box.

As with the Open dialog, much of the code in the Save As dialog is the same. Keep in mind that the names of the controls on both of these dialog boxes are the same, but because they are on two different forms, the names are local to those forms.

8. Open the Drive1_Change procedure and type the following. This action links the directory shown in the directory list to changes in the drive from the drive list.

```
Sub Drive1_Change ()
Dir1.Path = Drive1.Drive
End Sub
```

9. Open the Dir1_Change procedure and type the following. This links the file list to the directory selected in the directory list.

```
Sub Dir1_Change ()
File1.Path = Dir1.Path
End Sub
```

10. Open the CancelCmd_Click procedure and type the following. This command changes nothing, and returns control to Form1.

```
Sub CancelCmd_Click ()
SaveDialog.Hide
End Sub
```

11. Open the OKCmd_Click procedure and type

```
Sub OKCmd_Click ()
Dim thePath  As String
```

```
'Test for no file name    line 3
If FName.Text = "" Then
  MsgBox "Type a file name first"
  Exit Sub
End If
'Test for path     line 8
If InStr(FName.Text, "\") <> 0 Or InStr(FName.Text, ":") <> 0
Then
  MsgBox "File name only, no path"
  Exit Sub
End If
'Test for missing extension add .CKR if missing     line 13
FName.Text = LTrim$(RTrim$(FName.Text))
If InStr(FName.Text, ".") = 0 Then
  FName.Text = Left$(FName.Text,8) + ".CKR"
End If
thePath = Dir1.Path + "\" + FName.Text
'Check for existing file     line 19
If Dir$(thePath) <> "" Then
  Action = MsgBox("File exists, overwrite?", 257)
  If Action = 2 Then Exit Sub
End If
'Open the file and save the check register data     line 24
FileName = thePath
File1.Refresh
SaveIt
SaveDialog.Hide
End Sub
```

This OKCmd_Click procedure is a little more complex than that in the Open command, but only because it has to verify the file name before using it. The block of code from line 3 to line 7 checks to see whether you have typed a file name in the text box. If you haven't, it displays a Message box asking you to do so first, then exits the procedure with an Exit Sub statement. Lines 8 through 12 check to see whether you have typed a path in the text box as well as the file name by checking for the \ or : characters. Because you are going to create the path, you don't want users to type their own. A more complex Save As dialog could let users type their own paths.

Change the OKCmd procedure so users can type a complete path rather than a file name. If the user types a path without a file name, make the procedure change the Path properties of the file list box, the directory list box, and the Drive property of the drive list box, then exit. If the path includes a file name, change the Path properties and open the file. If a pattern is typed rather than a file name, change the Pattern property of the file list box to that pattern.

Lines 13 through 18 check to see whether the user has typed an extension on the file name by looking for the period. If not, the code block adds the .CKR extension in line 16. The LTrim$() and RTrim$() functions remove any blanks from the left or right sides of the file name. The Left$() function in line 16 extracts up to 8 characters from the left side of the file name, ensuring that the name part of the file name is no more than 8 characters long. In line 18, the complete path to the file is created by combining the directory path from the Path property of the directory box with a backslash and the file name from the text box.

Lines 19 through 23 check for an existing file using the Dir$() function. The Dir$() function returns the name of the file if it exists; otherwise it returns an empty string. If the file already exists, a Message box is displayed with an **OK** and a **Cancel** button (the 257 argument of the MsgBox statement; see Chapter 15, "Command Reference," for a list of codes). If the user presses **Cancel**, the Message box returns a value of 2, and the Exit Sub statement is called to exit the procedure without overwriting the file. If the point of execution reaches Line 24, the file can be created or opened, so pass the path to the Global variable FileName, and call the SaveIt Sub procedure to save the file.

12. Open the File1_Click procedure and type the following. This step puts a selected file name in the text box if the user clicks it in the file list box.

```
Sub File1_Click ()
FName.Text = File1.FileName
End Sub
```

13. Open the File1_DblClick procedure and type the following. This procedure makes double-clicking a file name in the file list box the same as clicking the file and pressing the **OK** button.

```
Sub File1_DblClick ()
OKCmd_Click
End Sub
```

This completes the Save As dialog box. Now create a module for the SaveIt, ClearIt and ReadIt Sub procedures.

14. Select the module, and create the SaveIt Sub procedure with the New Procedure command on the View menu. Type

```
Sub SaveIt ()
Dim I As Integer
'Open the file and save the contents of Register
Open FileName For Output As #1            'line 4
Write #1, Form1.Register.ListCount, CkNum, Balance,
➥InitialBalance
For I = 0 To Form1.Register.ListCount - 1            'line 6
  Print #1, Form1.Register.List(I)
Next I
Close #1
End Sub
```

This procedure saves the contents of the Register list box in the file specified by the Global variable FileName. Line 4 opens the file for sequential output. Line 5 writes the number of items in the list, and the value of CkNum, Balance, and InitialBalance. These three values also are needed to restart the program from a datafile. Note how the Register object on Form1 is accessed from this module by prefacing the object name with the form name. Unfortunately, you can't do this for user-defined variables, only Visual Basic objects. User-defined variables have to be passed through the module.

Note also that I have used the Write # statement to ensure that I can extract the values correctly later. Lines 6 through 8 loop through all the items in the list box, and print each item to the disk file. I use the Print statement here because I am writing complete lines to the file, not individual values. Line 9 closes the file.

15. Open the ClearIt Sub procedure and type (use the commented out statements with Version 1)

```
Sub ClearIt ()
'Clear the contents of Register
Form 1.Register.Clear
'While Form1.Register.ListCount > 0
'Form1.Register.RemoveItem 0
'Wend
End Sub
```

This procedure simply clears the contents of the Register list box on Form1. Note again how I have added the form name to the list box name, so I can access the object in Form1 from this module. The procedure uses the Clear method to clear the contents of the Register list box. The commented out statements in version 1 do the same thing. The commented out procedure works with a While/Wend loop that checks the number of items in the Register List box using the ListCount property. As long as there is still at least one item in the list, it executes the RemoveItem method on the first item (item number 0). It continues until there are no more items in the List box.

16. Open the ReadIt Sub procedure and type

```
Sub ReadIt ()
Dim NumEntries As Integer, aLine As String
'Open the file and read into Register
Open FileName For Input As #1
Input #1, NumEntries, CkNum, Balance, InitialBalance
For i = 1 To NumEntries
Line Input #1, aLine
Form1.Register.AddItem aLine
Next i
Close #1
End Sub
```

This procedure complements the SaveIt Sub procedure. It first opens the file that has its name in the global variable FileName for sequential input. You can use the same file number here (1) as you used in the SaveIt procedure because you close the file when you end that procedure. If that file were still open, you would have to use a different file number. After opening the file, the procedure reads the number of entries into NumEntries, then reads the three values saved with the Write # statement back into the same variables using the Input # statement. Using the NumEntries number, you will know exactly how many lines of data to read, so you won't need to use the EOF() function each time to check for the end of the file. In this case, loop over the number of entries that you previously wrote to the file. Because you wrote complete lines of text to the file, you can read them back with the Line Input # statement into the variable aLine, and then insert that line into the Register list box on Form1 using the AddItem method. Finally, close the file.

17. Save the project; it's done. Run the program and insert a few values, then execute the **Save** command on the **File** menu. Note that it brings up the Save **As** dialog box, as shown in Figure 9.3,

because you have not saved this data yet. Select a disk and directory by clicking the list boxes, type a file name (REG1), and press **OK**. The data is saved.

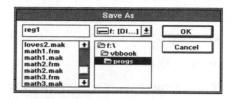

Figure 9.3. *The Save As dialog box.*

18. Change the data by adding a few more items, then execute Save again. This time the program doesn't bring up the Save **As** dialog because it already knows where to store the data.

19. Change the data again, then execute the Open command. The Open dialog, as shown in Figure 9.4, appears. Select the old file and click **OK**. The old data is read, replacing the data currently in the Register list box.

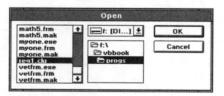

Figure 9.4. *The Open dialog box.*

You now have an operating check register program to keep track of your bank account. This program demonstrates linear record keeping or journaling, which attaches each new entry to the end of the file of data. This is just one possible type. A ledger, for example, requires randomly accessed files, which are discussed in Chapter 10, "Using Random Access Files."

What You Have Learned

Three types of disk files are available in Visual Basic, and this chapter investigated the most common, sequential access files. Random Access files

are discussed in Chapter 10, "Using Random Access Files." The third type, binary files, is used primarily with advanced applications. To access files within an application, you created Open and Save As dialog boxes and attached them to the Check Register program. In this chapter, you learned about

● Using `Open` to open or create sequential files.

● Writing sequential files with `Write #` and `Print #`.

● Reading sequential files with `Input #`, `Line Input #`, and `Input$()`.

● Creating file access dialog boxes using drive, folder, and file lists.

Using Random Access Files

The second most useful file type in Visual Basic is the random access file. A random access file is different from a sequential access file in that the individual records are read and written in any order, rather than only from the beginning to the end. The primary use of random access files is for database-type programs such as a general ledger or inventory manager.

In This Chapter

Random access files are opened and closed in much the same manner as sequential files, but the record length is fixed rather than variable like sequential files. This fixed record length is necessary so individual records can be located and accessed asynchronously. To implement the storing of values in fixed length records, use a record type variable composed of one or more standard type values, such as integers and strings. In this chapter, you will learn to

- Create user-defined record type variables
- Create and open random access files
- Read and write records in random access files
- Create a Datebook database program

Storing Data in Random Access Disk Files

Your computer actually reads data from a disk in fixed-length pieces called sectors, and a sector holds 512 bytes. If a record is 512 bytes long, or some number that is evenly divisible into 512 (a power of 2 = 1, 2, 4, 8, 16, 32, 64, 128...), then no record crosses a sector boundary. If a record crosses a sector boundary, the computer must read two sectors rather than one to get the whole record.

For example, if your record length is 500 bytes (a nice, round number), the first record is contained in the first 500 bytes of the first sector. The second record is in the last 12 bytes of the first sector and the first 488 bytes of the second. The third record uses the last 24 bytes of the second sector and the first 476 bytes of the third. On the other hand, if the record is just 12 bytes longer, every record is completely contained within a single sector. If you can't use the extra bytes, you are still only wasting about 2.5% of your disk space in exchange for cutting the access time in half. The trade-off is file space versus file access time. What you do depends on your application. If you have huge data files that don't get accessed often, you might want to sacrifice speed for reduced size. On the other hand, if your application spends too much time accessing the files, you might want to sacrifice some file space for increased speed.

Random access files, as the name implies, are not accessed in a linear fashion. They are accessed in fixed length blocks, known as records, in any order. Random access files are also text files, but you may not be able to read any of the numbers stored in them. Numbers are stored as binary data rather than character data. This procedure saves a considerable amount of memory, because a 5-digit integer takes at least 5 bytes to be stored as text, and only 2 bytes to be stored as a binary integer.

Record lengths in random access files are fixed, and the default length is 128 bytes. Although record lengths of any size (up to 32,767 bytes) are allowed, sizes that are powers of two are more efficient. The record length is specified when you open the file.

Defining Record Type Variables

In addition to the built-in variable types such as Integer and String, you can define your own variable types by combining other types. Then, a single variable name passes the whole contents of a record rather than a single value. To create a record type variable, you must first define the variable type with a Type statement. The Type statement defines which of the built-in or user-defined variable types make up the record, and in what order. The syntax of the Type statement is

```
Type newtypename
   elementname As typename
   elementname As typename
   .
   .
   .
End Type
```

Here, newtypename is the name you are giving to the type definition, elementname is the name you are giving to the element that is going to be a part of this type, and typename is the type of variable that elementname is. Typename can be any of the built-in types (Integer, Long, Single, Double, Currency, or String), or some other user-defined type.

For example, the following Type definition defines the variable type DayType, which consists of three elements. The first is theDate, which is a Double precision floating point number for storing a date. The second is an Integer named Flags, and the third is a fixed length String named Msg. Strings are normally variable length and might be so in a general, user-defined type; but because the record length in a random access file is fixed, the length of any strings that make up the record variable also must be fixed. Fixed length String variables are created by adding an asterisk (*) and the string length following the String type name.

10

```
Type DayType
  theDate As Double
  Flags As Integer
  Msg As String * 118
End Type
```

If you add up the number of bytes needed to store this new variable, you will notice that it adds up to 128 bytes exactly (8 bytes for the Double, 2 for the Integer, and 118 for the String), one of the efficient lengths for random access file records. The length of a record type variable must be less than or equal to the length of a record defined with the Open statement. After you have defined a new type, you must then define a variable with that type so you can use it. Defining a variable as a new type is done in exactly the same way as the built-in type definitions, by using Dim and Global statements. For example,

```
Dim aLine As String, Today as DayType
Global theMonth(1 To 31) As DayType
```

The first line defines aLine as a string variable and Today as the new variable type DayType. The second line defines an array named Month of 31 DayType variables. To access the parts of a user-defined variable type, combine the variable name with the element name, separated with a dot. For example,

```
Today.Flags = 2
Month(5).Msg = "Some interesting message"
Today.theDay = Now
```

The first line stores the number 2 in the Flags element of Today (the Integer), the second inserts a string in the Msg element of the fifth element of Month, and the third line uses the function Now to insert today's date and time into the theDay element of Today.

Opening A Random Access File

To open a random access file, use the Open statement, defined in Chapter 9, "Using Sequential Files," or use a mode of Random, and include the record length. For example,

```
Open "MYFILE.DBK" For Random As #1 Len = 128
```

opens the file MYFILE.DBK in the default directory as a random access file, with file number 1 and with a record length of 128 bytes. The default record length for random access files is 128 bytes, so the length argument could have been omitted. It is better to specify the length, however, so when you are reading the program, you immediately know what the record length is.

When you are done with this file, close it in exactly the same way as a sequential file, using a `Close #` statement:

```
Close #1.c.
```

Reading and Writing Random Records

Now that you have the file open, you have to be able to read and write records. Records from a random access file are read with the Get # statement. The Get # statement syntax is

```
Get [#] filenumber%,[recordnumber&],recordvariable
```

Here, the `filenumber%` is the file number used in the Open statement, `recordnumber&` is the number of the record you want to read, and `recordvariable` is the name of the record type variable that receives the data. If you omit the record number, you will get the next record in the file after the last one you read. For example,

```
Get #1,225,Today
```

reads record number 225 from file number 1 and stores it in the DayType record variable Today. After you have read a record into a record variable, you can access the contents of that record by accessing the elements of the record variable.

Records are written in exactly the same manner as they are read, using the Put # statement. The syntax and arguments are identical to those for the Get # statement,

```
Put [#] filenumber%,[recordnumber&],recordvariable
```

An example is

```
Put #1, 12, Month(3)
```

which stores the third element of the array of record variables, Month( ), in record 12 of file number 1. If that record doesn't exist yet, the file is automatically extended to include it.

10

The Datebook Program

The Datebook program is a year-long electronic calendar of important dates and notes. When it starts, it automatically checks a week ahead and beeps if any of the dates are marked important. It then displays the current month with important dates marked in shades of gray. Clicking a date brings up a second window that shows the note attached to that date. In that window, you can create or edit the note and save it in the database file. The program consists of two forms: one contains a monthly calendar showing the important dates with attached notes, and the other shows the note attached to the selected date.

The monthly calendar form is made with 37 labels arranged in five rows of seven, plus one row of two. This structure holds any month. Also on the form are two arrows, used to move forward or backward one month. The File menu contains commands to create a new yearly database, or to open a database other than the current year. A Month menu contains all the month names to move rapidly to a different month in the current year.

1. Open a new project, select the form, and change its properties to the following. This holds a calendar for one month, as shown in Figure 10.1.

```
Caption = Date Book
BorderStyle = 3 - Fixed Double
MaxButton = False
Height = 5500
Width = 5460
```

Setting the BorderStyle to 3 and MaxButton to False makes it impossible for other users to change the size of the Form, which would spoil your user-interface.

2. Draw a label at the top to hold the name of the current month, and set its properties to

```
Caption = Month
Name = MonthBox
Top = 0
Left = 1440
Height = 380
Width = 2415
Alignment = 2 - Center
BorderStype = 1 - Fixed Single
FontSize = 12
```

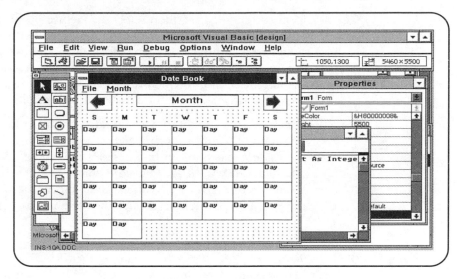

Figure 10.1. *Layout for Form1 of the Datebook program.*

The next step is to create the two arrow buttons to move the calendar forward or backward one month. Because there is no control that looks like an arrow, create one using a picture box or image control, an icon of the arrow, and a Click procedure.

A picture box has a Picture property into which you can load a drawing or icon, which is then displayed in the box. The types of picture files that can be loaded into a picture box include bitmap files (.BMP), icon files (.ICO), and Windows Metafile files (.WMF). One of the most common graphics file types is the bitmap file. Many programs create bitmap files, including most of the popular paint programs such as Paintbrush, included with Windows. An icon is simply a specialized bitmap file with a maximum size of 32 by 32 pixels. You can create your own icons, using the Iconwrks sample program included with Visual Basic (see Plate II).

The image control is similar to a picture box, but more limited in its capabilities. This control is faster than a picture box and uses fewer computer resources. You can draw on a picture box, attach controls to it, and do almost everything to the picture box that you can do with a form. You can attach a picture to an image control, but you can't draw on it or attach controls to it.

Visual Basic includes a small library of icons, including a whole list of arrows. To attach an icon to a picture box or image control (or a form), select the box, then select the Picture property. The type of attached picture, if there is one, shows in the Settings box. To the right of the Settings box is an ellipsis (...). When you click the ellipsis, an Open dialog box appears. Use that dialog box to select the file containing the picture or icon you want to use. To load a picture at run-time, use the LoadPicture function.

3. Draw a Picture box on the upper left with the following attributes. To set the Picture property, select it, and click the ellipsis on the right side of the Settings box to open a File Open dialog box. Locate the ARW07LT.ICO file containing the left arrow icon. It's located in the \VB\ICONS\ARROWS directory (the \VB directory is the Visual Basic directory). Click the file name and click OK.

```
Name = LeftArrow
Picture = ARW07LT.ICO
Top = -120
Left = 240
Height = 620
Width = 615
```

4. Draw a second Picture box on the upper right with the following attributes. Attach the right pointing arrow to it.

```
Name = RightArrow
Picture = ARW07RT.ICO
Top = -120
Left = 4440
Height = 620
Width = 615
```

5. Draw seven labels across the form containing the first letter of the days of the week, according to Table 10.1.

Table 10.1. Properties for Datebook Labels.

Caption	Left	Top	Height	Width
S	360	600	260	255
M	1080	600	260	255
T	1800	600	260	255
W	2520	600	260	255
T	3240	600	260	255

Caption	Left	Top	Height	Width
F	3960	600	260	255
S	4680	600	260	255

Now, create a control array of labels to form the calendar. Each label is a date square on the calendar, and also is a button to get access to the note attached to that date. Create the array by drawing the first box, then use the Copy and Paste commands on the Edit menu to create the rest.

6. Draw a label with the following properties.

```
Caption = Day
Name = DayButton
Top = 960
Left = 120
Height = 620
Width = 735
BorderStype = 1 - Fixed Single
```

7. Select the label and execute the Copy command, then execute the Paste command. A dialog box appears asking you whether you want to create a control array. Click Yes.

8. Select the newly pasted label and drag it to the right of the first one. Continue pasting and dragging until you have five rows of seven boxes and one row of two boxes, as shown in Figure 10.1.

There are two menus on this application. One is the standard file menu with New, Open, and Exit commands; the second is a Month menu with all the months of the year on it. The Month menu will quickly move you to any month in the current year.

9. Open the Menu Design window and create a File and a Month menu according to Table 10.2. The Month menu is a control array containing all the months of the year.

Table 10.2. Menu design for the Datebook program.

Caption	Name	# of indents	Index
&File	FileMenu	0	
&New	NewCmd	1	

continues

Table 10.2. continued

Caption	Name	# of indents	Index
&Open	OpenCmd	1	
-	SepBar1	1	
&Exit	ExitCmd	1	
&Month	MonthMenu	0	
&Jan	MonthCmd	1	1
&Feb	MonthCmd	1	2
Ma&r	MonthCmd	1	3
&Apr	MonthCmd	1	4
Ma&y	MonthCmd	1	5
J&un	MonthCmd	1	6
Ju&l	MonthCmd	1	7
Au&g	MonthCmd	1	8
&Sep	MonthCmd	1	9
&Oct	MonthCmd	1	10
&Nov	MonthCmd	1	11
&Dec	MonthCmd	1	12

10. Save the Form as DBOOK1.FRM.

This completes the design for the first form, which contains the calendar. Now, create a second form to use for reading and writing the notes being attached to the dates on the calendar.

11. Add a second form to the project with the New Form command on the File menu, and set its properties as follows.

```
Caption = Reminder
BorderStyle = 3 - Fixed double
MaxButton = False
MinButton = False
Height = 2740
Width = 5145
```

12. Draw a Text box on the form as shown in Figure 10.2, and set its properties. This is where you type the notes.

```
Name = Message
Top = 720
Left = 120
Height = 1340
Width = 3495
Text = " "
```

Figure 10.2. *Layout for Form2 of the Datebook program.*

Next, create a control array of three option buttons for setting the importance of a note. The array has three option buttons marked None, Routine, and Important. The None button clears the current note. The Routine button colors the date light blue (cyan) on the calendar, and the Important button colors the date red.

13. Create a control array of the following three option buttons. You can either create the first button, then Copy and Paste it to create the others, or draw three option buttons and give them all the same Name. Use Table 10.3 for the appropriate values for each button. These three buttons are used to indicate whether the attached note is routine or important.

Table 10.3. Values for the option buttons.

Caption	Left	Index	Value	Height	Width	Top
&None	120	0	True	500	1095	120
&Routine	1200	1	False	500	1095	120
&Important	2400	2	False	500	1095	120

There are two command buttons on this form. The first is the OK button, which attaches the note to the calendar and saves it in the disk file. The Cancel button discards any changes and returns you to the calendar.

14. Draw an OK command button with these properties:

```
Caption = OK
Name = OKCmd
Top = 120
Left = 3840
Height = 500
Width = 1095
Default = True
```

15. Draw a Cancel command button with these properties:

```
Caption = Cancel
Name = CancelCmd
Top = 720
Left = 3840
Height = 500
Width = 1095
Default = False
```

16. Draw a label below the Cancel button with these properties:

```
Caption = Reminder for
Top = 1320
Left = 3840
Height = 260
Width = 1215
```

17. Draw a label to hold the date with these properties:

```
Name = DateBox
BorderStyle = 1 - Fixed Single
Top = 1680
Left = 3840
Height = 380
Width = 1095
```

18. Save the Form as DBOOK2.FRM.

This completes the second form. Now attach code to the project. First is a module containing the definitions for asModal, a list of color definitions copied from the file CONSTANT.TXT included with Visual Basic and the definition for the DayType type. The type definition must come before any attempt to use it.

Next are some global variable definitions: FileName is a string variable that contains the name of the currently open file, theYear is an integer containing the current year as a number, theMonth contains the current month as a number, EOL holds the end-of-line characters—carriage return, and line feed. The variable ChangeDate is a record variable of type DayType; Months( ) is an array of 12 strings, each string containing the name of a month; thisMonth( ) is an array that holds the serial date numbers for each day in the current month; OldBackColor and OldForeColor are double precision variables to hold the values of the background and text colors.

Serial date numbers are used in Visual Basic to store dates and times. The date is stored in the integer part of the number as the integer number of days since 12/30/1899. Negative values describe dates back to 1/1/1753. The time is stored in the fractional part of the number as a fraction of a whole day; for example, 0.5 is noon. The functions Day( ), Weekday( ), Month( ), and Year( ) convert serial date numbers into integers representing the day of the month, day of the week, month of the year, and year. The function DateValue( ) converts a text representation of a date into a serial date number, and DateSerial(year,month,day) converts the three integers year, month, and day into a serial date number.

19. Create a new module named DBOOKM.BAS with the New Module command on the File menu and type

```
Global Const asModal = 1
Global Const BLACK = &H0&         'Colors from the file
Global Const RED = &HFF&          'CONSTANT.TXT
Global Const GREEN = &HFF00&
Global Const YELLOW = &HFFFF&
Global Const BLUE = &HFF0000
Global Const MAGENTA = &HFF00FF
Global Const CYAN = &HFFFF00
Global Const WHITE = &HFFFFFF
Global Const LT_GRAY = &H808080
Global Const DK_GRAY = &H404040
Type DayType                      'Type declaration for the
   TheDate As Double              'record DayType, 128 bytes
   Flags As Integer               'long
   Msg As String * 118
End Type
Global FileName As String         'The disk file name and path
Global theYear As Integer         'The current year
Global theMonth As Integer        'The current month
```

```
Global EOL As String          'End-Of-Line character
Global ChangeDate As DayType  'Serial date being changed
Global Months(1 To 12) As String    'Text names of the months
Global thisMonth(36) As Double     'Array to hold datenumbers
Global OldBackColor As Double    'Store old background color
Global OldForeColor As Double     'Store old text color
```

The Form_Load procedure sets up the problem. The first 15 lines define the EOL variable and fill the Months( ) array with the text of the 12 month names. Line 16 is a call to the ClearMonth procedure which initializes the 36 Labels on the calendar. Line 18 creates a file name from the current year by using the Now function to get the current serial date number, and the Year( ) function to extract the current year. The year (4 digits) is then combined with the .DBK file extension to form the file name. In line 19, the Dir$( ) function is used to see whether the file exists. If it doesn't, the procedure exits; otherwise, the file is opened as a random access file with file number 1 in line 20. In line 21, the Get # statement is used to extract the first record. The actual year stored in the file is extracted from the TheDate item of the aDay record variable in line 22 and the file is closed in line 23. This ensures that there actually is a file for the desired year.

In line 24, the Now function is used again with the Month( ) function to get the current month and store it in theMonth. In line 25, the FillMonth procedure is executed to insert the days and notes in the currently open year and month. In line 27, the LookAhead procedure is called with an argument of seven days. This procedure scans ahead the number of days specified, then beeps and prints a message if any day has the Important button set. The last two lines before the End Sub statement load Form2, then hide it. This gets Form2 into memory so it can be displayed when it is needed, and so its controls can be accessed before Form2 is displayed.

20. Select the first form, open the Form_Load procedure, and type

```
Sub Form_Load ()
Dim aDay As DayType
EOL = Chr$(13) + Chr$(10)     'End-of-line character
Months(1) = "January"       'Fill Months array
Months(2) = "February"
Months(3) = "March"
Months(4) = "April"
```

```
Months(5) = "May"
Months(6) = "June"
Months(7) = "July"
Months(8) = "August"
Months(9) = "September"
Months(10) = "October"
Months(11) = "November"
Months(12) = "December"
ClearMonth
'If a file for the current year exists, get it    line 17
FileName = Format$(Year(Now), "0000") + ".DBK"
If Dir$(FileName) = "" Then Exit Sub
Open FileName For Random As #1 Len = 128
Get #1, 1, aDay
theYear = Year(aDay.TheDate)
Close #1
theMonth = Month(Now)
FillMonth
'Look ahead one week for important days'
LookAhead (7)
Load Form2
Form2.Hide
End Sub
```

The New command creates a new year's data file. Lines 4 through 11 use an Input box so you can enter a year, and then test the value returned. If the value is a blank, the procedure exits. Otherwise, it stores the value in the variable theYear. Lines 11 through 18 convert the date into a file name, as before, and test to see whether a file already exists. If it does, the procedure sends a message to you, asking whether it is OK to overwrite the old file. If you do not want to overwrite it, press the Cancel button, and the procedure exits. Otherwise, it opens or creates the file. In lines 19 through 22, the record variable is filled with blank data, except for the first field, which contains the date of the record.

In lines 23 through 29, the file is opened, and the blank data is written out to it. This initializes the file by deleting any existing data in the file that could be mistaken for a message. The only thing that changes is the date, which is updated each pass through the loop. Finally, the procedure checks to see whether this is the current year. If it is, it switches to the current month. If not, it starts with January. FillMonth is called at the end to draw the current month.

21. Open the `NewCmd_Click` procedure, and type

```
Sub NewCmd_Click ()
Dim aDay As DayType, i  As Integer, aYear As String
Dim aMsg As String, Action As Integer
'Get a year from the user. Exit if blank.
theYear = 0
If theYear
< 1753 Or theYear > 2078 Then
  aYear = InputBox$("Type the year")
  If aYear = "" Then Exit Sub
  theYear = Val(aYear)
End If
'Make a file name with the year and check for an existing line 11
'file. Ask if it is OK to overwrite it.
FileName = Format$(theYear, "0000") + ".DBK"
If Dir$(FileName)
<> "" Then
  aMsg = "File already exists" + EOL + "Overwrite it?"
  Action = MsgBox(aMsg, 257)
  If Action = 2 Then Exit Sub   'If Cancel is pressed, exit
End If
'load the record variable    line 19
aDay.TheDate = DateSerial(theYear, 1, 1) - 1
aDay.Flags = 0
aDay.Msg = Space$(118)
'Open the file and fill with data.  line 23
Open FileName For Random As #1 Len = 128
For i = 1 To 366
  aDay.TheDate = aDay.TheDate + 1
  Put #1, i, aDay
Next i
Close #1
'If the new file is this year, display the current month
If theYear = Year(Now) Then
  theMonth = Month(Now)
Else
  theMonth = 1
End If
FillMonth
End Sub
```

The Open command works much the same way as the New command, but can be used only when the file already exists. The procedure first asks you for the year in line 10, using an Input box. When the year is validated, it uses the Dir$( ) function in line 17 to see whether the file exists. If it doesn't, a message box is displayed in line 18, asking you to use the New command instead.

If the file exists, it's opened as a random access file in line 24, and the first record is read in line 25. The current year is then extracted from the first record. In lines 28 through 34, the program determines if it is the current year, and displays the current month if it is.

22. Open the OpenCmd_Click procedure, and type

```
Sub OpenCmd_Click ()
Dim aDay As DayType, i  As Integer, aYear As String
Dim OldFileName As String, OldYear As Integer
'Save the old year in case the user changes his mind
OldYear = theYear
OldFileName = FileName
'Get a year from the user. Exit if it is a blank
theYear = 0
If theYear
< 1753 Or theYear > 2078 Then
  aYear = InputBox$('Type the year')
  If aYear = "" Then Exit Sub
  theYear = Val(aYear)
End If
'Make and validate a file name. Restore the old one and line 14
'exit if it doesn't exist.
FileName = Format$(theYear, "0000") + ".DBK"
If Dir$(FileName) = "" Then   'Check for existing file
  MsgBox 'File doesn't exist, use New'
  FileName = OldFileName
  theYear = OldYear
  Exit Sub
End If
'Open the file and get the correct year    line 23
Open FileName For Random As #1 Len = 128
Get #1, 1, aDay
theYear = Year(aDay.TheDate)
Close #1
```

```
'If it's this year, display the current month    line 28
If theYear = Year(Now) Then
  theMonth = Month(Now)
Else
  theMonth = 1
End If
FillMonth
End Sub
```

Set the right and left arrow picture boxes so they seem like real buttons; the buttons turn black when pressed with the mouse and white when released. To do this, use the MouseDown and MouseUp events rather than the Click event to activate the code. The MouseDown event is passed information about the state of the mouse, but changing the background color to black requires only the information that the mouse was pressed. In the MouseUp procedure, turn the background color back to white (or whatever it was). For the left arrow, subtract 1 from theMonth and for the right arrow, add 1. In both cases, make the value in theMonth wrap at 0 and 12 months so that pressing the left arrow in January causes a move to December, and pressing the right arrow in December moves to January. Finally, call the FillMonth procedure to draw the new month.

23. Open the LeftArrow_MouseDown procedure, and type

    ```
    Sub LeftArrow_MouseDown (Button As Integer, Shift As Integer,
        ➥X As Single, Y As Single)
    LeftArrow.BackColor = BLACK
    End Sub
    ```

24. Open the LeftArrow_MouseUp procedure, and type

    ```
    Sub LeftArrow_MouseUp (Button As Integer, Shift As Integer,
        ➥X As Single, Y As Single)
    LeftArrow.BackColor = WHITE
    theMonth = theMonth - 1
    If theMonth = 0 Then theMonth = 12
    FillMonth
    End Sub
    ```

25. Open the RightArrow_MouseDown procedure, and type

    ```
    Sub RightArrow_MouseDown (Button As Integer,
        ➥Shift As Integer, X As Single, Y As Single)
    ```

```
RightArrow.BackColor = BLACK
End Sub
```

26. Open the `RightArrow_MouseUp` procedure, and type

```
Sub RightArrow_MouseUp (Button As Integer,
    ➥Shift As Integer, X As Single, Y As Single)
RightArrow.BackColor = WHITE
theMonth = theMonth + 1
If theMonth = 13 Then theMonth = 1
FillMonth
End Sub
```

The `MonthCmd_Click` procedure is executed whenever one of the months is selected on the Month menu. The value of Index is equal to 1 for January, 2 for February, and so forth, so insert the value of Index into the variable `theMonth` and call `FillMonth` to draw the new month.

27. Open the `MonthCmd_Click` procedure, and type

```
Sub MonthCmd_Click (Index As Integer)
theMonth = Index
FillMonth
End Sub
```

28. Open the `ExitCmd_Click` procedure, and type

```
Sub ExitCmd_Click ()
End
End Sub
```

The labels that form the calendar are also buttons that open the appropriate note. They are handled in much the same way as the left-arrow and right-arrow buttons. The `DayButton_MouseDown` procedure changes the background color to black and the text color to white. The `DayButton_MouseUp` procedure reverses that step to make the button seem like it was pressed. In line 5, the record number containing the data for this date is calculated by subtracting the serial date number for January 1 of the current year from the selected date stored in the array `thisMonth( )`, plus 1. This gives the correct record number, because the records are stored in the file as sequential days starting with January 1. The program then reads the record, and inserts the data into the controls on Form2. Then the form is made visible as a modal Form.

243

29. Open the DayButton_MouseDown procedure, and type

```
Sub DayButton_MouseDown (Index As Integer,
    ➡Button As Integer, Shift As Integer, X As Single, Y As
            Single)
OldBackColor = DayButton(Index).BackColor
OldForeColor = DayButton(Index).ForeColor
DayButton(Index).BackColor = BLACK
DayButton(Index).ForeColor = WHITE
End Sub
```

30. Open the DayButton_MouseUp procedure, and type

```
Sub DayButton_MouseUp (Index As Integer, Button As Integer,
    ➡Shift As Integer, X As Single, Y As Single)
DayButton(Index).BackColor = OldBackColor
DayButton(Index).ForeColor = OldForeColor
Open FileName For Random As #1 Len = 128
RecNo = thisMonth(Index) - DateSerial(theYear, 1, 1) + 1
Get #1, RecNo, ChangeDate
Close #1
Form2.DateBox.Caption = Format$(ChangeDate.TheDate, "mm-dd-
yyyy")
Form2.Message.Text = ChangeDate.Msg
Form2.FlagOpt(ChangeDate.Flags).Value = True
Form2.Show 1
End Sub
```

31. Save the Form.

When Form2 appears, any existing data for the selected date is displayed on the form for you to edit or delete. Whenever any changes are made to the large text box on Form2, the Message_Change procedure is executed. It simply stores the changed message in the Msg item of the ChangeDate record variable. It then checks the option buttons, and automatically clicks the Routine button, (FlagOpt(1)), if the message was previously empty.

32. Select the Message_Change procedure and type

```
Sub Message_Change ()
ChangeDate.Msg = Message.Text
```

```
If FlagOpt(0).Value = True And Message.Text <>""
  ➡Then FlagOpt(1).Value = True
End Sub
```

The `FlagOpt_Click` procedure is called whenever one of the option buttons is pressed. When it is executed, it first stores the current state of the option buttons in the Flags item of the `ChangeDate` record variable. Next, it checks to see whether the **None** option button (Index = 0) was pressed, and if so, clears the contents of the Message text box. Finally, it moves the focus to the Message text box. The If statement is needed here to prevent this code from trying to move the focus while the form is hidden. Because the `DayButton` procedure makes changes to the values on this form before it makes the form visible, an error would be generated if this code attempted to set the focus while the form was hidden.

33. Select the `FlagOpt_Click` procedure and type

```
Sub FlagOpt_Click (Index As Integer)
ChangeDate.Flags = Index
If Index = 0 Then Message.Text = ""
If Message.visible Then Message.SetFocus
End Sub
```

After making any changes, you press the OK button. The OK button opens the data file, calculates the record number, and stores the edited record in the file. It then hides Form2 and calls the FillMonth procedure to redraw the month on Form1.

34. Select the second form, open the `OKCmd_Click` procedure, and type

```
Sub OKCmd_Click ()
Open FileName For Random As #1 Len = 128
RecNo = ChangeDate.TheDate - DateSerial(theYear, 1, 1) + 1
Put #1, RecNo, ChangeDate
Close #1
Form2.Hide
FillMonth
End Sub
```

The Cancel button simply hides Form2 without making any changes to the data file.

35. Select the CancelCmd_Click procedure and type

```
Sub CancelCmd_Click ()
Form2.Hide
End Sub
```

36. Save the Form.

Several procedures stored on the module do the real work of this program. The ClearMonth procedure loops over all the labels on Form1, deletes their captions, disables them, and resets the default background and foreground colors.

37. Select the DBOOKM.BAS form and create the ClearMonth procedure with the **New Procedure** command on the **View** menu and type

```
Sub ClearMonth ()
Dim I As Integer
For I = 0 To 36
Form1.DayButton(I).Caption = ""
Form1.DayButton(I).Enabled = False
Form1.DayButton(I).BackColor = WHITE
Form1.DayButton(I).ForeColor = BLACK
Next I
End Sub
```

The FillMonth procedure inserts the data for the current month into the calendar. It first clears the calendar using the ClearMonth procedure in line 5. In line 6, it inserts the name of the current month and the year into the MonthBox at the top of the form. In lines 7, 8, and 9, it loops over all the months in the Month menu and unchecks them. It's easier here just to uncheck every item on the menu rather than trying to figure out which item is checked. In line 10, the procedure checks the current month on the Month menu.

The next block of code inserts the data into the calendar. In line 11, the serial date number of the first day of the month is placed in the variable StartDate. Next, the data file is opened, and the record number containing the data for the first of the month is calculated. The record is read, the day is extracted from the serial date number (should be 1) in line 15, and the day of the week is extracted in line 16. The day of the week is used to determine which of the DayButton procedures on Form1 holds the dates for this month.

In line 18, a loop starts that continues until the serial date number advances to the next month; thus it cycles over all the days in the current month. In line 19, the current date is combined with an end-of-line (carriage return-line feed) and the current day's messages, and is inserted in the Caption property of the DayButton procedure. In line 20, the label is enabled, and in line 21, the current serial date number is stored in the array, theMonth( ). In lines 22 through 24, the day is checked to see whether it is today; if it is, it's marked with an asterisk (*) inserted before the date and colored yellow.

Lines 26 through 31 check the state of the option buttons to see whether this date has a note attached, and whether it's important. If a note is attached, the background color is changed to light blue (cyan). If the note is important, the background color is changed to dark gray and the text is changed to white. I used shades of gray here because they print better in a book, but you can use any of the colors defined in the module. Finally, this procedure increments the index for the next day, reads the next record, and extracts the day. This loop continues until the day is in the next month.

38. Create the FillMonth procedure and type

```
Sub FillMonth ()
Dim StartDate As Double, aDay As DayType
Dim theDay As Integer, RecNo As Integer
Dim Index As Integer, I  As Integer, FirstIndex As Integer
ClearMonth
Form1.MonthBox.Caption = Months(theMonth) + Str$(theYear)
For I = 1 To 12
  Form1.MonthCmd(I).Checked = False
Next I
Form1.MonthCmd(theMonth).Checked = true
StartDate = DateSerial(theYear, theMonth, 1)     _line 11
Open FileName For Random As #1 Len = 128
RecNo = StartDate - DateSerial(theYear, 1, 1) + 1
Get #1, RecNo, aDay
theDay = Day(aDay.TheDate)
FirstIndex = Weekday(StartDate) - 1     _line 16
Index = FirstIndex
While theMonth = Month(StartDate + Index - FirstIndex)
  Form1.DayButton(Index).Caption = Str$(theDay) + EOL + aDay.Msg
```

```
      Form1.DayButton(Index).Enabled = true
      thisMonth(Index) = aDay.TheDate
      If aDay.TheDate = Fix(Now) .Then
        Form1.DayButton(Index).Caption = _*_ +
        Form1.DayButton(Index).Caption
        Form1.DayButton(Index).BackColor = YELLOW
      End If
      If aDay.Flags = 1 Then      _line 26
        Form1.DayButton(Index).BackColor = CYAN
      ElseIf aDay.Flags = 2 Then
        Form1.DayButton(Index).BackColor = RED
        Form1.DayButton(Index).ForeColor = WHITE
      End If
      Index = Index + 1
      RecNo = RecNo + 1
      Get #1, RecNo, aDay
      theDay = Day(aDay.TheDate)
  Wend
  Close #1
  end sub
```

The `LookAhead` procedure is executed by the `Form_Load` procedure of Form1. It checks Days days ahead of the current day and beeps and displays a message box if it finds one with the Important option set. In line 6, the variable `StartDate` is set to the serial date number for today. The `Fix( )` function removes any fraction of a day returned by the `Now` function. Lines 10 through 14 loop over the number of days ahead to look, extract the records for each of those days, and check the state of the option buttons. In line 12, if a date is found that has the Important option set (`aDay.Flags = 2`), then `FoundIt` is set to `True`, and the program beeps. In line 19, if `FoundIt` was set to `True`, it will display a message box that tells you there are important messages.

39. Create the `LookAhead` procedure and type

```
Sub LookAhead (Days As Integer)
'Look ahead Days for messages and beep if important
Dim StartDate As Double, aDay As DayType
Dim RecNo As Integer, Foundit As Integer
Dim I  As Integer
StartDate = Fix(Now)
```

```
Open FileName For Random As #1 Len = 128
RecNo = StartDate - DateSerial(theYear, 1, 1) + 1
Foundit = False
For I = 1 To Days       'line 10
  Get #1, RecNo, aDay
  If aDay.Flags = 2 Then
    Foundit = true
    Beep
  End If
  RecNo = RecNo + 1
Next I
Close #1
If Foundit Then MsgBox "You have important dates this week"
End Sub
```

40. Save the module as DBOOKM.BAS, then save the project.

41. Run the program. The first time there is no data file, so execute the New command and give it the current year. When the program finishes creating the new data file, the calendar window looks something like Figure 10.3, with the current month visible, and the current day marked with an asterisk and a yellow background.

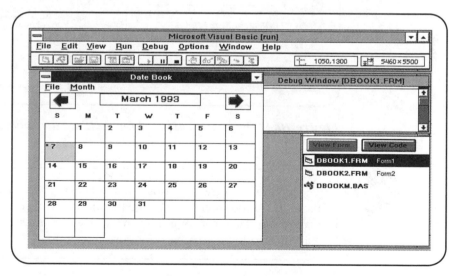

Figure 10.3. The Datebook program—startup at the current month.

42. Click a date and the Reminder window opens, as shown in Figure 10.4. In the Reminder window, click the **Important** Option button and type a note. Only the first couple of words show on the calendar window, so make sure they indicate what the note is about—see also Plate IV.

Click **OK** to add the note and return to the calendar window. After adding a few routine or important dates, the calendar window should look something like Figure 10.5.

This completes the Datebook program; use it for all your important dates.

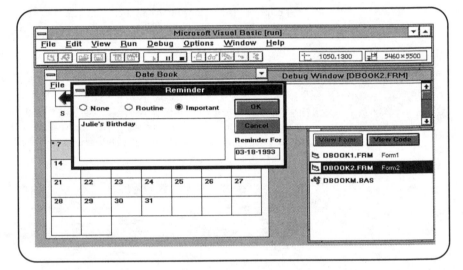

Figure 10.4. The Datebook program—adding an important date.

Try some of the other options, such as clicking the arrow buttons or using the Month menu to change the month. You could compile the program and make it a Windows startup document so every time you start up windows, you see your current calendar.

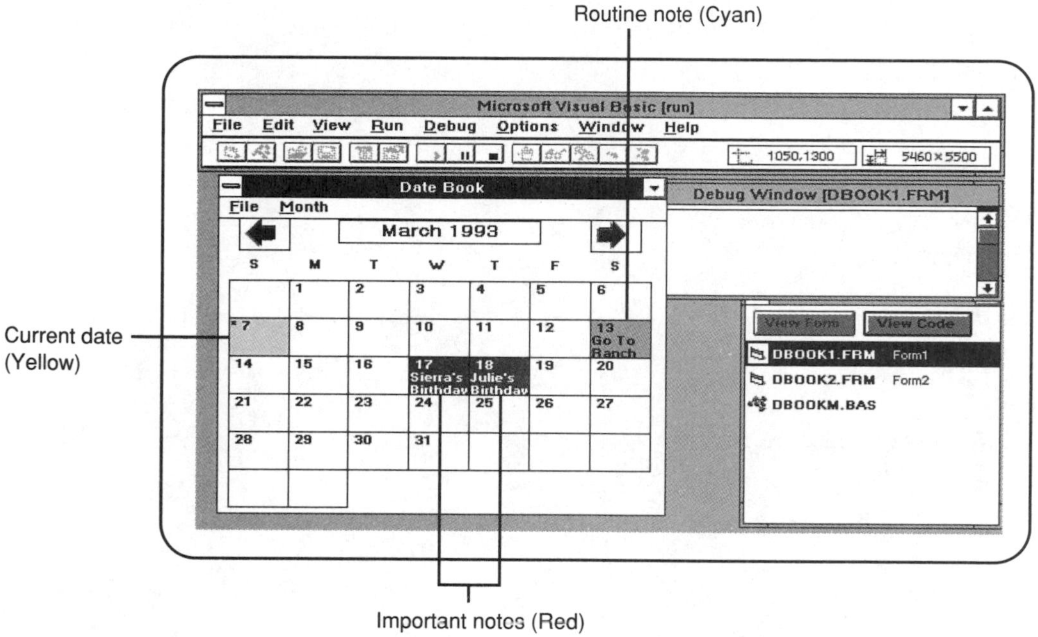

Routine note (Cyan)

Current date
(Yellow)

Important notes (Red)

Figure 10.5. *The Datebook program with notes added to some important dates.*

What You Have Learned

This chapter discussed the use of random access files. A random access disk file is one in which the individual records are read or written independently of all the other records in the file. All records are defined the same length when the file is opened. The contents of a record are determined by a record type variable defined with the Type statement. Specifically, this chapter investigated

- Using Type to create user-defined variables

- Using Open to open or create a random access disk file

- Reading and writing records with Get # and Put #

- Creating a Datebook database program to store important events

11

The Use of Color

Before you can draw graphics with Visual Basic, you have to set up the drawing environment. In addition to the obvious drawing properties such as the colors, the drawing environment includes setting the drawing mode, controlling the redrawing of windows when they have been uncovered, and setting the coordinate system. Redrawing of graphic windows is especially important in a window's environment where windows can be covered or uncovered at any time. The colors and drawing mode control how the drawing methods discussed in Chapter 12, "Drawing with Visual Basic," paint color on the screen, and the coordinate system determines what units you have to use when drawing on the screen.

In This Chapter

This chapter shows you how to manipulate color and the drawing properties, so you can control the drawing environment of Visual Basic. Properties exist to control the style of drawing, the colors used, and the scale of the drawing. Properties also exist to control redrawing of graphic images when a Form is uncovered. In this chapter, you will learn to

- Control redrawing of a graphic.
- Set the scale used when drawing.
- Set the colors.
- Set the drawing mode.
- Set the scale of a graphic.

Setting Drawing Properties

Drawing on the screen only occurs on a form or picture box; you cannot draw on any of the other controls. In addition to the screen, you can draw on the `Printer` object to obtain printed images. Forms and picture boxes have special properties, shown in Table 11.1, for controlling how and where drawing occurs on them. These properties set the default colors used for foreground and background objects, the initial drawing location, and the coordinate system used on a Form.

Table 11.1. Graphics properties of forms and picture boxes.

Property	Description
AutoRedraw	Sets the object to remember what was drawn on it
BackColor	Sets the background color
CurrentX	The current horizontal location
CurrentY	The current vertical location
DrawMode	Controls how new drawing is combined with old

Property	Description
DrawStyle	Controls line dashing
DrawWidth	Controls the width of lines
FillColor	Controls the color used to fill circles and rectangles
FillStyle	Controls the pattern used to fill circles and rectangles
ForeColor	Sets the foreground color
Image	Provides access to the persistent bitmap
Key Preview	Gives the form access to all key presses before they are passed to a control
Picture	Provides access to the displayed graphic image
ScaleHeight	The height of the drawing area in the scale units
ScaleLeft	The x coordinate of the left side of the drawing area
ScaleMode	The coordinate system to use in the drawing area
ScaleTop	The y coordinate of the top of the drawing area
ScaleWidth	The width of the drawing area in scale units

Controlling Redrawing of a Graphic

Whenever a form is covered and then uncovered by another window, its contents are erased by the covering window and have to be redrawn if you want to see them. Text boxes, labels, lists, and Combo boxes all contain the text drawn on them, so they automatically redraw themselves. File list boxes, directory list boxes and drive list boxes also contain the text they display, and also redraw themselves. Forms and picture boxes with graphic images loaded into them at design time contain those images, and automatically redraw themselves. However, forms and picture boxes with graphic images drawn on them at run time or with text printed on them do

not contain those images, and thus do not redraw themselves. Redrawing these objects must be handled by the Windows operating system or your program.

Although the file, directory, and drive list boxes automatically redraw themselves, their contents are not updated unless you change a directory. If you have added a file to a directory, or added a new subdirectory with your program, execute the Refresh method for that box to make it update its contents.

There are two ways to redraw a window, let the system do it, or do it yourself. The AutoRedraw property controls who does the redrawing when a window is uncovered. If AutoRedraw is set to True, then the Windows operating system stores a copy of everything drawn on the form or picture box in what is known as the persistent bitmap. It's persistent, because it isn't erased by an overlaying window. Whenever a form or picture box needs redrawing, the system paints a copy of the persistent bitmap on the screen, recreating the image.

If AutoRedraw is set to False, then uncovering a form or picture box causes a Paint event for that object, and, if you want the object redrawn, you must place code in the Paint event procedure to do so.

Accessing the Graphic Images

The Picture and Image properties provide a link to the graphic images displayed on a form, picture box, or image control. The Picture property is a link to the image displayed on the screen. It can be used to either load or store a graphic image. The Image property is a link to the persistent bitmap for a form or picture box, and is used to extract that image. The image control doesn't have an image property.

To store an image in a form, picture box or image control at design time, select the Picture property from the Properties list, then click the ellipses to the right of the Settings box. A File open dialog box appears for you to select the picture file. Only bitmaps (.PCX), icons (.ICO), Windows metafiles (.WMF), and device-independent bitmaps (.DIB) files can be stored in a form, picture box, or image control. To load these properties at run time, use the GetData method to copy a picture from the Clipboard, or the LoadPicture function to load one from a disk file. To save an image, use the SetData method to put it on the Clipboard, or the SavePicture statement to put it in a disk file. See Chapter 15, "Command Reference," for the details.

Although it is certainly more convenient to let the system redraw uncovered objects, especially if the image is difficult to reconstruct, there are some caveats to using the AutoRedraw property.

1. Persistent bitmaps can use up to 30K of memory. If you have only one graphic in an application, then it probably isn't a problem. If you have many forms and picture boxes that contain graphics, then it could become a problem, because each of those has its own persistent bitmap.

2. When AutoRedraw is True, drawing and printing is done on the persistent bitmap. When your drawing procedure finishes, and your program is in the *idle-loop*, the persistent bitmap is copied to the screen. (A program is in the idle-loop when it is waiting for you to do something, such as press a button.) If you have a graphic procedure that takes a long time to run, you won't see anything on the screen until it finishes.

3. You can override the problem in number 2 by executing the Refresh method for the object whenever you want the persistent bitmap copied to the screen. However, this slows down your program significantly by causing your whole drawing to be drawn multiple times; once on the persistent bitmap, and again on the screen every time you execute Refresh.

4. If you change AutoRedraw from True to False at run time, then everything in the persistent bitmap becomes the background of the form or picture box, and is not erased with the Cls method. If you later change AutoRedraw back to True, the image in the persistent bitmap replaces everything drawn since you changed AutoRedraw to False when the image is refreshed. The image isn't immediately refreshed, but waits until you make a change and enter the idle-loop, or until you execute the Refresh method.

> 5. You must set AutoRedraw to True if you want to print graphics drawn on a form or picture box using the PrintForm method.

Setting the Scale

The default scale used in a form or picture box is twips, measured from the upper-left corner of the drawing area (just below the title bar of a form). The horizontal or *x* coordinate is measured to the right from the left edge of the drawing area, and the vertical or *y* coordinate is measured down from the top edge of the drawing area. The location of the drawing point is stored in the CurrentX and CurrentY properties of the object that is being drawn. The drawing point is where the next drawing method will begin drawing, or where the next printed character will appear. Because this coordinate system is inverted, and uses units that most people are not used to, Visual Basic has the capability to redefine the coordinate system used on the drawing area of a form, picture box, or printer.

First is the ScaleMode property, which sets one of seven standard coordinate systems in a window (see Table 11.2). The origin is not changed by setting this property, but the unit system is. Setting this property does not change the size or physical location of any object drawn on a form or picture box, just the system used to measure it.

Table 11.2. Settings of the ScaleMode property.

Setting	Description
0	User-defined scale, automatically set when the scale is manually changed
1	Twips (default)
2	Points
3	Pixels
4	Characters
5	Inches

Setting	Description
6	Millimeters
7	Centimeters

In addition to these seven built-in scales, you can define your own scale with the ScaleLeft, ScaleTop, ScaleWidth, and ScaleHeight properties. ScaleLeft and ScaleTop define the coordinates of the upper-left corner of the drawing area. ScaleWidth and ScaleHeight then define the width and height of the drawing area. Setting the ScaleHeight property to a negative number, and setting the ScaleTop property to a positive number of the same magnitude, flips the coordinate system. This moves the origin to the lower-left corner, and also makes the vertical coordinate increase as you go upwards. The Scale method is a convenient way to set the ScaleHeight, ScaleWidth, ScaleLeft, and ScaleTop properties all at once. The syntax of the Scale method is

`[object.]`**Scale** `[(x1!,y1!) - (x2!,y2!)]`

where *object* is the object that has its four properties changed; *x1!, y1!* is the *x, y* location in the new scale of the upper-left corner of the window, and *x2!, y2!* are the *x, y* coordinates of the lower-left corner window. These values are then combined to create the four Scale properties. When you set any of the four Scale properties, or use the Scale method, the ScaleMode property of the object is automatically changed to 0 - User Defined.

Setting Screen Colors

The ForeColor and BackColor properties control the default colors used for foreground and background objects. Foreground objects consist of lines, text, and the borders of rectangles and circles. The background is the blank area of a form or picture box. Two other properties, FillColor and FillStyle, control the default color and pattern used in the two fillable drawing objects, rectangles and circles—see Chapter 15, "Command Reference," for a list of values.

Colors are set at design time using the Color Palette window, or at run time using either the defined colors from the CONSTANT.TXT file included with Visual Basic, or with the RGB() and QBColor() functions. You have

already set some of the colors using both the Color Palette window and color constants. Now, let's look at the numbers themselves. A color is stored as a single Long integer, but it actually contains four separate numbers stored in the four bytes of the Long integer.

The right-most three bytes contain the color in RGB format. The right-most byte contains the intensity of red, next is the intensity of green, and the third is blue. Each of the three intensities has a range of 0 to 255, where 0 is no color or black, and 255 is the brightest.

The simplest representations of these values are as hexadecimal numbers. Hexadecimal numbers are base 16, rather than base 10 like decimal numbers. The digits in a hexadecimal number range from 0 through 9, and then A through F to represent the numbers 10 through 16. In a hexadecimal number, each byte is represented by a pair of these digits. For example, &H02 is equal to 2 in decimal; the &H designator tells you that the following digits are hexadecimal and not decimal: &H09 = 9, &H0A = 10, &H0B = 11, &H0F = 15, &H10 = 16, &H11 = 17, and so on through &HFF = 255. Table 11.3 contains the hexadecimal values for the standard colors available in the file CONSTANT.TXT, included with Visual Basic. As you did in Chapter 10, "Using Random Access Files," the definitions can be loaded into the Global module and then used throughout a program.

Table 11.3. Hexadecimal color numbers for some standard colors.

Color	Hexadecimal Value
BLACK	&H000000
RED	&H0000FF
GREEN	&H00FF00
YELLOW	&H00FFFF
BLUE	&HFF0000
MAGENTA	&HFF00FF
CYAN	&HFFFF00
WHITE	&HFFFFFF

The right-most byte controls the meaning of the Long integer. If it is 0, the Long integer represents an RGB color as described above. If it has a hexadecimal value of &H80, the Long integer becomes a selector of one of the default system colors shown in Table 11.4. The default system colors are those set in the Windows control panel. Use these colors when you want parts of your application to appear the same as similar parts of the system.

Table 11.4. The hexadecimal color numbers for the system default colors.

System Color	Hexadecimal value
Gray area on Scroll bars	&H80000000
Desktop background	&H80000001
Caption of an active window	&H80000002
Caption of an inactive window	&H80000003
Menu background	&H80000004
Window background	&H80000005
Window frame	&H80000006
Menu text	&H80000007
Window text	&H80000008
Caption text	&H80000009
Border of an active window	&H8000000A
Border of an inactive window	&H8000000B
Background of MDI applications	&H8000000C
Selected items	&H8000000D
Selected text	&H8000000E
Command button	&H8000000F
Command button edge	&H80000010
Disabled text	&H80000011
Push buttons	&H80000012

The RGB() function is an alternate way of creating colors without using the constant values from CONSTANT.TXT. The RGB() function takes three

integer arguments, one each for the red, green, and blue intensities, and returns the number for that color. The syntax is

RGB(*red%*,*green%*,*blue%*)

where *red%*, *green%*, and *blue%* are integer values in the range 0 to 255. For example,

```
Color = RGB(255,0,0)
```

would give the variable `Color` the value &H0000FF, which, according to Table 11.3, is bright red.

A second function, `QBColor()`, sets the color value for the 16 standard Quick Basic colors. The color is set with a simple integer argument in the range 0 to 15 according to Table 11.5.

> The numbers and colors in Table 11.5 correspond to the QuickBasic, GW-BASIC, and BASICA color attributes.

Table 11.5. The color codes for use with the `QBColor` function.

Code	Color
0	Black
1	Blue
2	Green
3	Cyan
4	Red
5	Magenta
6	Yellow or Brown
7	White
8	Gray
9	Light Blue
10	Light Green
11	Light Cyan

Code	Color
12	Light Red
13	Light Magenta
14	Light Yellow
15	Bright White

Color Test Program

To look at some of these colors, create the Color Test program. This program allows you to set the colors and display the color values used in labels. Use scroll bars to set the values.

1. Open a new project, select Form1 and set its properties to

```
Height = 3700
Width = 4950
Caption = Color Test
```

2. Draw a picture box on the form, as shown in Figure 11.1, and set its properties to

```
Height = 1100
Width = 1095
Top = 360
Left = 120
```

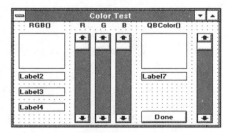

Figure 11.1. *Layout of the Color Test program.*

3. Draw a second picture box on the form and set its properties to

```
Height = 1100
Width = 1095
```

```
Top = 360
Left = 3000
```

4. Draw a label on the form and set its properties to

```
Caption = R       G       B
Height = 260
Width = 1215
Top = 0
Left = 1440
```

5. Draw three labels on the form and set their properties to

```
BorderStyle = 1 - Single
Height = 260
Width = 1095
Left = 120
Top = 1560, 2040, 2520
```

6. Draw a label above the `Picture1` box and set its properties to

```
Caption = RGB()
Height = 260
Width = 735
Top = 0
Left = 360
```

7. Draw a label above the `Picture2` box and set its properties to

```
Caption = QBColor()
Height = 260
Width = 855
Top = 0
Left = 3120
```

8. Draw a seventh label on the form and set its properties to

```
BorderStyle = 1 - Single
Height = 260
Width = 1095
Top = 1560
Left = 3000
```

9. Create a control array of three vertical scroll bars with the properties

```
Name = VScroll()
Height = 2780
```

```
Width = 375
Max = 255
Min = 0
Large Change = 10
Top = 360
Left(3 values) = 1440, 1920, 2400
```

 10. Draw a vertical scroll bar with the properties

```
Name = VScroll1
Height = 2780
Width = 375
Max = 15
Min = 0
Top = 360
Left = 4320
```

11. Draw a command button with the properties

```
Caption = Done
Height = 380
Width = 1095
Top = 2760
Left = 3000
```

12. Open the Command1_Click procedure and type

```
Sub Command1_Click ()
End
End Sub
```

The following procedure is for the control array of three vertical scroll bars. The procedure is executed whenever the thumb of one of the scroll bars is moved. In line 2, the Value properties of the three bars, and the RGB() function are used to set the intensity of Red, Green, and Blue in the background of the Picture1 picture box. In line 3, the text R = is combined with the intensity of Red and stored in the Caption property of Label2. Lines 4 and 5 do the same for Green and Blue.

13. Open the VScroll_Change procedure and type

```
Sub VScroll_Change (Index As Integer)
Picture1.BackColor = RGB(VScroll(0).Value, VScroll(1).Value,
➥VScroll(2).Value)
Label2.Caption = "R = " + Str$(VScroll(0).Value)
Label3.Caption = "G = " + Str$(VScroll(1).Value)
```

```
Label4.Caption = "B = " + Str$(VScroll(2).Value)
End Sub
```

The following procedure uses the Value property of the VScroll1 scroll bar to set the color code in the QBColor() function. That color is then used for the background of the Picture2 picture box. The contents of the Value property are displayed in Label7.

14. Open the VScroll1_Change procedure and type

```
Sub VScroll1_Change ()
Picture2.BackColor = QBColor(Int(VScroll1.Value))
Label7.Caption = Str$(VScroll1.Value)
End Sub
```

When the form first loads, the following procedure executes both of the Change procedures to insert the initial values and colors into the labels and picture boxes.

15. Open the Form_Load procedure and type

```
Sub Form_Load ()
VScroll_Change 0
VScroll1_Change
End Sub
```

16. Save the project as COLOR.MAK, and COLOR.FRM.

17. Run the program, and move the three Scroll bars on the RGB() side to see how the different combinations of red, green, and blue change the color of the first picture window. Move the Scroll bar on the QBColor() side and see what colors the 16 values of the argument give. The form should look something like Figure 11.2.

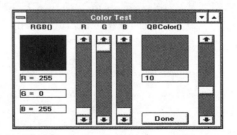

Figure 11.2. The Color Test program.

Controlling the Drawing Mode

Three picture properties control the drawing mode of the graphic pen; DrawMode, DrawStyle, and DrawWidth. The graphic pen is a convenient abstraction to understand drawing on a form or picture box. When foreground graphics are being created on a form or picture box, you can imagine a pen drawing those graphics. The three Draw properties described here control how the ink flows out of that fictitious pen. DrawMode is an Integer code that controls how the color being drawn on the graphic (the Pen) combines with what is already there (the Screen). The color numbers for the pen's color and the existing screen colors are combined using the logical formulas given in Table 11.6.

Table 11.6. Codes for the DrawMode property.

Code	Definition	Description
1	Black	Black
2	Not Merge Pen	NOT (Pen AND Screen)
3	Mask Not Pen	NOT Pen OR Screen
4	Not Copy Pen	NOT Pen
5	Mask Pen Not	Pen OR NOT Screen
6	Invert	NOT Screen
7	Xor Pen	Pen XOR Screen
8	Not Mask Pen	NOT (Pen OR Screen)
9	Mask Pen	Pen OR Screen
10	Not Xor Pen	NOT (Pen XOR Screen)
11	Transparent	Screen
12	Merge Not Pen	NOT Pen AND Screen
13	Copy Pen (Default)	Pen
14	Merge Pen Not	Pen AND NOT Screen
15	Merge Pen	Pen AND Screen
16	White	White

Of the 16 possible modes shown, only the following six give results that are easily predictable.

1 - Black, draw with a black pen.

6 - Invert, draw with the inverse of whatever is already there.

7 - XOR Pen, draw with the colors that are not common to both the pen and screen.

11 - Transparent, don't draw anything.

13 - Copy Pen, draw with the current ForeColor (default).

16 - White, draw with a white pen.

Drawing twice with mode 7 restores the screen to what it was before it was drawn on. The other 10 values are not easily predictable, so experimenting with them is the best way to see what they do.

A useful project would be to create a program like the Color Test program, that changes the DrawMode and DrawStyle for different foreground and background colors. You would need to draw a foreground object across the picture boxes to have something to combine with the background colors.

The DrawStyle property sets the style for lines drawn on a form or picture box. Table 11.7 lists the different line styles you can set with this property. Styles 1 through 4 work only if the DrawWidth property is set to 1; otherwise the setting defaults to 0 - Solid. That is, you cannot draw wide dotted or dashed lines.

Table 11.7. Values of the DrawStyle property.

Value	Definition
0	Solid (Default)
1	Dashed line
2	Dotted line
3	Dash-dot

Value	Definition
4	Dash-dot-dot
5	Invisible
6	Inside solid

The DrawWidth property controls the width of lines drawn on a form or picture box. Its value specifies the width of a line in pixels.

What You Have Learned

This chapter has dealt with the Visual Basic methods that draw on a form, and the properties and methods that set the colors to draw with and the modes in which colors are combined. Forms and picture boxes are the only screen objects that can be drawn on. The Printer object also can be drawn on to produce printed graphics. The image control can't be drawn on but can contain an image stored in its picture property. In detail, you have learned about

- Controlling the redrawing of a graphic.

- Loading and saving a graphic image.

- Setting the scale with the Scale method, and the ScaleHeight, ScaleWidth, ScaleLeft, and ScaleTop properties.

- Setting the foreground and background colors with constants, and the RGB( ) and QBColor( ) functions.

- Controlling how new drawing combines with what is already on a graphic.

- Drawing dotted and dashed lines.

Drawing with Visual Basic

Although Visual Basic does not have an extensive set of drawing tools, it does have a line and rectangle tool, a circle tool, and a point plotting tool. Using these simple tools, and the capability to set the screen colors, you can draw many useful figures. Or, using the graphic file importing capability, you can load a figure that has been created elsewhere directly into a Visual Basic window.

In This Chapter

This chapter shows you how to create graphics images with Visual Basic. At design time, you can draw on a form or picture box using the line and shape tools from the toolbox window. At runtime Visual Basic has three methods for drawing on the screen; Line, Circle, and PSet. The Line method draws lines and rectangles, the Circle method draws circles, and the PSet method

sets the color of a single point. In addition, Visual Basic can import several of the standard picture format files and display them on a Form or picture window.

In this chapter, you learn to

● Draw circles and pie sections.

● Draw lines and rectangles.

● Set the color of a point on the screen.

● Import and export pictures.

Drawing with the Toolbox Tools

There are two tools in the toolbox window for drawing on a form or picture box—the line and shape tools. As you might expect, you can draw lines with the line tool. Using the line's Properties window, you can change the color, thickness, or pattern of a line. If you make a short, thick line, you get a bar with rounded ends. The shapes tool creates filled shapes, with separately controlled borders (thickness and color) and fills (color and pattern). The possible shapes are

• Rectangle

• Square

• Oval

• Circle

• Rounded Rectangle

• Rounded Square

which are set with the Shape property. The background color and pattern are set with the BackColor and BackStyle properties. The foreground colors and patterns are set with the FillColor and FillStyle properties. The border is controlled with the BorderColor, BorderStyle, and BorderWidth properties. The properties of a line or shape can be set at run time like any other property. This attribute makes it possible to dynamically draw objects on the screen, or draw objects that can be selected and moved.

Draw a few objects on a form and try changing the values of the properties to get a feel for how the drawing tools work, and what their capabilities are.

Making Circles and Pie Slices

The `Circle` method is used to draw circles, filled circles, arcs, pie slices, and filled pie slices on forms, picture boxes, and the `Printer` object. The syntax of the `Circle` method is

```
[object.]Circle[Step](xc!,yc!),radius![,[color&],
[startang!][,[endang!][,aspect!]]]]
```

where `object` is the object to be drawn on, `(xc!,yc!)` is the location of the center of the circle, `radius!` is the radius of the circle, `color&` is the color to use to draw the outline of the circle or arc, `startang!` and `endang!` are the starting and ending angles (in radians) of the pie slice, and `aspect!` is the aspect ratio of the object. If you use the `Step` argument, the coordinates of the center of the circle are treated as relative to the current drawing location. If the `startang!` and `endang!` arguments are positive, they mark the end points of an arc. If they are negative, they still mark the end points of an arc, but a line also is drawn from the center of the circle to the end of the arc, creating a pie slice.

The Drawing Test Program

The drawing test program is a simple program used to experiment with the drawing tools. First add a picture box and some buttons to a form. Then attach code to the buttons to experiment with circles.

1. Open a new project and select `Form1`. Set its properties as follows.

   ```
   Caption = Drawing
   Height = 4100
   Width = 6240
   ```

2. Draw a picture box on the form with these properties.

   ```
   Name = BlackBoard
   Height = 2300
   Width = 4575
   ```

```
Top = 240
Left = 1440
```

3. Draw the Exit Command button on the Form as shown in Figure 12.1, with these properties.

```
Name = ExitCmd
Caption = Exit
Height = 380
Width = 615
Top = 2640
Left = 3400
```

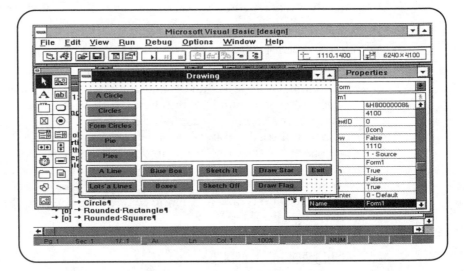

Figure 12.1. *Layout of the Drawing program.*

4. Open the `ExitCmd_Click` and `Form_Unload` procedures and type

```
Sub ExitCmd_Click ()
End
End Sub
Sub Form_Unload ()
End
End Sub
```

5. Add a module to the project with the New **M**odule command and type the following. The first block of color definitions comes from the CONSTANT.TXT file included with Visual Basic. The rest of the

definitions are used later in this example. The constant definitions could go in the form's declarations section but the Type statement can only go in a module.

```
' BackColor, ForeColor, FillColor (standard RGB colors:
➥form, controls)
Global Const BLACK = &H0&
Global Const RED = &HFF&
Global Const GREEN = &HFF00&
Global Const YELLOW = &HFFFF&
Global Const BLUE = &HFF0000
Global Const MAGENTA = &HFF00FF
Global Const CYAN = &HFFFF00
Global Const WHITE = &HFFFFFF
Global SketchMode As Integer
Type FlagType
        Xmin As Single
        Xmax As Single
        Ymin As Single
        Ymax As Single
        Stripe As Single
        Rbox As Single
End Type
```

6. Draw a command button on the form with the following properties.

```
Name = CircleCmd
Caption = A Circle
Height = 3
Width = 15
Top = 0
Left = 0
```

7. Open the `CircleCmd_Click` code window and type

```
Sub CircleCmd_Click ()
'Draw a Blue circle
BlackBoard.ScaleMode = 1            '  Twips
BlackBoard.DrawStyle = 0            '  Solid
BlackBoard.FillStyle = 0            '  Solid
BlackBoard.FillColor = BLUE
BlackBoard.Cls
BlackBoard.Circle (2000, 1000), 800, RED
End Sub
```

This procedure first resets ScaleMode to twips, in case it had been changed by another command. It then turns off-line and fill patterns by setting both DrawStyle and FillStyle to 0 - Solid. It sets the FillColor to blue, then executes the Cls method on the Picture box. The Cls, or Clear Screen, method clears any drawing in the box and sets the whole box to the background color. Finally, the Circle method is applied to the picture window. It draws a circle in the window centered on the point 2000 twips from the left side of the box and 1000 twips from the top. The radius of the circle is 800 twips, the outline color is red, and the fill color is blue.

8. Save the project as FLAG.MAK, FLAG1.FRM, and FLAGG.BAS (the reason for saving it with this name will be apparent soon). Run the program and click the **A Circle** button; the Form should look like Figure 12.2.

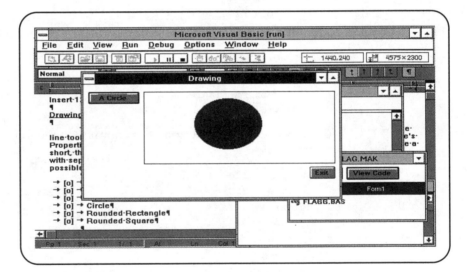

*Figure 12.2. Result of pressing the **A Circle** button.*

Now this isn't terribly exciting, even though it is a pretty blue circle with a bright red rim. Draw a few more circles to make things more interesting.

9. Add another command button below the first and set its properties to

```
Height = 380
Width = 1215
Top = 720
```

276

```
Left = 120
Caption = Circles
Name = CirclesCmd
```

10. Open the `CirclesCmd_Click` procedure and type

```
Sub CirclesCmd_Click ()
'Draw 100 random circles
Dim Color As Long, I As Integer
BlackBoard.ScaleMode = 1              ' - Twips
BlackBoard.DrawStyle = 0              ' - Solid
BlackBoard.FillStyle = 0              ' - Solid
BlackBoard.Cls
For I = 1 To 100
  XC = Rnd(1) * BlackBoard.ScaleWidth         'line 9
  YC = Rnd(1) * BlackBoard.ScaleHeight
  Radius = Rnd(1) * BlackBoard.ScaleHeight / 2
  Color = QBColor(Rnd(1) * 15)
  BlackBoard.FillColor = Color
  BlackBoard.Circle (XC, YC), Radius, Color
Next I
End Sub
```

The first few lines of this procedure are the same as in the
`CircleCmd_Click` procedure, where the drawing environment is set
up. In line 8, a `For/Next loop` starts that iterates the enclosed block
of statements 100 times, which draws 100 circles on the form. Just
drawing 100 circles won't be interesting, so set the arguments of
the `Circle` method using random numbers. In lines 9 and 10, a
random center for the circle is calculated. Because the random
number function `RND(1)` always returns a number between 0 and 1,
scale it with the `ScaleWidth` and `ScaleHeight` properties of the
picture box. This ensures that the center is always within the
picture box.

In line 11, calculate the radius of the circle and scale it to be a
maximum of one half the height of the picture box. In line 12, use
the `QBColor()` function and the `Rnd()` function to randomly select
one of the 16 standard colors. Finally, in line 13, the `Circle`
method is called to draw the circle.

You can be more creative and use the `RGB()` function rather than
`QBColor()`, because it's capable of creating over 16 million colors.

11. Save the program and run it. Press the **Circles** button and see what happens. You should see something like Figure 12.3 (kind of pretty, don't you think?).

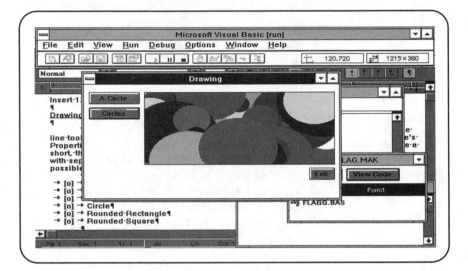

Figure 12.3. Execution of the Circles *program.*

You can draw on a form as well as on a picture box, as you will see.

12. Draw a command button and set its properties to

```
Height = 380
Width = 1215
Top = 1200
Left = 120
Caption = Form Circles
Name = FCirclesCmd
```

13. Open the CirclesCmd_Click procedure and copy everything but the first and last lines. Open the FCirclesCmd_Click procedure and paste it into the template, then edit it until it reads as follows. All you have to do is to remove the name of the picture box so that the drawing defaults to the form.

```
Sub FCirclesCmd_Click ()
'Draw 100 random circles on the form
Dim Color As Long, I As Integer
ScaleMode = 1 ' - Twips
```

```
DrawStyle = 0 ' - Solid
FillStyle = 0 ' - Solid
Cls
For I = 1 To 100
  XC = Rnd(1) * ScaleWidth
  YC = Rnd(1) * ScaleHeight
  Radius = Rnd(1) * ScaleHeight / 2
  Color = QBColor(Rnd(1) * 15)
  FillColor = Color
  Circle (XC, YC), Radius, Color
Next I
End Sub
```

14. Save the project and run it. Click the **Form Circles** button and circles appear on the form as shown in Figure 12.4. Note how they don't overwrite the buttons or the picture box, but are drawn behind them.

    The Circles method is capable of more than simply creating circles. It creates ellipses if you make the aspect! argument any number other than 1. It also creates arcs and filled pie slices if you use the startang! and endang! arguments. If startang! and endang! are positive, the method draws an arc. If they are negative, the method draws a filled pie slice.

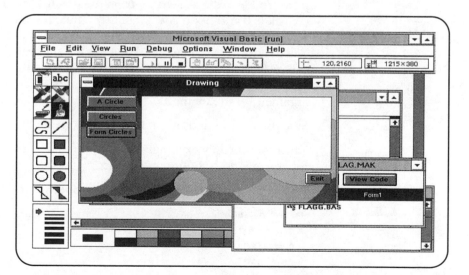

Figure 12.4. *Execution of the* Form Circles *program.*

15. Draw a command button and set its properties to

```
Height = 380
Width = 1215
Top = 1680
Left = 120
Caption = Pie
Name = PieCmd
```

16. Open the `PieCmd_Click` procedure and type the following. You can copy most of it from the previous procedure to save yourself some typing.

```
Sub PieCmd_Click ()
'Draw a Red pie slice
BlackBoard.ScaleMode = 1 ' - Twips
BlackBoard.DrawStyle = 0 ' - Solid
BlackBoard.FillStyle = 0 ' - Solid
BlackBoard.FillColor = RED
BlackBoard.Cls
BlackBoard.Circle (2000, 1000), 800, BLACK, -1, -2, 1
End Sub
```

This procedure works like the `Circle` program, with the addition of -1 and -2 for the starting and ending angles. The angles are measured in radians, starting from the positive x axis (that is, 3 o'clock is 0 and noon is $\pi/2$ radians). Thus, the arc is drawn from 1 radian ($1 \times 180/\pi = 57.3$ degrees) to 2 radians (114.6 degrees). The two values are negative, so lines also are drawn from the center of the circle to each end of the arc. The arc is filled with the `FillColor`, red, and outlined in black, as specified in the color argument of the method.

17. Save the project and run it. It should look like Figure 12.5.

Yawn, not terribly exciting, is it? But, if random circles were interesting, how about random pies?

18. Draw a command button and set its properties to

```
Height = 380
Width = 1215
Top = 2160
Left = 120
Caption = Pies
Name = PiesCmd
```

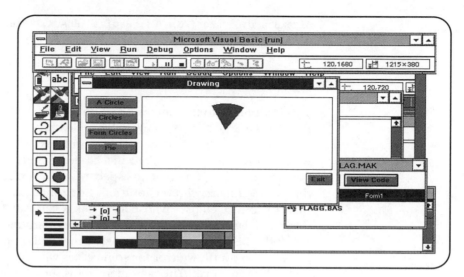

Figure 12.5. *Execution of the* Pie *program.*

19. Open the CirclesCmd_Click procedure and copy everything but the first and last lines. Open the PiesCmd_Click procedure and paste it into the template, then edit it until it reads as follows:

```
Sub PiesCmd_Click ()
'Draw 100 random pie slices
Dim Color As Long, I As Integer
Dim XC As Single, YC As Single
Dim Radius As Single
Dim PieStart As Single, PieEnd As Single
BlackBoard.ScaleMode = 1                        ' - Twips
BlackBoard.DrawStyle = 0                        ' - Solid
BlackBoard.FillStyle = 0                        ' - Solid
BlackBoard.Cls
For I = 1 To 100
  XC = Rnd(1) * BlackBoard.ScaleWidth
  YC = Rnd(1) * BlackBoard.ScaleHeight
  Radius = Rnd(1) * BlackBoard.ScaleHeight / 2 + 20
  Color = QBColor(Rnd(1) * 15)
  BlackBoard.FillColor = Color
  PieStart = Rnd(1) * 6
  PieEnd = Rnd(1) * 6
  Aspect = Rnd(1) * 2
  If Aspect * Radius > 10 Then
```

```
BlackBoard.Circle (XC, YC), Radius, BLACK, -PieStart,
    ➥-PieEnd, Aspect
    End If
Next I
End Sub
```

This is identical to the Circles program, with the addition of the PieStart, PieEnd, and Aspect variables. PieStart and PieEnd are given random values between 0 and 6 radians (6 is slightly less than 2π, the number of radians in a circle.) Aspect is given a value between 0 and 2. Note that an aspect of 1 is a circle, values less than 1 are ellipses with the long axis horizontal, and values greater than 1 produce ellipses whose long axis is vertical. Another difference is the addition of an `If` statement around the Circle method. There is a bug in Visual Basic that makes this method generate an overflow error for some cases where the aspect ratio and radius are small. This statement skips the `Circle` method if the product of the values is less than 10, which seems to prevent the method from crashing.

20. Save the project, run it, and press the **Pies** button. Yieoww! It looks like a Pac-Man attack—see Figure 12.6.

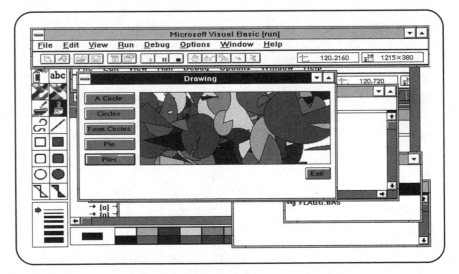

Figure 12.6. Execution of the `Pies` *program. (Look out, it's a Pac-Man attack!)*

Making Lines and Boxes

The `Line` method works much like the `Circle` method, except that it produces lines and filled rectangles rather than circles. The syntax of the Line method is

```
[object.]Line[[Step](xst!,yst!)]-
[Step](xen!,yen!)[,[color&],B[F]]]
```

Here, `object` is the form, picture box, or Printer to be drawn on; `xst!` and `yst!` are either the `x,y` coordinates to the start of a line or the upper-left corner of a box; `xen!` and `yen!` are the `x,y` coordinates of the end of the line, or the lower-right corner of a box. If the starting point is omitted, drawing starts from the current position specified by the `CurrentX` and `CurrentY` properties of the object. If `Step` is used, the coordinates are considered to be relative to the previous point plotted. The `B` parameter specifies that this is a box rather than a line, and the `F` parameter specifies that if it is a box, it is to be filled with the same color as the bounding line specified with `color&`, rather than using the `FillColor` property of the object. You can now draw a line on the form.

1. Draw a command button and set its properties to

   ```
   Height = 380
   Width = 1215
   Top = 2640
   Left = 120
   Caption = A Line
   Name = LineCmd
   ```

2. Open the `LineCmd_Click` procedure and type the following. You can copy most of it from the previous procedure and save yourself some typing.

   ```
   Sub LineCmd_Click ()
   'Draw a line
   BlackBoard.ScaleMode = 1  ' - Twips
   BlackBoard.DrawStyle = 0  ' - Solid
   BlackBoard.FillStyle = 0  ' - Solid
   BlackBoard.Cls
   BlackBoard.Line (200, 500)-(4000, 2000), BLUE
   End Sub
   ```

Here, the first few lines are the same as in the previous proce-
dures. The `Line` method in the next-to-last line draws a blue line
from a point 200 twips from the left and 500 twips from the top of
the drawing area to the point 4000 twips from the left and 2000
twips from the top.

3. Save the project, run it, and press the **A Line** button. It should
   look like Figure 12.7.

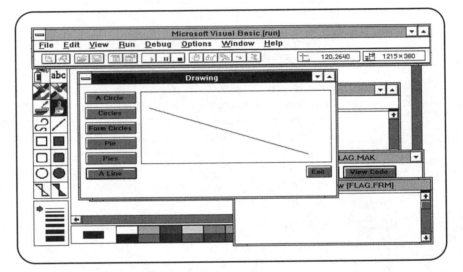

Figure 12.7. *Execution of the* A Line *program.*

4. Draw a command button and set its properties to

```
Height = 380
Width = 1215
Top = 3120
Left = 120
Caption = Lots'a Lines
Name = LinesCmd
```

5. Open the `LinesCmd_Click` procedure and type the following. You
   can copy most of it from the `Circles` procedure and save yourself
   some typing.

```
Sub LinesCmd_Click ()
'Draw 100 random Lines
Dim Color As Long, I As Integer
Dim XL As Single, XR As Single
```

```
Dim YL As Single, YR As Single
BlackBoard.ScaleMode = 1 ' - Twips
BlackBoard.DrawStyle = 0 ' - Solid
BlackBoard.FillStyle = 0 ' - Solid
BlackBoard.Cls
For I = 1 To 100
  XL = Rnd(1) * BlackBoard.ScaleWidth
  YL = Rnd(1) * BlackBoard.ScaleHeight
  XR = Rnd(1) * BlackBoard.ScaleWidth
  YR = Rnd(1) * BlackBoard.ScaleHeight
  Color = QBColor(Rnd(1) * 15)
  BlackBoard.Line (XL, YL)-(XR, YR), Color
Next I
End Sub
```

Here, you generate four random numbers to specify the x,y coordinates of the start and end of a line and another random number for the color. These values are then used as arguments to the Line method, which draws a line.

6. Save the project, run it, and press the **Lots'a Lines** button. It should look like Figure 12.8.

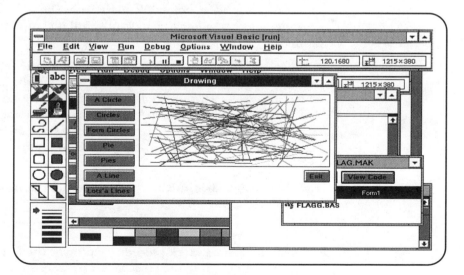

Figure 12.8. *Execution of the* `Lots'a Lines` *program.*

Now, try a box. Use the same procedure as the `LineCmd_Click`, but add the `B` parameter.

7. Draw a command button and set its properties to

```
Height = 380
Width = 1215
Top = 2640
Left = 1440
Caption = Blue Box
Name = BoxCmd
```

An interesting variation on the Lines program is one I call Spinners, shown in Plate III. As with all the examples, it uses the Drawing Test Program as a base. First, two pairs of points are selected randomly. Next, the program moves 1/20 of the distance from one point to the next in a pair, and a line is drawn from there to the equivalent point between the other pair of points. The program then steps another 1/20 of the distance and draws another line. This continues until it reaches the second point in each pair. Then, two new pairs of points are created with the second point from each of the original two pairs, plus two new random points added to them. The program continues drawing lines and adding new points until it completes 20 pairs of points.

Another variation is to draw multisided geometric figures. Set the program up to calculate points on a circle, input the angle through which to move each step, and draw a line. Continue rotating and drawing lines until you come back to your starting point. If you set the angle to 120 degrees, you get a triangle. If you set it to 90 degrees, you get a square. If you set it to 88 degrees, the program draws around in a circle 44 times.

There are many other variations; have fun with this program and see what you can come up with.

8. Open the `BoxCmd_Click` procedure and type the following. You can copy most of it from the `LineCmd_Click` procedure and save yourself some typing.

```
Sub BoxCmd_Click ()
'Draw a blue box
```

```
BlackBoard.ScaleMode = 1  ' - Twips
BlackBoard.DrawStyle = 0  ' - Solid
BlackBoard.FillStyle = 0  ' - Solid
BlackBoard.FillColor = BLUE
BlackBoard.Cls
BlackBoard.Line (200, 500)-(4000, 2000), BLACK, BF
End Sub
```

9. Save the project, run it, and click the **Blue Box** button. The window should now look like Figure 12.9.

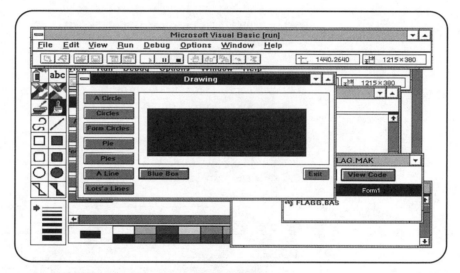

Figure 12.9. *Execution of the* Blue Box *program.*

Now, how about a bunch of boxes.

10. Draw a command button and set its properties to

```
Height = 380
Width = 1215
Top = 3120
Left = 1440
Caption = Boxes
Name = BoxesCmd
```

11. Open the BoxesCmd_Click procedure and type the following code. Copy most of it from the LinesCmd_Click procedure to save yourself some typing.

```
Sub BoxesCmd_Click ()
'Draw 100 random boxes
Dim Color As Long, I As Integer
Dim XL As Single, XR As Single
Dim YL As Single, YR As Single
BlackBoard.ScaleMode = 1 ' - Twips
BlackBoard.DrawStyle = 0 ' - Solid
BlackBoard.FillStyle = 0 ' - Solid
BlackBoard.Cls
For I = 1 To 100
  XL = Rnd(1) * BlackBoard.ScaleWidth
  YL = Rnd(1) * BlackBoard.ScaleHeight
  XR = Rnd(1) * BlackBoard.ScaleWidth
  YR = Rnd(1) * BlackBoard.ScaleHeight
  Color = QBColor(Rnd(1) * 15)
  BlackBoard.FillColor = Color
    BlackBoard.Line (XL, YL)-(XR, YR), Color, B
Next I
End Sub
```

12. Save the project, run it, and click the **Boxes** button. Psychedelic!
The window should now look like Figure 12.10.

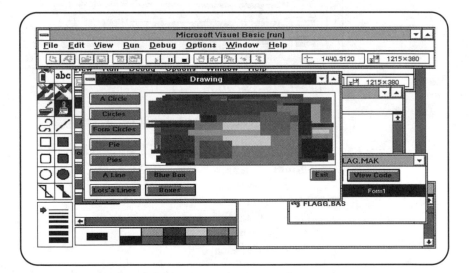

Figure 12.10. *Execution of the* Boxes *program.*

Drawing Points

Points on the screen are individually set with the PSet method, and read with the Point method. The syntax of the PSet method is

```
[object.]PSet [Step](x!,y!)[,color&]
```

Here, object is the form, picture box, or Printer to draw on, x! and y! give the x,y location of the point, and color& indicates the color you've chosen for the point. If Step is used, the point is relative to the previous point. If color& is omitted, the current foreground color is used. The syntax of the Point method is

```
[object.]Point (x!,y!)
```

The definitions of the arguments are the same as for the PSet method, except that this method returns the color rather than setting it.

To draw points on the screen, you need a way to select the point to color, and the mouse and the MouseMove event do the job. The MouseMove event is generated whenever the location of the mouse has changed after some short length of time. The MouseMove event procedure is passed the state of the mouse's buttons and its x,y location; use that information to make a black dot at the mouse location if the mouse button is down.

1. Draw a command button and set its properties to

   ```
   Height = 380
   Width = 1215
   Top = 2640
   Left = 2760
   Caption = Sketch It
   Name = SketchCmd
   ```

2. Draw a second command button below it and set its properties to

   ```
   Height = 380
   Width = 1215
   Top = 3120
   Left = 2760
   Caption = Sketch Off
   Name = UnSketchCmd
   ```

3. Open the `SketchCmd_Click` procedure and type the following code. This command initializes the picture box and sets the flag `SketchMode` to `True`.

```
Sub SketchCmd_Click ()
'Turn on sketch mode
SketchMode = True
BlackBoard.ScaleMode = 1   ' - Twips
BlackBoard.DrawStyle = 0   ' - Solid
BlackBoard.FillStyle = 0   ' - Solid
BlackBoard.ForeColor = BLACK
BlackBoard.Cls
End Sub
```

4. Open the `UnSketchCmd_Click` procedure and type the following code. This command sets the flag `SketchMode` to `False`.

```
Sub UnSketchCmd_Click ()
'Sketch Mode off
SketchMode = False
End Sub
```

5. Open the `BlackBoard_MouseMove` procedure and type

```
Sub BlackBoard_MouseMove (Button As Integer,
➥Shift As Integer, x As Single, y As Single)
If SketchMode = True And Button <> 0 Then
   BlackBoard.PSet (x, y)
End If
End Sub
```

Whenever the mouse moves, this command is executed. It checks to see that `SketchMode` is `True`, and that a mouse button is down. If this is `True`, it sets the point at the mouse location to the current foreground color (black).

6. Save the project, run it, and click the **Sketch It** button. Move the mouse into the picture box, press the button, and move the mouse.

   A trail of dots follows the mouse's motion. The spacing of the dots and the speed at which you move the mouse indicates how often Visual Basic checks to see whether the mouse has moved. The screen should look like Figure 12.11.

7. Click the **Sketch Off** button when you are done.

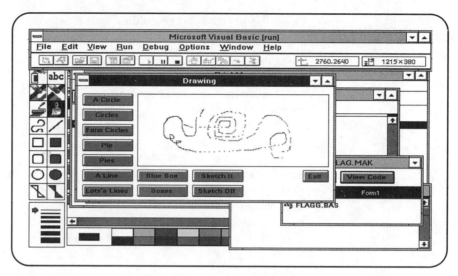

Figure 12.11. *Execution of the* Sketch It *program.*

Now that you know how to use the drawing programs, try something more interesting— drawing an American flag on the screen. The red and white stripes, a blue rectangle, and fifty white stars all can be drawn with the line method, the first two with the B option and the stars without this option.

The stars present a special problem, because they have to be filled with white, but there is no filled star method available, nor is there a Paint method. The Paint method is available in other BASICs, and it fills any enclosed area with a specific color. It isn't available in Visual Basic. Writing a Paint method would be an interesting evening's project, but you can live without it here, because the stars are going to be small, so you can fill them with lines. First create the star-drawing procedure. There is a Paint event, but it has nothing to do with filling in a graphic. The Paint event tells you when a window needs to be redrawn—see Chapter 11, "The Use of Color."

8. Draw a command button and set its properties to

```
Height = 380
Width = 1215
Top = 2640
Left = 4080
Caption = Draw Star
Name = StarCmd
```

9. Open the `StarCmd_Click` method and type

```
Sub StarCmd_Click ()
'Draw a star
Dim theFlag As FlagType
theFlag.Xmin = 0      'Bounding box
theFlag.Xmax = 44
theFlag.Ymin = 0
theFlag.Ymax = 26
theFlag.Stripe = 0    'Stripe height
theFlag.Rbox = 44     'Right side of the star box
ScaleIt theFlag, BlackBoard
BlackBoard.Cls
BlueRec theFlag, BlackBoard
Star 44 / 2, 26 / 2, 26 / 2, BlackBoard
End Sub
```

This procedure uses the `FlagType` record type, defined in the module, to save space while passing information to the `Sub` procedures. The `FlagType` type contains the *bounding box* of the rectangle to hold the flag, the width of a stripe, and the width of the blue rectangle. A bounding box is a rectangle that completely contains the flag. In this procedure, you want to draw a single star on a blue background, so set the stripe height to 0 and the width of the blue box to the width of the flag. After `theFlag` is loaded, the procedure calls the `ScaleIt` `Sub` procedure to scale the picture box. Note that the procedure is passed only the name of the record type variable `theFlag`, rather than each of its components. The components are still passed, but in the record type variable.

Next, the procedure clears the picture box, calls the `BlueRec` `Sub` procedure to draw the blue rectangle, and then calls the `Star` `Sub` pro-cedure to draw a star. The arguments to the `Star` `Sub` proce-dure are the `x,y` location of the center of the star, the length of a side, and the object to draw them on. Now, create those three `Sub` procedures.

10. Create a new `Sub` procedure named `ScaleIt` and type

```
Sub ScaleIt (C As FlagType, Pic As Control)
If TypeOf Pic Is PictureBox Then
  Pic.ScaleMode = 0              ' - User defined scale
  Pic.Scale (C.Xmin, C.Ymax)-(C.Xmax, C.Ymin)
End If
End Sub
```

Note, in the heading of this procedure, the `Pic As Control` clause. The `Control` type allows you to pass a control name as an argument to a `Sub` procedure. Line 2 tests the control passed to the procedure to make sure it is a `PictureBox`. The procedure then sets the `ScaleMode` to `0 - User Defined`, and uses the `Scale` method to set the scales of the picture box. The `Scale` method sets all the `Scale` properties at once.

11. Create a new `Sub` procedure named `BlueRec` and type

```
Sub BlueRec (C As FlagType, Pic As Control)
'Draw blue rectangle
Pic.Line (C.Xmin, 6 * C.Stripe)-(C.Rbox, C.Ymax), BLUE, BF
End Sub
```

This routine draws the blue rectangle in the upper-left corner of the flag. To do so, it uses the `Line` method with the `B` and `F` options to draw a filled, blue rectangle.

12. Create a new `Sub` procedure named `Star` and type

```
Sub Star (XC, YC, Slen As Single, Pic As Control)
'Draw a 5 pointed star, one point at a time.
Dim Lmin As Single, Lmax As Single
Lmin = Slen * .25
Lmax = Slen * .75
PointAng = 1.26    'radians, 2*Pi/5, the angle between points
HPointAng = PointAng / 2 'the half angle of a point
RotAng = 1.57    'radians, rotate star
For K = 1 To 5
  'x,y location of the point
  Xpt = Lmax * Cos(RotAng + (K - 1) * PointAng) + XC
  Ypt = Lmax * Sin(RotAng + (K - 1) * PointAng) + YC
  'x,y location of the right valley
  XptR = Lmin * Cos(RotAng - HPointAng + (K - 1) * PointAng) + XC
  YptR = Lmin * Sin(RotAng - HPointAng + (K - 1) * PointAng) + YC
  'x,y location of the left valley
  XptL = Lmin * Cos(RotAng + HPointAng + (K - 1) * PointAng) + XC
  YptL = Lmin * Sin(RotAng + HPointAng + (K - 1) * PointAng) + YC
  'x,y location of the opposite valley
  XptB = Lmin * Cos((K - 1) * PointAng - RotAng) + XC
  YptB = Lmin * Sin((K - 1) * PointAng - RotAng) + YC
  'Draw the three lines
```

293

```
     Pic.Line (XptR, YptR)-(Xpt, Ypt), WHITE
     Pic.Line (Xpt, Ypt)-(XptL, YptL), WHITE
     Pic.Line (Xpt, Ypt)-(XptB, YptB), WHITE
Next K
End Sub
```

This procedure first defines Lmin and Lmax as one quarter and three quarters of the point length SLen. It then defines PointAng as 1.26 radians, which is the angle between two points on a 5-pointed star; HPointAng, which is half PointAng; and RotAng, the angle through which you want to rotate the star before drawing it.

Using this data, the procedure starts a For/Next loop over the five points on a star. The block of code within the loop calculates the following four x,y locations on a star's point.

- Xpt,Ypt: The location of the tip of the point.

- XptR,YptR: The valley between two points to the right of the firs point.

- XptL,YptL: The location of the valley to the left of the first point.

- XptB, YptB: The location of the valley between two points, on the opposite side of the star from the point being drawn.

Finally, three lines are drawn on the object, one on each side of a point and one down the center. The line down the center fills the object when it is small. The loop causes five points to be drawn on the Picture window, rotating each to line up the valley points.

13. Save the procedure, run it, and press the **Draw Star** button. A star like the one in Figure 12.12 is drawn. Note how each point is made up of three lines. When they are drawn small, the points appear to be filled.

Now, draw the flag.

 14. Draw a command button and set its properties to

```
Height = 380
Width = 1215
Top = 3120
Left = 4080
Caption = Draw Flag
Name = FlagCmd
```

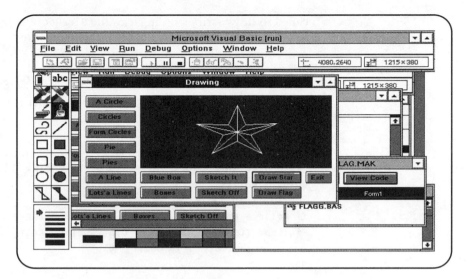

Figure 12.12. *Execution of the* Draw Star *program.*

15. Open the FlagCmd_Click procedure and type

```
Sub FlagCmd_Click ()
'Draw an American Flag
Dim theFlag As FlagType
theFlag.Xmin = 0        'Bounding box
theFlag.Xmax = 44
theFlag.Ymin = 0
theFlag.Ymax = 26
theFlag.Stripe = 2    'Stripe height
theFlag.Rbox = 26      'Right side of the star box
ScaleIt theFlag, BlackBoard
BlackBoard.Cls
DrawStripes theFlag, BlackBoard
BlueRec theFlag, BlackBoard
DrawStars theFlag, BlackBoard
End Sub
```

This time the theFlag record type variable is loaded with values that create a flag. The width of the bounding box is 44 user-defined units, and the height is 26; each stripe is 2 units tall, and the blue box is 26 units wide. After the record type variable is loaded, the ScaleIt procedure is called to scale the Picture box, Cls is called to clear it, and the DrawStripes Sub procedure is

called to draw stripes on it. Next, the `BlueRec` `Sub` procedure is
called to draw the blue rectangle, and finally, the `DrawStars` `Sub`
procedure is called to draw the stars.

16. Create a new procedure named `DrawStripes` and type

```
Sub DrawStripes (C As FlagType, Pic As Control)
'Draw stripes
Dim I As Integer, Color As Double
'Calculate the position of the stripes, and
'alternate the colors between RED and WHITE.
Color = WHITE
For I = 1 To 13
If Color = WHITE Then Color = RED Else Color = WHITE
Pic.Line (C.Xmin, (I - 1) * C.Stripe)-(C.Xmax, I *
          ➥C.Stripe), Color, BF
Next I
End Sub
```

This procedure draws the 13 alternating red and white stripes.
There are actually 6 long stripes and 7 short stripes, but draw 13
long stripes, and then draw the blue rectangle over them. The
procedure first defines the variable `Color` as white, and creates a
loop over the 13 stripes, starting at the bottom. The first statement
in the `For`/`Next` loop causes the value of `Color` to alternate between
red and white. The second uses the `Line` command with the `B` and
`F` options to draw a stripe.

17. Create a new procedure named `DrawStars` and type

```
Sub DrawStars (C As FlagType, Pic As Control)
Dim I As Integer, J As Integer
'Calculate the position of each star, then draw it.
DX = C.Rbox / 12
DY = 7 * C.Stripe / 10
'First the 5 rows of 6 stars
For I = 1 To 5
  For J = 1 To 6
    XC = -DX + J * 2 * DX
    YC = 6 * C.Stripe - DY + I * 2 * DY
    Star XC, YC, C.Stripe / 2, Pic
  Next J
Next I
'Next the 4 rows of 5 stars
For I = 1 To 4
```

```
    For J = 1 To 5
      XC = J * 2 * DX
      YC = 6 * C.Stripe + I * 2 * DY
      Star XC, YC, C.Stripe / 2, Pic
    Next J
  Next I
End Sub
```

This last procedure calculates the position of each star on the blue rectangle, and calls the Star Sub procedure to draw them. It does this by first calculating the positions of five rows of six stars, and then calculating the positions of the remaining four rows of five stars. In both cases nested For/Next loops are used. The first loop selects the five rows, and the second selects the six stars along each row. DX and DY are the star-to-star spacings in the horizontal and vertical directions.

18. Save the project, run it, and click the **Draw Flag** button. The flag appears, as shown in Figure 12.13 (see also Plate I), and makes you want to stand up and cheer.

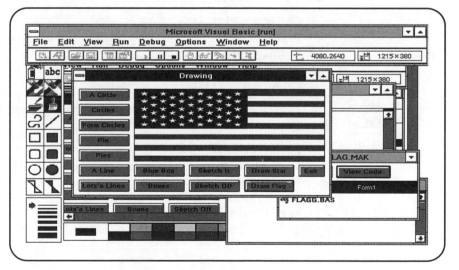

Figure 12.13. Execution of the Draw Flag *program.*

> If you look at Plates I and III, you will notice that they are similar to those developed in the text, but enlarged to full screen. They are actually the same program as the Drawing Test program. I expanded the form to full screen with the **Maximize** button, moved the buttons around and stretched the picture box to fill most of the screen. Since the picture box was used to scale the problem, no changes need to be made to the code. Try this variation, it's simple to do.

The Plot It Program

If you can tear yourself away from the circles and pies, you can put all this together and make something useful. The Plot It program is a simple data plotter that demonstrates the principles of creating a grid and plotting data. The program itself consists of two forms, one for the plot and the second for inputting the data. It's not a sophisticated plotting program, but could easily be expanded, or incorporated into another program.

1. Open a new project, select Form1, and set its properties to

   ```
   Caption = Plot It
   Height = 3700
   Width = 7650
   BorderStyle = 3 - Fixed Double
   MaxButton = False
   ```

2. Draw a picture box on the form as shown in Figure 12.14 and set its properties to

   ```
   Name = PlotPic
   Height = 2540
   Width = 5055
   Top = 240
   Left = 2160
   ```

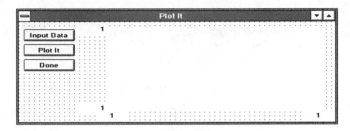

Figure 12.14. *Layout of the* Plot It *program.*

3. Draw a label on the form and set its properties to

```
Caption = 1
Name = YmaxLabel
Alignment = 1 - Right Justify
Height = 260
Width = 615
Top = 120
Left = 1440
```

4. Draw a label on the form and set its properties to

```
Caption = 1
Name = YminLabel
Alignment = 1 - Right Justify
Height = 260
Width = 615
Top = 2640
Left = 1440
```

5. Draw a label on the form and set its properties to

```
Caption = 1
Name = XminLabel
Alignment = 2 - Center
Height = 260
Width = 615
Top = 2880
Left = 1920
```

6. Draw a label on the form and set its properties to

```
Caption = 1
Name = XmaxLabel
Alignment = 2 - Center
```

Do It
Yourself

```
Height = 260
Width = 615
Top = 2880
Left = 6840
```

7. Draw a command button on the form and set its properties to

```
Caption = Input Data
Name = InputCmd
Height = 380
Width = 1215
Top = 240
Left = 120
```

8. Draw a command button on the form and set its properties to the following. Disable this button at the start, because you don't want to plot anything until some data has been inserted.

```
Caption = Plot It
Name = PlotItCmd
Enabled = False
Height = 380
Width = 1215
Top = 720
Left = 120
```

9. Draw a command button on the form and set its properties to

```
Caption = Done
Name = DoneCmd
Height = 380
Width = 1215
Top = 1200
Left = 120
```

10. Create a new module and type

```
Global xyData(500, 2) As Single          'x,y data
Global DataLen As Single                  'length of filled array
Global Xmin As Single, Xmax As Single    'x axis limits
Global Ymin As Single, Ymax As Single    'y axis limits
Global Const asModal = 1
```

The first line defines a large, two-dimensional array to hold the x,y data to be plotted. Next is DataLen, which contains the number of elements of xyData that have been filled with data. Xmin, Xmax, Ymin, and Ymax contain the upper and lower x and y limits for the plot. The last line defines the constant asModal.

11. Select Form1, open the InputCmd_Click procedure and type

```
Sub InputCmd_Click ()
InputDialog.Show Modal
PlotItCmd.Enabled = True
End Sub
```

This procedure displays the second Form as a Modal Form for inputting the data. When that procedure completes, this procedure enables the **Plot It** button.

12. Open the PlotItCmd_Click procedure and type

```
Sub PlotItCmd_Click ()
DrawAxes
PlotData
End Sub
```

This procedure simply calls two other procedures to create the plot, DrawAxes to draw the axes, and PlotData to plot the data.

13. Open the DoneCmd_Click and Form_Unload procedures and type

```
Sub DoneCmd_Click ()
End
End Sub
Sub Form_Unload
End
End Sub
```

14. Create a new procedure named DrawAxes and type

```
Sub DrawAxes ()
Dim VTic As Single, HTic As Single
Dim ShapeFac As Single
ScaleMode = 1
ShapeFac = PlotPic.Width / PlotPic.Height
VTic = .02 * (Ymax - Ymin)
HTic = .02 * (Xmax - Xmin) / ShapeFac
PlotPic.Scale (Xmin - HTic, Ymax + VTic)-(Xmax + HTic, Ymin - VTic)
PlotPic.Line (Xmin - HTic, Ymin)-(Xmax + HTic, Ymin)   'line 9
PlotPic.Line (Xmin, Ymin - VTic)-(Xmin, Ymax + VTic)
PlotPic.Line (Xmax, Ymin - VTic)-(Xmax, Ymax + VTic)
```

```
PlotPic.Line (Xmax / 2, Ymin - VTic)-(Xmax / 2, Ymin + VTic)
PlotPic.Line (Xmin - HTic, Ymax)-(Xmin + HTic, Ymax)
PlotPic.Line (Xmin - HTic, Ymax / 2)-(Xmin + HTic, Ymax / 2)
XminLabel.Caption = Str$(Xmin)                          'line 15
XmaxLabel.Caption = Str$(Xmax)
YminLabel.Caption = Str$(Ymin)
YmaxLabel.Caption = Str$(Ymax)
End Sub
```

This procedure draws the axes on the PlotPic picture box. In line 4, it resets the scale to twips, and then, in line 5, it calculates ShapeFac, a shape factor, from the width and height of the picture box. ShapeFac is used to adjust the length of horizontal lines so that they appear the same length as similar vertical lines, even though the box isn't square. Next, the routine defines VTic and HTic, the vertical and horizontal Tic mark lengths, as two percent of the height or width of the box, with HTic adjusted with ShapeFac.

Next, the routine uses the Scale method to set the scale of the picture box to that stored in Xmin, Xmax, Ymin, and Ymax. The minimum and maximum values are moved in from the edge of the picture box by the Tic amount so there is room to draw the Tic marks. In lines 9 through 14, the procedure uses the Line method to draw the x and y axes, and Tic marks at the ends and centers of each axis. In lines 15 through 18, the values of the upper and lower limits are inserted into the labels that mark those limits.

15. Create a new procedure named PlotData and type

```
Sub PlotData ()
Dim I As Integer
PlotPic.CurrentX = xyData(1, 1)
PlotPic.CurrentY = xyData(1, 2)
For I = 2 To DataLen
  PlotPic.Line -(xyData(I, 1), xyData(I, 2))
Next I
End Sub
```

The PlotData procedure plots the data on the existing grid. It first moves the drawing point to the first x,y data point by setting the values of the CurrentX and CurrentY properties. It then loops over all the data in the xyData array, using the Line method with only one data point to draw lines from the current position to that given in the argument to the method.

This completes the plotting portion of the program. Now it's time to plot some data. In this demonstration, I create a simple dialog box for inputting the data. Depending on your application, you might have the data produced by a calculation, or read from a data file. To make the plotting portion work, you have to fill the data array xyData(), put the number of data points in the DataLen variable, and set the plot limits in the Xmin, Xmax, Ymin, and Ymax variables.

16. Attach a new form to the project and set its properties to

```
Caption = Input Dialog
Name = Input Dialog
Height = 3700
Width = 5250
BorderStyle = 3 - Fixed Double
MinButton = False
MaxButton = False
```

17. Draw a text box on the form, as shown in Figure 12.15, and set its properties to

```
Name = DataBox
Height = 2540
Width = 2295
Top = 480
Left = 120
ScrollBars = 2 - Vertical
MultiLine = True
Text = ''
```

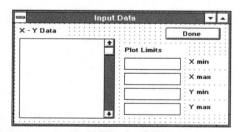

Figure 12.15. Layout of the Input dialog box.

18. Draw four text boxes to hold the plot limits, and set their properties according to Table 12.1.

Table 12.1. Properties for the four Text boxes.

Name	Height	Width	Left	Top	Text
XminBox	380	1335	2640	1080	" "
XmaxBox	380	1335	2640	1560	" "
YminBox	380	1335	2640	2040	" "
YmaxBox	380	1335	2640	2520	" "

19. Draw a label on the form and set its properties to

```
Caption = X-Y Data
Height = 260
Width = 1095
Top = 120
Left = 120
```

20. Draw another label on the form and set its properties to

```
Caption = Plot Limits
Height = 260
Width = 1455
Top = 720
Left = 2640
```

21. Draw four labels on the form and set their properties according to Table 12.2.

Table 12.2. Properties for the four Labels.

Caption	Height	Width	Left	Top
X min	260	855	4200	1080
X max	260	855	4200	1560
Y min	260	855	4200	2040
Y max	260	855	4200	2520

22. Draw a **Done** command button and set its properties to

```
Name = DoneCmd
Caption = Done
```

```
Height = 380
Width = 1335
Top = 120
Left = 3600
```

The following four procedures copy the values of Xmin, Xmax, Ymin, and Ymax from the text boxes into the variables whenever the user types in one of the boxes.

23. Open the XminBox_Change procedure and type

```
Sub XminBox_Change ()
Xmin = Val(XminBox.Text)
End Sub
```

24. Open the XmaxBox_Change procedure and type

```
Sub XmaxBox_Change ()
Xmax = Val(XmaxBox.Text)
End Sub
```

25. Open the YminBox_Change procedure and type

```
Sub YminBox_Change ()
Ymin = Val(YminBox.Text)
End Sub
```

26. Open the YmaxBox_Change procedure and type

```
Sub YmaxBox_Change ()
Ymax = Val(YmaxBox.Text)
End Sub
```

27. Open the DoneCmd_Click procedure and type

```
Sub DoneCmd_Click ()
Dim Start As Integer, End1 As Integer, End2 As Integer
'Check limit boxes
If (XmaxBox.Text = "" Or XminBox.Text = ""
  ➥Or YmaxBox.Text = "" Or YminBox.Text = "") Then
  MsgBox 'Type plot limits first.'
  Exit Sub
End If
'Load the data array
DataLen = 0
Start = 1
End1 = InStr(Start, DataBox.Text, ",")                    'line 11
End2 = InStr(End1 + 1, DataBox.Text, Chr$(13))
```

305

```
While End1 <> 0 And End2 <> 0                           'line 13
  DataLen = DataLen + 1
  xyData(DataLen, 1) = Val(Mid$(DataBox.Text, Start, End1 -
Start))
  xyData(DataLen, 2) = Val(Mid$(DataBox.Text, End1 + 1,
      ➥End2 - End1 - 1))
  Start = End2 + 1
  End1 = InStr(Start, DataBox.Text, ',')
  End2 = InStr(End1 + 1, DataBox.Text, Chr$(13))
Wend
InputDialog.Hide
End Sub
```

This procedure must take the data out of the text box, convert it to numbers, and store those numbers in the data array. You have to type x,y data into the text box, separating the x,y values with commas and pressing Enter after each y data value. In line 4, the procedure first checks the four plot limit boxes to see that the user has typed data in each one. If not, the procedure puts up an error message and exits. If data has been typed in all the boxes, the procedure begins looking for data in the DataBox text box.

Using the InStr() function in line 11, it locates the first comma in the Text property of DataBox and assigns the character number to End1. In line 12 it looks for the first carriage return (ASCII code 13) and assigns its location to End2. The x data should be between the beginning of the string and the comma, and the y data should be between the comma and the carriage return. In line 13, the procedure starts a While/Wend loop that continues until the InStr() functions don't find any more values. If a pair of values is found, the values are added to the data array.

In line 14, the value of DataLen is incremented. In line 15 the Mid$() function is used to extract the substring containing the x value from the Text property of DataBox. The value lies between character positions Start and End1. The extracted substring is immediately converted to a value with the Val() function and stored in xyData. Line 16 does the same for the y value. In line 17, the starting position stored in Start is moved to one character beyond the carriage return. The procedure then looks for another comma and carriage return. This loop continues until it can't find any more numbers. The procedure then hides itself, and returns to Form1 so you can plot the data.

28. Save the project as PLOT.MAK, PLOT1.FRM, PLOT2.FRM, and PLOTG.BAS.

29. Run the program, press the **Input Data** button and type some data, including the plot limits. The Input dialog box should look like Figure 12.16.

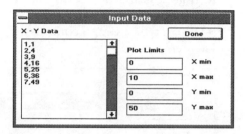

Figure 12.16. The Input dialog box for the Plot It *program.*

30. Click **Done** on the Input dialog box, then press the **Plot It** button on Form1. The data is plotted in the picture box, which should now look like Figure 12.17.

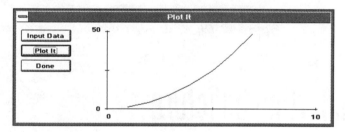

Figure 12.17. Plotting data with the Plot It *program.*

Many variations of this program can be created, because it is still in a primitive form. It lacks labels for the axes and a title, which could be loaded in the Input dialog box. It also automatically could calculate the plot limits by examining the maximum and minimum values in the data. How you change it depends on what you want it to do. Don't let the fact that this is a simple plot program make you think that it has limited scope. As Figure 12.18 shows, you can use this program to create a 3-D wireframe plot. In fact, the plot form is identical to that

continues

307

developed here in this text. The wireframe plot is created completely by manipulating the data. The plotted data is Cos(x π2)Cos (y π/2)Exp(xy/10).

The Pro Version of Visual Basic contains a graph control that is used to draw a graph object on a form. The type of graph is set by its properties, and includes bar charts, pie charts, line graphs, and a few 3-D chart types. Graph controls are also available from other manufacturers.

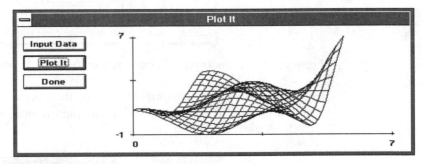

Figure 12.18. *A 3-D wireframe plot created with the* Plot It *program.*

Importing a Picture

Drawing pictures is fun, but you might have a more complicated illustration that you want to import into a picture box or a form. At design-time, you do this in exactly the same manner that you created the arrow keys in the Datebook program. Select the object you want to attach the drawing to, and select its Picture property. Click the ellipsis (...) in the Settings window and a File window opens for you to select the file containing the picture. When you select it, the picture is imported into your object and displayed.

You can do similar things at run-time, using the LoadPicture() function. The function has the syntax

```
LoadPicture[(path$)]
```

Here, *path$* is the path and name of the picture file to load. Equate the Picture Property of a form or picture box to this function to load it. Visual Basic currently recognizes bit map (.BMP), icon (.ICO), and Windows metafile (.WMF) files.

If you have a picture in a window and want to save it in a file, use the SavePicture statement. The SavePicture statement has the syntax

SavePicture *picturevariable, path$*

Here, the *picturevariable* argument is the Picture or Image property of a form or picture box, and *path$* is a string containing the path and file name of the file in which to store the picture. Pictures are saved as bit maps (.BMP) files.

What You Have Learned

In this chapter, you read about the Visual Basic methods that draw on a form. Forms and picture boxes are the only screen objects that can be drawn on. The Printer object also may be drawn on to produce printed graphics. In detail, you have read about

- Using the Circle method to draw circles and pie sections.

- Using the Line method to draw lines and rectangles.

- Using the PSet method to set the color of a point on the screen.

- Using the Point method to set the color of a point on the screen.

- Importing pictures with LoadPicture and saving pictures with SavePicture.

Debugging and Error Trapping

You've just completed your latest and greatest application that will surely bring the world rushing to your door, but when you run it, it does something entirely unexpected. Say hello to a programming bug. There is no way to completely avoid these little monsters, so now you must look at what you can do about them. (Kicking the computer might make you feel better, but won't make the bugs go away.).

In This Chapter

This chapter covers two related topics, debugging and error trapping. Although they sound similar, they are inherently different. Debugging is the process of eliminating known errors from a program. These errors include misspelled keywords, misplaced commas, and incorrect program logic. Error trapping is the process of handling errors that you cannot eliminate by changing the code. Errors which can be trapped include numeric

overflow and divide-by-zero. These types of errors are caused, for the most part, by unexpected values appearing in a formula. In this chapter, you learn how to

- Debug applications.
- Locate and fix syntax errors.
- Locate and fix logical errors.
- Use tools that find errors.
- Use error trapping.
- Handle trapped errors.

The Art of Debugging

Debugging computer programs is more art than engineering, which is often disconcerting to new programmers who are becoming used to the rigid structure of a computer language. But there is no rigorous method for locating programming bugs. Successfully locating logical errors in complex programs calls on all of a programmer's knowledge and experience. The more the programmer knows about the operation of the language, the nature of the problem to be solved, and even the basic electronic operation of a computer, the more quickly he or she can locate the problem. Fixing a problem is usually trivial compared to finding it.

However, now that I have worried you somewhat, I must add that being able to locate and fix a problem in a huge mass of code is an extremely rewarding experience, with nearly immediate gratification. When a bug is fixed, the program works, (well, most of the time) right now. In no other branch of engineering can you so quickly fix a problem and see the results.

Luckily, the complexity of your programs increases gradually with your experience and ability, so the increase in bugs you generate is gradual, too. Don't be overly worried about the bugs in your programs; finding them is part of the fun.

The first step in debugging is having well documented, modularized code. Keep code blocks and procedures reasonably small and as single-minded as possible. That is, make sure the function of each block or procedure is well defined and well known. Use remarks liberally, especially whenever you do something that isn't obvious. This adds to the work of creating a code, but it dramatically reduces the time needed to correct or change one.

The second step in debugging is to realize that a computer is completely logical, and does exactly what you tell it to do. A program bug can make a computer seem to have a peculiar mind of its own, but realize it is actually doing what you told it to do, literally. With that in mind, read on and discover bugs.

Syntax Errors

The most common bug is the syntax error, and it is also the easiest to find. Most syntax errors are found by the Visual Basic interpreter as soon as you type a line of code. Others show up as soon as you try to compile or run your code. Thus, syntax errors come in two flavors, design-time and compile-time.

Syntax errors are generated when you stray from the strict guidelines, or grammar, of the computer language. They involve misspelling key words, inserting the wrong number or type of arguments to a function, and inserting the wrong punctuation in a programming statement.

Design-Time Syntax Errors

Design-time errors are revealed to you when you are typing your code. They are errors that involve the syntax of a single line of code, such as missed punctuation or misspelled key words. The design-time interpreter looks at each line you type as soon as you move the cursor out of that line. It then compares what you have typed with the syntax of the language. It cannot check the value or type of variables in a statement, only the number and punctuation. If it can't make sense of what you have done, it tells you so.

You probably already have seen several of these errors as you have typed the example programs in this book. Either that, or you are a splendid typist, and never make a mistake. I wish I had that capability, but my fingers don't always seem to do what my head is telling them to do, so I generate syntax errors frequently. Luckily, I know right away when I have made an error, and can fix it.

13

313

Compile-Time Syntax Errors

The second type of syntax error is the compile-time error. Compile-time errors occur when you run a program in interpreted mode or compile it into an executable file. In both cases, the structure of a program is checked before attempting to run or compile it. Compile-time errors occur when you use the wrong type of argument in a function, or have incorrect block structures. Most Visual Basic functions and methods require specific variable types as arguments. If you give a function the wrong variable type, the compile-time syntax checker stops the program, displays the offending program line, and displays a message about possible corrections to the line. This can be done only when trying to run or compile code because the code that defines the variable types, in this case, the Dim and Global statements, is physically separated from the place the variable is actually used. For example,

```
Dim B as Integer
A = Val(B)
```

The Val() function expects B to be a String variable. As the point of execution reaches the first statement, B is defined as an Integer. When it reaches the second statement, Val() generates an error.

Another common compile-time error is misused block structures, such as a block If statement missing its End If statement, or a For/Next loop missing its Next statement. Again, these errors cannot be determined at design time, but are revealed when you attempt to run the code and check whether blocks are incorrectly set up. For example,

```
A = 3 * 5
Printer.Print A
Next I
```

The Next I statement has to have a matching For statement, so this code generates a compile-time error.

Run-time Errors

Run-time errors are those errors that occur in a running program. Arithmetic errors, such as overflow and divide-by-zero, are run-time errors. Most of these errors are determined by the hardware, and passed back to

Visual Basic, which stops the code and sends you a message. Arithmetic errors often result from a logical error in the program design, when the wrong values are inserted into a calculation. For example,

```
A = 3 * 0
B = 1/A
```

generates a divide-by-zero error because A is incorrectly set to zero.

File system errors occur when a requested file-related action cannot be completed (for example, when you open a file for input that does not exist, or print to a file that has not yet been opened). Again, these types of errors usually result from logical errors in a program's design. Table 13.1 contains a list of the Visual Basic run-time errors, and error numbers.

The first two columns of this table were generated with the following simple piece of code, which printed the table into the Immediate pane of the Debug window. The Error$() function produces Visual Basic's error message for the given error number used as an argument. If there is no error defined for a number, it returns "User-defined error." The If statement skips all the undefined error numbers.

```
Sub Form_Click ()
For I = 1 To 1000
  If Error$(I) <> "User-defined error" Then
    Debug.Print I, Error$(I)
  End If
Next I
End Sub
```

Table 13.1. Visual Basic run-time errors.

Code	Error	Description
3	Return without GoSub	A Return statement was encountered without a corresponding GoSub.
5	Illegal function call	This is usually caused by calling a function with invalid or out of range arguments (for example, Sqr(-1)).
6	Overflow	The result of some calculation was greater than the largest number that can be stored in the variable to receive that result.

continues

Table 13.1. continued

Code	Error	Description
7	Out of memory	Code and data storage have filled all available memory.
9	Subscript out of range	The value of an array subscript is not within the range defined in the Dim or Global statement.
10	Duplicate definition	A variable was defined with the same name as a variable that already exists.
11	Division by zero	A numeric calculation has a zero in the denominator.
13	Type mismatch	A string variable has been equated to a numeric variable, or a function argument is the wrong type.
14	Out of string space	All the strings in the modules or Forms use more than 64K bytes of memory.
16	String formula too complex	A string expression is too complicated to evaluate break it into smaller segments.
17	Can't continue	A change was made in break mode that prevents a code from being restarted.
19	No Resume	An On Error statement is active and missing its Resume statement.
20	Resume without error	A Resume statement was encountered without an active On Error statement.
28	Out of stack space	The memory reserved for storage of local variables and procedure calls is full.
35	Sub or Function not defined	An undefined procedure was called.

Code	Error	Description
48	Error in loading DLL	Something is wrong with a DLL library file that was accessed.
49	Bad DLL calling convention	Something is wrong with the interface to a DLL routine.
51	Internal error	An internal Visual Basic error, probably a bug in Visual Basic.
52	Bad file name or number	A file name or number is being used for a file that hasn't been opened yet.
53	File not found	An attempt has been made to access a file that doesn't exist.
54	Bad file mode	`Get#` or `Put#` was used with a sequential file, or `Input#` or `Print#` was used on files opened for Output only or Input only.
55	File already open	An attempt has been made to Open a sequential file that is already open, or to `Kill` an open file.
57	Device I/O error	A device driver has issued an error.
58	File already exists	A `Name` statement was used to change a file name to one that already exists.
59	Bad record length	A record variable is larger than the record length specified in the `Open` statement.
61	Disk full	A disk filled up while writing a file.
62	Input past end of file	An attempt has been made to read beyond the end-of-file marker on a file.
63	Bad record number	A negative record number was specified in a `Get#` or `Put#` statement.

continues

Table 13.1. continued

Code	Error	Description
64	Bad file name	A file name was specified that does not follow DOS conventions.
67	Too many files	The number of files open at any one time has been exceeded.
68	Device unavailable	A device, such as a printer, is currently off-line.
70	Permission denied	An attempt has been made to write to a locked or protected file.
71	Disk not ready	A floppy disk isn't inserted or the door on a drive isn't closed.
74	Can't rename with different drive	A Name statement attempted to move a file to a different drive.
75	Path/File access error	A path-file combination does not exist, or an attempt to write a write protected file occurred.
76	Path not found	A path does not exist.
91	Object variable not Set	The object variable you are using to install an object does not contain a valid object.
92	For loop not initialized	Jump into the middle of loop.
93	Invalid pattern string	The pattern string in a search operation is invalid.
94	Invalid use of Null	Attempting to take the value of a variable or expression that contains Null.
95	Cannot destroy active form instance	Attempting to destroy a form instance that contains active procedures.

Code	Error	Description
260	No Timer available	An attempt has been made to allocate more than 16 Timers.
280	DDE channel not closed	Awaiting response from foreign application. An attempt was made to start a new DDE connection before an old one was fully closed.
281	No More DDE channels	Too many DDE channels are open.
282	No foreign application responded to a DDE initiate	A DDE initiate request was sent to an external application and it didn't reply. The foreign application may be closed, slow or may not recognize the request.
283	Multiple applications responded to a DDE initiate	More than one application responded to a DDE initiate request.
284	DDE channel locked	An attempt was made to use a DDE link that is already in use.
285	Foreign application won't perform DDE method or operation	An operation was requested that a foreign application doesn't recognize.
286	Timeout while waiting for DDE response	A foreign application is not responding.
287	User pressed Alt key during DDE operation	The Alt key was pressed while a DDE conversation was in progress.
288	Destination is busy	The foreign application is busy and won't respond to a DDE request.
289	Data not provided in DDE operation	An unexpected error occurred during a DDE conversation.
290	Data in wrong format	Data returned by a foreign application is the wrong type.

continues

Table 13.1. continued

Code	Error	Description
291	Foreign application quit	The foreign application quit without ending the DDE link.
292	DDE conversation closed or changed	The foreign application unexpectedly closed the link.
293	DDE Method invoked with no channel open	A DDE method was executed on a nonexistent link.
294	Invalid DDE Link format	The foreign application sent data that is not in DDE link format.
295	Message queue filled; DDE message lost	When the DDE message queue is filled, new messages are lost.
296	PasteLink already performed on this control	An attempt to establish a link using the PasteLink command occurred to a control that is already involved in a link.
297	Can't set LinkMode; invalid LinkTopic	The LinkTopic is invalid in an attempt to change the LinkMode.
298	DDE requires ddeml.dll	The DDEML.DLL file, needed for DDE operations, cannot be located.
320	Can't use character device names in file names	A device name, like LPT1 was used as a file name.
321	Invalid file format	A Form file is damaged.
340	Control array element ' ' does not exist	A control array index is out of range.
341	Invalid object array index	A control array index is larger than 32,767 or less than 0.
342	Not enough room to allocate control array ' '	Not enough memory to create a control array.

Code	Error	Description
343	Object not an array	An index was applied to an object that is not a control array.
344	Must specify index for object array	A control array was accessed without an index.
345	Reached limit: cannot create any more controls for this Form	Created more than 255 controls on a Form.
360	Object already loaded	A control specified in a control array is already loaded.
361	Can't load or unload this object	An attempt was made to load or unload a system object, such as a Printer, or to unload a nonarray control.
362	Can't unload controls created at design time	An attempt was made to unload a control loaded at design time.
363	Custom control ' ' not found	A custom control on a Form is not yet attached to a project.
364	Object was unloaded	A Form was unloaded by its own `Form_Load` procedure.
365	Unable to unload within this context	A Form could not be unloaded.
366	No MDI Form available to load	No MDI Form is available to load
380	Invalid property value	An invalid value was applied to a property.
381	Invalid property array index	An index applied to a property that accepts an index is less than 0 or greater than 32,767.
382	' ' property cannot be set at run time	An attempt was made to change a property that only can be changed at design time.

continues

Table 13.1. continued

Code	Error	Description
383	'' property is read-only	An attempt was made to change a read-only property.
384	'' property can't be modified when Form is minimized or maximized	An attempt was made to change Top, Left, Height, or Width with the Form maximized or minimized.
385	Must specify index when using property array	An attempt was made to access the Fonts or List property, without using an array index.
386	'' property not available at run time	An attempt was made to access Name at run time.
387	'' property can't be set on this control	An attempt was made to check a top level menu, or make all submenus invisible.
388	Can't set Visible property from a parent menu	A submenu head cannot set the visible property of a submenu item.
389	Invalid key	
390	No Defined Value	
391	Name not available	A custom control attempted to get the name of an object from an executable (.EXE) file. Names are only available in interpreted codes.
392	MDI child forms cannot be hidden	Attempted to hide an MDI child form with Hide or by setting the Visible property to False.
393	'' property cannot be read at run time	Attempted to read a design-time only property.
394	'' property is write-only	Attempted to read a property that can only be written.
395	Can't use separator bar as menu name	Attempted to use as a menu name.

Code	Error	Description
400	Form already displayed; can't show modally	An attempt was made to make a Form modal that was already visible.
401	Can't show non-modal Form when modal Form is displayed	An attempt was made to show a nonmodal Form while a modal Form is visible.
402	Must close or hide topmost modal Form first	An attempt was made to hide or unload a modal Form that has other modal Forms above it. Modal Forms must be unloaded from the top down.
403	MDI forms cannot be shown modally	MDI parent forms cannot be modal.
404	MDI child forms cannot be shown modally	MDI child forms cannot be modal.
420	Invalid object reference	An object was referenced on an unloaded Form.
421	Method not applicable for this object	An inappropriate method was applied to an object.
422	Property '' not found	A property was referenced that does not apply to the object in the reference.
423	Property or control '' not found	A property or control was referenced that is not part of the referenced Form.
424	Object required	A property was used in a reference where an object should be.
425	Invalid object use	An attempt was made to assign a value to a control or Form rather than to a property.

continues

Table 13.1. continued

Code	Error	Description
426	Only one MDI Form allowed	Only one MDI parent form is allowed in an application.
460	Invalid Clipboard format	The specified Clipboard format is incompatible with the method being used.
461	Specified format does not match format of data	The specified Clipboard format does not match the data being transferred.
480	Can't create `AutoRedraw` image	Not enough memory to create the persistent bit map.
481	Invalid picture	Data assigned to the `Picture` property isn't a recognizable picture.
482	Printer error	There is some problem with the printer.
520	Can't empty Clipboard	Another application is using the Clipboard and won't release it.
521	Can't open Clipboard	Another application is using the Clipboard and won't release it.
600	Set value not allowed on collections	Attempted to set the property of a member of a collection.
601	Get value not allowed on collections	Attempted to get the value of a property of a member of a collection.
602	General ODBC error: ' '	General database error.
603	ODBC— SQLAllocEnv failure	Unable to allocate a database handle. Probably insufficient memory.
604	ODBC— SQLAllocConnect failure	Unable to allocate a database handle. Probably insufficient memory.
605	OpenDatabase— invalid connect string	An invalid connection string was used with the OpenDatabase call.

Code	Error	Description
606	ODBC—SQLConnect failure: ' '	Unable to connect to a database.
607	Access attempted on unopened DataBase	An operation was requested on a database that has not yet been opened.
608	ODBC—SQLFree Connect error	Unable to free a database handle.
609	ODBC—GetDriverFunctions failure	Unable to determine the functions of a database driver.
610	ODBC—SQLAllocStmt failure	Unable to allocate a handle for a database statement. Probably insufficient memory.
611	ODBC—SQLTables (TableDefs.Refresh) failure: ' '	Unable to get database tables.
612	ODBC—SQLBindCol failure	Unable to bind database to memory.
613	ODBC—SQLFetch failure: ' '	Unable to get a record from the database.
614	ODBC—SQLColumns (Fields.Refresh) failure: ' '	Unable to determine the fields in a database.
615	ODBC—SQLStatistics (Indexes.Refresh) failure: ' '	Unable to get the index to a database.
616	Table exists—append not allowed	Attempting to append a table that already exists. Try changing the table's name.
617	No fields defined—cannot append table	Attempting to append a table that does not contain any fields. Append fields to the table first.

13

Table 13.1. continued

Code	Error	Description
618	ODBC— SQLNumResultCols (CreateDynaset) failure: ' '	Can not determine the number of columns in a Dynaset.
619	ODBC— SQLDescibeCol (CreateDynaset) failure: ' '	Cannot get the type of columns in a Dynaset.
620	Dynaset is open— Create Dynaset method not allowed	Only one Dynaset may be open at a time.
621	Row-returning SQL is illegal in ExecuteSQL method	Row-returning SQL functions are not allowed in this method.
622	CommitTrans/ Rollback illegal— Transactions not supported	The database driver does not allow these transactions.
623	Name not found in this collection	A column name is not in an object collection.
624	Unable to Build Data Type Table	OpenDatabase command cannot determine data types. Possibly insufficient memory.
625	Data type of field ' ' not supported by target database	The database does not support a field of this type.
626	Attempt to Move past EOF	A record was requested beyond the end of file.
627	Dynaset can't be updated or Edit method has not been invoked	Attempted to update a Dynaset that can't be updated.

Code	Error	Description
628	'' Dynaset method illegal — no scroll-able cursor support	The Move method was requested, which is not allowed.
629	Warning: (ODBC — SQLSetConnect-Option failure)	Something failed.
630	Property is read-only	Attempted to set a read-only property.
631	Zero rows affected by Update method	Update was called, but nothing was changed.
632	Update illegal without previous Edit or AddNew method	Update was called without editing or adding a new record.
633	Append illegal— Field is part of a TableDefs collection	A field was appended to a table when it is already a part of a table.
634	Property value only valid when Field is part of a Dynaset	A Field property was accessed and the Field was not part of a Dynaset.
635	Cannot set the property of an object which is part of a Database object	Attempted to change the value of a property of an open database.
636	Set field value illegal without previous Edit or AddNew method	Edit or AddNew must be issued before changing the Value property of a Field.
637	Append illegal— Index is part of a TableDefs collection	An index was appended to an object, and it is already a part of another object.

continues

13

Table 13.1. continued

Code	Error	Description
638	Access attempted on unopened Dynaset	A Dynaset must be opened before it can be accessed.
639	Field type is illegal	A Field type was specified that is not allowed.
640	Field size illegal for specified Field Type	The specified Field size is illegal.
641	Illegal—no current record	Edit or Delete called without a current record.
642	Reserved parameter must be FALSE	The Exclusive argument of an OpenDatabase call must be FALSE.
643	Property Not Found	A property was accessed that does not exist.
644	ODBC— SQLConfigData Source error ' '	A RegisterDatabase call failed.
645	ODBC Driver does not support exclusive access to Dynasets	Exclusive access requested for a Dynaset and the driver does not allow it.
646	GetChunk: Offset/ Size argument combination illegal	The size or the offset in a GetChunk operation is invalid.
647	Delete method requires a name argument	A Delete was executed without specifying a name.
648	ODBC Objects require VBODBCA.DLL	The VBODBCA.DLL file could not be found.
708	File not found: ' '	The indicated file could not be found. Check the name and path.

Logical Errors

Logical errors occur when the computer is doing what you told it to do, but not what you wanted it to do. When you are lucky, the cause is obvious and you fix it. More often, these errors are hard to find, because the cause can be far from the statement that produced the outward appearance. For example, if you get a divide-by-zero error, the statement that made the divisor zero can be far from the statement where the division operation occurred. A logical error might not even generate an error message, but result in an incorrect value calculated and printed by a program. Here's where your experience and intuition come into play.

The Timer Program

This simple little program illustrates a logical bug—see whether you can find it. The program uses the timer control on the Toolbox window. The timer is basically an alarm clock that runs in the background and generates a Timer event whenever its time runs out. The timer's Interval property stores the amount of time to wait, in milliseconds, before generating a Timer event. Using the Timer to generate one-second events, this program counts those events, and displays the value of the counter in a label.

1. Open a new project, select Form1, and set its properties to

```
Caption = The Timer
Height = 1340
Width = 5130
BorderStyle = 3 - fixed double
ControlBox = False
MaxButton = False
MinButton = False
```

2. Draw a label on the form, as shown in Figure 13.1, with these properties:

```
Height = 620
Width = 3015
Top = 120
Left = 720
Caption = ""
FontSize = 24
```

Figure 13.1. *Layout for the Timer program.*

 3. Draw a command button on the form with these properties:

```
Name = OnCmd
Height = 500
Width = 855
Top = 120
Left = 3960
Caption = On/Off
```

 4. Draw a timer to the left of the label. The location isn't important because the timer is invisible in the running application. Set its properties to

```
Interval = 1000
Enabled = False
```

5. Open the Timer1_Timer procedure and type

```
Sub Timer1_Timer ()
Dim I As Integer
I = I + 1
Label1.Caption = Str$(I)
End Sub
```

This procedure is executed whenever the Timer event occurs, which is once per second. When executed, it increments the value of I by 1 and inserts that number in the Caption property of the label; thus the label counts seconds whenever the timer is running.

6. Open the OnCmd_Click procedure and type

```
Sub OnCmd_Click ()
Timer1.Enabled = Not Timer1.Enabled
End Sub
```

This procedure turns the timer on and off by applying the Not logical operator on the timer's Enabled property. The Not operator changes True to False or False to True.

7. Save the project as TIMER.MAK and TIMER.FRM.

8. Run the program and click the **On/Off** button.

What happens? The timer doesn't count, but displays a 1 all the time. This isn't what you told the computer to do—or is it? In the next few sections, you will learn how to track down the problem.

To locate a logical error, gather all the information you have about it—where it occurred: what did you do, step-by-step, just before the error occurred, what the program was doing, what was the error, or whatever you have. Use this information to estimate the most probable cause of the error and then check that piece of code. If that doesn't work, try using some of the debugging tools (discussed in the next section) to get more information about the bug and what it's doing. Keep gathering information and looking at the code until you find out what is happening.

Debugging Tools

Not all of debugging is done through intuition and magic. There are some excellent tools built into Visual Basic that greatly reduce the amount of work involved in locating and fixing programming bugs. In fact, it's much easier to debug Visual Basic programs than those in most other high-level languages, primarily because Visual Basic is an interpreted language. This means you can make changes and adjustments in the code and immediately run it to see the results. In fact, you can make adjustments while the code is running by issuing the Break command, making the change, then issuing the Continue command.

The difference between a compiler and an interpreter is found in the way they convert and execute code. An interpreter directly executes the text file containing the code you have written, while a compiler converts it into a file of machine language codes first, then executes those machine language codes. Machine language codes are the numeric codes that the microprocessor in your computer executes. Interpreters still have to convert the text version of a code into machine language, but they do it one line at a time. An interpreter reads a single line of code, converts it to machine language, executes it, then continues with the next line of code. A compiler converts the whole code into machine language first, then it executes the machine language.

Breaking a Running Code

There are six ways to break a running code:

- Pressing the Break tool on the toolbar.

- Pressing Ctrl-Break.

- Selecting Brea**k** on the **R**un menu.

- Encountering a Stop statement in a program.

- Encountering a breakpoint inserted with the Toggle **B**reakpoint command on the **D**ebug menu.

- Having a condition occur that was set in a watchpoint.

A seventh way is encountering a run time error, which automatically breaks the code at the line where the error occurs.

When a program is in Break mode you can examine code in the code windows, print values in the Immediate pane of the Debug window, change the values of variables, and even change code. When you are done, issue the **C**ontinue command on the **R**un menu, and your code starts up where it left off.

To break a code using the Break tool, Ctrl-Break, or the Brea**k** command on the **R**un menu, the code must first be running. These three commands are somewhat imprecise about their stopping points in code, because as soon as you issue one of these commands, it immediately stops execution, opens a code window, and displays the next line it is going to execute surrounded by a black box. You see something similar when a code encounters a run time error, but then you know the boxed statement is the one causing the error.

The Stop statement and Toggle **B**reakpoint command cause a code to stop in a specific place. You use these when you think you know where a problem is, and want to stop the execution at that spot. The Stop statement is like any other Visual Basic statement. You type it into your code, and when it is executed, the code stops. It is different from the End statement for interpreted code. When an End statement is encountered, the code is stopped and unloaded, and all the variables are erased. You must restart the code from scratch if you use End. Stop, however, simply halts the code. Everything is still in memory and can be restarted from the stopping point.

If you compile the code, though, the Stop statement behaves exactly the same way as an End statement.

To use the Toggle **B**reakpoint command, select the statement where you want the code to stop, and click the Toggle **B**reakpoint command. Your code behaves exactly as if you had inserted a Stop statement there. To remove a breakpoint, select the statement and press Toggle **B**reakpoint again, or click the Clear **A**ll Breakpoints command to remove them all. Breakpoints are not saved with a program, so you don't have to worry about clearing them before saving your program.

Watchpoints are another method to break a running code, but are not attached to a specific location, but to a specific value. A watchpoint can simply display a value, or the result of a formula in the top of the Debug window, or it can initiate a Break in a running code. A watchpoint is inserted with the **A**dd Watch command on the **D**ebug menu. To make a watchpoint break a running code, type a value or a logical equation in the Add Watch dialog box, and click Break when expression is **T**rue, or Break when expression has **C**hanged. When the expression changes as you have indicated in the dialog box, the code is stopped and placed in break mode.

Watchpoints are especially useful when debugging loops. A breakpoint will stop every time it is encountered, while a watchpoint waits only for a condition. For example, if a loop counter is I, and you set the watch equation to I>9 with the option Break when the expression is True; when run, the loop executes 9 times, and on the tenth time it stops and goes into break mode.

Examining and Changing Things

When your code is in Break mode, you can examine code and variables, and even change things. To change code while in Break mode, simply type the changes in the appropriate code window. You can change most statements without affecting the running code. A few things that you can't change are

- Variable definitions, such as those in Dim and Global statements.

- Loop control statements, such as For/Next.

- Sub and Function procedure calls.

If you change these things, your code becomes inconsistent and must be restarted rather than continued. Visual Basic warns you when a change will force a restart.

To examine the values of variables, open the Debug window, Immediate pane and type `Print`, `?`, or the variable name; then press Enter, and the value of the variable is printed. For example, to see the value of a variable called count, type `Print count` or `? count` in the Debug window.

To change the value of a variable, type an assignment statement in the Debug window equating the variable to its new value. For example, to reset the value of count, you could type `count=0` in the Debug window. You can examine or change only those variables in the active call chain. The active call chain includes procedures currently being executed, and those which call procedures that are being executed. Examining and changing any other procedures makes no sense anyway. For example, why would you want to examine a variable that hasn't even been defined yet? Its value has no meaning until it is in the active call chain.

You also can use the Debug window to experiment with functions and formulas. The program executes just about any statement you type, and you can print the results using `Print`. The only restriction is that it can execute only a single line at a time, although you can stack several statements, separated by colons, on one line to execute a short piece of code.

Use the Break mode to figure out what is wrong with the Timer program (bear with me if you have already figured it out).

1. The problem is probably in the `Timer1_Timer` procedure, so open it, insert the cursor in the first executable statement (`I = I + 1`), and execute the Toggle **Breakpoint** command. The statement is displayed in reversed video, as shown in Figure 13.2, to indicate it has a breakpoint set.

2. Run the program and click the **On/Off** button. The program stops at the breakpoint and displays the Code window—see Figure 13.3.

3. Select the Debug window, either by clicking it, or selecting it from the Windows menu. Type `Print I` and press Enter. The value 0 is printed in the Debug window, as you would expect, the first time this procedure is executed.

4. As I mentioned, you can try almost anything in this window. Type `Print Sin(5)`, and the value of the sine of 5 radians appears, as shown in Figure 13.4.

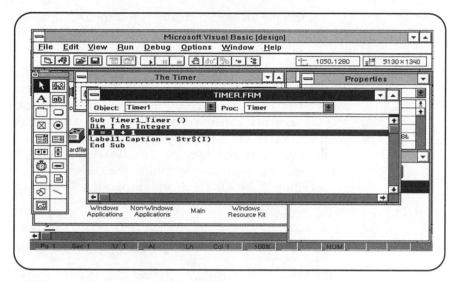

Figure 13.2. *Setting a breakpoint.*

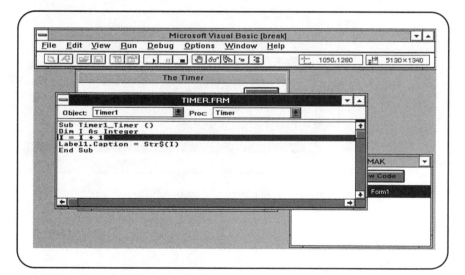

Figure 13.3. *Stopped at a breakpoint.*

5. Select the Continue command from the Run menu or click the start tool on the toolbar. The code runs for a moment, and then

hits the breakpoint again. Select the Debug window and type **Print I** again. It still returns 0. Do this step several times; the value of I is zero every time.

In addition to breakpoints, watchpoints and the Debug window, there is also the Calls window, which lists all the procedures in the current call chain. The call chain is the list of procedures in the currently executing application that have not run to completion. A procedure that calls another procedure stays in the call chain until the other procedure returns and the calling procedure completes. The Calls window is displayed with the **Calls** command on the **Debug** menu. In the Calls window, you can select any procedure in the call chain and display it's Code window by clicking the Show button.

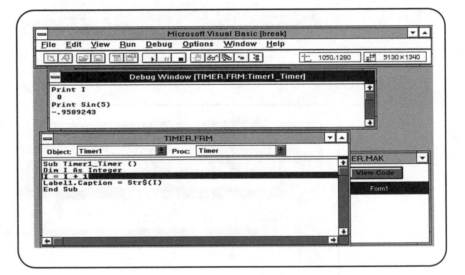

Figure 13.4. *Using the Immediate window.*

Step Mode

Rather than pressing Continue to continue running a program after it has been in Break mode, you can click the **S**ingle Step command on the Debug menu, click the Single Step tool in the toolbar, or press the F8 key to execute one statement of the program and return to Break mode. You use these commands to step through a program, one step at a time, so you can watch the execution and examine the value of the variables at each step.

The **Procedure** Step command on the Debug menu or the procedure Step tool on the toolbar works the same way as the **Single** Step command, except when it reaches a call to another procedure. The **Single** Step command moves to the called procedure and begins executing code there, one step at a time. The **Procedure** Step command runs all the code in the procedure and returns to Break mode only when the called procedure returns to the procedure that called it. Thus, the **Single** Step command moves you throughout your program, but the **Procedure** Step command takes you step by step through a single procedure.

Also useful here are the Show Next Statement and Set **Next** Statement commands on the **Debug** menu. In Break mode, the Show Next Statement command draws a black box around the next statement to be executed. Use it to see where you are in a program. The Set **Next** Statement command changes the execution point to a different statement. Use it to reexecute a statement or block of statements after making a change, and to see the effect of that change.

1. Click the Single Step tool and the execution point moves to the next statement, as shown in Figure 13.5. Select the Debug window and type **Print I**, and the value 1 is returned as you would expect.

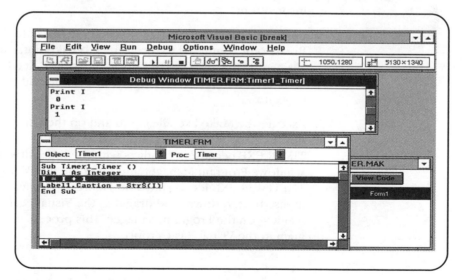

Figure 13.5. *Single stepping to the next statement and checking I again.*

2. Click the **Single Step** tool again, and the execution point moves to the End Sub statement. click the tool a third time and it exits the procedure, waits for the next Timer event, reenters the Timer1_Timer procedure, and stops at the first executable statement (the I = I + 1 statement.) Select the Debug window and type **Print I**, and the value 0 is returned again. I is being incremented as it is supposed to, but it is reset to 0 each time the procedure is called.

   The problem should be obvious by now: Each time a procedure ends, all its local variables are lost and reset to 0 when the procedure is called again. The variable I is local to this procedure because it was defined in the Dim statement at the beginning of the procedure. To make this program work, you must make the value of I persist from one call of the procedure to the next. One way to do that is to move the definition of I to the declarations area of the Form. A simpler way that keeps I local is to change the Dim statement to a Static statement.

3. Select the Timer1_Timer procedure, select the Dim statement, and change the word Dim to Static. Click elsewhere in the procedure and Visual Basic puts up a message that informs you to restart the program—see Figure 13.6. You must restart because you have changed a variable definition, making the running application inconsistent.

4. Click **OK**, select the I = I + 1 statement, execute the Toggle Breakpoint command to turn off the breakpoint, run the program again and click the **On/Off** button. It works!!! See Figure 13.7. Click the End tool or execute the End command to quit the program.

5. Execute the **Make Exe File** command on the **File** menu and compile the program as THETIMER.EXE. You can't use the name TIMER.EXE because it conflicts with the timer driver. Switch to the Windows Program Manager and open the File Manager. Find the THETIMER.EXE file as shown in Figure 13.8, click it, hold the left mouse button down, and drag it to the Visual Basic program group window on the Program Manager. This process installs the program in the Visual Basic group.

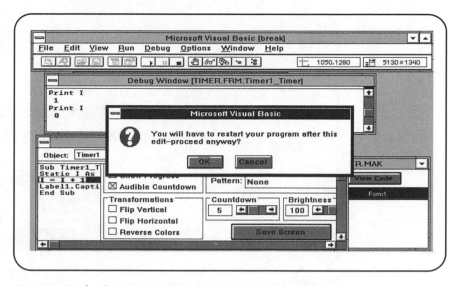

Figure 13.6. *Changing a Dim statement in break mode causes a restart.*

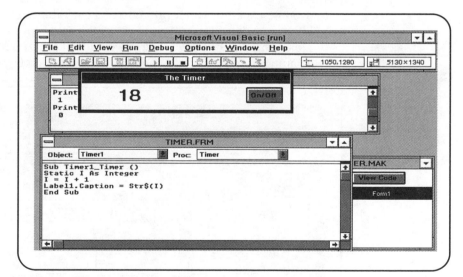

Figure 13.7. *The Timer program, working at last.*

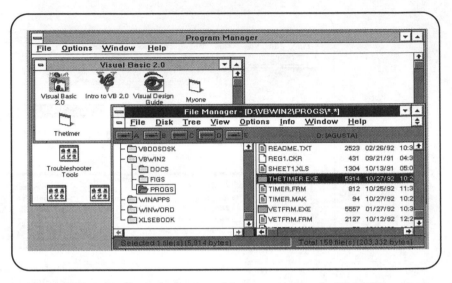

Figure 13.8. *Installing the executable program in the Visual Basic group window.*

6. Double-click the Timer program and click the **On/Off** button. You have a working Timer. Double-click the Timer program a few more times and you can have multiple copies of the Timer running simultaneously, each doing its own timing—see Figure 13.9.

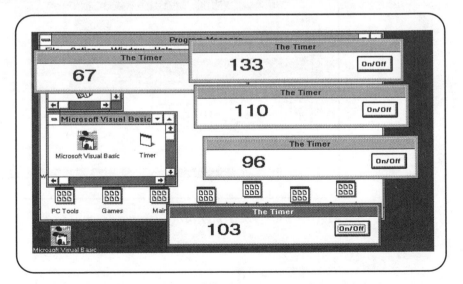

Figure 13.9. *Multiple copies of the Timer program.*

7. End the Timer programs and continue. Oh, oh! Another logical error. There is no way to turn them off.

There is no **Quit** or **Exit** command in the code, and you disabled the form's control box in Step 1. Luckily, there is no way for these programs to hurt anything. They merrily run in the background until you quit Windows, at which time they are deleted. In fact, they have been running the whole time I have been typing these last few pages. Actually, you can get rid of the programs by pressing Ctrl-Esc to open the Windows task list, selecting the Timer, and pressing End Task.

Sounds

When debugging a program, often you don't want many details about a program's execution; you just want to know when it reaches a particular location in the code. In this situation, the Beep statement is very useful. Simply insert it in an interesting area and your code beeps at you when it reaches that point. You can get more elaborate by inserting different beep codes at different points in your program to signal where you are.

Unfortunately, you can't string several Beeps in a row. The sounds all run together and you get a buzz rather than a beep, so you can't tell how many beeps you have. To create multiple beeps in a code, you can insert a simple procedure like this one:

```
Sub Beeper (NumBeeps As Integer)
Dim I As Integer, J As Integer
For I = 1 To NumBeeps
  Beep
  For J = 1 To 10000
  Next J
Next I
End Sub
```

Call this procedure in every location where you want to hear a marker. Follow the procedure name by the number of beeps you want to hear. That number is passed to the variable NumBeeps, which is used as the upper limit on a For/Next loop. The procedure executes a Beep, then executes a second For/Next loop. Note that the Next statement in the second loop immediately follows the For statement, so this loop does nothing but waste some time

to create a pause between beeps. You might have to adjust the upper limit of the second loop so you can discern the number of beeps. The value 10,000 seems to work well for my machine, but the number you use is machine-dependent. Pick a number just large enough so you can hear the number of beeps.

An alternate for the second loop is a `While`/`Wend` loop that watches the value of the `Timer()` function. The `Timer()` function returns the number of seconds since midnight, so if you wait until its integer value changes, you get a one-second pause, though I find this too long.

```
Sub Beeper (NumBeeps As Integer)
Dim I As Integer, J As Integer
For I = 1 To NumBeeps
Beep
J = Timer
While J = Int(Timer)
Wend
Next I
End Sub
```

For example, in the nonworking version of the Timer program, you could insert the first `Beeper` procedure with `I` as the argument. Then the program would beep the value of `I` to you each time it executes. Try it and see.

Debugging Code

A final method of tracing bugs is the insertion of debugging code. Debugging code usually consists of `Print` statements strategically placed in a code to print their location and the values of important variables. Visual Basic makes this easy by including the `Debug` object. Anything printed to the Debug object appears on the Immediate pane of the Debug window, so as your code runs, you can monitor the printed values to watch for suspicious changes.

If you have more than one `Debug` statement, be sure to include a short piece of text to identify the location of the statement doing the printing. In a large code, with many `Debug` statements, put a global `Debug` flag in the module and use it in an `If` statement to control the execution of the Debug statements. For example,

```
If DebugFlag Then Debug.Print "I am here",J
```

Here, this statement does nothing if the value of DebugFlag is False. If it is True, it prints I am here, then the value of the variable J. This way you can leave the Debug statements in your code and they won't do much but slow it down a little. When you want to print the Debug values, either insert a statement at the beginning of your code that sets DebugFlag to True, or break the code, and type DebugFlag = -1 in the Debug window. When you click Continue, the Debug statements are activated.

The Role of Error Trapping

Debugging involves searching for the causes of an error. When you figure it out, you fix your code and (you hope) never have that error again. Some errors you can't control—for example, trying to open a file for input that doesn't exist. If the user of your code does this, an error message appears and the code stops in break mode. If you are running a compiled version of your code, it quits and is removed from memory. Generally, you would prefer that did not happen—just as you would be thoroughly upset if, right after you had typed your Magnum Opus, your word processor quit without letting you save anything, just because you mistyped a file name. To handle problems like this, use error trapping.

Error trapping allows your program to take control when an error occurs. All of the run time errors listed in Table 13.1 are "trappable" by your program (they can be captured by your code and handled internally). When an error occurs, your error trap code takes control, checks to see what the error is, fixes it if possible, and then returns you to the place where the problem occurred. Each procedure has its own specific error-handling procedure. The error handler is enabled with the On Error statement. When enabled, if a run time error occurs, the block of code pointed to by the On Error statement is executed.

How Visual Basic Traps Errors

When Visual Basic encounters a run time error, it puts the error number from Table 13.1 in the variable Err, and checks whether any error handler is available. If so, it executes the handler, and lets it take care of the error.

13

If the handler also generates an error, Visual Basic checks the procedure that called the procedure with the error, to see whether the calling procedure has an error handler. If no error handler is available, or if none can handle the error, the code quits and displays an error message concerning the original error.

If you are running the program in interpreted mode, it displays the error message, then displays the offending statement. If you are running a compiled version of the code, it quits after displaying the error message from Table 13.1.

Setting a Trap for Errors

To set up an error trap, insert an `On Error Goto` statement near the beginning of a procedure with the errors you want to trap. This statement must be placed before any statement that might cause a "trappable" error. The syntax of the statement is

```
On Error {GoTo label ¦ Resume Next ¦ GoTo 0}
```

If you use the `GoTo label` clause, where *label* is a valid Label within the same procedure, the block of code following that Label is set as the current error handling procedure. Control isn't passed to the error handler with this statement; the statement is only marked as where to go if an error occurs. While an error handler must be in the same procedure as the `On Error` statement, it might immediately call some other procedure to handle the error. This way you can combine all similar error handling in a `Sub` or `Function` procedure, then pass control to it from the different error handlers in a program.

If you use the `Resume Next` clause, your code skips the statement that caused the error and continues running with the next one. This statement does not define an error handler. Be careful of this, because skipping statements can make your code inconsistent. The main use for the `Resume Next` clause is to save an error to handle later. If you are doing something that should not be stopped to handle an error, such as receiving data in a telecommunications program, use the `Resume Next` statement. Note that only the last error encountered is stored in `Err`, so if you encounter a second error before handling the first, the error number of the first error is lost.

The last clause, `GoTo 0`, disables error trapping in this routine. Use this clause to turn off error checking after the vulnerable statements have been executed.

To test an error trap, use the `Error` statement. The `Error` statement takes a single number as its argument, and that number is the code for the error you want to simulate. Whenever Visual Basic executes an `Error` statement, it simulates getting the error specified by that argument and either displays an error dialog or executes your error trapping code. The `Error` statement also is used to create your own errors. For example, in a File Open dialog box, if you already have an error handler for file-not-found errors that warns the user and requests a new file name, you can use the existing mechanism to handle files with an incorrect file type by creating a user-defined error. Otherwise, you will have to write practically the same block of code to handle the file type errors as you do for file-not-found errors.

You can use any of the missing numbers from Table 13.1 as user-defined errors, but make sure that if you have a user-defined error, you also have an error trap enabled to handle it. Also note that future versions of Visual Basic might use some of these unused error numbers.

Getting Information About an Error

After you have trapped an error, you must get information about it, such as what error occurred, and where it occurred. When error checking is not enabled, Visual Basic displays a dialog box that informs you what error occurred; and then, if you are running in interpreted mode, it displays the error message.

After an error has occurred, the variable `Err` contains the error number—see Table 13.1. To get the text of an error message, call the `Error$()` function with the error number as its argument. The function returns the text description of the error. This is the same description you get when Visual Basic displays an error message. Getting the location of the error is more difficult. In older versions of BASIC, each line in a program was consecutively numbered. If you number your lines, the number of the closest line to the line containing the error will be in `Erl`. Because Visual Basic programs rarely use line numbers, this might not be very useful unless you specifically number the statements with which you expect to have problems.

The `Err` and `Erl` functions are valid only in the procedure where the error occurs, and are reset to 0 whenever you execute a `Resume` or `On Error`

statement. They also might be reset if you call some other procedure, so save the values they return at the beginning of your error handler if you plan to use them.

Creating an Error Handler

As mentioned previously, an error handler must reside in the same procedure as the On Error statement that activated it. However, you usually don't want it in a position where it can be executed during the normal operation of your procedure. A good place to put it is at the end of your procedure, separated from the rest of the procedure with an Exit Sub or Exit Function statement.

An error handler can contain whatever you choose; the only requirement is that it end with a Resume statement. Commonly, error handlers first use the Err function to see what the error is, and then use a block If statement to decide what to do in each case. Rarely would you code an error handler for all of the possible errors listed in Table 13.1. Usually, you write code for the errors you expect and then write an Else clause for the rest that prints an error message and ends the program, or at least exits that procedure.

Every error handler must end with a Resume, Resume Next, or Resume *label* statement. The Resume statement returns the execution point to the statement that caused the problem, and tries to execute it again. This is the most common case: the handler corrects the problem and lets the program try again. The Resume Next statement returns execution to the next statement after the one that caused the problem. In this case, the error handler must handle the work of the statement that caused the problem, then skip it. The Resume *label* statement resumes execution at the statement following the Label.

For example, a formula that contains a division operation runs the risk of having zero as the divisor. An important case is the integrand of the Sine Integral Si(x). The integrand is equal to the sine of x divided by x. At x equals zero, the integrand is zero divided by zero, which is one; however, Visual Basic gives a divide-by-zero error. To make this work correctly, trap the divide-by-zero error and replace the result with one.

```
Function Si(x As Single) As Single
'function to calculate the sine integral
```

```
'statements to integrate sin(x)/x from x to infinity
  .
  .
  .
Integrand = Sin(xint)/xint
  .
  .
  .
End Function
```

Because the integral can pass through 0, xint equals 0 and the routine crashes. To fix this, create an error handler this way:

```
Function Si(x As Single) As Single
'function to calculate the sine integral
'statements to integrate sin(x)/x from x to infinity
On Error GoTo FixSin      'turn the error handler on
  .
  .
  .
Integrand = Sin(xint)/xint
  .
  .
.Exit Function
FixSin:
If Err = 11 Then
  Integrand = 1
Else
  MsgBox Error$(Err)
  Stop
End If
Resume Next
End Function
```

The error handler is enabled by line 4. If line 8 is executed and no error is encountered, the procedure continues normally. If an error is encountered, control passes to the block of code following the FixSin: Label. The error handler first checks whether the error is the expected divide-by-zero (error number 11.) If it is a divide-by-zero error, the procedure sets the value of Integrand to 1 and resumes with the statement after the one with the divide-by-zero error. If it isn't a divide-by-zero error, this procedure

sends the error message to the user and ends. You might want to move the On Error statement down to a position just before the Integrand statement and put an On Error GoTo 0 statement after it. This assures you that the Integrand statement is the one with the problem and not some other statement with a division error.

The Pies procedure on the Drawing Test Program in Chapter 12, "Drawing with Visual Basic," found a small bug in Visual Basic. To work around that bug, I had to put the Circle method within a block If statement so I could check the input values and skip drawing the pie slice if the numbers looked bad. If you remove that protection and press the Pies button a few times, it eventually crashes with an overflow error. An overflow error occurs when numbers get too large to be represented by a variable.

1. Open the Drawing Test program (FLAG.FRM), open the PiesCmd_Click procedure, and remove the If and End If statements that surround the Circle method. One way to remove a line without actually deleting it from a program is to insert a Rem or ' at the beginning of the line, turning it into a comment (the changed lines are bold).

```
Sub PiesCmd_Click ()
'Draw 100 random pie slices
Dim Color As Long, I As Integer
Dim XC As Single, YC As Single
Dim Radius As Single
Dim PieStart As Single, PieEnd As Single
BlackBoard.ScaleMode = 1          ' - Twips
BlackBoard.DrawStyle = 0          ' - Solid
BlackBoard.FillStyle = 0          ' - Solid
BlackBoard.Cls
For I = 1 To 100
  XC = Rnd(1) * BlackBoard.ScaleWidth
  YC = Rnd(1) * BlackBoard.ScaleHeight
  Radius = Rnd(1) * BlackBoard.ScaleHeight / 2 + 20
  Color = QBColor(Rnd(1) * 15)
  BlackBoard.FillColor = Color
  PieStart = Rnd(1) * 6
  PieEnd = Rnd(1) * 6
  Aspect = Rnd(1) * 2
```

```
Rem  If Aspect * Radius > 10 Then
    BlackBoard.Circle (XC, YC), Radius, BLACK, -PieStart, -
PieEnd, Aspect
Rem  End If
Next I
End Sub
```

2. Run the program. Press the **Pies** button a few times and it eventually crashes, as shown in Figure 13.10.

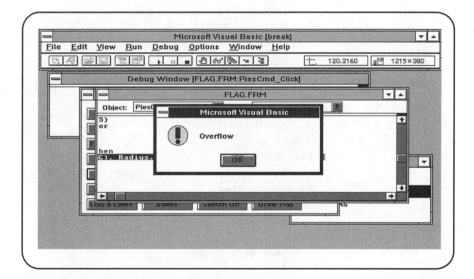

Figure 13.10. *Crashing the Pies procedure.*

3. Insert an error trap into the procedure so it reads as follows (the changed and added lines are bold).

```
Sub PiesCmd_Click ()
'Draw 100 random pie slices
Dim Color As Long, I As Integer
Dim XC As Single, YC As Single
Dim Radius As Single
Dim PieStart As Single, PieEnd As Single
BlackBoard.ScaleMode = 1            ' - Twips
```

```
BlackBoard.DrawStyle = 0          ' - Solid
BlackBoard.FillStyle = 0          ' - Solid
BlackBoard.Cls
On Error GoTo PieFix     'Enable error trapping
For I = 1 To 100
  XC = Rnd(1) * BlackBoard.ScaleWidth
  YC = Rnd(1) * BlackBoard.ScaleHeight
  Radius = Rnd(1) * BlackBoard.ScaleHeight / 2 + 20
  Color = QBColor(Rnd(1) * 15)
  BlackBoard.FillColor = Color
  PieStart = Rnd(1) * 6
  PieEnd = Rnd(1) * 6
  Aspect = Rnd(1) * 2
  Rem If Aspect * Radius > 10 Then
    BlackBoard.Circle (XC, YC), Radius, BLACK, -PieStart, -
PieEnd, Aspect
      Rem End If
  Next I
Exit Sub
PieFix:        'this is the error handler
If Err = 6 Then
  Debug.Print "Got one"
  Resume Next
Else
  MsgBox Error$(Err)
  Stop
End If
End Sub
```

The Debug statement in the error handler prints Got one on the Immediate window whenever it traps an error. If it does trap an overflow error, it executes the Resume Next statement to skip drawing the pie slice with the Circle method.

4. Save the program, run it, and press **Pies** several times. The error trapping procedure now captures any errors and skips the Circle method, as shown in Figure 13.11. Note the Got ones printed on the Debug window.

5. Remove the Debug statement from the error handler and save the project.

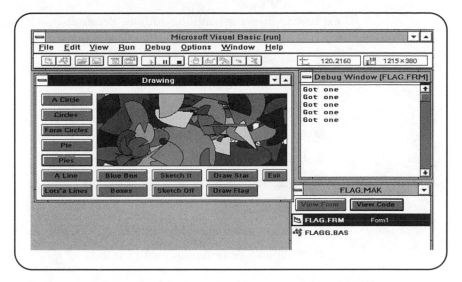

Figure 13.11. *Trapping run-time errors in the Pies procedure.*

What You Have Learned

This chapter discussed debugging programs and trapping errors. Debugging is finding and removing errors from a program, while error trapping is writing code to correct situations when the error can't be avoided. The types of errors involved in debugging are syntax, run time, and logical errors. Syntax errors occur because you have incorrectly applied the grammar of the Visual Basic language. Run-time errors are usually caused by supplying incorrect values to Visual Basic functions or operators. Logical errors occur when your code does what you told it to do, but not what you wanted it to do. Error trapping can trap only run-time errors, and is used to capture errors that would normally crash an application. After it is

captured, an error-handling routine determines what is to be done to correct the error. Specifically, this chapter discussed

- Syntax errors.

- Run-time errors.

- Logical errors.

- Examining a program in Break mode.

- Using sounds to mark sections of code.

- Using debugging code and the Debug window.

- Error trapping with the `On Error` statement.

- Getting information about an error with `Err` and `Erl`.

- Exiting an error handler with `Resume`.

Advanced Language Features

The advanced features of Visual Basic are somewhat beyond the scope of an introductory book. However, they represent important capabilities that you might eventually want to include in your programs. These features include control of the DOS file system, Dynamic Data Exchange (DDE), and Dynamic Link Libraries (DLL). As your understanding of Visual Basic and Windows programming increases, you probably will want to use these capabilities, so I briefly discuss them here. Note that some of these capabilities are only available in the professional version of Visual Basic. You can work out the details as you need them.

In This Chapter

Visual Basic has several advanced features, including Dynamic Data Exchange (DDE), Dynamic Link Libraries (DLL), and the use of Binary files.

This chapter discusses

- Dynamic Data Exchange.
- Object Linking and Embedding.
- Dynamic Link Libraries.
- Open database connectivity.
- Custom controls.
- Multiple Document Interface.
- Help compiler.
- Binary files.
- Dragging and dropping.
- File system management.

Using Dynamic Data Exchange

Dynamic Data Exchange (DDE) is a windows capability that allows two running programs to exchange data. The programs must be especially equipped to handle DDE and set up a link with another program. Visual Basic has this capability built in, so you only have to enable it.

Servers and Clients

Every DDE link has two ends, the *server* and *client*. The server provides data for the client and the client receives the data. The linking is generally between two similar objects in the two programs, or at least between two objects that understand the same type of data. For example, a cell in a Microsoft Excel worksheet and a text box in Visual Basic can be linked in a DDE link. If Excel is the server and Visual Basic is the client, then whenever the contents of the worksheet cell changes, that change is passed to the text box. If Visual Basic is the server and Excel is the client, then changing the contents of the text box changes the contents of the worksheet cell.

In any DDE exchange, a program can be both a server and a client, depending on the needs of the communication. For example, a worksheet cell could be a server for a label, and a text box could be a server for a worksheet cell. Thus, the two programs can pass data between them. Be careful with this; don't make the same item both a server and a client. If you do, an unending loop is set up with one program changing the other, and the change in the other initiating a change in the first. If you have to send data to a server, and if the server is capable of accepting data as well as sending it, a `LinkPoke` method is available. See Chapter 15, "Command Reference," for more details.

Hot and Cold Links

DDE links come in two temperatures, hot and cold. A hot DDE link updates the client's data whenever the data changes in the server. Because this is not ideal in some cases, the DDE link also can be cold: the client's data is updated only when the client asks for it with the `LinkRequest` method. For example, pictures contain a large amount of data that must be transferred over the link. If the link between two pictures is hot, the whole picture is sent every time you change a single bit on the picture on the server. With a cold link, you can wait until you have finished changing the picture before sending it over the link.

Initiating a Link

A client-server relationship is initiated by the client asking the server for service. To establish the link, a LinkOpen request must first be passed to the Windows operating system. Windows then passes the request to the selected program. A LinkOpen request contains the following data:

```
application¦topic!item
```

The `application` is the name of the server application. This name can be different from the name of the running application. For example, the application name for Microsoft Excel is Excel. The application name for a Visual Basic program running in the Visual Basic environment is the name of the Project window minus the .MAK extension. If the Visual Basic program is compiled, the application name is the name of the executable file minus the .EXE extension.

14

The topic is usually the name of the document that contains the needed data. For Excel, it is the name of the worksheet window. In Visual Basic, it's the name of the form (see the FormName property).

The item is a reference to the object containing the data. In Excel, it is a reference to the cell containing the data in RC format; that is, R3C5 stands for the cell at the intersection of row 3 and column 5. For Visual Basic, the item is the name of the label, text box or picture box that contains the data.

To initiate a DDE link with Visual Basic as the client, change the LinkTopic property of a form, label, picture box, or text box to application¦topic, the LinkItem property to item, and the LinkMode property to 1 (Hot), or 2 (Cold). Your Visual Basic program then attempts to establish a link with the external application. You don't have to do anything else. To close the link, change the LinkMode property of the form or control back to 0 (none).

For example, the following procedure establishes a link between an Excel worksheet and Visual Basic (Microsoft Excel is needed for this example). Whenever the **Command1** button is pressed, the following short procedure establishes a link between the Text1 text box and cell B2 (R2C2) on Sheet1.XLS of an Excel worksheet. Figure 14.1 shows both the cell in the worksheet and the text box in Visual Basic. Changing the contents of the cell causes the text box to change, as well.

Because Microsoft Excel is needed for this example, and you might not have it, check the documentation of some of your other Windows programs to see how they handle DDE and use them instead. Another option is to create a second Visual Basic application to respond to your DDE requests, as is done later in this chapter.

1. Open a new project and draw a command button and text box on the form.

2. Open the Command1_Click procedure and type

```
Sub Command1_Click ()
Text1.LinkTopic = "Excel¦Sheet1.XLS"
Text1.LinkItem = "R2C2"
Text1.LinkMode = 1
End Sub
```

3. Run Microsoft Excel, type some text in cell B2, and save the worksheet as Sheet1.XLS.

4. Run the Visual Basic program and click the **Command1** button. The contents of the Excel worksheet should appear in the Text1 text box. You will note two little bar-like symbols next to the text. They are markers for the carriage return-line feed that Excel appended to the text. Because the box is a single line box (Multiline = False) the carriage return-line feed appears as symbols. If Multiline were True, the symbols would make the cursor move down a line.

5. Switch to Excel and change the contents of cell B2. See what happens in the Text1 text box.

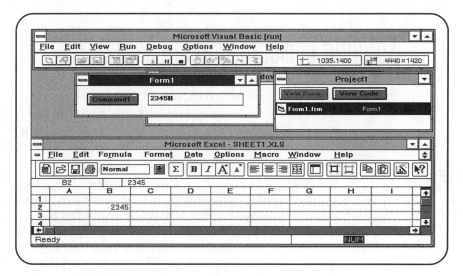

Figure 14.1. *A Dynamic Data Link between cell B2 on an Excel worksheet and a text box.*

Sending Data to the Server

Excel can accept a Poke event, so add the following command button to the program. When you press the button, the data in the Text1 text box is sent to the worksheet, changing the value of the linked cell in the worksheet.

6. Add another command button to the form, open the
   `Command2_Click` procedure and type

```
Sub Command2_Click ()
Text1.LinkPoke
End Sub
```

7. Excel should still be running, so run the Visual Basic program and
   click the **Command1** button to initiate the link. The `Text1` text box
   and cell `B2` should contain the same thing.

8. Change the contents of the `Text1` text box. Nothing happens in the
   worksheet because the text box is the client, not the server. Click
   the **Command2** button and the contents of the text box is sent to
   cell `B2` on the worksheet.

Sending Commands to the Server

In addition to linking data, some DDE servers can accept commands from
the client. For example, Excel accepts any valid macro commands, surrounded by square brackets, from a linked client. Using macro commands,
Excel can be asked to open files, change settings, change data, and so forth.

For example, the following procedure informs Excel to select cell `D2`
and change its value to `Good Morning`. Note that double quotation marks are
needed in the command strings, so they have to be created with `Chr$(34)`
and concatenated into the command string. The comments show what the
command string looks like. The first command informs Excel to activate
Sheet1.XLS, the second command selects cell `D2` (`R2C4`), and the third
command changes its value to Good Morning. The result is shown in Figure
14.2.

9. Add another button to the Form, open the `Command3_Click` procedure and type

```
Sub Command3_Click ()
    'Send the command: [ACTIVATE("SHEET1.XLS")]
Text1.LinkExecute "[ACTIVATE(" + Chr$(34) + "SHEET1.XLS" +
➡ Chr$(34) + ")]"
    'Send the command: [SELECT( "R2C2" )]
Text1.LinkExecute "[SELECT(" + Chr$(34) + "R2C4" +
➡ Chr$(34) + ")]"
```

```
              'Send the command: [FORMULA("Good Morning")]
              Text1.LinkExecute "[FORMULA(" + Chr$(34) +              "Good
           ➡ Morning" + Chr$(34) + ")]"
              End Sub
```

10. Run the program, press **Command1** to establish the link, then press **Command3** to send the macro commands to Excel.

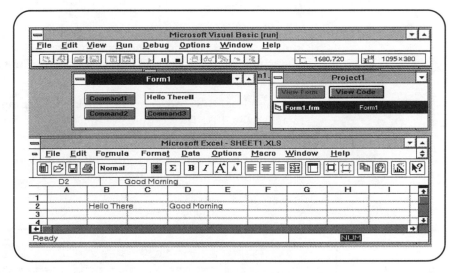

Figure 14.2. *Sending commands to a DDE server (Excel).*

Making Visual Basic the Server

To make a Visual Basic program the server in a DDE link, the LinkMode property of the form you want to be the server must be set to 1 - Server. Note that this is the default setting, so you don't have to do anything to make a Visual Basic program a server. Any program that attempts to link to it sends Visual Basic a link request with the proper application, topic, and item. In Excel, the cell formula is =application¦Topic!Item.

For example, run a copy of the Timer program, then link to the label using another Visual Basic program, and a cell in an Excel worksheet. All three cells count together, as shown in Figure 14.3.

1. Open a new project and draw a command button and Text box on the form.

2. Open the `Command1_Click` procedure and type

```
Sub Command1_Click ()
Text1.LinkTopic = "TheTimer¦Form1"
Text1.LinkItem = "Label1"
Text1.LinkMode = 1
End Sub
```

3. Run a compiled version of the Timer program from Chapter 13, _Debugging and Error Trapping, and click the **On/Off** button to start it counting.

4. Run the Visual Basic program and click the **Command1** button to establish the link. The contents of the `Text1` text box now counts along with the label on the Timer.

5. Select Excel, and set cell B3 to the following command. Now it, too, is counting along with the Timer.

```
=TheTimer¦Form1!Label1
```

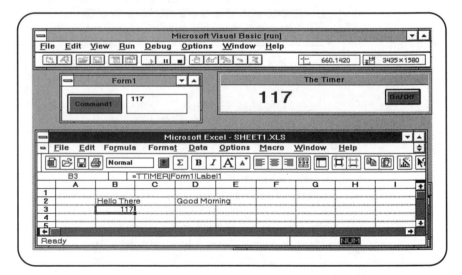

***Figure 14.3.** A Dynamic Data Link between two Visual Basic programs and an Excel worksheet.*

Object Linking and Embedding

> *Object linking and embedding*, or *OLE*, is much the same as DDE, except the link to the server application is different. Where DDE provides the data to the client application, which the client must display, an OLE link provides an image of the data in the server's native format. Thus, the client application has only to display it. This is especially useful for server applications like Excel, where the data is displayed in a grid. With DDE you have to put the data in a grid yourself, while in OLE, Excel does it for you. With DDE, the client application receives the data and does any needed editing. With OLE, the server application is opened whenever you need to edit the data.

Deciding to use OLE or DDE depends on what you want to do. If you plan to display or use the data from the server, or to control the server application from Visual Basic, then DDE is easier to implement. If you just want to display the data and let the server application display and edit it, then use OLE.

OLE is implemented with the OleClient control. The OleClient control is a custom control, so it must be attached to a project to use it. Attach a custom control to a project with the Add File command on the File menu, and search for files with the VBX extension. Whenever you start a new project, both the Grid and OleClient controls are automatically attached. The OleClient control is contained in the file OLECLIEN.VBX, and needs the library files OLECLI.DLL and SHELL.DLL files to operate.

To use OLE, draw an OLE window on a form and set the OLEClient properties that define the Class, Protocol, SourceDoc, SourceItem, and ServerType. Each of these properties is needed to create the link to the server application.

Class—This is the type of document that can be linked to. For example, ExcelWorksheet is the class for a Microsoft Excel worksheet.

Protocol—This is the type of editing or interaction that the server allows. The default for most applications is StdFileEditing.

SourceDoc—This is the name and path of the document to be displayed.

SourceItem—This is data within the document to be displayed. In a worksheet, this is a range reference to the cells to be displayed.

ServerType—This determines how the linked document is stored. A server type of 0 - Linked stores the document in the server application, while a type 1 - Embedded stores the data in the OLE object created in the Visual Basic application.

The settings of these properties depend on the server application, so you must consult the documentation to see what is allowed. Most of the allowed settings are registered with Windows, and can be viewed with the REGVIEW.MAK sample program included with Visual Basic.

Once the link is established with the properties just mentioned, the Action property is used to make the connection, display the data, and invoke the native application for editing. For example, create a small application to link the Excel worksheet created in the DDE example.

1. Open a new project and draw a command button and an OLEClient window on the form. Make the OLEClient window about 5415 twips wide by 1100 twips tall.

2. Open the declarations section and type the following definitions. These definitions may be copied from the file CONSTANT.TXT, included with Visual Basic. These are the allowed values of the Action property.

```
'Action values
Const OLE_CREATE_NEW = 0
Const OLE_CREATE_FROM_FILE = 1
Const OLE_COPY = 4
Const OLE_PASTE = 5
Const OLE_UPDATE = 6
Const OLE_ACTIVATE = 7
Const OLE_EXECUTE = 8
Const OLE_CLOSE = 9
Const OLE_DELETE = 10
Const OLE_SAVE_TO_FILE = 11
```

```
Const OLE_READ_FROM_FILE = 12
Const OLE_CONVERT_TO_TYPE = 13
'Server types
Const OLE_LINKED = 0
Const OLE_EMBEDDED = 1
Const OLE_STATIC = 2
```

On the command button, attach code to define the Class, Protocol, SourceDoc, SourceItem and ServerType properties. For the SourceDoc property, use the path and directory for where you stored the worksheet file used in the DDE example. Next execute the OLE_CREATE_FROM_FILE action, which tells Excel to startup and open the indicated file, and then the OLE_UPDATE action which tells Excel to send the item to the client.

3. Open the Command1_Click procedure and type,

```
Sub Command1_Click ()
OleClient1.Class = "ExcelWorksheet"
OleClient1.Protocol = "StdFileEditing"
OleClient1.SourceDoc = "D:\EXCEL\Sheet1.XLS"
OleClient1.SourceItem = "R1C1:R4C6"
OleClient1.ServerType = OLE_LINKED
OleClient1.Action = OLE_CREATE_FROM_FILE
OleClient1.Action = OLE_UPDATE
End Sub
```

To open the server application for editing of the data, insert an OLE_ACTIVATE action in a double click procedure for the OLEClient.

4. Open the OleClient1_DblClick procedure and type,

```
Sub OleClient1_DblClick ()
OLEClient1.Action = OLE_ACTIVATE
End Sub
```

Run the program and click the command button. The Excel program is started in the background, the file Sheet1.XLS is loaded and the contents of cells A1 to F4 are displayed on the form as shown in Figure 14.4. Double click the OLEClient window and the Excel worksheet is displayed for editing. Make some changes in cell D4, and they immediately appear on the form as shown in Figure 14.5.

14

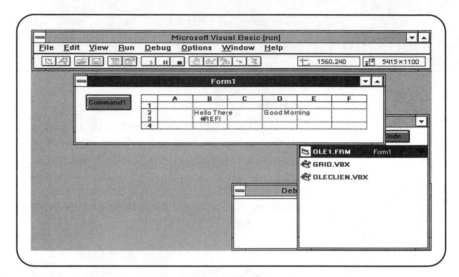

Figure 14.4. *A Visual Basic form with an embedded Excel worksheet.*

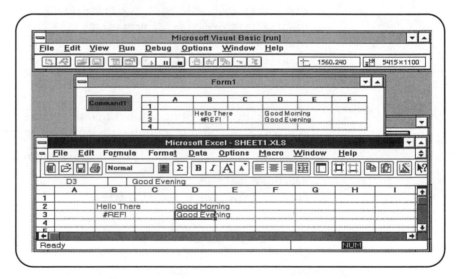

Figure 14.5. *Editing the image in the OLE server (Excel).*

Linking to Dynamic Link Libraries

A Dynamic Link Library is a special library of functions external to Visual Basic. Dynamic Link Libraries all have the .DLL extension. To use the functions in a DLL, you first must have the library documentation. There are several libraries that come with Windows, and the documentation is in the *Microsoft Windows Programmers Reference* by Microsoft Press or the Windows Software Development Kit (SDK). The Professional version of Visual Basic contains a Help file that lists all the Windows functions. The Visual Basic DLLs are in the VBRUN200.DLL run-time library and include the Visual Basic procedures. Many of the Windows and Visual Basic procedures are defined in the examples included with Visual Basic.

Armed with this description of the library interface, add a `Declare` statement to the global module to tell Visual Basic the names and argument types. After it is declared, you can use the function like any other internal `Sub` or `Function` procedure. Call the function with any numeric types, and Visual Basic converts the numbers to the correct types and passes them to the library routine.

For example, the following declares the interface to the DLL function `InvertRect`, in the library User.DLL. It has two arguments, `hdc` which is passed by value, and a user-defined type `lpRect`, passed by address.

```
Declare Function InvertRect Lib "User" (ByVal hdc, lpRect
As RECT)
```

The `InvertRect` function could now be used in a program, such as

```
Rval = InvertRect(Ctrl.hdc, rect)
```

Here, `Rval` is a dummy variable that receives any value returned by `InvertRect`.

Open Database Connectivity

Open Database Connectivity or *ODBC* is a capability for accessing database files with many different structures, using a standard system of commands and controls. This capability is achieved by creating an object-oriented database structure, and binding a real database to that structure using a database driver. Visual Basic provides a complete library of functions and statements for accessing a database. These functions and statements interact with the database driver which knows how to access the real database on disk. Because databases are not identical in their capabilities, not all the database commands and functions can be applied to all databases.

An ODBC database is made of collections of objects, where a collection is like an array variable or a control list. At the highest level is the Database object, which is defined when the database file is opened with the OpenDatabase function. A Database object is made of a collection of Tables, and a Table is a collection of Fields and Indexes. To understand Tables, imagine a multi-column table on a spreadsheet. Each column of the table is a Field, and each row is a Record. The column headings are stored in the Name property of each Field. When a Database is first opened, there is no data in the Tables, only the field names. One or more Indexes are also associated with each Table, and an Index is a method for selecting records in the table.

To access the data in a database, you must create a Dynaset, where a Dynaset is a temporary copy of one of the tables in the database. Once a Dynaset is created, each Field gets a Value property which contains the current Record's data for that Field. At this point, you can access or change the Value of a Field. To access the data in the next Record, apply the MoveNext method to the Dynaset. To move to the first record in the database, close the Dynaset and then open it again. There also are methods for adding or deleting Records from the Dynaset. To access a field, use the following syntax:

```
aValue = myDB.Tables(1).Fields(3).Value
```

Here, myDB is a database object, Tables() is the Tables collection for the database, and Fields() is the Fields collection for the Table. In this example, you are accessing the fourth Field of the second Table, because the collection indexes start with 0.

To store the data in the Dynaset back into the actual database file, use the Transactions property of the database. If the Transactions property equals auto-commit, then every change you make to the Dynaset is automatically made to the underlying database file. The default when you first open a database file is auto-commit. If you change the Transactions property to True, then changes in the database are stored as a series of transactions, which are not written to the database file. You start storing transactions after applying the BeginTrans method to the database. Once you have made your changes and decide to keep them, execute the `CommitTrans` method to make the changes permanent. If you don't execute the `CommitTrans` method, the changes are ignored and the database is unchanged.

There is more detail to using the ODBC capability to access a database file. See the *ODBC Object Reference* and the examples included with Visual Basic.

Custom Controls

The Control Development Kit (CDK) is included in the Pro version of Visual Basic. The kit is a collection of examples, libraries, and documentation for creating a custom control. To create a custom control, you must have a compiler for a computer language other than Visual Basic that can create .DLL library files. You must also have a familiarity with programming in the Windows environment. Your control must know how to draw and what to do if it is activated. A control is passed events that occur to it, and the control must handle each event. For example, when a button is passed a Click event, it must change its image to simulate a button being pressed. It can change its properties to indicate it was pressed, and can then, if it needs to, pass the event on to the event procedure written by the Visual Basic programmer. The Click event is usually passed on to the programmer, while something like a Paint event is completely handled by the control.

See the *Control Development Guide* in the Pro version of Visual Basic for more information.

14

Multiple Document Interface Programs

You have already used several Multiple Document Interface (MDI) programs in the Windows environment. The Program Manager and the File Manager applications are both MDI programs. An MDI program has a single MDI parent form that forms the background of the application with one or more child forms attached to it. The child forms are only visible within the body of the parent form, and only the parent form can have menus. Child

forms never leave the body of the parent form, and if they are minimized, the icon appears within the body of the parent form instead of at the bottom of the screen, as shown in Figure 14.6. MDI programs are most useful for situations where multiple documents are open at the same time.

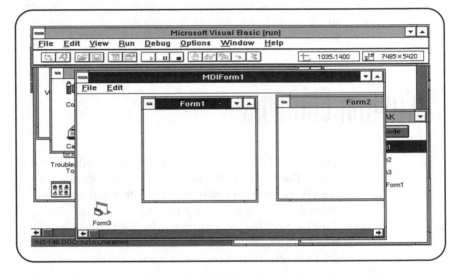

Figure 14.6. *An MDI program showing the parent and child forms, and a minimized child form.*

To create an MDI application, first create an MDI form with the New MDI Form command on the File menu. There can be only one MDI form in a single application. Next, add one or more child forms with the New Form command on the File menu, then change the MDIChild property on each child form to true. After you have created your forms, use Visual Basic to create your application.

Help Compiler

The Pro version of Visual Basic includes a copy of the Windows help compiler. The help compiler is a special application that creates Windows type help files that can be used and displayed with the Windows help system. A help file is essentially a group of pages of text, with each page discussing a topic. On any page are hidden buttons that activate drop-down windows for more information on a topic, or that institute a jump elsewhere in the help file to a related topic.

The first page of a help file is usually a table of contents showing the contents of the help file, and having a jump from the name of each topic to the topic itself. Following the table of contents are the topics. Each topic should be a page or two, at most, in length, and should discuss some aspect of your application. Place related topics together so that a reader can use the browse controls to read other topics related to the one he was reading.

When you have written all your topics, combine them together into a help project file and compile them with the help compiler. The WinHelp application is then used to display and browse the compiled help file. To call WinHelp from within a Visual Basic application, use the `WinHelp` function. The `WinHelp` function must be declared in a module before you use it because it is in an external .DLL library.

In addition to opening a standard help file, Visual Basic applications can have context sensitive help. To create an application with context sensitive help, you must insert context numbers into your help file. Each number uniquely defines a topic in the help file. Then, for each object in your application that will have context sensitive help, set the `HelpContextID` property to the number of the help topic you want displayed. When the user presses F1, the topic associated with the currently selected object is displayed. Set the name of the help file to use with the **P**roject command on the **O**ptions menu.

14

Binary Files

Binary data files are actually any data file type opened with the Binary file type in the `Open` statement. When a file is opened `As Binary`, every byte of the file is accessible and changeable as if it were a random access file with one-byte-long records. Use this file type when you have to look at the raw bytes of a file. A virus checker would be one such program, because it needs to search the contents of an executable file for a particular sequence of bytes. Any file can be opened as Binary, including executable (.EXE and .COM) files.

Use the `Get` and `Input$` statements to read data from the Binary file and the Put statement to store data. When using Get and Put, the number of bytes read or written is equal to the number of bytes in the variables used as arguments to the statements.

Dragging and Dropping

If you want movable controls rather than fixed ones on a form, you have two options, change the `DragMode` property of the control to `1 - Automatic`, or use the `Drag` method in the controls `MouseDown` event procedure. Whichever of these methods you use, when you place the mouse pointer on the control and press the mouse button you can drag an outline of the control around the form. To actually move the control, use the Move method in the form's `DragDrop` event procedure. For example, drag a picture box around on a form.

1. Draw a small picture box on a form, and set its `DragMode` property to `1 - Automatic`.

2. Run the program, place the mouse pointer on the picture box, press the left mouse button, and drag an outline of the picture box around the screen.

   When you release the mouse button to drop picture box, the picture box jumps back to its original location, because you have not moved the Picture box; you have only dragged its outline around. To actually move it, add a `Move` method to the form's `DragDrop` procedure.

3. End the program, open the `Form_DragDrop` procedure and type the following.

   ```
   Sub Form_DragDrop (Source As Control, X As Single,
   ➥Y As Single)
   Source.Move X, Y
   End Sub
   ```

   The `DragDrop` event occurs whenever a control is dragged over a form (or other control) and dropped. The `Source` argument contains the name of the control (the picture box) that was dragged over and dropped on the form. The X and Y arguments contain the location of the mouse pointer when the control was dropped. The Move method is used here to actually move the control to the new coordinates. A difficulty here is that the upper-left corner of the control is moved to the x,y location supplied by the DragDrop procedure. The x,y location is not the upper-left corner of the outline being dragged around the form but the location of the mouse pointer on that outline. When you Run this program you will see what I mean.

4. Run the program and drag and drop the picture box around on the form. Note where the outline is and where the picture box moves when you release the mouse button. End the program when you are done.

   If you want the dragged control to align with the outline when it is moved, you must capture the x,y coordinates of the MouseDown event on the control and subtract that location from the x,y coordinates in the DragDrop procedure.

5. Open the general procedure on the form and define the variables for the x and y offsets. Also, define two constants to be used later.

```
Dim XOffset As Single
Dim YOffset As Single
Const StartDrag = 1
Const Drop = 2
```

6. Select the Picture1_MouseDown procedure and type the following.

```
Sub Picture1_MouseDown (Button As Integer,
➡Shift As Integer, X As Single, Y As Single)
XOffset = X
YOffset = Y
Picture1.Drag StartDrag
End Sub
```

   This procedure stores the location of the MouseDown event on Picture1, and manually initiates dragging with the Drag method.

7. Select the Form_DragDrop procedure and change it to the following.

```
Sub Form_DragDrop (Source As Control, X As Single, Y As
➡Single)
Source.Drag Drop
Source.Move X - XOffset, Y - YOffset
End Sub
```

This procedure ends manual dragging and moves the picture box. The procedure offsets that move by the location of the initial `MouseDown` on the picture box.

8. Click the **View Form** button on the Project window, select the `Picture1` picture box and change its `DragMode` property to **0 - Manual**.

9. Run the program and drag and drop the picture box. Again, note where the outline is and where the picture box moves when the mouse button is released. Now they should align. End the program when you are done and save it if you like.

This method works for all controls that have a `MouseDown` event, which includes list boxes, labels, file list boxes and picture boxes. For all other controls, such as command buttons, you can either manually insert the values of `XOffset` and `YOffset` that offset the move to the center of the control (the most obvious place to click a control before dragging it), or use a custom icon stored in the controls `DragIcon` property. The custom icon is always centered on the mouse pointer so you can manually insert the size of the offset. See the "Command Language Reference" included with Visual Basic for more information on using these properties.

File System Management

File system control is not truly an advanced feature, but it is covered here because it is not widely used in BASIC anymore. The original BASICs were the operating systems for several early machines, and, as such, had to be able to control the file system. Current BASICs are programming environments within the current operating system, so they rarely have to move and copy files, but the capability from the earlier versions still exists. The DOS file system is controlled from within a Visual Basic program with commands similar to the DOS system commands. The following statements and functions can be used in any Visual Basic program to control the file system. See the descriptions of the individual commands in Chapter 15, Command Reference, for more information.

ChDir	Change to a different default directory
ChDrive	Change the current drive
CurDir$	Get the current directory path
Dir$	Return a list of files
Kill	Delete a file
MkDir	Create a subdirectory
Name As	Change the name of a file or move it to a different directory
RmDir	Delete a subdirectory

What You Have Learned

This chapter points you to some of the advanced capabilities of Visual Basic. These features are somewhat beyond the scope of an introductory book, but I expect that you will eventually want to use them, if only to experiment with the capabilities of Visual Basic. To try them out, create some simple applications like those in this chapter and experiment with the functions and methods. Note that some of these capabilities are only available in the Por version of Visual Basic. This chapter examined

- Linking Applications with DDE and OLE.
- Using DLL Libraries.
- Using ODBC.
- Creating custom controls.
- Creating MDI applications.
- Creating custom help files.
- Using Binary files.
- Dragging and dropping.
- Managing the file system.

14

Congratulations to all of you who have made it to the end of Part II. By now, you should be able to use the essential capabilities of Visual Basic. Part III shows the complete development of a Visual Basic application from initial design to final application. Here is where you put everything you have learned together to create a useful application.

Part III

A Comprehensive Example

written by Gary Entsminger

Creating an Application

By now you should have a good general understanding of how Visual Basic works. It's both a language (similar to many high-level structured programming languages) and a system of objects and tools for creating applications. You use the objects to create an application's user interface and use the Visual Basic language to create the application's procedures. See Figure 15.1.

The interface can be simple, consisting of a single form, or complex, consisting of forms, controls, and menus. The application's general procedures can reside in one or more modules.

Regardless of the size of the intended application, you follow the same basic steps to create it.

1. Create a form for each window in your application.

2. Draw the controls for each form.

3. Design a menu bar for the main form.

4. Set the form and control properties.

5. Write event and general procedures.

6. Test and debug.

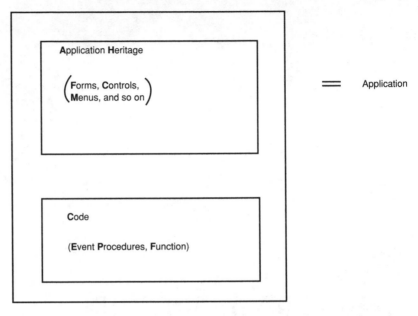

Figure 15.1. An application = an interface + code.

During and in between each step, you save the forms, controls, menu bar, and code as a project. (The first time you save a project, you specify names for the form, module, and project files.)

Using a project makes it easier to keep track of the application's components. Use the project to organize both the interface and the code. You can create a general procedure file for procedures you use frequently and include them in any project that needs them, without rewriting code.

When you're satisfied with the application, you're ready for the last step.

7. Create an executable file to turn the project into an application.

Each application in this section follows a similar set of steps.

Putting Windows and Visual Basic Together

When you start Visual Basic, it automatically displays an empty form. It opens default form and project files where the application's code can be saved. These files are called form1.frm, and project1.prj until the first time you save the application. When you first save, you should specify new, meaningful names for these files. All the files that make up a project are displayed in the project window. See Figure 15.2.

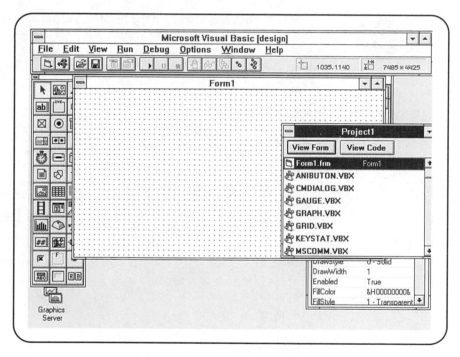

Figure 15.2. Startup project window.

Any time you add a new module (using the New **M**odule option from the **F**ile menu) or form (using the New **F**orm option from the **F**ile menu) to a project, it appears in this project window. By clicking a filename or the View Code or View Form commands, you can switch between the files and components of a project.

Any application you create will consist of at least a form and its accompanying code. The form has the underlying capability of connecting your application to Windows. A default, empty form is opened

15

automatically, so you don't have to do anything to get the first form required by any application. An application that uses only this form, without any accompanying controls or additional modules, is as simple to develop as its corresponding DOS (text-based) counterpart. Let me show you.

Let's start with a simple application that writes text to a form. Because a default form already exists, step 1 is done for you. To keep this application ultra-simple, we won't add any controls (step 2) or a menu bar (step 3). Also, let's use the default property settings (step 4), which brings us to step 5, writing the code.

Double-click anywhere on the form. In response to the double-click, the form's accompanying Code window (or form) opens, automatically displaying the form's first event procedure, Load. (Note: in VB 1.0 the Click event procedure was the first procedure shown by default. In VB 2.0, the Load event procedure is shown by default.) See Figure 15.3.

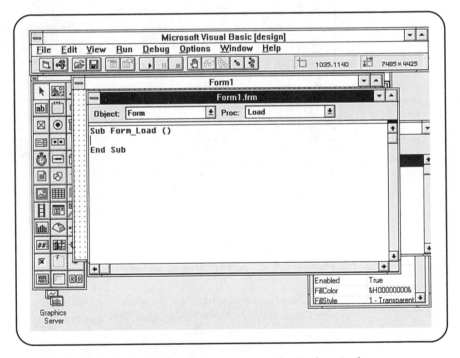

Figure 15.3. Double-click a form to get to the Code window.

> Double-clicking any form or control during design mode opens the accompanying code form (a Visual Basic window) for the selected form or control.

Notice in the code window:

1. The template for the load procedure, and

2. The object and proc dropdown boxes near the top of the window.

The Object box lists all the objects that are part of the current application. The Proc box lists all the event procedures for a form. You can either specify actions as event procedures or as general procedures. Any project, by default, consists of at least two objects—a form and a general procedures object. A project can have as many as 512 distinct objects (up from 255 in VB 1.0). As you add controls and other forms to a project, they are added automatically to the object list. General procedures are executed only when called by another procedure. An event procedure is invoked automatically in response to some action—either a user's or the system's.

Let's suppose that you want to write a string to a form whenever the user clicks the mouse. Scroll the Proc bar to get to the Click (event) procedure template and simply enter the following code:

```
Print "This text is strange."
```

See Figure 15.4.

Then Run the application from the Main menu. Figure 15.5 shows the application that results from this code.

Look familiar? It should; it's simply the form with its accompanying code hidden. In order to print This text is strange., click anywhere on the form. Figure 15.6 shows the result.

If you continue to click the form, This text is strange. is displayed for each click. See Figure 15.7.

To exit, click the command button in the upper-left part of the form and select Close, or press Alt-F4 or F10, press the down arrow, and select Close. These exit options and everything else about the form are the form's default components.

Figure 15.4.
*Enter Code
in the code
window.*

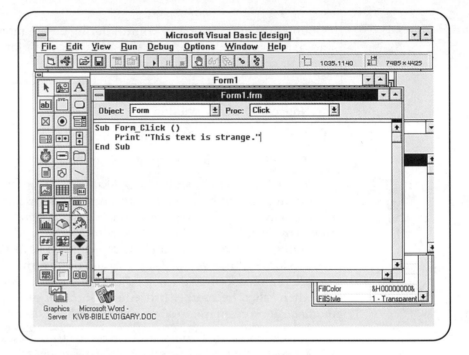

Figure 15.5.
*Application
"Print Strange
Text" running,
before clicking
on form.*

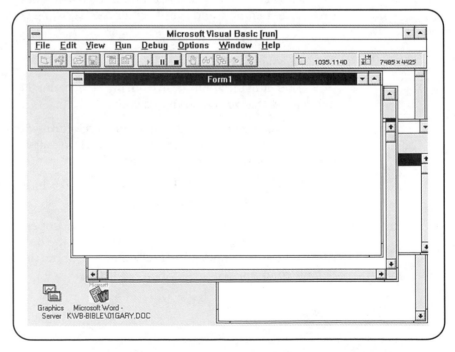

A form is your window to Windows. It knows how to interact with Windows, so you can ignore most of the interfacing details. You just write the procedural part of the application, instructing the application to respond to the events channeled to the application via its form. In the strange text application, we wrote a single event response procedure for the Click event.

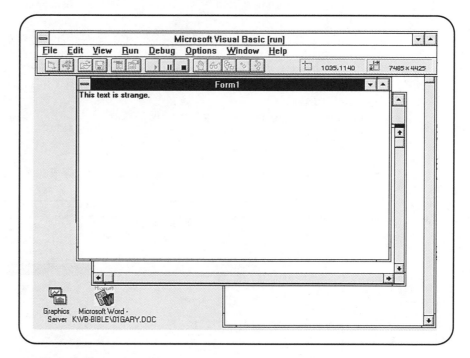

Figure 15.6. *Application "Print Strange Text," after click.*

The events that a form can respond to are specified in the form's procedure list.

Adding code to any event procedure is similar. Select the event from the drop-down proc box and add the code. For example, to have text generated as part of a random loop in response to a click, proceed as follows:

1. Select the form's click event.

2. Enter this code within the code window template:

```
Sub Form_Click ()
Dim Y As Integer, X As Integer          ' Declare variables
                                        ' locally

    Randomize                           ' Initialize random num
                                        ' generator

    X = Int(10 * Rnd + 1)               ' Generate X in the
                                        ' range 1-10

    Y = Int(10 * Rnd + 1)               ' Generate Y in the
                                        ' range 1-10

    If X > Y Then                       ' Compare X and Y
        Form1.Print "yes"; X; " "; Y    ' Print results
    Else
        Print "no "; X; " "; Y          ' Print results
    End If
End Sub
```

Run and click the form. Figure 15.8 shows the results.

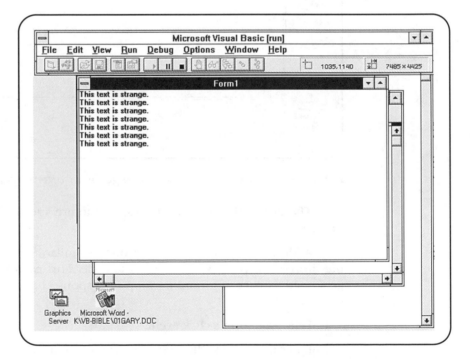

Figure 15.7. *Application "Print Strange Text," repeated clicking.*

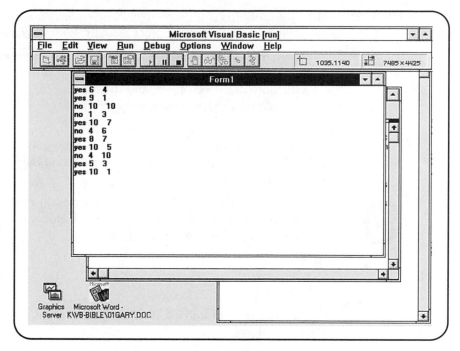

Figure 15.8. *Application "Random" running.*

Let's look a bit closer at this code before moving on. First, how does it work? Each time a user clicks the form, the event procedure Form.Click() responds by generating random numbers for X and Y, comparing them, and printing the results. Until the user closes the form (by using the control menu in the upper-left corner of the form or by pressing Alt-F4), the event procedure continues to respond to a click. Even if the user switches away from this form to another application, when the user switches back and clicks the form again, this event procedure responds to the click.

Note also that two different lines are used to print the results of the comparison of X and Y:

```
Form1.Print "yes";  X; " "; Y
Print "no ";  X; " "; Y
```

In this example, both lines print to the same location—the form. Form1.Print explicity directs output to the form. Print implicity directs it to the form, because if no object is specified for output, Print outputs to the currently selected object. Print is a polymorphic method. In other

words, many objects (forms, controls, and so on) share the Print name for generating output. But each object actually Prints in its own way.

When matters are simple, as in this example (a single form), you do not need to specify the object explicitly. In most situations, however, you deal with more than one object, and thus you need to name the object in order to guarantee that the output created by Print goes where you want it to.

While we're at it, let's modify this little piece of code (which, incidentally, is a complete application from Visual Basic's perspective) to use a user-defined type.

There isn't much to it. First, declare the type in a module (Note, in VB 1.0 you were required to define types in the global module. The global module no longer exists in VB 2.0):

```
Type U1
    X As Integer
End Type
```

and then use it by modifying the Form_Click event procedure you used earlier, as follows:

```
Sub Form_Click ()
Dim Y As Integer
Dim UseU1 As U1                        ' Declare an instance of
                                       ' type

    Randomize
    UseU1.X = Int(10 * Rnd + 1)        ' Use the type's field
    Y = Int(10 * Rnd + 1)
    If UseU1.X > Y Then
        Form1.Print "yes"; UseU1.X; " "; Y
    Else
        Print "no "; UseU1.X; " "; Y
    End If
End Sub
```

You define the type. Then you declare an instance of the type in the module or procedure that uses it.

Creating an Interface with the Toolbox

Let's move into something a little more complicated—adding controls to a form. To add a control to a form, simply double-click the control (in the toolbox) that you want to add to the form. It appears in the center of the form. See Figure 15.9.

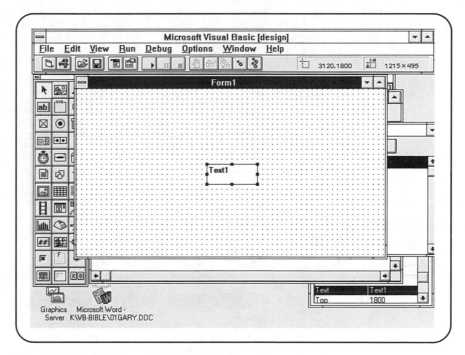

Figure 15.9. *Add a text box control to a form.*

Next, using the mouse pointer, resize and move the control to the desired location. See Figure 15.10.

To attach code to the control, follow the same procedure you followed to attach code to a form. First, select the control (click it with the mouse pointer), then double-click it to bring up the Code window. See Figure 15.11.

387

Figure 15.10.
Move the text
box control.

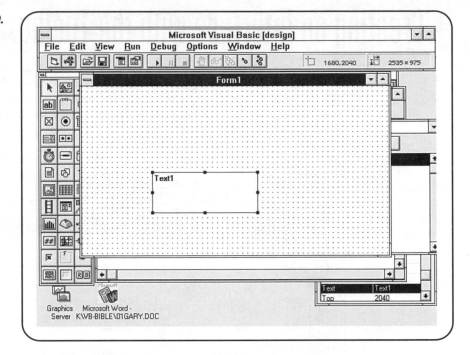

Figure 15.11.
Double-click
the control to
get to the Code
window.

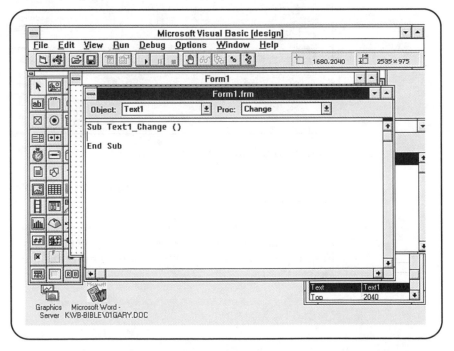

Then add the code for the event procedures you want the control to respond to.

Use the Object and Proc bars to select the objects and event procedures that you want to add code to. See Figure 15.12.

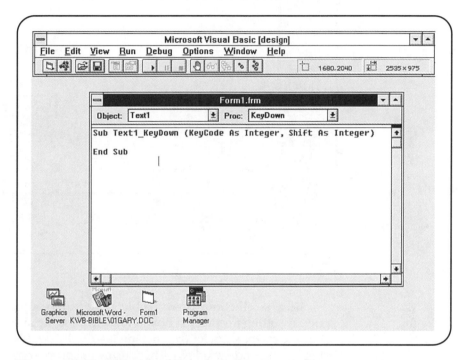

Figure 15.12. Object and Proc bars for a control.

You can use controls to manipulate the properties of other forms. For example, you can use one control to show or hide another control. Figure 15.13 shows a form with two controls—a command button and a text box. At startup, the form and the command button are visible. By clicking the command button, you can show the text box (make it visible).

First, create the two controls using the toolbox. Double-click a command button, move it to its location, then double-click on a text box and move it to its location. See Figure 15.13.

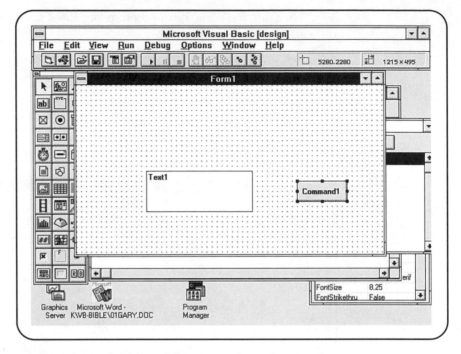

Figure 15.13. Command button and text box.

Because all controls are visible by default, you need to change the property setting for the text box to make it invisible at startup. To do this, select the textbox object (by clicking it—*not* by double-clicking it, which brings up the Code window). Then, using the properties bar just below the Visual Basic main menu bar, select the Visible property and change it to False, hiding the text box at startup. See Figure 15.14.

Next, attach code to the command button to make the text box visible when the command button is clicked. First, select the command button by clicking it. Then double-click it to bring up the Code window. Add the following code to the command button's Click event procedure:

```
Sub Command1_Click ()
    Text1.Visible = -1    ' See Visible to True
End Sub
```

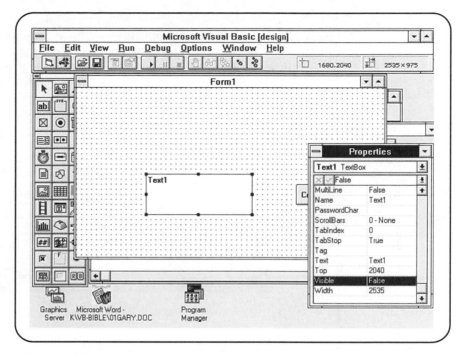

Figure 15.14. *Text box visible property - > False.*

Note that you use the control names of the command button (Command1 and Text1) to specify the control you want to manipulate or use. Command1 and Text1 are default names. As your applications become more complex, you should change these names to something more meaningful to your application.

Note also that you use the numbers 0 and -1 to represent values for the Booleans, True and False. To set a property to True in code, always use -1. To set a property to False, use 0. Figures 15.15 and 15.16 show the form before and after clicking the command button. When you click the command button, the text box becomes visible.

You could also use the command button to alternately make the text box visible and invisible. Each time the user presses the command button, its code checks to see if the text box is visible. If so, it makes it invisible. If it's already invisible, it makes it visible. The following code does the trick:

```
Sub Command1_Click ()
If Text1.Visible = 0       ' Is it invisible?
     Text1.Visible = -1    ' Set Visible to True
Else
      Text1.Visible = 0    ' Set Visible to False.
End If
End Sub
```

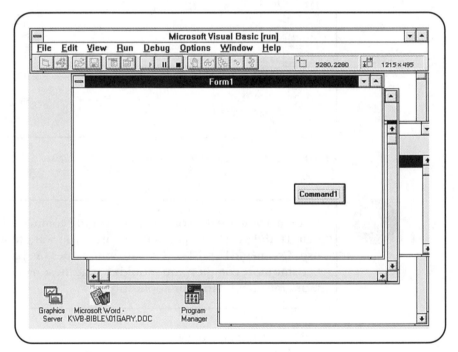

Figure 15.15. Form before the command button: textbox not visible.

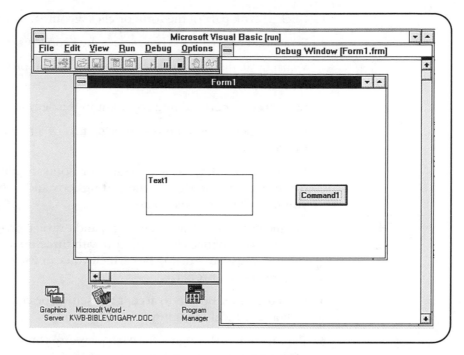

Figure 15.16. *Form after the command button: text box visible.*

Properties

Objects (forms and controls) have properties that are always set to something by default. Properties are the named attributes of a form or control. They define an object's characteristics (size, color, and screen location) or behavior (whether a property is enabled or not).

In simple cases, you can use these objects without changing any of the default property settings. As your projects become more complex, you will manipulate objects through their properties to great advantage.

In sum, you can set properties with the properties bar at design time and by code at run time.

To set form or control properties with the properties bar at design time, follow these steps:

1. Click a blank part of the form or click a control to select the form.

2. From the Properties list box, select the property you want.

   Visual Basic displays the current setting for the property in the Settings box.

3. Enter the property setting you want in the Settings box.

   For a property that requires entering text or a number, type the information.

   For a property that has enumerated or Boolean values, click the down arrow to the right of the Settings box and select the option you want from the combo box.

   For the `BackColor`, `ForeColor`, `Icon`, and `Picture` properties, the down arrow changes into a button with three dots. Click this button to display a dialog box which you can use to select the settings for the property.

4. Click the Enter button to accept the setting or click the Cancel button to cancel the setting.

5. Repeat steps 2 through 4 for each property you want to set for the selected form or control.

   To set form or control properties at run time, place a reference to the property (`object.property`) on the left side of an assignment statement:

```
Text1.Text = "Say anything"
```

> When you use an assignment statement, both sides of the statement must be either string or numeric values.

Forms and Code

In sum, the code you attach to a form or a control is called an event procedure. Every form and control has a set of predefined events that it recognizes automatically. You attach event procedures only for the events that you want a form or a control to respond to in some specific way.

To attach an event procedure to a form or a control, follow these steps:

1. Double-click a blank part of the form to open the form's Code window. Or, to attach code to a control, double-click the control.

2. In the Procedure box, select the event to which you want to attach code.

3. Enter the code you want within the template.

4. Repeat steps 2 and 3 if you need to in order to attach additional event procedures to the item.

You also can select controls or the form itself from the Object box in the Code window. The information displayed in the Procedure box changes to reflect the predefined events for the object you select. Bold text in the Code window's Procedure box indicates event procedures that you have attached to a form or a control.

Instead of using the template provided by Visual Basic, you also can create a new procedure by typing Sub *ProcedureName* in the Code window. Visual Basic will figure out what you have in mind and create the procedure for you.

Designing Menus

One of the flashiest and most important objects you can add to a form is a menu bar. The menu bar you create with Visual Basic looks very similar to the Visual Basic menu bar. It contains a horizontal list of menu names. See Figure 15.17.

Each menu name represents a menu of commands that appear in a drop-down box below each name. The user of the application can, in turn, use these drop-down boxes of commands to control the application (entirely or in part).

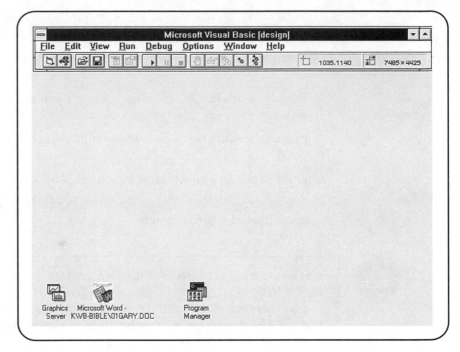

Figure 15.17. The Visual Basic menu bar.

You use the Menu Design window to create a menu bar that displays the menu names available in the active window. You also can write code that lets a menu respond dynamically to user selections and preferences or to run-time conditions. One simple and useful example is to enable and disable a menu command in response to a control or a situation.

All menu names and commands have the property `Enabled`. `Enabled` is a Boolean property; that is, it can take on either of two values: True or False. Suppose that you design a menu that contains the command `OpenFileCom`. You can disable that command (thereby making it appear in shadow) by setting the command's `Enable` property to False:

```
OpenFileCom.Enabled = 0
```

You can do many other things to and with menus and commands, such as checking a menu item, or even adding or deleting a menu item at run time.

To create a menu bar, follow these steps:

1. Click the form that will be attached to the menu bar.

2. From the Visual Basic Window menu, select Menu Design Window, and the Menu Design window appears. See Figure 15.18.

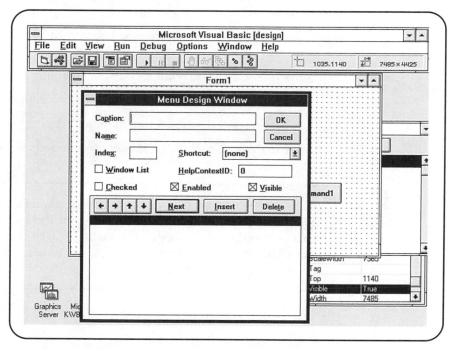

Figure 15.18. *The Menu Design window.*

3. In the Caption text box, enter the menu item caption you want displayed on the menu bar.

   To include a separator bar in your menu, type a single hyphen (–) in the Caption text box.

   To give a user a keyboard shortcut (that is, via Alt+*underlined letter*) to a menu item, type an ampersand (&) before the letter you want to specify as the shortcut (access) key. At run time, this letter is underlined, and the user can access the menu or command by using the keyboard shortcut.

4. Enter the control name (in the CtlName text box) that you will use to refer to the menu item in code. This name will always have a default value of the form Command1, Text2, and so on. A CtlName can be identical to the caption (that is, the Caption property).

15

5. Use the left- or right-arrow keys to change the level of a menu item (from a higher level to a lower level or vice versa). There can be as many as six levels of menus.

   Use the up or down arrows to change the position of a menu item (up or down in the list box).

   Select **Next** to move to the next line and add another item to the menu.

   Select **Insert** to add a line before the currently selected line.

   Select **Delete** to delete the currently selected line.

6. Repeat steps 3 through 5 to add menu items.

7. Select **Done** to accept the changes for the selected form.

> The menu you created is visible at design time, but no events are generated until you write code to carry out the menu commands. This is a handy feature, because it enables you to create and experiment with the look and feel of a menu (or menus) before actually writing the code for the menu.

A Menu has eight properties:

- Caption
- Checked
- CtlName
- Enabled
- Index
- Parent
- Tag
- Visible

and can respond to one event, a Click.

Input Boxes and Message Boxes

Two other boxes that result from the use of functions can be important in both simple and complex applications. These two boxes, an InputBox and a message box (MsgBox), enable you to communicate with users easily. Use an input box to get user input, and use a message box to communicate information to the user.

To put a message in the center of a form, use a MsgBox statement. For example, if you want to display a message when a form is clicked, write an event procedure for the form that displays the message:

```
Sub Form1_Click ()
    MsgBox "Here's a message, coming at you."
End Sub
```

Figure 15.19 shows the message box.

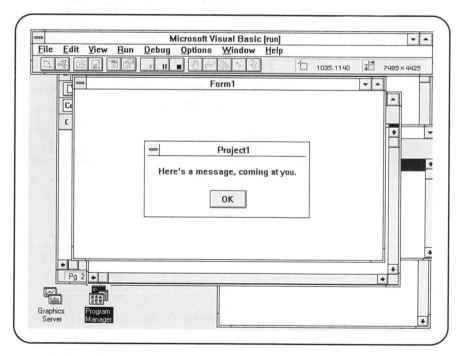

Figure 15.19. *A message box.*

You can alternatively use the MsgBox function to display a message and return a value indicating which button the user selected. The MsgBox function differs from the MsgBox statement primarily in that it returns a value.

The MsgBox function looks like this:

```
MsgBox(msg$ [, type% [, title$] ] )
```

where:

msg$ = The message in the dialog (or message) box;

type% determines the buttons and icons to display in the dialog (message) box;

title$ indicates the Title to be displayed in the title bar of the dialog (message) box.

MsgBox displays a maximum of 1024 characters. Any message longer than that is truncated after the 1024th character. If a message (which is a string) is longer than 255 characters and includes no spaces (to allow line breaks), it will be truncated after the 255th character.

MsgBox breaks lines automatically at the right edge of the dialog box. If you want to specify your own line breaks, use Chr$(13) (carriage return) and Chr$(10) (line feed character) before the text that you want to begin a new line.

The parameter type% is the sum of values that describe the number and type of buttons to display, the icon style, and the identification of the default button. Table 15.1 shows how these summed values work. I've put them in three groups (indicating buttons, icons, and ID system, respectively).

Table 15.1. Message box button, icon, and ID system.

type% *Value*	*Action*
Group 1	
0	Display OK button only.
1	Display OK and Cancel buttons.

type% *Value*	*Action*
2	Display Abort, Retry, and Ignore buttons.
3	Display Yes, No, and Cancel buttons.
4	Display Yes and No buttons.
5	Display Retry and Cancel buttons.
——— *Group 2* ———	
16	Display Critical Message icon.
32	Display Warning Query icon.
48	Display Warning Message icon.
64	Display Information Message icon.
——— *Group 3* ———	
0	First button is default.
256	Second button is default.
512	Third button is default.

The first group (1-5) indicates how many and what kind of buttons are displayed in the dialog box, the second group (16-64) describes the icon, and the third group determines which button is the default.

> You can use only one number from each group with each message box.

By default, if you omit type%, MsgBox displays one OK button in the dialog box and makes it the default button. No icon is the default display.

The return value of the MsgBox function indicates which button the user pressed. Table 15.2 shows how to interpret the return values.

Table 15.2. MsgBox function return values.

Value	Button Pressed
1	OK
2	Cancel
3	Abort
4	Retry
5	Ignore
6	Yes
7	No

If you omit the `title$`, MsgBox uses the default title, `Microsoft Visual Basic`.

InputBox$ Function

When you want to get information from a user, you can use any of several approaches. Perhaps the easiest approach (particularly if you want to get only a little bit of information) is to use an input box. An input box displays a prompt in a dialog box, waits for the user to input some text or select a button, and returns the contents of the edit box (where the user inputs the text).

An InputBox has the following syntax:

`InputBox$(prompt$ [, title$ [, default$[, xpos%, ypos% ] ] ])`

where:

`prompt$` = the message you want to display in the dialog box;

`title$` = the title you want to display in the title bar of the dialog box;

`default$` = the default response displayed in the edit box;

`xpos%` = the horizontal distance, in *twips,* of the left edge of the dialog box from the left edge of the screen;

ypos% = the vertical distance, in twips, of the upper edge of the dialog box from the top of the screen.

A twip is 1/20 of a printer's point. There are 72 printer's points to an inch. Thus, 1440 twips equal an inch. By default, all Visual Basic sizing, movement, and graphical/drawing statements use twips.

For example, to bring up an input box to the default position on a form, use an event procedure for the form (say Click) which contains InputBox$ code:

```
Sub Form1_Click()
    In$ = InputBox$ (" What's the first thing that comes to
    ➥mind?", "Please Respond")
End Sub
```

Figure 15.20 shows the input box that results from this code.

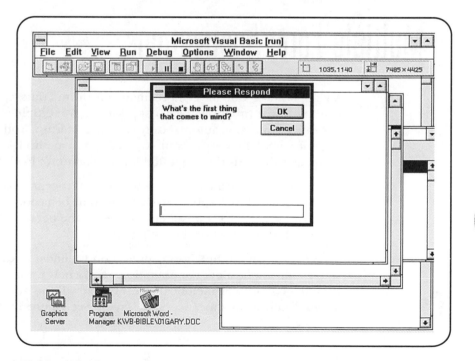

Figure 15.20. Input box.

The length of prompt$ is restricted to approximately 255 characters, depending on the width of the characters used in prompt$ (which varies depending on your choice of font). If you want prompt$ to have more than one line, add a carriage return (Chr$(13)) and a line-feed character (Chr$(10)) after each line. For example:

```
Msg$ = "Hi" + Chr$(13) + Chr$(10) + "you."    ' Add carriage
                                              ' return
In$ = InputBox$ (Msg$, "Please Respond")
```

If you omit the parameter title$, the title bar is empty. If you omit default$, the edit box is displayed empty. If you omit xpos%, you must also omit ypos%. When xpos% and ypos% are omitted, the dialog box is centered horizontally and positioned vertically approximately one-third of the way down the screen (the default position for an input box).

If the user selects the OK button or presses Enter, InputBox$ returns whatever is in the edit box. If the user selects the Cancel button, InputBox$ returns a null string ("").

Multiple-Form Applications

An application can have more than one form, thus creating a multi-windowed (or "multiple-form") application. A multiple-form application has one form that is automatically shown at startup. You then can show other forms whenever you want to use the Show method. The Show method automatically loads the requested form if you don't load it explicitly.

Whenever a form is shown, several events occur: Load, Resize, Paint, and GotFocus. Thus, if you want to specify some behavior for the form when it's shown—a listbox, for example—specifiy the behavior in one of these events. I'll show you how in a moment.

Creating a multiple-form application is almost as easy as creating a single form application. For example, to add a new form to an application, from the Visual Basic menu bar select the New Form option from the File menu. A new form appears on the screen. See Figure 15.21.

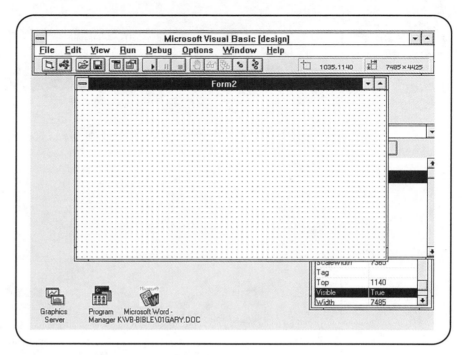

Figure 15.21. *Add a new form.*

To establish a switching connection between the forms, add a command control to each form and attach code to each command button for switching between the forms. Figure 15.22 shows Form1 with a command button control. Figure 15.23 shows Form2 with a command button control.

In order to switch forms each time the command control is clicked, send a message to the Show method for the form you want displayed. The following code shows Form2 in response to a command control click on Form1:

```
Sub Command1_Click ()
    Form2.Show
End Sub
```

The following code shows Form1 in response to a command control click on Form2:

```
Sub Command1_Click ()
    Form1.Show
End Sub
```

Figure 15.22.
Form1 with a
command
button
control.

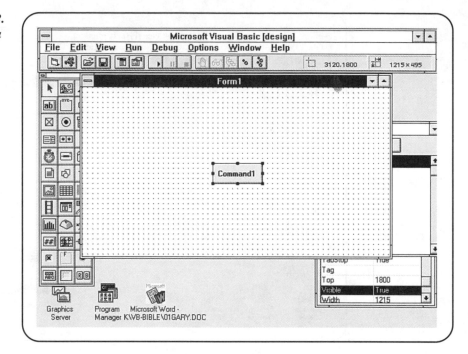

Figure 15.23.
Form2 with a
command
button
control.

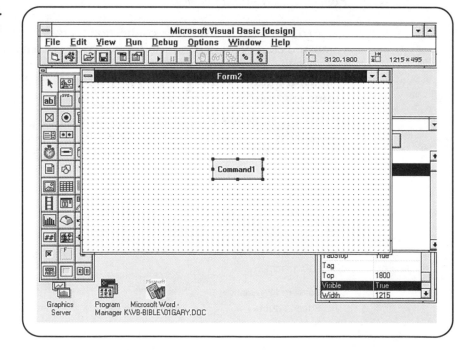

Figures 15.24 and 15.25 show the forms switched in response to command control clicks on each form.

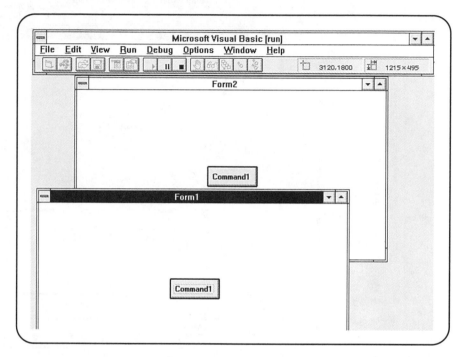

Figure 15.24. *Switching between forms.*

You also can hide a form when you show another form. The following code handles that step:

```
Sub Command1_Click ()
    Form1.Hide
End Sub
```

Figure 15.26 shows Form2, after a Form1 command control click, with Form1 hidden.

If you want to specify some behavior for the form when it is shown, specify it in either the Load, Resize, Paint, or GotFocus event for the form. For example, to add several items to a list box when the form is shown, follow steps 1-6 (following Figure 15.26).

Figure 15.25.
Switching between forms.

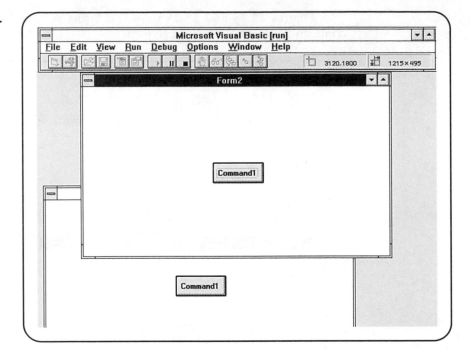

Figure 15.26.
Form2 is visible; Form1 is hidden.

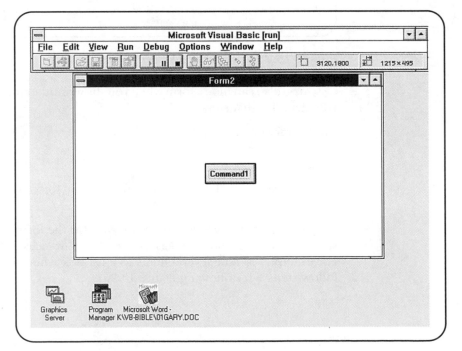

1. Add a list box to Form2 (see Figure 15.27).

2. Call it `CustomList` (by changing its `CtlName` property; see Figure 15.28).

3. Double-click the form to bring up the Code window.

4. Select the `Load` event from the proc bar (see Figure 15.29).

5. Add the following code to `Form2_Load()`:

```
Sub Form2_Load ()
    CustomList.AddItem " skiing "        ' Add items to list.
    CustomList.AddItem " kayaking"
End Sub
```

See Figure 15.30.

6. Run the application and click the command button of Form1.

   Figure 15.31 shows the resulting screen.

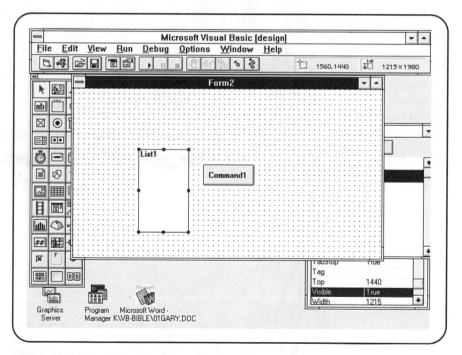

Figure 15.27. Add a list box.

Figure 15.28.
Change
CtlName
property
setting.

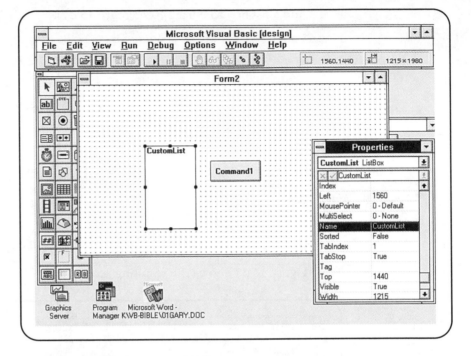

Figure 15.29.
Select Load
event from the
proc bar.

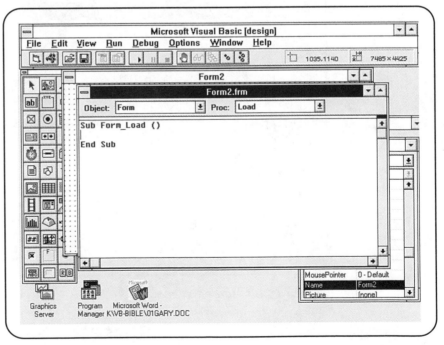

Figure 15.30.
Edit Load
event.

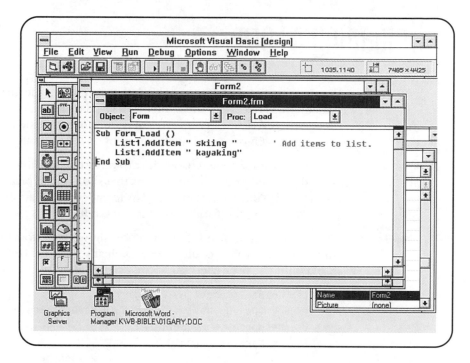

Figure 15.31.
Application
"Add List"
running.

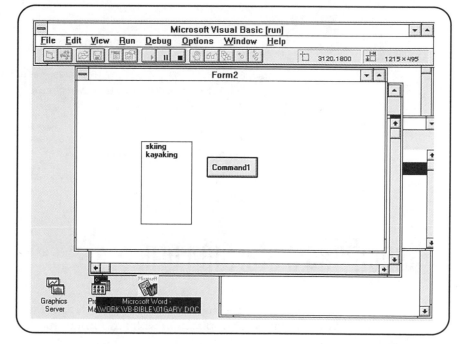

Unloading a Form

Use the Form_Unload event to unload (that is, remove) a form from the screen. If that form is reloaded, the contents of all its controls are reinitialized. This event is triggered by user action (closing the form using the control menu icon in the upper-left corner of the form) or by an Unload statement.

Use an Unload event procedure to verify that the unloading of the form should proceed or to specify actions that should take place when the form is unloaded. You also can include any form-level validation code you might need for closing the form or saving data in it.

For example, the following code shows how you might handle an unload event, which could occur explicitly after an Unload message or implicitly if the user used the form's system menu to close the form:

```
Sub Form_Unload (Cancel As Integer)
    Msg$ = "Do you want to save data before closing?"
    UserResponse% = MsgBox(Msg$, 3 + 32, "Save Dialog")
    Select Case Response%
        Case 2                        ' 2 = cancel (see Table 15.2)
            ' Do not allow close.
            Cancel = -1
            Msg$ = "Command cancelled."

        Case 6                        ' 6 = yes (see Table 15.2)
            ' Write code to handle save here.
            Msg$ = "Data saved."

        Case 7                        ' 7 = no (see Table 15.2)
            Msg$ = "Data not saved."
    End Select
End Sub
```

Specifying a Startup Form

An application does not have to start up with the first form in the project. You can start your application with any form or module.

To specify a startup form, follow these steps:

1. Select the Set Startup Form option from the **R**un menu. Visual Basic displays a dialog box.

2. Select the form you want your application to start with using the Set Startup Form option from the **R**un menu.

3. Select OK.

Instead of loading a form, Visual Basic can invoke a procedure. To specify a startup module, follow these steps:

1. Code a general procedure and save it under the filename Main.

2. Select the Set Startup Form option from the **R**un menu. Visual Basic displays a dialog box.

3. Select Sub Main from the list box.

4. Select OK.

> You can assign a special icon to any form that the user can minimize at run time. A special icon can give the user a visual cue for the behavior of a form or an application. Visual Basic's Icon Library is a good source for icons. Figure 15.32 shows several icons displayed using the Object Packager that comes with Windows.

Creating an .EXE

15

To create an executable file from your project, follow these steps:

1. Select the Make EXE File option from the File menu. Visual Basic checks to make sure there are no syntax or other compile errors in your code. If your code is OK (that is, if it has no syntax or other compile errors), Visual Basic displays a default .EXE filename in the File Name text box.

2. Enter a filename in the text box or accept the default if you're satisfied with that name. Your filename replaces the default name when you begin typing a new name. Visual Basic automatically adds the required .EXE extension.

3. Specify the title for your application (in the title box), or accept the default (the project name). This title will appear as the application name in the Windows Task Manager Task List.

4. In the Use Icon From List box, select an icon for the application. You can either use one of those you've assigned to the other forms in the project or accept the displayed icon (the default icon for the startup form). If you want to use a special icon for the application, you must first use the special icon to indicate a form in the project. The application icon must be one of the project's form icons.

   This Application icon is displayed when the application is mini-mized, and in the Windows Program Manager.

5. Select OK to create an executable version of your project.

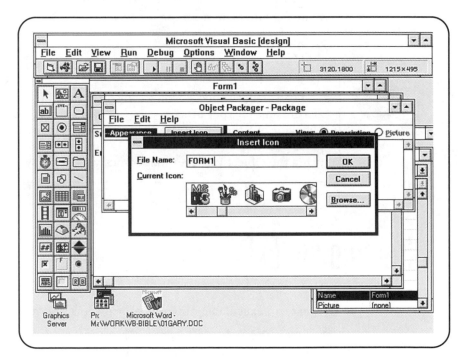

Figure 15.32. *Several Icons displayed using the Object Packager.*

Running an Executable File

Use this procedure to run an application Visual Basic project you have compiled into an executable file. Before you run your application, be sure that you have included the Visual Basic runtime DLL (VBRUN100.DLL if you're using VB 1.0 and VBRUN200.DLL if you're using VB 2.0) in your current path.

To run a Visual Basic application from Microsoft Windows, double-click the icon for your application's .EXE file.

To run a Visual Basic application from DOS, at the command prompt type `win filename`, where `filename` indicates your application's .EXE file.

Summary

That's about enough of the application development basics. You should be able to use what you've learned in this chapter to create many and various kinds of applications. From this point on, you'll use the techniques you've learned in this chapter as a basis for creating more and more complex applications.

In the next four chapters you explore application development in more detail and create several simple applications, which explore more advanced techniques and features of Visual Basic. In general, use the blueprint we developed in this chapter to design your applications:

1. Create a form for each window in your application.

2. Draw the controls for each form.

3. Design a menu bar for the main form.

4. Set form and control properties.

5. Write event procedures and general procedures.

6. Test and debug.

Then, after you're satisfied with the application,

7. Create an executable file to turn the project into an application.

Don't hesitate to vary these steps when you need to: It's just a plan, but a good one to start with.

16

Mouse Events and Responding to Commands

So far, you've used event procedures to tell your applications how to respond to a mouse click (event). Responding to Mouse Clicks and DoubleClicks is an important way to communicate with users. The mouse system, however, can be much more powerful.

For example, you can design applications so that your users can create and manipulate graphic images and move controls using a mouse pointer. In other words, users of your applications can manipulate and customize their own interfaces at runtime.

Visual Basic makes this possible through several mouse events, the DragMode and DragIcon properties, and the Drag method.

In this chapter, you develop several small example applications that utilize different aspects of these events, properties, and methods. The first example you develop is a simple painting application.

A Painting Application

Forms and several controls (file listbox, label, listbox, and picture box) can respond (through event procedures) to three mouse events: MouseDown, MouseUp, and MouseMove.

A MouseDown event occurs when the user presses a mouse button.
A MouseUp event occurs when the user releases a mouse button.
A MouseMove event occurs when the user moves the mouse.

Typically, you use these events in conjunction. For example, you might have some action occur while a MouseButton is down, but before it's released.

In the first part of this chapter, you develop two versions of a painting application (called Mouse1 and Mouse1b). Both use the MouseDown event procedure with a related MouseMove procedure to paint when any mouse button is pressed. The MouseUp procedure turns off the paintbrush. Mouse1 sets up the basic machinery for the paint application. Mouse1b changes the painting surface from a form to a picture box. Mouse1b also uses an input box to allow the user to vary the DrawWidth and DrawStyle properties.

Mouse1

Use the Step system you developed in Chapter 15, "Creating an Application," to develop this application.

Step 1—Open a new project. (Remember, you don't have to do anything to begin a new project. Visual Basic automatically opens a new project for you, with a new form when you start up Visual Basic.) This project will only have one form, so you're ready to go.

Step 2—Draw the controls for each form. (No controls for Mouse1, so on to Step 3.)

Step 3—Design a menu bar for the main form. (No menu bar for Mouse1, so on to Step 4.)

Step 4—Set form and control properties. (We'll just use the defaults for now, so on to Step 5.)

Step 5—Write event and general procedures. (Now you have to do something!)

The first go at the paint application (which is Mouse1) needs event procedures for the form.

First, the application needs a Load procedure. You can specify some default behavior for a form by putting it in Form_.Load(). This works because Visual Basic always calls the Load event procedure for the Startup (or Main, for C programmers) form when it starts the application. If you don't add any behavior to the Load event procedure, the form still gets loaded with its default values. Also, even if you add some behavior to any event procedure, only the behaviors you change or add are affected. All other default values and settings for the object (in this case, a form) retain their defaults.

Now you set two of the form's properties, DrawWidth and ForeColor, but leave every other property unchanged. The following code handles this task.

```
Sub Form_Load ()
    DrawWidth = 7                ' Use wider paintbrush; default = 1
    ForeColor = RGB(0, 0, 255)
End Sub
```

Figure 16.1 shows this code in the project's code window.

Notice you didn't have to specify an object for DrawWidth or ForeColor. By default, Visual Basic assumes that an unspecified property refers to the current object. In this case the current object is a form, so Form does not have to be specified. You could specify it, though, as shown in the following code.

```
Sub Form_Load ()
    Form1.DrawWidth = 7          ' Use wider paintbrush; default = 1
    Form1.ForeColor = RGB(0, 0, 255)
End Sub
```

Next, write the code for the three mouse events. Visual Basic automatically sends a message to the selected object (in this case a form) through the MouseDown event procedure, notifying it that a mouse button has been pressed. If you want to implement some specific response behavior to the MouseDown event, do it in the MouseDown event procedure. In Mouse1, the MouseDown event procedure notifies the rest of the application that a mouse button has been pressed. The following code accomplishes this:

419

```
Sub Form_MouseDown (Button As Integer, Shift As Integer, X As
➥Single, Y As Single)
    MouseIsDown = -1          ' MouseIsDown.
End Sub
```

Figure 16.2 shows this code in the project's code window.

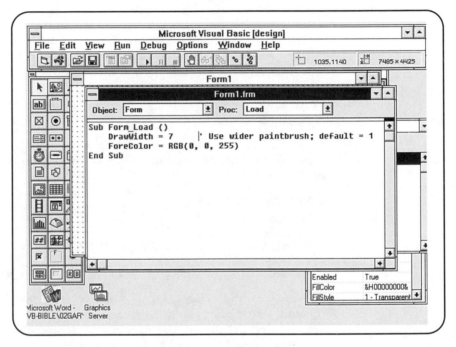

Figure 16.1. The project's code window.

Before you attach any more code to the other mouse event procedures, ponder for a moment how the MouseDown code you just wrote notifies the application that the user wants to paint.

The MouseDown event procedure is called when a mouse button has been pressed and the current object gets this message. Notice the object-oriented nature of this message processing. Each object that can respond to a MouseDown event has its own version of MouseDown. For example, there's Form_MouseDown and PictureBox_MouseDown.

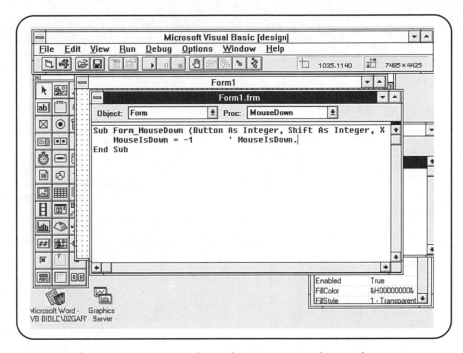

Figure 16.2. *MouseDown code in the project's code window.*

This is object-oriented programming's polymorphism feature in action. Powerful, flexible, yet something you as a Visual Basic programmer need not worry about. You simply add the code to the event procedure for the object that you want to respond to the mouse event. You don't have to think about how the message gets routed to the correct object. Mouse2, later in this chapter, illustrates this concept in a bit more detail. For now (and really, for always), you don't have to worry about this matter. Visual Basic takes care of it.

Polymorphism actually came into play earlier in this chapter with the DrawWidth and ForeColor properties. Both of these property names (and many others) are shared by several objects. Usually, you'll just take polymorphism for granted. It's a great Visual Basic feature that you don't need to worry about.

The `MouseIsDown` variable informs the application that the mouse button has been pressed. For the application to recognize this variable, you must declare it either globally (so that all modules in the application get the message) or in the declarations section of the form (as a form-level variable, so all the procedures attached to the form get the message). Figure 16.3 shows how variable scoping works in Visual Basic.

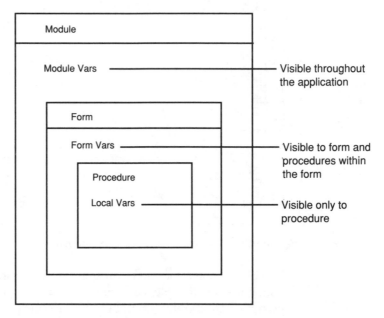

Figure 16.3. The scope of variables in an application.

Because the current application has only one module, it really doesn't matter where you declare the variable `MouseIsDown`. Figure 16.4 shows it declared as a general procedure in the code window.

The next step is to write an event procedure for `Form_MouseUp()` that informs the rest of the application, through the variable `MouseIsDown`, that the mouse is no longer down. `Form_MouseUp()` sets `MouseIsDown` to False (0). The following code does it.

```
Sub Form_MouseUp (Button As Integer, Shift As Integer, X As
➡Single, Y As Single)
    MouseIsDown = 0        ' MouseIsDown set to false (0)
End Sub
```

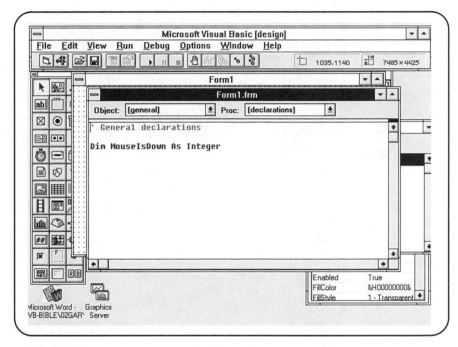

Figure 16.4. A general procedure declaration in the code window.

Now you can use the MouseMove event to actually paint. Form_MouseMove()
checks to see if the mouse button is down. If it is, it sets the current point
(the location of the mouse pointer) using PSet. The following code does
this.

```
Sub Form_MouseMove (Button As Integer, Shift As Integer, X As
➡Single, Y As Single)
    If MouseIsDown Then     ' If mouse is down
        PSet (X, Y)         ' draw the point
    End If
End Sub
```

423

Figure 16.5 shows the results of the application at the current development stage, after the user clicks the form and moves the mouse around a bit.

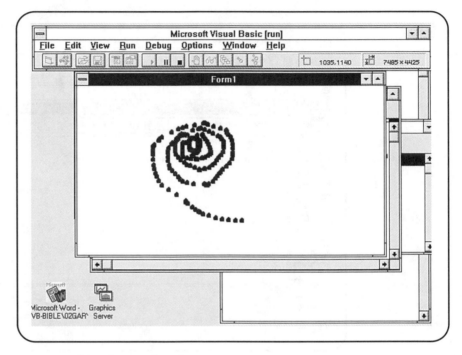

Figure 16.5. *The results of Mouse1.*

There's something else of interest in Figure 16.5. It's a screen capture, and only half of the form looks as if it's drawn on. I ran the application, and then switched to my screen program (Collage) to capture the image so I could use it in this book. The image I actually drew with the application is the one in Figure 16.6.

What's happening? Well, by default, the contents of a form are not automatically redrawn when the form is covered by another application window (or form). My screen capture program partially covers the form (the right half), so when this program captures the screen, it only correctly captures the part of the form that isn't covered. Why? Because the form is not automatically redrawn when Collage switches back to it to capture the image.

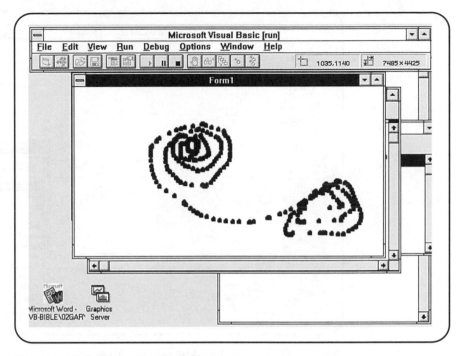

Figure 16.6. Mouse1—the full image.

So, how did I capture the correct image? Simple. I set the form's AutoReDraw property to True. Thus, when I switch back to the form, it's contents are automatically redrawn. (Actually, the contents are redrawn at other times as well. More on that in a moment.) Figure 16.7 shows the property bar and new setting for AutoReDraw.

When I switched back to the form (from Collage), the form's contents were redrawn.

Unfortunately, AutoReDraw slows down the performance of the mouse because the AutoReDraw occurs more often than needed (even when you're still painting on the form; for example, between mouse events).

So can you handle the redrawing of the form's contents another way? Yes, by storing the points that are already drawn (using Pset). Then, when you need to redisplay the contents of a form, they can be redrawn (again using Pset).

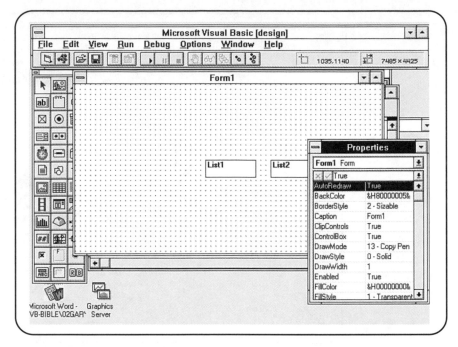

Figure 16.7. *Form.ReDraw is set to True.*

How does this work? Good question. The key to this solution is knowing what happens each time the Windows switches back to your application. For a more detailed description, check out your Visual Basic manual: *The Visual Basic Programmer's Guide.*

Whenever the AutoReDraw property for a form is set to False (0), the form's Paint method gets sent a message by Windows. So the redrawing of points should occur in the Paint method. So how do you save and redraw points?

You can use any of several variable structures to store points for later display. One interesting (and easy) structure, the listbox, has already been set up for you, so use it in this example.

First, create two listboxes by double-clicking the listbox control (in the Toolbox) twice. Two listboxes (one on top of the other) appear on the form. Place them on the form (see Figure 16.8).

But you don't really need to see the boxes at runtime; you just want to use the list properties of the listbox. Set the Visible property for each of the listboxes to False using the property bar (see Figure 16.9).

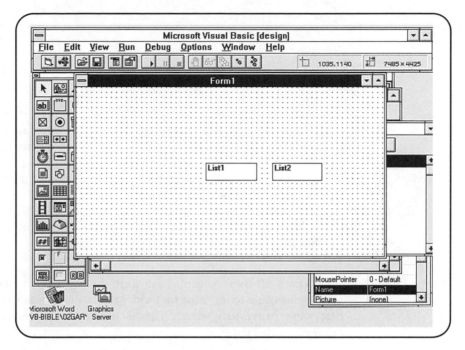

Figure 16.8. Two listboxes on the form.

Now you have two invisible listboxes that you can use at run time for storing and retrieving points. Store the points at the same time you draw them by rewriting the MouseMove event procedure, as follows:

```
Sub Form_MouseMove (Button As Integer, Shift As Integer, X As
➡Single, Y As Single)
    If MouseIsDown Then
        PSet (X, Y)                ' Draw the point
        List1.AddItem Str$(X)      ' Save the X coordinate
        List2.AddItem Str$(Y)      ' and Y coordinate for later
    End If
End Sub
```

Notice that you're using one list to store the X coordinate and the other list to store the Y coordinate. Also, AddItem is a predefined method, which the listbox (and also combo boxes) can use.

To replay MouseMoves, retrieve the points from the list and redraw them (using PSet again) when the form's Paint method gets a message. The following code does the trick:

```
Sub Form1_Paint()
    ReDrawPoints                            ' general procedure
End Sub


Sub ReDrawPoints ()
    Cls                                     ' Clear the screen
    For I = 0 To List1.ListCount - 1        ' Redraw all the
                                            ' points stored in the
                                            ' lists

        X = Val(List1.List(I))              ' Get X from list1
        Y = Val(List2.List(I))              ' Get Y from list 2
        Form1.PSet (X, Y)                   ' Actually draw the
                                            ' point

    Next
End Sub
```

That's all there is to it. Each time the form is uncovered, Windows sends a message to its Paint method. Paint calls ReDraw to draw the points that were previously saved. This is much more efficient than setting AutoReDraw to True.

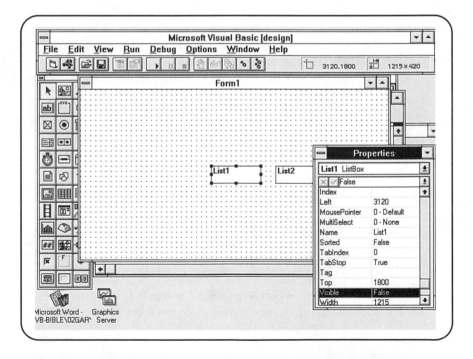

Figure 16.9. The Visible property for the listboxes is set to False.

> Remember, you must set the AutoReDraw property to False for the
> Paint method to get the message.

Listing 16.1 shows the complete code for the Mouse1 application.
Figure 16.10 shows the lists updated after a mouse move.

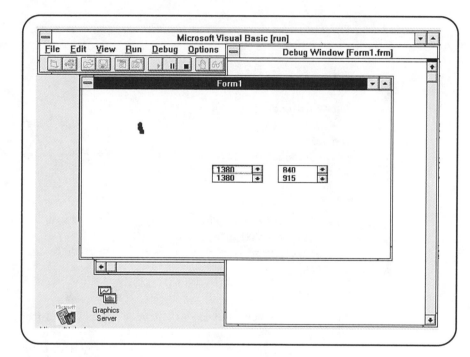

Figure 16.10. *List update after a mouse move.*

Listing 16.1. Mouse1.

```
' General declarations


Dim MouseIsDown As Integer


' general procedures
```

continues

Listing 16.1. continued

```
Sub ReDrawPoints ()
    Cls
    For I = 0 To List1.ListCount - 1
        X = Val(List1.List(I))              ' get X from List1
        Y = Val(List2.List(I))              ' Get Y from List2
        Form1.PSet (X, Y)                   ' Actually draw the point
    Next
End Sub



' Event procedures for form

Sub Form_Load ()
    DrawWidth = 7                           ' Use wider paintbrush.
Default = 1
    ForeColor = RGB(0, 0, 255)              ' Set color (optional)
End Sub



Sub Form_MouseDown (Button As Integer, Shift As Integer, X As
➥Single, Y As Single)
    MouseIsDown = -1                        ' MouseIsDown.
End Sub



Sub Form_MouseUp (Button As Integer, Shift As Integer, X As
➥Single, Y As Single)
    MouseIsDown = 0                         ' MouseIsUp.
End Sub


Sub Form_MouseMove (Button As Integer, Shift As Integer, X As
➥Single, Y As Single)
    If MouseIsDown Then
        PSet (X, Y)
        List1.AddItem Str$(X)               ' Store X and Y in List1
                                            ' and List2

        List2.AddItem Str$(Y)
    End If
End Sub
```

Notice you don't write any code for manipulating the list at a low level. Visual Basic takes care of managing the list for you. You just add things (using AddItem) and get things back (using List). Pretty nifty, Visual Basic.

Painting to a Picture

16

It's also a simple matter to rewrite the previous application to allow painting to go to a picture rather than a form. Add a picture box to the form (using the Toolbox). Listing 16.2, Mouse1b, shows the new code.

Listing 16.2. Mouse1b.

```
' general declarations


Dim MouseIsDown As Integer


' general procedures

Sub ReDrawPoints ()
    Picture1.Cls
    For I = 0 To List1.ListCount - 1
        X = Val(List1.List(I))          ' Get X and Y values from
                                        ' Lists1& 2
        Y = Val(List2.List(I))
        Picture1.PSet (X, Y)            ' Draw the point on a
                                        ' picture.
    Next
End Sub


' Form event procedures

Sub Form_Load ()
    Picture1.DrawWidth = 7             ' Set the picture box
                                       ' instead of the form.
```

continues

Listing 16.2. continued

```
        Picture1.ForeColor = RGB(0, 0, 255)
End Sub


Sub Form_Paint ()              ' Paint will be called anytime the form
                               ' needs
    ReDrawPoints               ' to be repainted
End Sub


' Picture box event procedures           ' Let the picture box
                                          ' instead of the form
                                          ' respond to the mouse
                                          ' so write Picture mouse
                                          ' event procedures

Sub Picture1_MouseDown (Button As Integer, Shift As Integer, X As
➡Single, Y As Single)
    MouseIsDown = -1
End Sub


Sub Picture1_MouseUp (Button As Integer, Shift As Integer, X As
➡Single, Y As Single)
    MouseIsDown = 0
End Sub


Sub Picture1_MouseMove (Button As Integer, Shift As Integer, X As
➡Single, Y As Single)
    If MouseIsDown Then
        Picture1.PSet (X, Y)
        List1.AddItem Str$(X)            ' Save point coordinates
        List2.AddItem Str$(Y)
    End If
End Sub
```

Figure 16.11 shows the results.

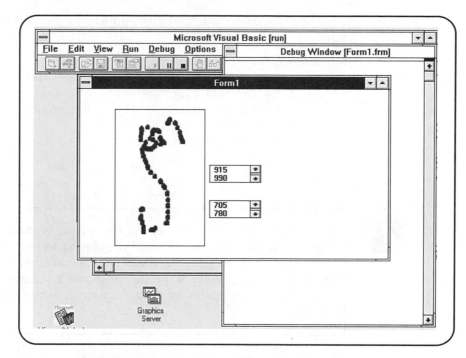

Figure 16.11. *Painting to a picture box.*

Notice how this new version of the code differs from the first version of the painting application (Mouse1). Instead of directing output to the form, all output is now directed to the picture box.

```
Sub Picture1_MouseMove (Button As Integer, Shift As Integer, X As
➥Single, Y As Single)
    If MouseIsDown Then
        Picture1.PSet (X, Y)              ' Set point in picture box
        List1.AddItem Str$(X)
        List2.AddItem Str$(Y)
    End If
End Sub
```

Rather than specifying DrawWidth and ForeColor properties for the form, you specify them for the picture box when the form is loaded, as shown in the following lines of code:

```
Sub Form_Load ()
    Picture1.DrawWidth = 10              ' set picture box properties
    Picture1.ForeColor = RGB(0, 0, 255)
End Sub
```

433

ReDrawPoints now refers all its output to the picture box instead of the form.

```
Sub ReDrawPoints ()
    Picture1.Cls                       ' Clear picture1
    For I = 0 To List1.ListCount - 1
        X = Val(List1.List(I))         ' Get points
        Y = Val(List2.List(I))
        Picture1.PSet (X, Y)
    Next
End Sub
```

> PSet is polymorphic—that is, the name PSet is shared by several objects. In this example, Picture1 (an object) and Form1 (an object) both use a PSet method. The actual implementations of PSet differs. Form1.PSet sets a point at the current X and Y relative *to the form*. Picture1.PSet sets a point at the current X and Y relative *to the picture*.

DrawWith and DrawStyle

Two other improvements on the painting application complete this general picture, which you can use as a model for many applications. You add two command buttons that control the display of an input box. You also use the input box to let users modify the width and style of the paintbrush.

Add the command buttons and reset their caption properties to DrawWidth and DrawStyle. See Figure 16.12.

Write Click event procedures for the command buttons:

The code following Figure 16.12 is for Command1 and Command2 button click event procedures.

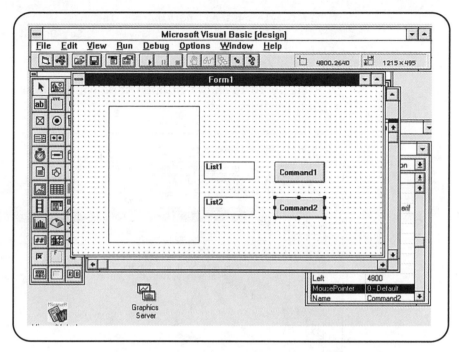

16

Figure 16.12. *The* DrawWidth *and* DrawStyle *command buttons.*

```
For Command1_Click():
```

```
Sub Command1_Click ()
    DWidth = Val(InputBox$("Enter new DrawWidth value.",
"DrawWidth Property"))
    If DWidth >= 1 And DWidth <= 255 Then
        Picture1.DrawWidth = DWidth    ' Set DrawWidth property
    End If
End Sub
```

```
For Command2_Click():
```

```
Sub Command2_Click ()
    DStyle = Val(InputBox$("Enter new DrawStyle value.",
"DrawStyle Property"))
```

```
        If DStyle >= 1 And DStyle <= 6 Then
            Picture1.DrawStyle = DStyle    ' Set DrawStyle property
        End If
    End Sub
End Sub
```

Figure 16.13 shows an open code window with a command click event procedure.

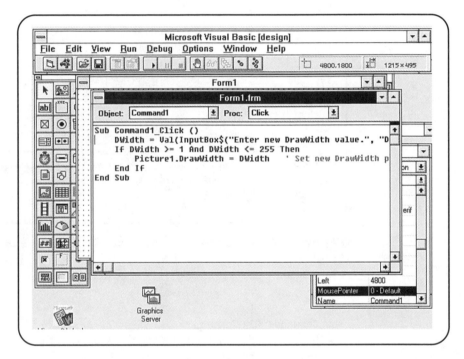

Figure 16.13. *The open code window.*

Figure 16.14 shows the running application with the DrawWidth input box open.

Figure 16.15 shows the running application with the DrawStyle input box open.

Figure 16.16 shows new DrawWidth and DrawStyle properties in use.

Listing 16.3 contains the complete code for Mouse1C.

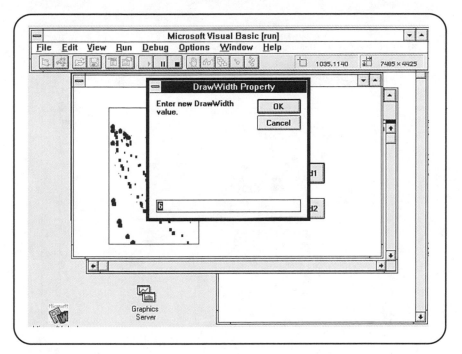

Figure 16.14.
The open
DrawWidth
input box.

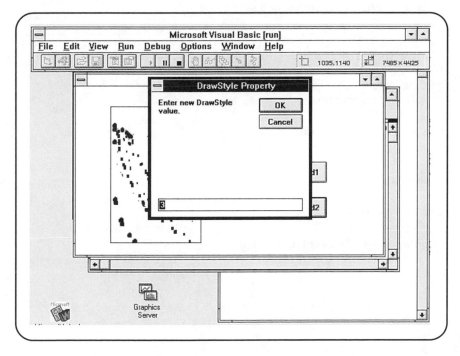

Figure 16.15.
The open
DrawStyle
input box.

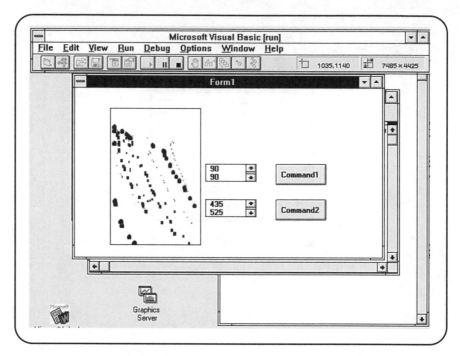

Figure 16.16. *Using* DrawWidth *and* DrawStyle.

Listing 16.3. The Paint application using DrawWidth and DrawStyle input boxes.

```
'general declarations

Dim MouseIsDown As Integer



' general procedures

Sub ReDrawPoints ()
    Picture1.Cls                        ' Clear picture box
    For I = 0 To List1.ListCount - 1
        X = Val(List1.List(I))          ' Get X and Y from Lists 1
                                        ' and 2
        Y = Val(List2.List(I))
        Picture1.PSet (X, Y)            ' Set the point in the
                                        ' picture box
```

```
        Next
End Sub


' form event procedures


Sub Form_Load ()
    Picture1.DrawWidth = 7            ' Set picture box properties
    Picture1.ForeColor = RGB(0, 0, 255)
End Sub


' Command button event procedures

Sub Command1_Click ()
    DWidth = Val(InputBox$("Enter new DrawWidth value.",
"DrawWidth Property"))
    If DWidth >= 1 And DWidth <= 255 Then
        Picture1.DrawWidth = DWidth    ' Set new DrawWidth property
    End If
End Sub


Sub Command2_Click ()
    DStyle = Val(InputBox$("Enter new DrawStyle value.",
"DrawStyle Property"))
    If DStyle >= 1 And DStyle <= 6 Then
        Picture1.DrawStyle = DStyle    ' Set new DrawStyle property
    End If
End Sub


' Picture box event procedures

Sub Picture1_MouseDown (Button As Integer, Shift As Integer, X As
➡Single, Y As Single)
    MouseIsDown = -1                   ' True
End Sub
```

continues

439

Listing 16.3. continued

```
Sub Picture1_MouseUp (Button As Integer, Shift As Integer, X As
➡Single, Y As Single)
    MouseIsDown = 0                    ' False
End Sub



Sub Picture1_MouseMove (Button As Integer, Shift As Integer, X As
➡Single, Y As Single)
    If MouseIsDown Then
        Picture1.PSet (X, Y)           ' Set the point
        List1.AddItem Str$(X)          ' Save the point
        List2.AddItem Str$(Y)
    End If
End Sub
```

If you run this code as is, it works great except for one glitch: when the form needs to be repainted, it updates the picture box display somewhat incorrectly. It puts the points where it should, but not in the correct width or style. It uses the last width or style for the form when it repaints the points. This is probably not what you want. It should reproduce the display exactly. You need to set the DrawWidth and DrawStyle each time you set a point, which also means that you need to save their values each time you save a point. Back to the drawing board.

A simple solution to this new problem is to create two more lists (List3 and List4): List3 holds the DrawWidth property each time a point is saved. List4 holds the DrawStyle property. Add two more listbox controls and make them invisible (unless you want to see these values on the form). Modify the Picture1.MouseMove event procedure as follows:

```
Sub Picture1_MouseMove (Button As Integer, Shift As Integer, X As
➡Single, Y As Single)
    If MouseIsDown Then
        Picture1.PSet (X, Y)
        DWidth = Picture1.DrawWidth
        DStyle = Picture1.DrawStyle
        List1.AddItem Str$(X)          ' X
        List2.AddItem Str$(Y)          ' Y
        List3.AddItem Str$(DWidth)     ' Save DrawWidth property
        List4.AddItem Str$(DStyle)     ' Save DrawStyle property
```

```
        End If
End Sub
```

This saves the Picture1.DrawWidth and DrawStyle values and adds these values to List3 and List4.

You need to modify the general procedure ReDrawPoints to read these values back from the list each time a point needs to be redisplayed. The new ReDrawPoints code is shown here.

```
Sub ReDrawPoints ()
    Picture1.Cls
    For I = 0 To List1.ListCount - 1
        X = Val(List1.List(I))
        Y = Val(List2.List(I))
        DWI% = Val(List3.List(I))      ' Get DrawWidth for point
        DSI% = Val(List4.List(I))      ' Get DrawStyle for point
        Picture1.DrawWidth = DWI%      ' Set DrawWidth
        Picture1.DrawStyle = DSI%      ' Set DRawStyle
        Picture1.PSet (X, Y)
    Next
End Sub
```

The complete listing for this version of the Paint application is given in Listing 16.4.

Listing 16.4. Mouse1d—Paint, including Save DrawWidth & DrawStyle.

```
'general declarations

Dim MouseIsDown As Integer



' general procedures

Sub ReDrawPoints ()
    Picture1.Cls
    For I = 0 To List1.ListCount - 1
        X = Val(List1.List(I))          ' Save X, Y, DrawWidth,
                                        ' DrawStyle
        Y = Val(List2.List(I))          ' for each point
```

continues

441

Listing 16.4. continued

```
        DWI% = Val(List3.List(I))
        DSI% = Val(List4.List(I))
        Picture1.DrawWidth = DWI%        ' Set DrawWidth, DrawStyle,
                                         ' Point
        Picture1.DrawStyle = DSI%
        Picture1.PSet (X, Y)
    Next
End Sub



' form event procedures



Sub Form_Load ()
    Picture1.DrawWidth = 7              ' Set picture box properties
    Picture1.ForeColor = RGB(0, 0, 255)
End Sub



' Command button event procedures

Sub Command1_Click ()
    DWidth = Val(InputBox$("Enter new DrawWidth value.",
    ➥"DrawWidth Property"))
    If DWidth >= 1 And DWidth <= 255 Then
        Picture1.DrawWidth = DWidth    'Set DrawWidth after test
    End If
End Sub



Sub Command2_Click ()
    DStyle = Val(InputBox$("Enter new DrawStyle value.",
    ➥"DrawStyle Property"))
    If DStyle >= 1 And DStyle <= 6 Then
        Picture1.DrawStyle = DStyle    ' Set DrawStyle after test
    End If
End Sub
```

```
' Picture box event procedures

Sub Picture1_MouseDown (Button As Integer, Shift As Integer, X As
➡Single, Y As Single)
    MouseIsDown = -1                    ' True
End Sub


Sub Picture1_MouseUp (Button As Integer, Shift As Integer, X As
➡Single, Y As Single)
    MouseIsDown = 0                     ' False
End Sub


Sub Picture1_MouseMove (Button As Integer, Shift As Integer, X As
➡Single, Y As Single)
    If MouseIsDown Then
        Picture1.PSet (X, Y)
        DWidth = Picture1.DrawWidth     ' Get DrawWidth & DrawStyle
                                        ' properties
        DStyle = Picture1.DrawStyle
        List1.AddItem Str$(X)           ' Add X, Y, DrawWidth,
                                        ' DrawStyle
        List2.AddItem Str$(Y)           ' for point
        List3.AddItem Str$(DWidth)
        List4.AddItem Str$(DStyle)
    End If
End Sub
```

Moving Controls at Run time

You can also use mouse events to manipulate controls. For example, the
following code demonstrates how you can animate a control. This application uses a control that moves about the screen in response to a MouseDown
event. When the mouse button is released (a MouseUp event), the control
rests until the mouse is pressed again.

To develop this application, use the step system you developed in Chapter 15, "Creating an Application."

Step 1—Begin with a form.

Step 2—Add a control (a picture box, for example) to a form. Double-click the picture box tool in the Toolbox. To make the picture box more interesting, add a picture to it. To load a picture from a file to the picture box, first select the picture box to make it active. Then go to its property bar and change its picture setting to a file (see Figure 16.17).

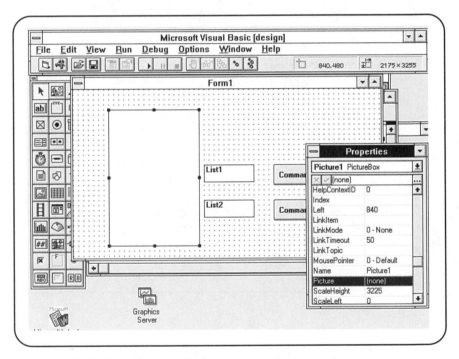

Figure 16.17. The property bar setting for a picture box.

When you change this setting to a file, a file dialog box opens and you can select a file to load from disk (see Figure 16.18).

Select the file. If you selected a bitmap, the file now appears in the picture box (see Figure 16.19).

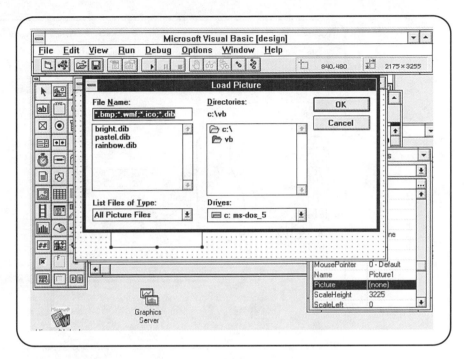

Figure 16.18. *The picture box dialog.*

Next, write the event procedures for Form_MouseDown, Form_MouseUp, and Form_MouseMove. MouseDown and MouseUp are the same as in the last application: Mouse1(Mouse1a,Mouse1b,Mouse1c, and Mouse1d).

Form_MouseDown

looks like this:

```
Sub Form_MouseDown (Button As Integer, Shift As Integer, X As
➥Single, Y As Single)
    MouseIsDown = -1
End Sub
```

Just as in Mouse1, the MouseDown event simply notifies the application that a mouse button has been pressed by setting the variable MousePressed to True (–1). Because MousePressed needs to be recognized by more than one event procedure, it cannot be declared locally (within a procedure). Recall the discussion when you designed Mouse1, and declare the event either in the global module, where it is recognized by the entire application, or in the declarations section of the form, where this event is recognized by all the procedures attached to the form. Refer back to Figure 16.3.

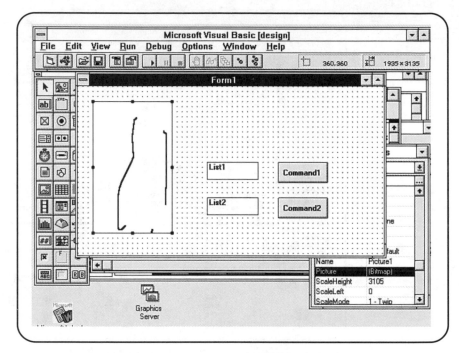

Figure 16.19. *A picture (bitmap file) loaded into a picture box.*

Declare MouseIsDown in the declarations section for the form:

```
Dim MouseIsDown As Integer
Form_MouseUp
```

looks like this:

```
Sub Form_MouseUp (Button As Integer, Shift As Integer, X As
➥Single, Y As Single)
    MouseIsDown = 0
End Sub
```

Again, the real work occurs in the Mouse_Move event procedure. Form_MouseMove randomly moves the picture box (containing a picture) around in the form. The code for this action is shown here.

```
Sub Form_MouseMove (Button As Integer, Shift As Integer, X As
➥Single, Y As Single)
        If MouseIsDown = -1 Then
```

```
              Randomize                   ' Initialize Random Num ' '
                                          ' generator
         X = Int(7500 * Rnd + 1)
         Y = Int(4500 * Rnd + 1)
         Picture1.Move X, Y
      End If
End Sub
```

It first tests `MouseIsDown`. If the button is down, it randomly moves the picture box about the form, using the `Move` method.

> `Move` is another polymorphic method that forms and controls share. Each object's implementation of `Move` is slightly different; each one knows how to move the object (form or control) that it belongs to. You—and this is one of the beautiful things about object-oriented programming—don't need to know the details of how each object implements `Move`. You just use it with the object (`Form1.Move X, Y` or `Picture1.Move X, Y`, for example).

Alternatively (and more usefully), you could have the user control the movement of the picture box depending on where the mouse pointer is located. The following `Mouse_Move` event procedure handles this alternative:

```
Sub Form_MouseMove (Button As Integer, Shift As Integer, X As
➡Single, Y As Single)
      If MouseIsDown = -1 Then
         Picture1.Move X, Y
      End If
End Sub
```

Simple, isn't it? Listing 16.5 shows the complete application.

Listing 16.5. Mouse2.

```
' general declarations

Dim MouseIsDown As Integer
Dim UserControlled As Integer
```

continues

447

Listing 16.5. continued

```
' form event procedures

Sub Form_MouseDown (Button As Integer, Shift As Integer, X As
➥Single, Y As Single)
    MouseIsDown = -1
End Sub



Sub Form_MouseUp (Button As Integer, Shift As Integer, X As
➥Single, Y As Single)
    MouseIsDown = 0
End Sub



Sub Form_MouseMove (Button As Integer, Shift As Integer, X As
➥Single, Y As Single)
  If MouseIsDown = -1 Then
    If UserControlled = 0 Then      ' Not user controlled, since
                                    ' 0 = False
        Randomize                   ' So, randomize movement.
        X = Int(7500 * Rnd + 1)
        Y = Int(4500 * Rnd + 1)
        Picture1.Move X, Y
    Else                            ' Is user controlled.
        Picture1.Move X, Y          ' Move the picture to where
                                    ' the user has
    End If                          ' placed the pointer
  End If
End Sub



' Picture box event procedures

Sub Picture1_Click ()          ' If single click, then Random
    UserControlled = 0         ' UserControlled = False
End Sub

Sub Picture1_DblClick ()       ' If double click,
    UserControlled = -1        ' UserControlled = True
End Sub
```

16

You can manipulate any control in a similar manner by using these three mouse event procedures. The way you just used these mouse events, however, was to test if *any* mouse button was pressed. What if you want to distinguish between buttons? Was it a left or a right button? You can determine the answer by testing the first parameter (Button) in the call to the event procedure. Each mouse event procedure gets this information when it's invoked in the first parameter (of 4). Notice the syntax of MouseUp and MouseDown in the code that follows.

```
Sub Form_MouseDown (Button As Integer, Shift As Integer, X As
➥Single, Y As Single)
```

```
Sub Form_MouseUp (Button As Integer, Shift As Integer, X As
➥Single, Y As Single)
```

Table 16.1 completely describes these parameters.

Table 16.1. MouseDown **and** MouseUp**.**

Parameter	Description
Button	A button was pressed (MouseDown) or released (MouseUp), causing an event. The Button parameter is a bit field with bits corresponding to the left button (bit 0), right button (bit 1), and middle button (bit 2). These relative values are 1 (left), 2 (right), and 4 (middle). With each event, one (and only one) of the bits is set, indicating the button that caused the event.
Shift	This indicates the state of the Shift, Ctrl, and Alt keys when the button was pressed or released. A bit is set in the Shift parameter if either of these keys is down. The Shift parameter's bits correspond to the values 1, 2, and 4, indicating Shift (1), Ctrl (2), Alt (4). Some, all, or none of the bits can be set, indicating that some, all, or none of the keys were pressed when the mouse event occurred.
X, Y	Current position of the mouse pointer. X and Y are always expressed in terms of the coordinate system set by the ScaleHeight, ScaleWidth, ScaleLeft, and ScaleTop properties of the object.

Modify the previous example application (Mouse2) to allow random movement of the picture box if the left button is pressed, and user-controlled movement if the right button is pressed. The new code, which assumes a two-button mouse, is in Listing 16.6.

Listing 16.6. Mouse Control 2b.

```
' general declarations

Dim MouseIsDown As Integer
Dim UserControlled As Integer


' form event procedures

' Sub Form_MouseDown

Sub Form_MouseDown (Button As Integer, Shift As Integer, X As
➥Single, Y As Single)
        MouseIsDown = -1              ' A button has been
                                     ' pressed.
        If Button = 1 Then           ' Test Button. Is it the
                                     ' left?
                LeftButtonDown = -1  ' Yes, so set a status '
                                     ' variable
                                     ' for the rest of the
                                     ' application
        Else
                RightButtonDown = -1 ' Right.
        End If
End Sub


' MouseUp hasn't changed.


' Sub Form_MouseUp

Sub Form_MouseUp (Button As Integer, Shift As Integer, X As
➥Single, Y As Single)
    MouseIsUp = 0                    ' Indicate that the mouse button was
                                     ' released.
```

```
End Sub


' Sub Form_MouseMove


Sub Form_MouseMove (Button As Integer, Shift As Integer, X As
➥Single, Y As Single)
    If MouseIsDown = -1 Then                    ' Is a button down?
            If RightButtonDown = 0 Then         ' Was it the right
                                                ' button?
                Randomize
                X = Int(7500 * Rnd + 1)
                Y = Int(4500 * Rnd + 1)
                Picture1.Move X, Y              ' Move randomly.
            Else    If LeftButtonDown           ' Or the left?
                        Picture1.Move X, Y ' Move where the
                                                ' user indicates.
                    End If
            End If
    End If
End Sub



' picture box event procedures

Sub Picture1_Click ()
    UserControlled = 0
End Sub
```

16

A Taste of Dragging and Dropping

Although I don't build an application around it in this chapter, you should
be aware that Visual Basic offers another alternative to moving controls
around in a form. This alternative uses the DragMode and DragIcon properties, the DragDrop and DragOver events, and the Drag method.

For example, the following fragment enables you to drag a command button on a form, showing the button in outline, until you release the mouse button.

```
Sub Form_Click ()

    If Command1.DragMode = 0 Then     ' Check DragMode.
        Command1.DragMode = 1         ' Turn it on.
    Else
        Command1.DragMode = 0         ' Or turn it off.
    End If

End Sub
```

After the mouse is released, the command button returns to its original position. If you want the control to stay at its new location, appear highlighted as it's dragged, and so on, use the DragOver and DragDrop procedures.

Mouse Facts

Here are a few other facts about Click, DblClick, and MouseMove events that I didn't emphasize in the applications in this chapter.

If you press a mouse button while the pointer is over a form or control, that object essentially captures the mouse and receives all mouse events up to and including the last MouseUp event. This suggests, at least, that the X, Y mouse pointer coordinates given by a mouse event may not always be in the client area of the object that receives them. Explore this yourself to suit your own applications.

If you press mouse buttons in succession, the object that captures the mouse after the first press receives all mouse events until you release all buttons.

The MouseMove event is generated continually as the mouse pointer moves across objects. Unless another object captures the mouse, an object recognizes a MouseMove event whenever the mouse appears within its borders.

If you need to test for the Button or Shift parameters, you can declare constants that define the bits within the parameter by loading the CONSTANT.TXT file into the global module. This isn't necessary; you can test the values directly, as you've done in this chapter. If you use CONSTANT.TXT, these mouse button constants have the values specified in Table 16.2.

Table 16.2. The mouse button constants.

Constant	Value
LEFT_BUTTON	1
RIGHT_BUTTON	2
MIDDLE_BUTTON	4
SHIFT_MASK	1
CTRL_MASK	2

These constants can act as bit masks, which you can use to test for any combination of buttons without having to figure out the unique bit-field value for each combination. You test for a condition by first assigning each result to a temporary integer variable, and then comparing the Button or Shift parameters to a bit mask. Use the And operator with each parameter to test if the condition is greater than zero, indicating the key or button is pressed. For example:

```
LeftDown% = (Button And LEFT_BUTTON) > 0

CtrlDown% = (Shift And CTRL_MASK) > 0
```

Then, in a procedure, you can test for any combination of conditions. For example:

```
If LeftDown% And CtrlDown% Then

    ' Act accordingly here.
```

Summary

Use a MouseDown or MouseUp procedure to prescribe actions to occur when a mouse button is pressed or released. The MouseDown and MouseUp events, unlike the Click and DblClick events, enable you to determine whether the left, right, or middle mouse button was pressed. You can also determine and utilize whether a mouse-keyboard combination (using the Shift, Ctrl, and Alt keyboard modifiers) is the current event.

17

Files, Directories, and an Editor

Now you move from graphics applications to reading, writing, and editing files in a more text-like mode. Graphics and text are interwoven in Windows and in Visual Basic. Visual Basic definitely handles text as graphics, because it appears in a font form on a graphics screen, but still handles text more generally than graphic images. That is, Visual Basic handles text by character and line rather than by pixel or point—the way DOS basically handles text.

Visual Basic supplies the controls for handling the reading, writing, and editing of text. Putting these controls together can be complicated, however, so in this and the next two chapters you study some variation detail. The application in this chapter (EDITOR) is a full-window (or screen) text editor that uses two forms and six controls: a text box, a file list box, a directory box, a drive box, and two command buttons. It enables you to select a file from any drive or directory in a system and then edit and save the file. Use it as is to edit files and as the basis for more complex applications.

In Chapter 18, "Errors, Error Handling, and an Editor (Take 2)," you expand the text editor to include numerous error-handling capabilities. Chapter 19, "From Application to Application (Using DDE)," wraps it up using Visual Basic's DDE (Dynamic Data Exchange) to add Cut and Paste capabilities to the editor. The more polished version of the editor (EDITOR3, listed in the DDE chapter) is probably the one from which you want to build your own applications, if they need such sophisticated capabilities.

Start by creating the forms and controls you need. You learn how the pieces of the applications fit together as you go along. You also learn about reading and writing text to files in route. If you need only those capabilities and not the editor, pay particular attention to the FileInFo form, which works with or without the Editor form.

Remember, Visual Basic encourages the building, testing, and working of applications piece by piece. If you separate functionality as the examples in this book encourage and/or demonstrate, you quickly can prototype code and easily reuse code without extensive rewriting. This application emphasizes the separation of functionality.

An Editor Application: Take 1

The Editor application uses two forms: one to control the application and one to control file I/O. A good reason for separating functionality (note that you don't have to separate them) is to make it easier to use the file I/O controls without the editor. You might want to let the user browse the files on a disk without actually loading a selected file into an editor. You might want to use the FileInFo form to get the name and path of a file to run an application or to compare files. You can use the FileInFo form in many ways.

Thus, the easiest solution to implement puts all the file I/O controls on a separate form that the editor (or any other application) loads when needed. The file I/O form then takes care of any file-related tasks and returns (via global variables) drive, directory, and file information. Then the application calling the FileInFo form determines whether to use the generated information.

In this application, the editor form uses that information to load a file into a text box for editing. Later, when a user requests to save the text box contents, the editor uses the `FileInFo` information again to Save the file.

Step 1—Create the forms.

1. An Editor form (form1).

2. A FileInfo form (form2).

Step 2—Add controls.

1. Add a text box to the editor (see Figure 17.1).

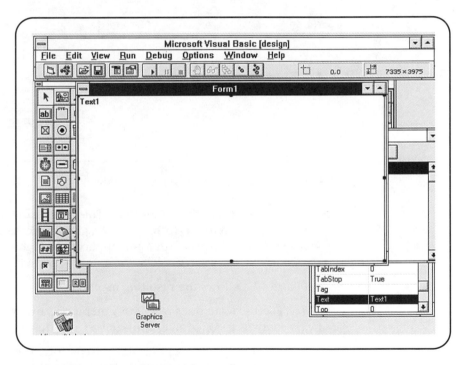

Figure 17.1. Editor form with text box.

2. Add drive, directory, and file listboxes to the FileInfo form. Also, add two command buttons to OK or cancel action (see Figure 17.2).

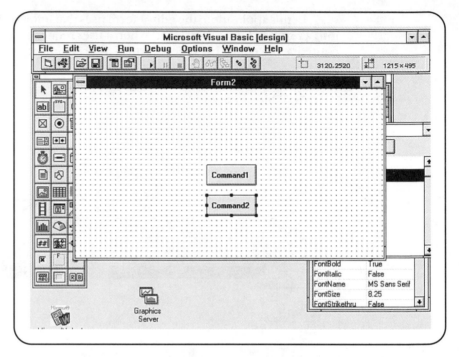

Figure 17.2. FileInfo form with controls.

Step 3—Add a menu to the Editor form. This menu can include any of the commands you want in this form. For now, give it commands for Opening and Saving files and for Quitting the application. Figure 17.3 shows the Editor form in menu design.

Figure 17.4 shows the resulting menu bar.

The File I/O form does not have a menu because the Form invoking it always controls it. Of course, you can vary this design scheme.

Step 4—Change properties. In this discussion, the text box is the FileTextBox, so change this property. Remember also to set its MultiLine property to True so it can handle input from a file.

Step 5—Write the event and general procedure code for the forms. (Plenty of work here.) Begin by writing the event procedure for OpenCom_Click(). This procedure is what you want to happen when the user clicks the File/Open menu. In short, you want the File/Open click command (OpenCom_Click()) to do the following:

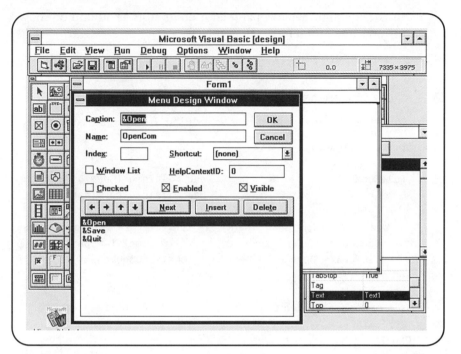

Figure 17.3.
Menu design.

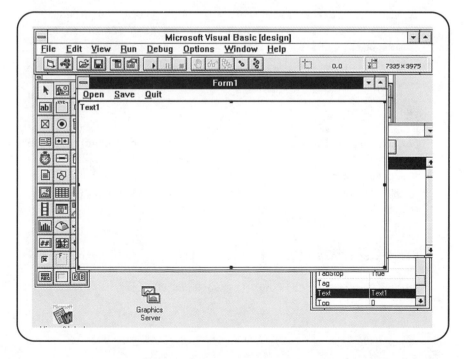

Figure 17.4.
Editor menu
bar.

1. Invoke the FileInFo form and let it do its stuff. (You find out how it works in a moment.)

2. Use the return values from the FileInFo form as the Path and FileName.

3. Verify and Open the file.

4. Read the file into the text box for editing. It looks like this:

```
Sub OpenCom_Click ()

    FileForm                        'Load FileInfo (Form & Controls)
                                    ' Use FileInfo form results.

    If WorkingFileName <> "" Then  ' Is there a file? If so, process.
        OpenMode% = LOADFILE              ' We want to open it.
        FileNum% = OpenAFile(WorkingFileName, OpenMode%, 0)
    End If

    If FileNum% = 0 Then                   ' If 0, no file opened.
        Exit Sub
    End If

    If LOF(FileNum%) > 32000 Then      ' A text box can't handle
                                       ' more than 32k or so
        MsgBox$ = "File too large."    ' Tell user file is too
                                       ' large.
        Exit Sub                         ' And exit Open
                                         ' event. Back to menu.
    End If

    Do Until EOF(FileNum%)              ' We have a good file. So
                                       ' read it.
        Line Input #FileNum%, NextLine$
        LineFromFile$ = LineFromFile$ + NextLine$ + Chr$(13) +
➥Chr$(10)
    Loop

    FileTextBox.Text = LineFromFile$ ' Load the file into the text
                                     ' box.
    Editor.Caption = "Editing: " + WorkingFileName
```

```
    Close FileNum%                          ' Close the file.
End Sub
```

Notice that you declare the variable WorkingFileName and other variables throughout the project in the general purpose module MODULE1.BAS. Create this module with the File/New Module menu command.

There's a great deal going on here, so consider how OpenCom_Click() works.

First, it calls the FileForm procedure. (See the sidebar for a brief discussion of scope in conjunction with the FileForm procedure.)

Scope and *FileForm( )*

FileForm() is general procedure for the application. In other words, any procedure within any form in the application that must invoke the FileInFo form should be capable of doing that. Make FileForm a global procedure. To do this, you must declare FileForm (or any other global procedures) in a separate module, not in the general procedures part of a form (see Figure 17.5).

Therefore, declare the variables that obtain the information generated by the FileInFo form in a general purpose module. (For the following example, MODULE1.BAS: Create this module with the File/New Module command.) Declare and define any procedures the entire application must recognize in a module included in the project. Visual Basic supplies a file of constant definitions useful for many applications, including those that open and close files. This file is CONSTANT.TXT. In this application, use the constants defined for LOADFILE (=2), REPLACEFILE (= and so on). Either copy the following constants to the declarations section of a module (in this case, MODULE1.BAS) or insert the entire CONSTANT.TXT file in MODULE1.BAS:

```
' Constants to rerepresent the file-access modes.

Global Const SAVEFILE = 1
Global Const LOADFILE = 2
Global Const REPLACEFILE = 1
```

continues

```
Global Const READFILE = 2
Global Const ADDTOFILE = 3
Global Const RANDOMFILE = 4
Global Const BINARYFILE = 5
```

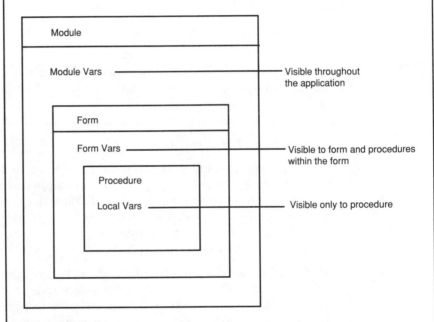

Figure 17.5. Scope revisited.

Then, add the following variables, which represent the file the user selects (with the file dialog box), the path of the file (from the directory box), the file form title (indicates what the FileI/O form is invoked to do), and the WorkingFileName (= the path + the file name):

```
Global TheFileName As String
Global TheNewPath As String
Global FileInfoTitle As String
Global WorkingFileName As String
```

Besides the FileForm procedure you just saw, you might implement the OpenAFile procedure as a global procedure. This is a general procedure you should probably implement as a global procedure, because many applications use the FileForm. You don't have to implement it this way. It can be form-specific, however. In this application, you can code it as a general procedure for the Editor form. The OpenAFile function in this Editor application takes the more general approach.

After OpenCom_Click() returns from FileForm, it uses the information generated by FileForm to determine if the user selected a file. This information is in the variable WorkingFileName. It then tries to open the file by calling the function OpenAFile:

```
If WorkingFileName <> "" Then    ' Is there a file? If so, process.
    OpenMode% = LOADFILE          ' We want to open it.
    FileNum% = OpenAFile(WorkingFileName, OpenMode%, 0)
End If
```

OpenAFile looks like this:

```
Function OpenAFile (NameToUse$, Mode%, RecordLen%) As Integer
    FileNum% = FreeFile
    Select Case Mode
        Case REPLACEFILE
            Open NameToUse For Output As FileNum%
        Case READFILE
            Open NameToUse For Input As FileNum%
        Case ADDTOFILE
            Open NameToUse For Append As FileNum%
        Case RANDOMFILE
            Open NameToUse For Random As FileNum% Len = RecordLen%
        Case BINARYFILE
            Open NameToUse For Binary As FileNum%
        Case Else
            Exit Function
    End Select

    OpenAFile = FileNum%
End Function
```

OpenAFile is straightforward. It calls the Visual Basic FreeFile function, which returns the next valid unused file number.

As a general practice, anytime you open a file, get a file number for it. This enables you (1) to have a convenient number to associate with the file (the number belongs to the file until it's closed) and (2) to verify a file can indeed be open—FreeFile returns a 0 if the operating system can't allocate a file number. If it can, FreeFile returns a number between 1 and 255 to represent the file. When you close the file, the number is free for reuse by another file in the application.

Next, OpenAFile opens a file in a designated mode. The Select Case statement in OpenAFile lists each of the possible modes. Notice this application only requires two modes: REPLACEFILE and READFILE. The others are included to indicate how you can generalize this application to read records (ADDTOFILE and RANDOMFILE) and binary files (BINARYFILE). Future applications that use the FileForm and OpenAFile need only pass the desired mode. The function won't change.

It makes good design sense to anticipate additions and modifications to existing applications. Anything you write for public consumption changes, so think generally from the beginning.

Finally, it returns the file number (for the file).

Now, back to OpenCom_Click(), which uses the file number to verify that a file was open:

```
If FileNum% = 0 Then              ' If 0, no file opened.
    Exit Sub
End If
```

If the file cannot open, it bails out (Exit Sub).

If the file is open, it checks to be sure the file isn't too large for the text box (about 64K is the maximum file a text box can handle).

Then, it reads the file one line at a time (using the Visual Basic Line Input # statement) into a string variable (NextLine$) and builds a string of the combined lines (using another variable, LineFromFile$):

```
Do Until EOF(FileNum%)              ' We have a good file. So read it.
    Line Input #FileNum%, NextLine$
    LineFromFile$ = LineFromFile$ + NextLine$ + Chr$(13) +
Chr$(10)
Loop
```

Notice, the `Line Input #` statement doesn't read the carriage return/
line feeds into the string (`NextLine$`), so you must add them manually using
the `Chr$` function.

`OpenAFile` then loads the file into the text box, sets the edit form
(window) caption, and closes the file:

```
FileTextBox.Text = LineFromFile$ ' Load the file into the text
box.
Editor.Caption = "Editing: " + WorkingFileName
Close FileNum%                        ' Close the file.
```

After the file is in the text box, you're homefree until it's time to save
the file. The text box in multiline mode (change the `Multiline` property to
TRUE, –1) enables the user to add, delete, and change text and to move
from line to line and from top to bottom. It even wraps the text in the text
box to fit the box or into 255 character segments. If you don't specify a
horizontal scroll bar for the text box, lines wrap to fit the current width of
the text box. If you specify a horizontal scroll bar, text doesn't wrap until
the maximum line length (255 characters).

When users want to save, they select the File/Save menu item.
`SaveCom_Click()` looks like this:

```
Sub SaveCom_Click ()
    SaveAFile FileTextBox
End Sub
```

This invokes a general procedure called `SaveAFile` and passes it the
name of the text box the contents of which it wants to save. Notice, you're
passing a control as an argument to a procedure. This is perfectly legitimate
in Visual Basic, and as you might expect, very handy.

The following procedure (`SaveAFile`) handles the save:

```
Sub SaveAFile (ThisTextBox As Control)
    FileNum% = OpenAFile((WorkingFileName), ReplaceFile, 0)
    If FileNum% = 0 Then
        Exit Sub
    End If
```

```
        Print #FileNum%, ThisTextBox.Text
        Close FileNum%
End Sub
```

SaveAFile also uses the OpenAFile general procedure to open the file. SaveAFile gets a FileNum back from OpenAFile, as did the OpenCom_Click() event procedure, and uses it to verify that the file was opened.

If a file doesn't open, it bails out. If a file is open, it overwrites the contents of the file specified by the WorkingFileName and closes the file.

Notice, overwriting a file is handled in one line that uses a Print # statement. That's all it takes. Also, notice the WorkingFileName is the same WorkingFileName obtained when the user opened the file to edit. In other words, this save uses the file's existing name. If you want to allow a user to modify the name, show an input box (for a name) or use some other method—for example, use the FileInFo form again to obtain a new name. This brings you back to the FileInFo form and its procedures.

The FileInfo Form

The FileInfo form has five controls: a drive, a directory, file dialog boxes, and two command buttons for accepting or canceling the status of these dialog boxes. These dialog boxes work together. Figure 17.6 shows these controls on form2, the FileInfo form.

In other words, a change in the status of one box can instigate a change in the status of another box. For example, a change of directories in the directory box notifies the file dialog box of the change, enabling it to change the files it displays. Similarly, a drive box status change notifies the directories box.

This sounds complicated, but it isn't, thanks to the built-in capability of these dialog boxes. Mainly, you write the code for the Change events for these dialog boxes, keeping in mind they work together (as a unit, of sorts).

For example, the directory box Change event procedure looks like this:

```
Sub Dir1_Change ()
    File1.Path = Dir1.Path
    File1.SetFocus
```

```
      If File1.ListCount Then
          File1.ListIndex = 0
      End If
End Sub
```

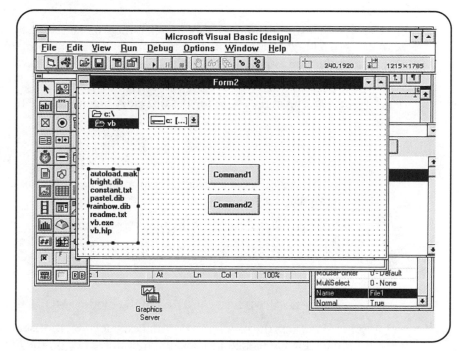

Figure 17.6. *The FileInfo form with controls.*

A Change event indicates a change in the contents of a control. There is a catch, however. When you actually note this change (when the Change event is called) varies from control to control. For example, the directory {listbox} Change event is called when the user double-clicks a new directory or when you change the path property for the directory in code. The previous event is then called only after you double-click the directory box.

After the double-click, the file dialog box path gets set to the directory box path. Then the file dialog box receives the focus. If there are files in the file listbox, the first one is selected.

The Drive box change event works similarly. The change event is called, however, each time you move the cursor or mouse over a drive:

```
Sub Drive1_Change ()
    Dir1.Path = Drive1.Drive
End Sub
```

This sets the directory box path to match the new (changed) drive box path.

Nothing much happens when the user clicks a list item in a directory or a file. A Click signifies a selection, but not a commitment to process. The selection is noted for later processing, after a file box double-click or a command button OK.

The Click event for the directory box looks like this:

```
Sub Dir1_Click ()
    LastChange = DIRSBOXCLICK
End Sub
```

LastChange is a variable in module1.bas. DIRSBOXCLICK is a constant in MODULE1.BAS.

The Click event for the file box looks like this:

```
Sub File1_Click ()
    LastChange = FileFormCLICK
End Sub
```

FileFormClick is declared in the module MODULE1.BAS.

When the user is ready to make a selection, the user can either double-click the file listbox or click OK. A double-click on the file listbox calls the command click event:

```
Sub File1_DblClick ()
    Command1_Click
End Sub
```

The command click event sets the global variables, indicating a file is selected:

```
Sub Command1_Click ()
    TheNewPath = Dir1.Path
    If Right$(TheNewPath, 1) <> "\" Then
        TheNewPath = TheNewPath + "\"
    End If
    TheFileName = File1.FileName
    FileInfo.Hide
End Sub
```

After setting the global variables, `Command1_Click` hides the `FileInfo` form.

If the user selects the Cancel button (Command2), the form is hidden and there's no updating of the file and path variables:

```
Sub Command2_Click ()
    FileInfo.Hide
End Sub
```

The general procedure `FileForm()` shows the form and sets two global variables: one indicates the `FileInfo` form is being opened in `OpenFile` mode and the other combines `TheNewPath` with `TheFileName` obtained from the `FileInfo` form:

```
Sub FileForm ()
    FileInfoTitle = "Open File"
    FileInfo.Show MODAL
    WorkingFileName = TheNewPath + TheFileName
End Sub
```

Listing 17.1 shows the complete code for this version of EDITOR. It includes the code for both the Editor and `FileInfo` forms and for all global procedures (in EDITOR.BAS).

Listing 17.1. EDITOR, Version 1.

```
' general declarations in module1

Global TheFileName As String
Global TheNewPath As String
Global FileInfoTitle As String
Global WorkingFileName As String

Global Const SAVEFILE = 1
Global Const LOADFILE = 2
Global Const REPLACEFILE = 1
Global Const READFILE = 2
Global Const ADDTOFILE = 3
Global Const RANDOMFILE = 4
Global Const BINARYFILE = 5

Const FileFormCLICK = 0
Const TEXTBOXCHANGE = 1
```

continues

Listing 17.1. continued

```
Const DIRSBOXCLICK = 2
Dim LastChange As Integer


' editor form


Sub OpenCom_Click ()

    FileForm                          'Load FileInfo (Form & Controls)

    If WorkingFileName <> "" Then
        OpenMode% = LOADFILE
        FileNum% = OpenAFile(WorkingFileName, OpenMode%, 0)
    End If
    If FileNum% = 0 Then
        Exit Sub
    End If


    If LOF(FileNum%) > 32000 Then
        Msg$ = "File too large."
        Exit Sub
    End If

    Do Until EOF(FileNum%)
        Line Input #FileNum%, NextLine$
        LineFromFile$ = LineFromFile$ + NextLine$ + Chr$(13) +
        ➡Chr$(10)
    Loop

    FileTextBox.Text = LineFromFile$
    Editor.Caption = "Editing: " + WorkingFileName
    Close FileNum%
End Sub

Sub SaveCom_Click ()
    SaveAFile FileTextBox
End Sub
```

```
Sub ExitCom_Click ()
    End
End Sub


Function OpenAFile (NameToUse$, Mode%, RecordLen%) As Integer
    FileNum% = FreeFile
    Select Case Mode
        Case ReplaceFile
            Open NameToUse For Output As FileNum%
        Case READFILE
            Open NameToUse For Input As FileNum%
        Case ADDTOFILE
            Open NameToUse For Append As FileNum%
        Case RANDOMFILE
            Open NameToUse For Random As FileNum% Len = RecordLen%
        Case BINARYFILE
            Open NameToUse For Binary As FileNum%
        Case Else
            Exit Function
    End Select

    OpenAFile = FileNum%
End Function

Sub FileForm ()
    FileInfoTitle = "Open File"
    FileInfo.Show MODAL
    WorkingFileName = TheNewPath + TheFileName
End Sub

Sub SaveAFile (ThisTextBox As Control)
    ' Note!! If you haven't opened a file.
    ' This routine will crash. See improved version
    ' in next chapter.
    FileNum% = OpenAFile((WorkingFileName), ReplaceFile, 0)
    If FileNum% = 0 Then
        Exit Sub
    End If
```

17

continues

Listing 17.1. continued

```
        Print #FileNum%, ThisTextBox.Text
        Close FileNum%
End Sub



' FileInfo form

Sub Drive1_Change ()
        Dir1.Path = Drive1.Drive
End Sub

Sub Dir1_Change ()
        File1.Path = Dir1.Path
        File1.SetFocus
        If File1.ListCount Then
                File1.ListIndex = 0
        End If
End Sub

Sub Dir1_Click ()
        LastChange = DIRSBOXCLICK
End Sub

Sub File1_Click ()
        LastChange = FileFormCLICK
End Sub

Sub File1_DblClick ()
        Command1_Click
End Sub

Sub Command1_Click ()
        TheNewPath = Dir1.Path
        If Right$(TheNewPath, 1) <> "\" Then
                TheNewPath = TheNewPath + "\"
```

```
        End If
        TheFileName = File1.FileName
        FileInfo.Hide
End Sub

Sub Command2_Click ()
        FileInfo.Hide
End Sub
```

Figures 17.7, 17.8, and 17.9 show the application in various stages of operation.

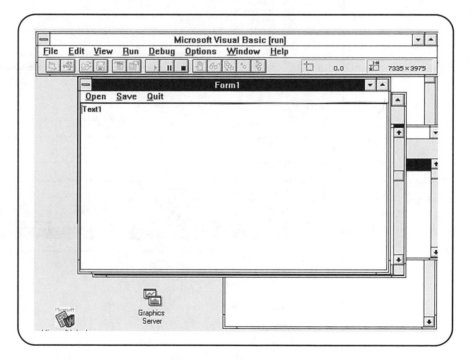

Figure 17.7. Editor: StartUp.

Figure 17.8.
Editor: Open
a file.

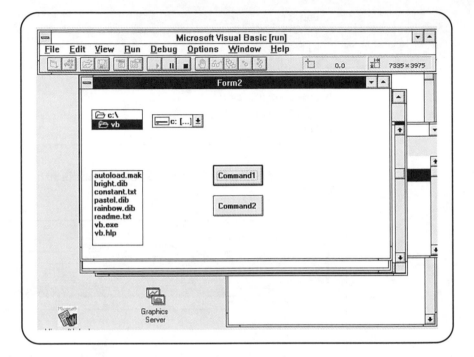

Figure 17.9.
Editor: Edit a
file.

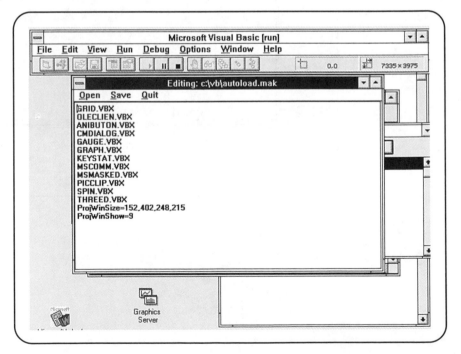

Summary

This concludes the first go at an Editor/File application. It works, but it isn't a strong editor yet. There's too much room for error, and it lacks some basic Cut/Paste capability. You should be getting the idea that a text editor is not difficult to implement with Visual Basic. It's just a text box plus features.

In the next chapter, you add features, beginning with the error problem. In the following chapter, you add some DDE capability.

18

Errors, Error Handling, and an Editor (Take 2)

In Chapter 17, "Files, Directories, and an Editor," you learned to use a multiform design to create a file I/O system and an editor that uses this system to open and save files. This system works fine, if there are no disk or file errors. What if the system encounters an unexpected error?

Unfortunately, as last chapter's Editor application stands, the system crashes after a disk or file error, a bad file name, and so on. The application (and you) grind to a halt.

Fortunately, you can avert some disasters by using Visual Basic's extensive error-handling capability to trap and recover from disk and file errors.

To trap errors, set up an error handler that takes control of the application when an error occurs. If the error handler can handle the error, the application resumes at or just after the point of the error. Visual Basic makes this kind of error handling easy by supplying several functions to

handle the low-level work. The functions talk to the operating system for you. You decide how you want the application to proceed.

In this chapter, you develop a version of the Editor application from the last chapter that implements an easy, but useful, error handler. It uses many of Visual Basic's error-handling techniques and demonstrates a general approach to error handling. It enables you to build from or readily adapt it to your applications.

Before you dive into the application, review what you must know about errors in general and the various kinds of errors your Visual Basic applications might encounter.

Compile-time Errors

Errors fall into two broad categories: compile-time and run-time. A compile-time error occurs when you run an application. It can be caused by an incorrectly blocked control structure, such as an EndIf statement used without a corresponding If statement. Syntax errors (that is, misuse of the Visual Basic language) is also a compile-time error—for example, if you misspell a word or omit a separator.

When it checks syntax, the Visual Basic Code menu checks each line of your code as you work. Each time you enter a return (<Enter>), Visual Basic checks the previous line for errors and notifies you if it finds any.

When you select the Make Exe File command from the File menu or the Start command from the Run menu, Visual Basic also automatically checks your code for errors. If a line contains code Visual Basic doesn't understand, it displays an error message.

When you get a compile-time error, you must correct it before the application can continue. You can also get context-sensitive help about an error by pressing F1 while the error message is on the screen. This is particularly useful when you haven't the foggiest notion of what's going on.

In response to the F1, Visual Basic displays a topic with possible causes for the error. It also suggests ways of resolving the type of error it detected. Notice it doesn't suggest anything about your particular error; it's responding to the type of error.

You also can get Help about the syntax of Visual Basic functions, statements, properties, events, and methods while you're working in the Code window. Type or select the keyword, the property, event, or method name and (again) press F1 for Help.

Run-time Errors

A run-time error is more complicated. A run-time error occurs while an application is running, which can be long after you've given it up—and even longer after the checks for it stop.

When Visual Basic encounters an untrapped run-time error, it halts the application, displays an error message, and places the insertion point in a box that surrounds the statement in which the error occurred. As with compile errors, you can use online Help to get information about the possible causes of the error and suggestions for resolving it. (Notice, the insertion point is the location in a form or window where the cursor appears after a form or window gets the focus.)

While your application is halted, you can open files or change variable values in the Immediate window, correct your code, modify the next statement to be executed, and so on. After you've corrected the error, to continue running the application at the statement after the stop, press F5. To restart the application from the beginning, press Shift+F5.

If you must change the form (controls, properties, and so on) or make major changes to your code, select the End command from the Run menu to end execution and return to design mode. Often, when you try to make a change, Visual Basic prompts you to restart the application and dumps you back to design mode.

These code/debug design mode sessions can generate run-time errors (file and disk problems, and so on), but it's easy to recover from them. <Ctrl+Break> can get you out of almost anything.

If a run-time error occurs while you run an executable file (.EXE version of the application), you can't recover without preparing for it yourself. To keep an application running at this juncture, you need an error-handling routine.

That brings us to the hands-on part of this chapter.

Trappable Errors

The kinds of errors you've been reading about are, fortunately, trappable errors. Again, these are the ones that can occur while an application is running, whether it's running in the Visual Basic environment or as a stand-alone executable. You can test and respond to them using the On Error statement and the Err function, which you soon read about.

Trappable errors can generate during file and disk I/O—while you manipulate object properties and with control arrays and timer functions, and so on. You can trap almost anything. Table 18.1 lists Visual Basic's trappable errors and their accompanying error messages.

All numbers do not have an error message associated with them.

Microsoft suggests when implementing your own error-handling messages, begin with 32,767 and work down. This prevents your error messages and Visual Basic's from colliding, because Visual Basic is working up from 0.

Table 18.1. Visual Basic error messages.

Error Code	Message
(compile or run-time errors)	
3	Return without GoSub.
5	Illegal function call.
6	Overflow.
7	Out of memory.
9	Subscript out of range.
10	Duplicate definition.

Error Code	*Message*
11	Division by zero.
13	Type mismatch.
14	Out of string space.
16	String formula too complex.
17	Can't continue.
19	No Resume.
20	Resume without error.
28	Out of stack space.
35	Sub or Function not defined.
	(disk/file errors)
48	Error in loading DLL.
51	Internal error.
52	Bad file name or number.
53	File not found.
54	Bad file mode.
55	File already open.
57	Device I/O error.
58	File already exists.
59	Bad record length.
61	Disk full.
62	Input past end of file.
63	Bad record number.
64	Bad file name.
67	Too many files.
68	Device unavailable.
70	Permission denied.

continues

18

Table 18.1. continued

Error Code	Message
71	Disk not ready.
74	Can't rename with different drive.
75	Path/File access error.
76	Path not found.
	(DDE errors)
260	No timer available.
280	DDE channel not fully closed; awaiting response from foreign application.
281	No more DDE channels.
282	No foreign application responded to a DDE initiate.
283	Multiple applications responded to a DDE initiate.
284	DDE channel locked.
285	Foreign application won't perform DDE method or operator.
286	Timeout while waiting for DDE response.
287	User pressed Alt during DDE operation.
288	Destination is busy.
289	Data not provided in DDE operation.
290	Data in wrong format.
291	Foreign application quit.
292	DDE conversation closed or changed.
293	DDE method invoked with no channel open.
294	Invalid DDE Link format.

Error Code	Message
295	Message queue filled; DDE message lost.
296	PasteLink already performed on this control.
297	Can't set LinkMode; Invalid LinkTopic.

(misc—object, property, array errors)

Error Code	Message
320	Can't use character device names in filenames: 'item'.
321	Invalid file format.
340	Control array element 'item' does not exist.
341	Invalid object array index.
342	Not enough room to allocate control array 'item'.
343	Object not an array.
344	Must specify index for object array.
345	Reached limit: cannot create any more controls for this form.
360	Object already loaded.
361	Can't load or unload this object.
362	Can't unload controls created at design time.
363	Custom control 'item' not found.
364	Object was unloaded.
365	Unable to unload in this context.
380	Invalid property value.
381	Invalid property array index.
382	'item' property can't be set at run time.

continues

18

Table 18.1. continued

Error Code	Message
383	'item' property is read-only.
384	'item' property can't be modified when form is minimized or maximized.
385	Must specify index when using property array.
386	'item' property not available at run time.
387	'item' property can't be set on this control.
388	Can't set Visible property from a parent menu.
400	Form already displayed; can't show form modally.
401	Can't show nonmodal form when a modal form is being displayed.
402	Must close or hide topmost modal form first.
420	Invalid object reference.
421	Method not applicable for this object.
422	Property 'item' not found.
423	Property or control 'item' not found.
424	Object required.
425	Invalid object use.
430	No currently active control.
431	No currently active form.
(misc—Clipboard, Printer, etc. errors)	
460	Invalid Clipboard format.
461	Specified format does not match format of data.
480	Can't create AutoRedraw image.

Error Code	Message
481	Invalid picture.
482	Printer error.
520	Can't empty Clipboard.
521	Can't open Clipboard.

Error Handler: Setting the Trap

How do you set up the error handler and spring the trap?

Here's one approach:

1. Set an error trap that tells the application where to GOTO when it encounters an error. Use the On Error statement to set (or enable) the trap. For example:

```
Sub AProcedure
    On Error GoTo ErrorHandler
    .
    .
    .
End Sub
```

2. Write a routine, in the procedure, to handle the specific errors you expect your application to encounter. For example:

```
Sub AProcedure
    On Error GoTo ErrorHandler          ' Turn on error trap
    .
    . (other code here )
    .
ErrorHandler:                           ' Branch to here if
                                        ' error
    If ...... Then
    .
    .
    End If
End Sub
```

485

3. Exit the error-handling procedure, using a Resume statement. For example:

```
Sub AProcedure
    On Error GoTo ErrorHandler        ' Turn on error trap
    .
    .
    .
ErrorHandler:                         ' Branch here if
                                      ' error
    If ...... Then
    .
    .
    End If
    Resume                            ' Resume after error
```

Notice, Resume returns to the statement with the error that caused the jump to the error handler. Resume next (another option) returns to the statement following the one with the error. Figure 18.1 shows how the error handler's flow of control works.

Now, read a few details.

The On Error GoTo Statement

The On Error GoTo statement enables error-handling and tells the application where to go, in the procedure, to analyze the error.

Its syntax looks like this:

```
On Error { GoTo line ¦ Resume Next ¦ GoTo 0 }
```

where:

GoTo line enables the error-handling routine beginning at line. If a run-time error occurs, the application branches to line.

The line (specified by a name or number) must be in the same procedure as the On Error statement. If line isn't in the same procedure, Visual Basic generates an error message.

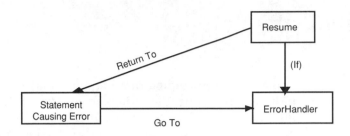

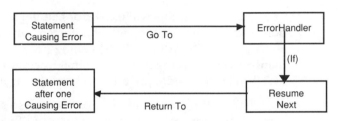

Figure 18.1. *Error handling—flow of control.*

Resume indicates control returns to the statement generating the error.

Resume Next indicates control returns to the statement immediately following the statement where the error occurred. If you must obtain the run-time error code, use Err.

GoTo 0 disables the enabled error handler.

If you don't use On Error GoTo statements to implement error handling, you significantly increase the chance a run-time error might crash your application. Visual Basic generates an error message (after the error), but it then halts the application.

Nitty Gritty Details

Some people (including those at Microsoft) use the term "enabled" to indicate an error handler is implemented (enabled) by an `On Error GoTo` line statement. After an error handler is enabled, a run-time error causes application control to jump to the enabled error-handling routine. The error handler then has control of the application. An error handler is active (in control) from the time a run-time error is trapped until the error handler reaches a `Resume` statement.

If an error occurs while an error handler is active (after the error and before the `Resume` statement), the current procedure's error handler is automatically DISABLED. If the calling procedure has an enabled error handler, control returns to the calling procedure, and its error handler is ACTIVATED to handle the error. (If not, the application will likely crash.)

If the calling procedure's error handler is also ACTIVE, control passes through any previous calling procedures until an INACTIVE error handler is located. If no inactive error handler is found, the error is fatal at the point where it occurred. (Again, at this point the system likely crashes.)

At each point where the error handler passes control back to the calling procedure, the calling procedure becomes the current procedure. After an error handler handles an error in any procedure, the application resumes in the current procedure at the point the `Resume` statement designates.

Whew! It's the error within the error within the error scenario you hope your applications never reach. Notice, at least, all this recasting of control can enable an application to recover from virtually any error.

Error-handling routines use the error status returned by the `Err` function to determine the cause of the error. The error-handling routine tests or saves this value before doing anything else, because another error corrupts this value. The value in `Err` reflects only the last error. You also can use the `Error$` function to return the error message associated with any run-time error number returned by `Err`.

The `On Error GoTo 0` statement disables error handling. However, it doesn't specify line 0 as the start of the error handling code, as you might expect. Even if the procedure contains a line numbered 0, `On Error GoTo 0` doesn't use it. If a procedure doesn't use an `On Error GoTo 0` statement (to disable the error handler), the error handler automatically is disabled when the procedure (containing the error handler) is exited.

Remember, the error handler is code within the procedure. Thus, the procedure can reach the error handler by executing sequential statements as well as by a jump. Generally, don't enable the procedure to reach the error handler by sequential statements, but only when an error occurs. You accomplish this by putting an `Exit Sub` or `Exit Function` statement immediately before the error-handling routine. For example:

```
Sub DoSomething(Var1, Var2, Var3)
    On Error GoTo ErrorHandler
    TheNextProcedure         ' Resume here
    .
    .
    Exit Sub                 ' Exit here before going into
ErrorHandler:                ' the error handler.
    .
    .
    .
    Resume Next
End Sub
```

In this example, the Error Handler is called if there's an error. Then, when it's finished processing, control returns to the statement following the call to the error handler. Just before the `ErrorHandler` code, the procedure is exited. If the exit statement isn't there, the `ErrorHandler` is called again (although there's no error). Even if the error handler is successful, the procedure loops indefinitely. Not good.

Using Err and Erl

After an error, the `Err` function returns an integer indicating the run-time error code for the error that occurred. The `Erl` function returns an integer indicating the line number where the error occurred—or the nearest line number before the line where the error occurred.

Because `Err` and `Erl` return meaningful values only after an error occurs, you only use them in error-handling routines to determine the error status values. The values returned by `Err` and `Erl` are also not

meaningful across procedure calls (either `Sub` or `Function`) or after any of the following statements:

```
On Error GoTo
```

```
On Error Resume Next
```

```
Resume Next
```

If you implement an error handler using `On Error GoTo` and that error handler calls another procedure, the value of `Err` and `Erl` might be reset to 0. The value of `Err` and `Erl` definitely resets to 0 if you execute any of the following:

1. `On Error GoTo`.

2. `On Error Resume Next`.

3. `Resume`.

Be sure you save the values returned by `Err` or `Erl` in variables before calling another procedure or executing any of the three statements that reset `Err` and `Erl`.

Notice, the `Erl` function returns a line number only, not a line label. Line numbers greater than 65,529 are treated as line labels and won't be returned by `Erl`. If your application has no line numbers or if there's no line number in the application before the point where an error occurs, `Erl` returns 0.

Because the `Erl` function isn't used in applications in this section, you find an example of its use from the *Microsoft Visual Basic Programming Guide*.

The example uses the `Err` function to return the run-time error code for a `Division by zero` error. It uses the `Erl` function to report the line number where the error occurred. Notice, the number 1020 on the procedure line that is most likely to encounter an error. If you do use a line number in this fashion, you can determine precisely where an error occurred. For example:

```
Sub ErrErlDemo ()
1000    On Error GoTo ErrHandler      ' Set up an error handler.
1010    B% = 1
1020    A% = B% \ C%                  ' Cause a "Divide by Zero"
                                      ' error.
1030    Exit Sub
```

```
ErrHandler:
    Msg$ = "Error number " + Ltrim$(Str$(Err)) + " occurred at
    ➡line "
    Msg$ = Msg$ + Ltrim$(Str$(Erl))
    MsgBox Msg$                              ' Display error informa-
                                             ' tion.

    Resume Next
End Sub
```

Back to the Editor

Now, implement an error handler for the Editor application you created last chapter. Because the editor uses the FileInFo form to get the file name and path, start there.

One problem is immediately obvious. If you change the drive and select a floppy disk drive, it's possible the drive either won't have a disk in it or the drive door is open.

The simplest solution is to use an `On Error Resume Next` statement during the drive change event procedure as follows:

```
Sub Drive1_Change ()
    On Error Resume Next         ' Set the error trap
    Dir1.Path = Drive1.Drive     ' If no error, allow the drive
                                 ' change

    If Err Then                  ' If Err
        MsgBox Error$            ' Report error
        Drive1.Drive = Dir1.Path ' Reset drive to previous state
                                 ' before error

    End If
End Sub
```

If there's an error, the next line (the one immediately after the error) is executed after the procedure resumes execution. If there's an error (returned by `Err`), the drive status is reset to its previous state (before the error).

You might also consider the following alternative, an `On Error GoTo` as follows:

```
Sub Drive1_Change ()
    On Error GoTo ErrorHandler    ' Set the error trap
    If Err Then                   ' If Err, exit Sub
     Exit Sub
    End If
    Dir1.Path = Drive1.Drive      ' If no error, allow the drive
                                  ' change
    Exit Sub                      ' Exit before error han-
                                  ' dler is reached


ErrorHandler:                     ' Error Handler
    If Err Then                   ' If Err
        MsgBox Error$             ' Report error
        Drive1.Drive = Dir1.Path  ' Reset drive to previous state
                                  ' before error
    End If
    Resume                        ' Resume application
End Sub
```

This code works too, but it's more verbose. Notice, if you omit the Exit Sub statement, the code falls through into the error handler and into an indefinite loop. For fun, you might comment out that line and give it a try. Remember, a Ctrl+Break breaks the loop.

The File Handling Problem

The other immediate potential problem in the Editor application concerns files, and it's a general one. Many things can go wrong when an application tries to open a file. The file might not exist. The operating system might not allow another file to open. If you try to save a file, you must know whether the file already exists—if it does, it will be overwritten. The list goes on.

The *Visual Basic Programmer's Guide* suggests a general-purpose error handler to handle file errors and to decide what action to take after an error. EDITOR2 takes this approach, adding two functions to the application: one called FileErrors, which determines the error; and one called ConfirmFile, which takes action.

Because you want to make both of these accessible to the entire application, code them in a module accessible to the entire application. EDITOR2 adds them to MODULE1.BAS—the general purpose module for the project you created in the last chapter.

FileErrors looks like this:

```
Function FileErrors (errVal As Integer) As Integer
    msgType% = MB_EXCLAIM                     ' Constant in
                                              ' CONSTANT.TXT

    Select Case errVal
        Case Err_DeviceUnavailable           ' Error #68
            Msg$ = "Device unavailable"
            msgType% = MB_EXCLAIM + 4
        Case Err_DiskNotReady                ' Error #71
            Msg$ = "Drive not ready."
        Case Err_DeviceIO                    ' Error #57
            Msg$ = "Internal disk error"
            msgType% = MB_EXCLAIM + 4
        Case Err_DiskFull                    ' Error #61
            Msg$ = "Disk full."
            msgType% = 35
        Case Err_BadFileName                 ' Error #64
            Msg$ = "File name is illegal"
        Case Err_BadFileNameOrNumber         ' Error #52
            Msg$ = "File name is illegal"
        Case Err_PathDoesNotExist            ' Error #76
            Msg$ = "Path does not exist."
        Case Err_BadFileMode                 ' Error #54
            Msg$ = "Can't open file in current mode."
        Case Err_FileAlreadyOpen             ' Error #55
            Msg$ = "File already open"
        Case Err_InputPastEndOfFile          ' Error #62
            Msg$ = "Attempting to read past EOF"
        Case Else
            FileErrors = 3
            Exit Function
    End Select
```

18

```
    Response% = MsgBox(Msg$, msgType%, "Disk Error")
    Select Case Response%
        Case 1, 4                          ' OK, Retry buttons
            FileErrors = 0                 ' Send this info
                                           ' back to the

        Case 5                             ' Ignore buttons
            FileErrors = 1                 ' calling proce-
                                           ' dure: 0,1,2, or 3

        Case 2, 3                          ' Cancel, abort buttons
            FileErrors = 2
        Case Else
            FileErrors = 3
    End Select
End Function
```

FileErrors puts all the errors the application can identify in one place, rather than in each function. Thus, you don't have to repeat code in your application if several functions need this information.

FileErrors identifies the error. (It uses constants declared in the CONSTANT.TXT file you must add to your project. In this case, copy the constants you need to MODULE1.BAS, the general purpose module for this project.) Then, FileErrors returns a response to the error. The calling procedure (the one that called FileErrors) still sets up the error trap, which calls the FileErrors function. The calling procedure then decides what to do with the error information returned by FileErrors. For example, OpenAFile (in the Editor application) sets up the error trap (using On Error GoTo), which calls FileError as follows:

```
Function OpenAFile (NameToUse$, Mode%, RecordLen%) As Integer
    FileNum% = FreeFile
    On Error GoTo OpenFileError        ' Set up error trap

    Select Case Mode
        Case ReplaceFile
            Open NameToUse For Output As FileNum%
        Case READFILE
            Open NameToUse For Input As FileNum%
        Case ADDTOFILE
            Open NameToUse For Append As FileNum%
        Case RANDOMFILE
            Open NameToUse For Random As FileNum% Len = RecordLen%
        Case BINARYFILE
            Open NameToUse For Binary As FileNum%
```

```
        Case Else
            Exit Function
    End Select
    OpenAFile = FileNum%
    Exit Function                       ' Don't bump into the
                                        ' error handler


OpenFileError:                          ' Error Handler
    Action% = FileErrors(Err)           ' Identify the error
    Select Case Action%                 ' Act accordingly
        Case 0                          ' OK, continue
            Resume
        Case Else
            OpenAFile = 0               ' Open failed
            Exit Function
        End Select
End Function
```

Notice that OpenFileError, the error handler, is still in the procedure. The error handler calls FileErrors, not otherwise. Also, notice the Resume statement is dependent now on the type of error encountered. If the file can't open now, the Resume doesn't occur. Instead, the function exits.

The other function you add to the editor in this chapter is ConfirmFile. It handles several problems, including overwriting a file. It also uses an OnError GoTo statement to turn on the error trap. In each case, it requests you to confirm your intention. It looks like this:

```
Function ConfirmFile (TheName As String, Operation As Integer) As
➥Integer
    On Error GoTo ConfirmFileError      ' Turn on Error Trap
    TheFile$ = Dir$(TheName)            ' Does file
                                        ' exist?
    On Error GoTo 0                     ' Turn Error Trap
                                        ' off

    If TheFile$ <> "" And Operation = ReplaceFile Then
        Msg$ = "File exists. Do you want to overwrite?"
        Confirmation% = MsgBox(Msg$, 65, "File Message")
    ElseIf TheFile$ = "" And Operation = READFILE Then
        Msg$ = "File doesn't exist. Create it?"
        Confirmation% = MsgBox(Msg$, 65, "File Message")
```

18

```
    ElseIf TheFile$ = "" Then
        If Operation = RANDOMFILE Or Operation = BINARYFILE Then
            Confirmation% = 2
        End If
    End If

    If Confirmation% > 1 Then              ' evaluate confirma-
                                           ' tion
        ConfirmFile = 0
    Else ConfirmFile = 1
    End If

    If Confirmation% = 1 Then
        If Operation = LOADFILE Then
            Operation = ReplaceFile
        End If
    End If
    Exit Function                          ' Exit if you get
                                           ' this far.


ConfirmFileError:                          ' Error handler
    Action% = FileErrors(Err)              ' Call FileErrors to
                                           ' determine error type
    Select Case Action%                    ' Act accordingly.
        Case 0
            Resume
        Case 1
            Resume Next
        Case 2
            Exit Function
        Case Else
            Error Err
    End Select
End Function
```

Notice it, too, calls FileErrors to determine the error from within the error handler. In addition, it conditionally resumes, if you confirm an action.

This is a general purpose function that applies to use of other kinds of files, as well as the simple test files in the Editor application.

The procedure `SaveAFile` in EDITOR2 uses `ConfirmFile` to verify your intention, but it doesn't set up an Error trap. It doesn't have to trap errors, only confirm decisions:

```
Sub SaveAFile (ThisTextBox As Control)
    If ConfirmFile((WorkingFileName), ReplaceFile) Then
        FileNum% = OpenAFile((WorkingFileName), ReplaceFile, 0)
        If FileNum% = 0 Then
        Exit Sub
        End If
        Print #FileNum%, ThisTextBox.Text
        Close FileNum%
    End If
End Sub
```

The complete code for the EDITOR2 application is in Listing 18.1.

Listing 18.1. EDITOR2.

```
' general declarations in module1


Global TheFileName As String
Global TheNewPath As String
Global FileInfoTitle As String
Global WorkingFileName As String

Global Const SAVEFILE = 1
Global Const LOADFILE = 2
Global Const REPLACEFILE = 1
Global Const READFILE = 2
Global Const ADDTOFILE = 3
Global Const RANDOMFILE = 4
Global Const BINARYFILE = 5


Const FileFormCLICK = 0
Const TEXTBOXCHANGE = 1
Const DIRSBOXCLICK = 2
Dim LastChange As Integer
' event procedures for the FileInFo form
```

continues

497

Listing 18.1. continued

```
Sub Drive1_Change ()
On Error GoTo ErrorHandler      ' Set the error trap
    If Err Then                 ' If Err, exit Sub
    Exit Sub
    End If
    Dir1.Path = Drive1.Drive    ' If no error, allow the drive
                                ' change
    Exit Sub     ' Make sure the error handler isn't called at the
                                ' wrong time


ErrorHandler:                   ' Error Handler
    If Err Then                 ' If Err
     MsgBox Error$              ' Report error
     Drive1.Drive = Dir1.Path   ' Reset drive to previous state
                                ' before error

    End If
    Resume                      ' Resume application at error
End Sub


Sub Dir1_Change ()
    File1.Path = Dir1.Path
    File1.SetFocus
    If File1.ListCount Then
     File1.ListIndex = 0
    End If
End Sub

Sub Dir1_Click ()
    LastChange = DIRSBOXCLICK
End Sub

Sub File1_Click ()
    LastChange = FileFormCLICK
End Sub

Sub File1_DblClick ()
    Command1_Click
End Sub
```

```
Sub Command1_Click ()
    TheNewPath = Dir1.Path
    If Right$(TheNewPath, 1) <> "\" Then
     TheNewPath = TheNewPath + "\"
    End If
    TheFileName = File1.FileName
    FileInfo.Hide
End Sub


Sub Command2_Click ()
    FileInfo.Hide
End Sub


' Editor form

Function OpenAFile (NameToUse$, Mode%, RecordLen%) As Integer
    FileNum% = FreeFile
    On Error GoTo OpenFileError

    Select Case Mode
        Case ReplaceFile
            Open NameToUse For Output As FileNum%
        Case READFILE
            Open NameToUse For Input As FileNum%
        Case ADDTOFILE
            Open NameToUse For Append As FileNum%
        Case RANDOMFILE
            Open NameToUse For Random As FileNum% Len = RecordLen%
        Case BINARYFILE
            Open NameToUse For Binary As FileNum%
        Case Else
            Exit Function
    End Select
    OpenAFile = FileNum%
    Exit Function

OpenFileError:
    Action% = FileErrors(Err)
    Select Case Action%
        Case 0
```

continues

Listing 18.1. continued

```
            Resume
        Case Else
            OpenAFile = 0          'Open failed
            Exit Function
        End Select
End Function


Sub FileForm ()
    FileInfoTitle = "Open A File"
    FileInfo.Show MODAL
    WorkingFileName = TheNewPath + TheFileName
End Sub


Sub SaveAFile (ThisTextBox As Control)
    If ConfirmFile((WorkingFileName), ReplaceFile) Then
        FileNum% = OpenAFile((WorkingFileName), ReplaceFile, 0)
        If FileNum% = 0 Then
        Exit Sub
        End If
        Print #FileNum%, ThisTextBox.Text
        Close FileNum%
    End If
End Sub


Function FileErrors (errVal As Integer) As Integer  ' Translate
                                                    ' error values
    msgType% = MB_EXCLAIM                            ' to English
    Select Case errVal
        Case Err_DeviceUnavailable                  ' Error #68
            Msg$ = "Device unavailable"
            msgType% = MB_EXCLAIM + 4
        Case Err_DiskNotReady                       ' Error #71
            Msg$ = "Drive not ready."
        Case Err_DeviceIO                           ' Error #57
            Msg$ = "Internal disk error"
            msgType% = MB_EXCLAIM + 4
        Case Err_DiskFull                           ' Error #61
            Msg$ = "Disk full."
            msgType% = 35
```

```
        Case Err_BadFileName            ' Error #64
            Msg$ = "File name is illegal"
        Case Err_BadFileNameOrNumber  'Error #52
            Msg$ = "File name is illegal"
        Case Err_PathDoesNotExist       ' Error #76
            Msg$ = "Path does not exist."
        Case Err_BadFileMode            ' Error #54
            Msg$ = "Can't open file in current mode."
        Case Err_FileAlreadyOpen        ' Error #55
            Msg$ = "File already open"
        Case Err_InputPastEndOfFile     ' Error #62
            Msg$ = "Attempting to read past EOF"
        Case Else
            FileErrors = 3
            Exit Function
    End Select

    Response% = MsgBox(Msg$, msgType%, "Disk Error") ' Tell the
                                                     ' user what's
                                                     ' happening.
    Select Case Response%                  ' User responds.
        Case 1, 4   ' OK, Retry buttons       ' Interpret the
                                               ' user's response.
            FileErrors = 0
        Case 5          ' Ignore buttons
            FileErrors = 1
        Case 2, 3    ' Cancel, abort buttons
            FileErrors = 2
        Case Else
            FileErrors = 3
    End Select
End Function

Function ConfirmFile (TheName As String, Operation As Integer) As
Integer
    On Error GoTo ConfirmFileError      'Turn on Error Trap
    TheFile$ = Dir$(TheName)            'Does file exist?
    On Error GoTo 0                     'Turn Error Trap off

    If TheFile$ <> "" And Operation = ReplaceFile Then
        Msg$ = "File exists. Do you want to overwrite?"
```

continues

Listing 18.1. continued

```
        Confirmation% = MsgBox(Msg$, 65, "File Message")
    ElseIf TheFile$ = "" And Operation = READFILE Then
        Msg$ = "File doesn't exist. Create it?"
        Confirmation% = MsgBox(Msg$, 65, "File Message")
    ElseIf TheFile$ = "" Then
        If Operation = RANDOMFILE Or Operation = BINARYFILE Then
            Confirmation% = 2
        End If
    End If


    If Confirmation% > 1 Then
        ConfirmFile = 0
    Else ConfirmFile = 1
    End If


    If Confirmation% = 1 Then
        If Operation = LOADFILE Then
            Operation = ReplaceFile
        End If
    End If
    Exit Function                   ' Don't fall into error handler.

ConfirmFileError:                   ' Error handler for the
➥ConfirmFileError
    Action% = FileErrors(Err)
    Select Case Action%
        Case 0
            Resume
        Case 1
            Resume Next
        Case 2
            Exit Function
        Case Else
            Error Err
    End Select
End Function




Sub OpenCom_Click ()

    FileForm                        ' Load FileInfo (Form & Controls)
```

```
        If WorkingFileName <> "" Then
            OpenMode% = LOADFILE
            FileNum% = OpenAFile(WorkingFileName, OpenMode%, 0)
        End If
        If FileNum% = 0 Then
            Exit Sub
        End If


        If LOF(FileNum%) > 32000 Then
            Msg$ = "File too large."
            Exit Sub
        End If

        Do Until EOF(FileNum%)
            Line Input #FileNum%, NextLine$
            LineFromFile$ = LineFromFile$ + NextLine$ + Chr$(13) +
            ➡Chr$(10)
        Loop

        FileTextBox.Text = LineFromFile$
        Editor.Caption = "Editing: " + WorkingFileName
        Close FileNum%
    End Sub


Sub SaveCom_Click ()
    SaveAFile FileTextBox
End Sub

Sub ExitCom_Click ()
    End
End Sub
```

Figures 18.2, 18.3, and 18.4 show EDITOR2 in various stages of operation.

Figure 18.2.
EDITOR2:
StartUp.

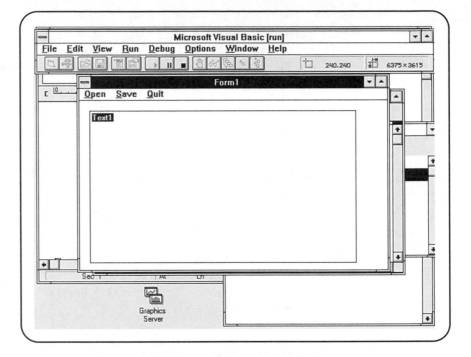

Figure 18.3.
EDITOR2:
Responding to
a Save error.

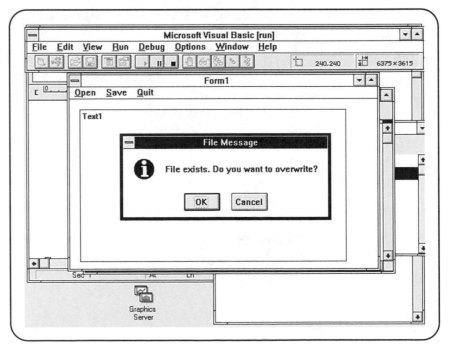

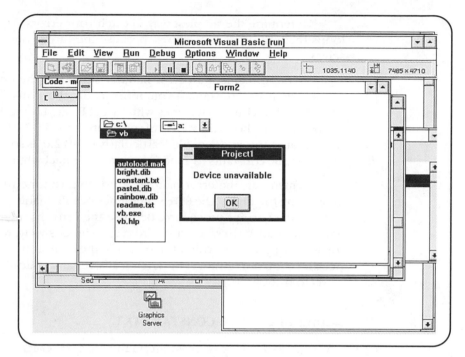

Figure 18.4. *EDITOR2: Responding to a drive-not-ready error.*

Summary

To wrap up this error-handling chapter, review a few general observations. If your application, like the Editor in this chapter, can use a drive or open a file, implement an error handler.

If your application does calculations that can lead to division by zero, and so on, implement an error handler.

If you can, make the error handler as general as possible. If you do this, you can easily reuse it with other applications without rewriting a great deal of code. For example, the FileErrors procedure you implement in this chapter lumps commonly used information.

Determine the simplest way to catch your errors. Try to avoid error loops that call other procedures, because they are prone to errors themselves.

If you implement an error handler similar to the one in this chapter—which uses constants—you must code the constant or use the CONSTANT.TXT file that comes with Visual Basic. Listing 18.2, at the end of this chapter, shows the variety of constants in the VB 2.0 CONSTANT.TXT file. Because this constant file, particularly in VB 2.0, is so large, you might copy specific constants to a module in your project when you need them.

Remember, the error handler must be a routine in the procedure generating the error. The GoTo statement doesn't enable you to GoTo code outside the current procedure. Because the error handler depends on a GoTo, this is always a restriction. From a designer's view, however, it's not too great a limitation. You want to handle the code as near the problem as possible. You don't want to be GoToing all over an application. That usually leads to trouble.

Listing 18.2. VB 2.0 CONSTANT.TXT.

```
' Visual Basic global constant file. This file can be loaded
' into a code module.
' Some constants are commented out because they have
' duplicates (e.g., NONE appears several places).
' If you're updating a Visual Basic 1.0 program to run in
' Visual Basic 2.0, you should replace your global constants
' with the constants in this file.  Note that True and False
' are now built into Visual Basic so are no longer defined in
' this file.
' General
' Clipboard formats
Global Const CF_LINK = &HBF00
Global Const CF_TEXT = 1
Global Const CF_BITMAP = 2
Global Const CF_METAFILE = 3
Global Const CF_DIB = 8
Global Const CF_PALETTE = 9

' DragOver
Global Const ENTER = 0
Global Const LEAVE = 1
Global Const OVER = 2
```

```
' Drag (controls)
Global Const CANCEL = 0
Global Const BEGIN_DRAG = 1
Global Const END_DRAG = 2

' Show parameters
Global Const MODAL = 1
Global Const MODELESS = 0

' Arrange Method
' for MDI Forms
Global Const CASCADE = 0
Global Const TILE_HORIZONTAL = 1
Global Const TILE_VERTICAL = 2
Global Const ARRANGE_ICONS = 3

'ZOrder Method
Global Const BRINGTOFRONT = 0
Global Const SENDTOBACK = 1

' Key Codes
Global Const KEY_LBUTTON = &H1
Global Const KEY_RBUTTON = &H2
Global Const KEY_CANCEL = &H3
Global Const KEY_MBUTTON = &H4          ' NOT contiguous with L &
                                        ' RBUTTON

Global Const KEY_BACK = &H8
Global Const KEY_TAB = &H9
Global Const KEY_CLEAR = &HC
Global Const KEY_RETURN = &HD
Global Const KEY_SHIFT = &H10
Global Const KEY_CONTROL = &H11
Global Const KEY_MENU = &H12
Global Const KEY_PAUSE = &H13
Global Const KEY_CAPITAL = &H14
Global Const KEY_ESCAPE = &H1B
Global Const KEY_SPACE = &H20
Global Const KEY_PRIOR = &H21
Global Const KEY_NEXT = &H22
Global Const KEY_END = &H23
Global Const KEY_HOME = &H24
```

18

continues

Listing 18.2. continued

```
Global Const KEY_LEFT = &H25
Global Const KEY_UP = &H26
Global Const KEY_RIGHT = &H27
Global Const KEY_DOWN = &H28
Global Const KEY_SELECT = &H29
Global Const KEY_PRINT = &H2A
Global Const KEY_EXECUTE = &H2B
Global Const KEY_SNAPSHOT = &H2C
Global Const KEY_INSERT = &H2D
Global Const KEY_DELETE = &H2E
Global Const KEY_HELP = &H2F

' KEY_A thru KEY_Z are the same as their ASCII equivalents: 'A'
' thru 'Z'
' KEY_0 thru KEY_9 are the same as their ASCII equivalents: '0'
' thru '9'

Global Const KEY_NUMPAD0 = &H60
Global Const KEY_NUMPAD1 = &H61
Global Const KEY_NUMPAD2 = &H62
Global Const KEY_NUMPAD3 = &H63
Global Const KEY_NUMPAD4 = &H64
Global Const KEY_NUMPAD5 = &H65
Global Const KEY_NUMPAD6 = &H66
Global Const KEY_NUMPAD7 = &H67
Global Const KEY_NUMPAD8 = &H68
Global Const KEY_NUMPAD9 = &H69
Global Const KEY_MULTIPLY = &H6A
Global Const KEY_ADD = &H6B
Global Const KEY_SEPARATOR = &H6C
Global Const KEY_SUBTRACT = &H6D
Global Const KEY_DECIMAL = &H6E
Global Const KEY_DIVIDE = &H6F
Global Const KEY_F1 = &H70
Global Const KEY_F2 = &H71
Global Const KEY_F3 = &H72
Global Const KEY_F4 = &H73
Global Const KEY_F5 = &H74
Global Const KEY_F6 = &H75
```

```
Global Const KEY_F7 = &H76
Global Const KEY_F8 = &H77
Global Const KEY_F9 = &H78
Global Const KEY_F10 = &H79
Global Const KEY_F11 = &H7A
Global Const KEY_F12 = &H7B
Global Const KEY_F13 = &H7C
Global Const KEY_F14 = &H7D
Global Const KEY_F15 = &H7E
Global Const KEY_F16 = &H7F

Global Const KEY_NUMLOCK = &H90

' Variant VarType tags

Global Const V_EMPTY = 0
Global Const V_NULL = 1
Global Const V_INTEGER = 2
Global Const V_LONG = 3
Global Const V_SINGLE = 4
Global Const V_DOUBLE = 5
Global Const V_CURRENCY = 6
Global Const V_DATE = 7
Global Const V_STRING = 8


' Event Parameters

' ErrNum (LinkError)
Global Const WRONG_FORMAT = 1
Global Const DDE_SOURCE_CLOSED = 6
Global Const TOO_MANY_LINKS = 7
Global Const DATA_TRANSFER_FAILED = 8

' QueryUnload
Global Const FORM_CONTROLMENU = 0
Global Const FORM_CODE = 1
Global Const APP_WINDOWS = 2
Global Const APP_TASKMANAGER = 3
Global Const FORM_MDIFORM = 4
```

continues

18

Listing 18.2. continued

```
' Properties

' Colors
Global Const BLACK = &H0&
Global Const RED = &HFF&
Global Const GREEN = &HFF00&
Global Const YELLOW = &HFFFF&
Global Const BLUE = &HFF0000
Global Const MAGENTA = &HFF00FF
Global Const CYAN = &HFFFF00
Global Const WHITE = &HFFFFFF

' System Colors
Global Const SCROLL_BARS = &H80000000      ' Scroll-bars gray
                                           ' area.
Global Const DESKTOP = &H80000001          ' Desktop.
Global Const ACTIVE_TITLE_BAR = &H80000002 ' Active window
                                           ' caption.
Global Const INACTIVE_TITLE_BAR = &H80000003 ' Inactive window
                                           ' caption.
Global Const MENU_BAR = &H80000004         ' Menu background.
Global Const WINDOW_BACKGROUND = &H80000005 ' Window back-
                                           ' ground.
Global Const WINDOW_FRAME = &H80000006     ' Window frame.
Global Const MENU_TEXT = &H80000007        ' Text in menus.
Global Const WINDOW_TEXT = &H80000008      ' Text in windows.
Global Const TITLE_BAR_TEXT = &H80000009   ' Text in caption,
                                           ' size box,
                                           ' scroll-bar
                                           ' arrow box.

Global Const ACTIVE_BORDER = &H8000000A    ' Active window
                                           ' border.
Global Const INACTIVE_BORDER = &H8000000B  ' Inactive window
                                           ' border.
Global Const APPLICATION_WORKSPACE = &H8000000C ' Background color
                                           ' of multiple
                                           ' document inter-
                                           ' face (MDI)
                                           ' applications.
```

```
Global Const HIGHLIGHT = &H8000000D          ' Items selected
                                             ' item in a control.
Global Const HIGHLIGHT_TEXT = &H8000000E     ' Text of item
                                             ' selected in a
                                             ' control.
Global Const BUTTON_FACE = &H8000000F        ' Face shading on
                                             ' command buttons.
Global Const BUTTON_SHADOW = &H80000010      ' Edge shading on
                                             ' command buttons.
Global Const GRAY_TEXT = &H80000011          ' Grayed (disabled)
                                             ' text.  This color
                                             ' is set to 0 if the
                                             ' current display
                                             ' driver does not
                                             ' support a solid
                                             ' gray color.
Global Const BUTTON_TEXT = &H80000012        ' Text on push
                                             ' buttons.


' Enumerated Types

' Align (picture box)
Global Const NONE = 0
Global Const ALIGN_TOP = 1
Global Const ALIGN_BOTTOM = 2

' Alignment
Global Const LEFT_JUSTIFY = 0   ' 0 - Left Justify
Global Const RIGHT_JUSTIFY = 1  ' 1 - Right Justify
Global Const CENTER = 2         ' 2 - Center

' BorderStyle (form)
'Global Const NONE = 0          ' 0 - None
Global Const FIXED_SINGLE = 1   ' 1 - Fixed Single
Global Const SIZABLE = 2        ' 2 - Sizable (Forms only)
Global Const FIXED_DOUBLE = 3   ' 3 - Fixed Double (Forms only)

' BorderStyle (Shape and Line)
'Global Const TRANSPARENT = 0   ' 0 - Transparent
'Global Const SOLID = 1         ' 1 - Solid
'Global Const DASH = 2          ' 2 - Dash
'Global Const DOT = 3           ' 3 - Dot
```

continues

18

Listing 18.2. continued

```
'Global Const DASH_DOT = 4        ' 4 - Dash-Dot
'Global Const DASH_DOT_DOT = 5 ' 5 - Dash-Dot-Dot
'Global Const INSIDE_SOLID = 6 ' 6 - Inside Solid

' MousePointer
Global Const DEFAULT = 0          ' 0 - Default
Global Const ARROW = 1            ' 1 - Arrow
Global Const CROSSHAIR = 2        ' 2 - Cross
Global Const IBEAM = 3            ' 3 - I-Beam
Global Const ICON_POINTER = 4     ' 4 - Icon
Global Const SIZE_POINTER = 5     ' 5 - Size
Global Const SIZE_NE_SW = 6       ' 6 - Size NE SW
Global Const SIZE_N_S = 7         ' 7 - Size N S
Global Const SIZE_NW_SE = 8       ' 8 - Size NW SE
Global Const SIZE_W_E = 9         ' 9 - Size W E
Global Const UP_ARROW = 10        ' 10 - Up Arrow
Global Const HOURGLASS = 11       ' 11 - Hourglass
Global Const NO_DROP = 12         ' 12 - No drop

' DragMode
Global Const MANUAL = 0           ' 0 - Manual
Global Const AUTOMATIC = 1        ' 1 - Automatic

' DrawMode
Global Const BLACKNESS = 1        ' 1 - Blackness
Global Const NOT_MERGE_PEN = 2 ' 2 - Not Merge Pen
Global Const MASK_NOT_PEN = 3 ' 3 - Mask Not Pen
Global Const NOT_COPY_PEN = 4 ' 4 - Not Copy Pen
Global Const MASK_PEN_NOT = 5 ' 5 - Mask Pen Not
Global Const INVERT = 6           ' 6 - Invert
Global Const XOR_PEN = 7          ' 7 - Xor Pen
Global Const NOT_MASK_PEN = 8     ' 8 - Not Mask Pen
Global Const MASK_PEN = 9         ' 9 - Mask Pen
Global Const NOT_XOR_PEN = 10     ' 10 - Not Xor Pen
Global Const NOP = 11             ' 11 - Nop
Global Const MERGE_NOT_PEN = 12 ' 12 - Merge Not Pen
Global Const COPY_PEN = 13        ' 13 - Copy Pen
Global Const MERGE_PEN_NOT = 14 ' 14 - Merge Pen Not
Global Const MERGE_PEN = 15       ' 15 - Merge Pen
Global Const WHITENESS = 16       ' 16 - Whiteness
```

```
' DrawStyle
Global Const SOLID = 0            ' 0 - Solid
Global Const DASH = 1            ' 1 - Dash
Global Const DOT = 2            ' 2 - Dot
Global Const DASH_DOT = 3        ' 3 - Dash-Dot
Global Const DASH_DOT_DOT = 4 ' 4 - Dash-Dot-Dot
Global Const INVISIBLE = 5       ' 5 - Invisible
Global Const INSIDE_SOLID = 6 ' 6 - Inside Solid

' FillStyle
' Global Const SOLID = 0                ' 0 - Solid
Global Const TRANSPARENT = 1         ' 1 - Transparent
Global Const HORIZONTAL_LINE = 2    ' 2 - Horizontal Line
Global Const VERTICAL_LINE = 3      ' 3 - Vertical Line
Global Const UPWARD_DIAGONAL = 4    ' 4 - Upward Diagonal
Global Const DOWNWARD_DIAGONAL = 5 ' 5 - Downward Diagonal
Global Const CROSS = 6               ' 6 - Cross
Global Const DIAGONAL_CROSS = 7     ' 7 - Diagonal Cross

' LinkMode (forms and controls)
' Global Const NONE = 0             ' 0 - None
Global Const LINK_SOURCE = 1      ' 1 - Source (forms only)
Global Const LINK_AUTOMATIC = 1 ' 1 - Automatic (controls only)
Global Const LINK_MANUAL = 2     ' 2 - Manual (controls only)
Global Const LINK_NOTIFY = 3     ' 3 - Notify (controls only)

' LinkMode (kept for VB1.0 compatibility, use new constants in-
' stead)
Global Const HOT = 1     ' 1 - Hot (controls only)
Global Const SERVER = 1 ' 1 - Server (forms only)
Global Const COLD = 2    ' 2 - Cold (controls only)


' ScaleMode
Global Const USER = 0        ' 0 - User
Global Const TWIPS = 1       ' 1 - Twip
Global Const POINTS = 2      ' 2 - Point
Global Const PIXELS = 3      ' 3 - Pixel
Global Const CHARACTERS = 4 ' 4 - Character
Global Const INCHES = 5      ' 5 - Inch
```

continues

18

513

Listing 18.2. continued

```
Global Const MILLIMETERS = 6  ' 6 - Millimeter
Global Const CENTIMETERS = 7  ' 7 - Centimeter

' ScrollBar
' Global Const NONE      = 0  ' 0 - None
Global Const HORIZONTAL = 1  ' 1 - Horizontal
Global Const VERTICAL = 2    ' 2 - Vertical
Global Const BOTH = 3        ' 3 - Both

' Shape
Global Const SHAPE_RECTANGLE = 0
Global Const SHAPE_SQUARE = 1
Global Const SHAPE_OVAL = 2
Global Const SHAPE_CIRCLE = 3
Global Const SHAPE_ROUNDED_RECTANGLE = 4
Global Const SHAPE_ROUNDED_SQUARE = 5

' WindowState
Global Const NORMAL = 0     ' 0 - Normal
Global Const MINIMIZED = 1  ' 1 - Minimized
Global Const MAXIMIZED = 2  ' 2 - Maximized

' Check Value
Global Const UNCHECKED = 0  ' 0 - Unchecked
Global Const CHECKED = 1    ' 1 - Checked
Global Const GRAYED = 2     ' 2 - Grayed

' Shift parameter masks
Global Const SHIFT_MASK = 1
Global Const CTRL_MASK = 2
Global Const ALT_MASK = 4

' Button parameter masks
Global Const LEFT_BUTTON = 1
Global Const RIGHT_BUTTON = 2
Global Const MIDDLE_BUTTON = 4

' Function Parameters
' MsgBox parameters
Global Const MB_OK = 0                    ' OK button only
Global Const MB_OKCANCEL = 1              ' OK and Cancel buttons
```

```
Global Const MB_ABORTRETRYIGNORE = 2    ' Abort, Retry, and Ignore
                                        ' buttons
Global Const MB_YESNOCANCEL = 3         ' Yes, No, and Cancel
                                        ' buttons
Global Const MB_YESNO = 4               ' Yes and No buttons
Global Const MB_RETRYCANCEL = 5         ' Retry and Cancel buttons

Global Const MB_ICONSTOP = 16           ' Critical message
Global Const MB_ICONQUESTION = 32       ' Warning query
Global Const MB_ICONEXCLAMATION = 48    ' Warning message
Global Const MB_ICONINFORMATION = 64    ' Information message

Global Const MB_APPLMODAL = 0           ' Application Modal Message
                                        ' Box
Global Const MB_DEFBUTTON1 = 0          ' First button is default
Global Const MB_DEFBUTTON2 = 256        ' Second button is default
Global Const MB_DEFBUTTON3 = 512        ' Third button is default
Global Const MB_SYSTEMMODAL = 4096      ' System Modal

' MsgBox return values
Global Const IDOK = 1                   ' OK button pressed
Global Const IDCANCEL = 2               ' Cancel button pressed
Global Const IDABORT = 3                ' Abort button pressed
Global Const IDRETRY = 4                ' Retry button pressed
Global Const IDIGNORE = 5               ' Ignore button pressed
Global Const IDYES = 6                  ' Yes button pressed
Global Const IDNO = 7                   ' No button pressed

' SetAttr, Dir, GetAttr functions
Global Const ATTR_NORMAL = 0
Global Const ATTR_READONLY = 1
Global Const ATTR_HIDDEN = 2
Global Const ATTR_SYSTEM = 4
Global Const ATTR_VOLUME = 8
Global Const ATTR_DIRECTORY = 16
Global Const ATTR_ARCHIVE = 32

'Grid
'ColAlignment,FixedAlignment Properties
```

18

continues

515

Listing 18.2. continued

```
Global Const GRID_ALIGNLEFT = 0
Global Const GRID_ALIGNRIGHT = 1
Global Const GRID_ALIGNCENTER = 2

'Fillstyle Property
Global Const GRID_SINGLE = 0
Global Const GRID_REPEAT = 1

'OLE Client Control
'Action
Global Const OLE_CREATE_NEW = 0
Global Const OLE_CREATE_FROM_FILE = 1
Global Const OLE_COPY = 4
Global Const OLE_PASTE = 5
Global Const OLE_UPDATE = 6
Global Const OLE_ACTIVATE = 7
Global Const OLE_EXECUTE = 8
Global Const OLE_CLOSE = 9
Global Const OLE_DELETE = 10
Global Const OLE_SAVE_TO_FILE = 11
Global Const OLE_READ_FROM_FILE = 12
Global Const OLE_CONVERT_TO_TYPE = 13

'ServerType
Global Const OLE_LINKED = 0
Global Const OLE_EMBEDDED = 1
Global Const OLE_STATIC = 2

'UpdateOptions
Global Const OLE_AUTOMATIC = 0
Global Const OLE_FROZEN = 1
Global Const OLE_MANUAL = 2

'Update Event Constants
Global Const OLE_CHANGED = 0
Global Const OLE_SAVED = 1
Global Const OLE_CLOSED = 2
Global Const OLE_RELEASE = 3
```

```
'-----------------------------------------------------------

'       Table of Contents for Visual Basic Professional
'
'       1.  3-D Controls
'           (Frame/Panel/Option/Check/Command/Group Push)
'       2.  Animated Button
'       3.  Common Dialog Section
'       4.  Gauge Control
'       5.  Graph Control Section
'       6.  Key Status Control
'       7.  Spin Button
'       8.  MCI Control (Multimedia)
'       9.  Masked Edit Control
'       10. Comm Control
'       11. ODBC Constants
'-----------------------------------------------------------



'-----------------------------------------------------------------
--
'3D Controls
'-----------------------------------------------------------------
--
'Alignment (Check Box)
Global Const SSCB_TEXT_RIGHT = 0         '0 - Text to the right
Global Const SSCB_TEXT_LEFT = 1          '1 - Text to the left

'Alignment (Option Button)
Global Const SSOB_TEXT_RIGHT = 0         '0 - Text to the right
Global Const SSOB_TEXT_LEFT = 1          '1 - Text to the left

'Alignment (Frame)
Global Const SSFR_LEFT_JUSTIFY = 0       '0 - Left justify text
Global Const SSFR_RIGHT_JUSTIFY = 1      '1 - Right justify text
Global Const SSFR_CENTER = 2             '2 - Center text

'Alignment (Panel)
Global Const SSPN_LEFT_TOP = 0           '0 - Text to left and top
Global Const SSPN_LEFT_MIDDLE = 1        '1 - Text to left and
                                         ' middle
```

continues

18

Listing 18.2. continued

```
Global Const SSPN_LEFT_BOTTOM = 2          '2 - Text to left and
                                           ' bottom
Global Const SSPN_RIGHT_TOP = 3            '3 - Text to right and
                                           ' top
Global Const SSPN_RIGHT_MIDDLE = 4         '4 - Text to right and
                                           ' middle
Global Const SSPN_RIGHT_BOTTOM = 5         '5 - Text to right and
                                           ' bottom
Global Const SSPN_CENTER_TOP = 6           '6 - Text to center and
                                           ' top
Global Const SSPN_CENTER_MIDDLE = 7        '7 - Text to center and
                                           ' middle
Global Const SSPN_CENTER_BOTTOM = 8        '8 - Text to center and
                                           ' bottom


'Autosize (Command Button)
Global Const SS_AUTOSIZE_NONE = 0          '0 - No Autosizing
Global Const SSPB_AUTOSIZE_PICTOBUT = 1    '0 - Autosize Picture to
                                           ' Button
Global Const SSPB_AUTOSIZE_BUTTOPIC = 2    '0 - Autosize Button to
                                           ' Picture


'Autosize (Ribbon Button)
'Global Const SS_AUTOSIZE_NONE      = 0     '0 - No Autosizing
Global Const SSRI_AUTOSIZE_PICTOBUT = 1    '0 - Autosize Picture to
                                           ' Button
Global Const SSRI_AUTOSIZE_BUTTOPIC = 2    '0 - Autosize Button to
                                           ' Picture


'Autosize (Panel)
'Global Const SS_AUTOSIZE_NONE      = 0     '0 - No Autosizing
Global Const SSPN_AUTOSIZE_WIDTH = 1       '1 - Autosize Panel width
                                           ' to Caption
Global Const SSPN_AUTOSIZE_HEIGHT = 2      '2 - Autosize Panel
                                           ' height to Caption
Global Const SSPN_AUTOSIZE_CHILD = 3       '3 - Autosize Child to
                                           ' Panel


'BevelInner (Panel)
Global Const SS_BEVELINNER_NONE = 0        '0 - No Inner Bevel
```

```
Global Const SS_BEVELINNER_INSET = 1      '1 - Inset Inner Bevel
Global Const SS_BEVELINNER_RAISED = 2     '2 - Raised Inner Bevel

'BevelOuter (Panel)
Global Const SS_BEVELOUTER_NONE = 0       '0 - No Outer Bevel
Global Const SS_BEVELOUTER_INSET = 1      '1 - Inset Outer Bevel
Global Const SS_BEVELOUTER_RAISED = 2     '2 - Raised Outer Bevel

'FloodType (Panel)
Global Const SS_FLOODTYPE_NONE = 0        '0 - No flood
Global Const SS_FLOODTYPE_L_TO_R = 1      '1 - Left to light
Global Const SS_FLOODTYPE_R_TO_L = 2      '2 - Right to left
Global Const SS_FLOODTYPE_T_TO_B = 3      '3 - Top to bottom
Global Const SS_FLOODTYPE_B_TO_T = 4      '4 - Bottom to top
Global Const SS_FLOODTYPE_CIRCLE = 5      '5 - Widening circle

'Font3D (Panel, Command Button, Option Button, Check Box, Frame)
Global Const SS_FONT3D_NONE = 0           '0 - No 3-D text
Global Const SS_FONT3D_RAISED_LIGHT = 1   '1 - Raised with light
                                          ' shading
Global Const SS_FONT3D_RAISED_HEAVY = 2   '2 - Raised with heavy
                                          ' shading
Global Const SS_FONT3D_INSET_LIGHT = 3    '3 - Inset with light
                                          ' shading
Global Const SS_FONT3D_INSET_HEAVY = 4    '4 - Inset with heavy
                                          ' shading


'PictureDnChange (Ribbon Button)
Global Const SS_PICDN_NOCHANGE = 0        '0 - Use 'Up'bitmap with
                                          ' no change
Global Const SS_PICDN_DITHER = 1          '1 - Dither 'Up'bitmap
Global Const SS_PICDN_INVERT = 2          '2 - Invert 'Up'bitmap

'ShadowColor (Panel, Frame)
Global Const SS_SHADOW_DARKGREY = 0       '0 - Dark grey shadow
Global Const SS_SHADOW_BLACK = 1          '1 - Black shadow

'ShadowStyle (Frame)
Global Const SS_SHADOW_INSET = 0          '0 - Shadow inset
Global Const SS_SHADOW_RAISED = 1         '1 - Shadow raised
```

continues

Listing 18.2. continued

```
'-------------------------------------
'Animated Button
'-------------------------------------
'Cycle property
Global Const ANI_ANIMATED = 0
Global Const ANI_MULTISTATE = 1
Global Const ANI_TWO_STATE = 2

'Click Filter property
Global Const ANI_ANYWHERE = 0
Global Const ANI_IMAGE_AND_TEXT = 1
Global Const ANI_IMAGE = 2
Global Const ANI_TEXT = 3

'PicDrawMode Property
Global Const ANI_XPOS_YPOS = 0
Global Const ANI_AUTOSIZE = 1
Global Const ANI_STRETCH = 2

'SpecialOp Property
Global Const ANI_CLICK = 1

'TextPosition Property
Global Const ANI_CENTER = 0
Global Const ANI_LEFT = 1
Global Const ANI_RIGHT = 2
Global Const ANI_BOTTON = 3
Global Const ANI_TOP = 4


'-------------------------------------
'Common Dialog Control
'-------------------------------------
'Action Property
Global Const DLG_FILE_OPEN = 1
Global Const DLG_FILE_SAVE = 2
Global Const DLG_COLOR = 3
Global Const DLG_FONT = 4
```

```
Global Const DLG_PRINT = 5
Global Const DLG_HELP = 6

'File Open/Save Dialog Flags
Global Const OFN_READONLY = &H1&
Global Const OFN_OVERWRITEPROMPT = &H2&
Global Const OFN_HIDEREADONLY = &H4&
Global Const OFN_NOCHANGEDIR = &H8&
Global Const OFN_SHOWHELP = &H10&
Global Const OFN_NOVALIDATE = &H100&
Global Const OFN_ALLOWMULTISELECT = &H200&
Global Const OFN_EXTENTIONDIFFERENT = &H400&
Global Const OFN_PATHMUSTEXIST = &H800&
Global Const OFN_FILEMUSTEXIST = &H1000&
Global Const OFN_CREATEPROMPT = &H2000&
Global Const OFN_SHAREAWARE = &H4000&
Global Const OFN_NOREADONLYRETURN = &H8000&

'Color Dialog Flags
Global Const CC_RGBINIT = &H1&
Global Const CC_FULLOPEN = &H2&
Global Const CC_PREVENTFULLOPEN = &H4&
Global Const CC_SHOWHELP = &H8&

'Fonts Dialog Flags
Global Const CF_SCREENFONTS = &H1&
Global Const CF_PRINTERFONTS = &H2&
Global Const CF_BOTH = &H3&
Global Const CF_SHOWHELP = &H4&
Global Const CF_INITTOLOGFONTSTRUCT = &H40&
Global Const CF_USESTYLE = &H80&
Global Const CF_EFFECTS = &H100&
Global Const CF_APPLY = &H200&
Global Const CF_ANSIONLY = &H400&
Global Const CF_NOVECTORFONTS = &H800&
Global Const CF_NOSIMULATIONS = &H1000&
Global Const CF_LIMITSIZE = &H2000&
Global Const CF_FIXEDPITCHONLY = &H4000&
Global Const CF_WYSIWYG = &H8000&          'must also have
                                           ' CF_SCREENFONTS &
                                           ' CF_PRINTERFONTS
```

18

continues

Listing 18.2. continued

```
Global Const CF_FORCEFONTEXIST = &H10000
Global Const CF_SCALABLEONLY = &H20000
Global Const CF_TTONLY = &H40000
Global Const CF_NOFACESEL = &H80000
Global Const CF_NOSTYLESEL = &H100000
Global Const CF_NOSIZESEL = &H200000

'Printer Dialog Flags
Global Const PD_ALLPAGES = &H0&
Global Const PD_SELECTION = &H1&
Global Const PD_PAGENUMS = &H2&
Global Const PD_NOSELECTION = &H4&
Global Const PD_NOPAGENUMS = &H8&
Global Const PD_COLLATE = &H10&
Global Const PD_PRINTTOFILE = &H20&
Global Const PD_PRINTSETUP = &H40&
Global Const PD_NOWARNING = &H80&
Global Const PD_RETURNDC = &H100&
Global Const PD_RETURNIC = &H200&
Global Const PD_RETURNDEFAULT = &H400&
Global Const PD_SHOWHELP = &H800&
Global Const PD_USEDEVMODECOPIES = &H40000
Global Const PD_DISABLEPRINTTOFILE = &H80000
Global Const PD_HIDEPRINTTOFILE = &H100000

'Help Constants
Global Const HELP_CONTEXT = &H1            'Display topic in
                                           ' ulTopic
Global Const HELP_QUIT = &H2               'Terminate help
Global Const HELP_INDEX = &H3              'Display index
Global Const HELP_CONTENTS = &H3
Global Const HELP_HELPONHELP = &H4         'Display help on using
                                           ' help
Global Const HELP_SETINDEX = &H5          'Set the current Index
                                           ' for multi index help
Global Const HELP_SETCONTENTS = &H5
Global Const HELP_CONTEXTPOPUP = &H8
Global Const HELP_FORCEFILE = &H9
Global Const HELP_KEY = &H101              'Display topic for
                                           ' keyword in offabData
Global Const HELP_COMMAND = &H102
```

```
Global Const HELP_PARTIALKEY = &H105        'call the search engine
                                            ' in winhelp


'Error Constants
Global Const CDERR_DIALOGFAILURE = &HFFFF

Global Const CDERR_GENERALCODES =&H0
Global Const CDERR_STRUCTSIZE = &H1
Global Const CDERR_INITIALIZATION = &H2
Global Const CDERR_NOTEMPLATE = &H3
Global Const CDERR_NOHINSTANCE = &H4
Global Const CDERR_LOADSTRFAILURE = &H5
Global Const CDERR_FINDRESFAILURE = &H6
Global Const CDERR_LOADRESFAILURE = &H7
Global Const CDERR_LOCKRESFAILURE = &H8
Global Const CDERR_MEMALLOCFAILURE = &H9
Global Const CDERR_MEMLOCKFAILURE = &HA
Global Const CDERR_NOHOOK = &HB

'Added for CMDLG.VBX
Global Const CDERR_CANCEL = &HC
Global Const CDERR_NODLL = &HD
Global Const CDERR_ERRPROC = &HE
Global Const CDERR_ALLOC = &HF
Global Const CDERR_HELP = &H10

Global Const PDERR_PRINTERCODES = &H1000
Global Const PDERR_SETUPFAILURE = &H1001
Global Const PDERR_PARSEFAILURE = &H1002
Global Const PDERR_RETDEFFAILURE = &H1003
Global Const PDERR_LOADDRVFAILURE = &H1004
Global Const PDERR_GETDEVMODEFAIL = &H1005
Global Const PDERR_INITFAILURE = &H1006
Global Const PDERR_NODEVICES = &H1007
Global Const PDERR_NODEFAULTPRN = &H1008
Global Const PDERR_DNDMMISMATCH = &H1009
Global Const PDERR_CREATEICFAILURE = &H100A
Global Const PDERR_PRINTERNOTFOUND = &H100B

Global Const CFERR_CHOOSEFONTCODES = &H2000
Global Const CFERR_NOFONTS = &H2001
```

continues

Listing 18.2. continued

```
Global Const FNERR_FILENAMECODES = &H3000
Global Const FNERR_SUBCLASSFAILURE = &H3001
Global Const FNERR_INVALIDFILENAME = &H3002
Global Const FNERR_BUFFERTOOSMALL = &H3003

Global Const FRERR_FINDREPLACECODES = &H4000
Global Const CCERR_CHOOSECOLORCODES = &H5000


'---------------------------------------
'GAUGE
'---------------------------------------
'Style Property
Global Const GAUGE_HORIZ = 0
Global Const GAUGE_VERT = 1
Global Const GAUGE_SEMI = 2
Global Const GAUGE_FULL = 3


'---------------------------------------
'Graph Control
'---------------------------------------
'General
Global Const G_NONE = 0
Global Const G_DEFAULT = 0

Global Const G_OFF = 0
Global Const G_ON = 1

Global Const G_MONO = 0
Global Const G_COLOR = 1

'Graph Types
Global Const G_PIE2D = 1
Global Const G_PIE3D = 2
Global Const G_BAR2D = 3
Global Const G_BAR3D = 4
Global Const G_GANTT = 5
Global Const G_LINE = 6
Global Const G_LOGLIN = 7
```

```
Global Const G_AREA = 8
Global Const G_SCATTER = 9
Global Const G_POLAR = 10
Global Const G_HLC = 11

'Colors
Global Const G_BLACK = 0
Global Const G_BLUE = 1
Global Const G_GREEN = 2
Global Const G_CYAN = 3
Global Const G_RED = 4
Global Const G_MAGENTA = 5
Global Const G_BROWN = 6
Global Const G_LIGHT_GRAY = 7
Global Const G_DARK_GRAY = 8
Global Const G_LIGHT_BLUE = 9
Global Const G_LIGHT_GREEN = 10
Global Const G_LIGHT_CYAN = 11
Global Const G_LIGHT_RED = 12
Global Const G_LIGHT_MAGENTA = 13
Global Const G_YELLOW = 14
Global Const G_WHITE = 15
Global Const G_AUTOBW = 16

'Patterns
Global Const G_SOLID = 0
Global Const G_HOLLOW = 1
Global Const G_HATCH1 = 2
Global Const G_HATCH2 = 3
Global Const G_HATCH3 = 4
Global Const G_HATCH4 = 5
Global Const G_HATCH5 = 6
Global Const G_HATCH6 = 7
Global Const G_BITMAP1 = 16
Global Const G_BITMAP2 = 17
Global Const G_BITMAP3 = 18
Global Const G_BITMAP4 = 19
Global Const G_BITMAP5 = 20
Global Const G_BITMAP6 = 21
Global Const G_BITMAP7 = 22
Global Const G_BITMAP8 = 23
```

18

continues

Listing 18.2. continued

```
Global Const G_BITMAP9 = 24
Global Const G_BITMAP10 = 25
Global Const G_BITMAP11 = 26
Global Const G_BITMAP12 = 27
Global Const G_BITMAP13 = 28
Global Const G_BITMAP14 = 29
Global Const G_BITMAP15 = 30
Global Const G_BITMAP16 = 31

'Symbols
Global Const G_CROSS_PLUS = 0
Global Const G_CROSS_TIMES = 1
Global Const G_TRIANGLE_UP = 2
Global Const G_SOLID_TRIANGLE_UP = 3
Global Const G_TRIANGLE_DOWN = 4
Global Const G_SOLID_TRIANGLE_DOWN = 5
Global Const G_SQUARE = 6
Global Const G_SOLID_SQUARE = 7
Global Const G_DIAMOND = 8
Global Const G_SOLID_DIAMOND = 9

'Line Styles
'Global Const G_SOLID = 0
Global Const G_DASH = 1
Global Const G_DOT = 2
Global Const G_DASHDOT = 3
Global Const G_DASHDOTDOT = 4

'Grids
Global Const G_HORIZONTAL = 1
Global Const G_VERTICAL = 2

'Statistics
Global Const G_MEAN = 1
Global Const G_MIN_MAX = 2
Global Const G_STD_DEV = 4
Global Const G_BEST_FIT = 8

'Data Arrays
Global Const G_GRAPH_DATA = 1
```

```
Global Const G_COLOR_DATA = 2
Global Const G_EXTRA_DATA = 3
Global Const G_LABEL_TEXT = 4
Global Const G_LEGEND_TEXT = 5
Global Const G_PATTERN_DATA = 6
Global Const G_SYMBOL_DATA = 7
Global Const G_XPOS_DATA = 8
Global Const G_ALL_DATA = 9


'Draw Mode
Global Const G_NO_ACTION = 0
Global Const G_CLEAR = 1
Global Const G_DRAW = 2
Global Const G_BLIT = 3
Global Const G_COPY = 4
Global Const G_PRINT = 5
Global Const G_WRITE = 6


'Print Options
Global Const G_BORDER = 2

'Pie Chart Options                '
Global Const G_NO_LINES = 1
Global Const G_COLORED = 2
Global Const G_PERCENTS = 4


'Bar Chart Options                '
'Global Const G_HORIZONTAL = 1
Global Const G_STACKED = 2
Global Const G_PERCENTAGE = 4
Global Const G_Z_CLUSTERED = 6


'Gantt Chart Options              '
Global Const G_SPACED_BARS = 1


'Line/Polar Chart Options          '
Global Const G_SYMBOLS = 1
Global Const G_STICKS = 2
Global Const G_LINES = 4
```

continues

Listing 18.2. continued

```
'Area Chart Options              '
Global Const G_ABSOLUTE = 1
Global Const G_PERCENT = 2

'HLC Chart Options               '
Global Const G_NO_CLOSE = 1
Global Const G_NO_HIGH_LOW = 2


'-------------------------------------------
'Key Status Control
'-------------------------------------------
'Style
Global Const KEYSTAT_CAPSLOCK = 0
Global Const KEYSTAT_NUMLOCK = 1
Global Const KEYSTAT_INSERT = 2
Global Const KEYSTAT_SCROLLLOCK = 3


'-------------------------------------------
'MCI Control (Multimedia)
'-------------------------------------------
'Mode Property
Global Const MCI_MODE_NOT_OPEN = 11
Global Const MCI_MODE_STOP = 12
Global Const MCI_MODE_PLAY = 13
Global Const MCI_MODE_RECORD = 14
Global Const MCI_MODE_SEEK = 15
Global Const MCI_MODE_PAUSE = 16
Global Const MCI_MODE_READY = 17

'NotifyValue Property
Global Const MCI_NOTIFY_SUCCESSFUL = 1
Global Const MCI_NOTIFY_SUPERSEDED = 2
Global Const MCI_ABORTED = 4
Global Const MCI_FAILURE = 8

'Orientation Property
Global Const MCI_ORIENT_HORZ = 0
Global Const MCI_ORIENT_VERT = 1
```

```
'RecordMode Property
Global Const MCI_RECORD_INSERT = 0
Global Const MCI_RECORD_OVERWRITE = 1

'TimeFormat Property
Global Const MCI_FORMAT_MILLISECONDS = 0
Global Const MCI_FORMAT_HMS = 1
Global Const MCI_FORMAT_FRAMES = 3
Global Const MCI_FORMAT_SMPTE_24 = 4
Global Const MCI_FORMAT_SMPTE_25 = 5
Global Const MCI_FORMAT_SMPTE_30 = 6
Global Const MCI_FORMAT_SMPTE_30DROP = 7
Global Const MCI_FORMAT_BYTES = 8
Global Const MCI_FORMAT_SAMPLES = 9
Global Const MCI_FORMAT_TMSF = 10


'----------------------------------------
'Spin Button
'----------------------------------------
'SpinOrientation
Global Const SPIN_VERTICAL = 0
Global Const SPIN_HORIZONTAL = 1


'----------------------------------------
'Masked Edit Control
'----------------------------------------
'ClipMode
Global Const ME_INCLIT = 0
Global Const ME_EXCLIT = 1


'----------------------------------------
'Comm Control
'----------------------------------------
'Handshaking
Global Const MSCOMM_HANDSHAKE_NONE = 0
Global Const MSCOMM_HANDSHAKE_XONXOFF = 1
Global Const MSCOMM_HANDSHAKE_RTS = 2
Global Const MSCOMM_HANDSHAKE_RTSXONXOFF = 3
```

18

continues

Listing 18.2. continued

```
'Event constants
Global Const MSCOMM_EV_SEND = 1
Global Const MSCOMM_EV_RECEIVE = 2
Global Const MSCOMM_EV_CTS = 3
Global Const MSCOMM_EV_DSR = 4
Global Const MSCOMM_EV_CD = 5
Global Const MSCOMM_EV_RING = 6
Global Const MSCOMM_EV_EOF = 7

'Error code constants
Global Const MSCOMM_ER_BREAK = 1001
Global Const MSCOMM_ER_CTSTO = 1002
Global Const MSCOMM_ER_DSRTO = 1003
Global Const MSCOMM_ER_FRAME = 1004
Global Const MSCOMM_ER_OVERRUN = 1006
Global Const MSCOMM_ER_CDTO = 1007
Global Const MSCOMM_ER_RXOVER = 1008
Global Const MSCOMM_ER_RXPARITY = 1009
Global Const MSCOMM_ER_TXFULL = 1010



'-------------------------------------------------
' VBMAPIM CONTROL CONSTANTS (MAPI SESSION CONTROL)
'-------------------------------------------------
'Action
Global Const SESSION_SIGNON = 1
Global Const SESSION_SIGNOFF = 2



'-------------------------------------------------
' VBMAPIM CONTROL CONSTANTS (MAPI MESSAGE CONTROL)
'-------------------------------------------------
'Action
Global Const MESSAGE_FETCH = 1          ' Load all messages
                                        ' from message store
Global Const MESSAGE_SENDDLG = 2        ' Send mail bring up
                                        ' default mapi dialog
Global Const MESSAGE_SEND = 3           ' Send mail without
                                        ' default mapi dialog
```

```
Global Const MESSAGE_SAVEMSG = 4           ' Save message in the
                                           ' compose buffer
Global Const MESSAGE_COPY = 5              ' Copy current message
                                           ' to compose buffer
Global Const MESSAGE_COMPOSE = 6          ' Initialize compose
                                           ' buffer (previous
                                           ' data is lost)
Global Const MESSAGE_REPLY = 7            ' Fill Compose buffer
                                           ' as REPLY
Global Const MESSAGE_REPLYALL = 8         ' Fill Compose buffer
                                           ' as REPLY ALL
Global Const MESSAGE_FORWARD = 9          ' Fill Compose buffer
                                           ' as FORWARD
Global Const MESSAGE_DELETE = 10          ' Delete current
                                           ' message
Global Const MESSAGE_SHOWADBOOK = 11      ' Show Address book
Global Const MESSAGE_SHOWDETAILS = 12     ' Show details of the
                                           ' current recipient
Global Const MESSAGE_RESOLVENAME = 13     ' Resolve the display
                                           ' name of the recipient
Global Const RECIPIENT_DELETE = 14        ' Fill Compose
                                           ' buffer as FORWARD
Global Const ATTACHMENT_DELETE = 15       ' Delete current
                                           ' message


'------------------------------------------------
'  ERROR CONSTANT DECLARATIONS (MAPI CONTROLS)
'------------------------------------------------
Global Const SUCCESS_SUCCESS = 32000
Global Const MAPI_USER_ABORT = 32001
Global Const MAPI_E_FAILURE  = 32002
Global Const MAPI_E_LOGIN_FAILURE = 32003
Global Const MAPI_E_DISK_FULL = 32004
Global Const MAPI_E_INSUFFICIENT_MEMORY = 32005
Global Const MAPI_E_ACCESS_DENIED = 32006
Global Const MAPI_E_TOO_MANY_SESSIONS = 32008
Global Const MAPI_E_TOO_MANY_FILES = 32009
Global Const MAPI_E_TOO_MANY_RECIPIENTS = 32010
Global Const MAPI_E_ATTACHMENT_NOT_FOUND = 32011
Global Const MAPI_E_ATTACHMENT_OPEN_FAILURE = 32012
```

continues

Listing 18.2. continued

```
Global Const MAPI_E_ATTACHMENT_WRITE_FAILURE = 32013
Global Const MAPI_E_UNKNOWN_RECIPIENT = 32014
Global Const MAPI_E_BAD_RECIPTYPE = 32015
Global Const MAPI_E_NO_MESSAGES = 32016
Global Const MAPI_E_INVALID_MESSAGE = 32017
Global Const MAPI_E_TEXT_TOO_LARGE = 32018
Global Const MAPI_E_INVALID_SESSION = 32019
Global Const MAPI_E_TYPE_NOT_SUPPORTED = 32020
Global Const MAPI_E_AMBIGUOUS_RECIPIENT = 32021
Global Const MAPI_E_MESSAGE_IN_USE = 32022
Global Const MAPI_E_NETWORK_FAILURE = 32023
Global Const MAPI_E_INVALID_EDITFIELDS = 32024
Global Const MAPI_E_INVALID_RECIPS = 32025
Global Const MAPI_E_NOT_SUPPORTED = 32026

Global Const CONTROL_E_SESSION_EXISTS = 32050
Global Const CONTROL_E_INVALID_BUFFER = 32051
Global Const CONTROL_E_INVALID_READ_BUFFER_ACTION = 32052
Global Const CONTROL_E_NO_SESSION = 32053
Global Const CONTROL_E_INVALID_RECIPIENT = 32054
Global Const CONTROL_E_INVALID_COMPOSE_BUFFER_ACTION = 32055
Global Const CONTROL_E_FAILURE = 32056
Global Const CONTROL_E_NO_RECIPIENTS = 32057
Global Const CONTROL_E_NO_ATTACHMENTS = 32058


'-------------------------------------------------
'  MISCELLANEOUS GLOBAL CONSTANT DECLARATIONS (MAPI CONTROLS)
'-------------------------------------------------
Global Const RECIPTYPE_ORIG = 0
Global Const RECIPTYPE_TO = 1
Global Const RECIPTYPE_CC = 2
Global Const RECIPTYPE_BCC = 3

Global Const ATTACHTYPE_DATA = 0
Global Const ATTACHTYPE_EOLE = 1
Global Const ATTACHTYPE_SOLE = 2
```

```
'------------------------------------------------
'   ODBC
'------------------------------------------------
'field type constants
Global Const FT_TRUEFALSE = 1
Global Const FT_BYTE = 2
Global Const FT_INTEGER = 3
Global Const FT_LONG = 4
Global Const FT_CURRENCY = 5
Global Const FT_SINGLE = 6
Global Const FT_DOUBLE = 7
Global Const FT_DATETIME = 8
Global Const FT_STRING = 10
Global Const FT_MEMO = 12
```

18

19

From Application To Application (Using DDE)

Another beauty of Windows is that it allows applications to exchange data through a protocol called Dynamic Data Exchange (DDE). As you've come to expect, Visual Basic makes it easy for you to tap into DDE and exchange data with any application that supports DDE, including the versatile Clipboard that comes with Windows.

Although many high-level programming languages (C and Pascal, for example) enable you to use the Windows DDE, no high-level language (that I know) makes it as direct as Visual Basic.

In this chapter, a DDE capability is added to the Editor you are developing. You use the Editor to cut, copy, and paste to the Clipboard

(using DDE). You add an optional picture box to the Editor form, which enables a user to paste and copy pictures to and from the form. Pasting text and pictures are two sides of the same coin. This new application, EDITOR3, includes the FileInFo form you developed earlier, as well as the error handler you added to the editor in the last chapter.

Working with Text

The easiest way to use DDE is with the Clipboard, so that's what this discussion concentrates on (for a more lengthy study see *Secrets of the Visual Basic Masters*, Sams Publishing 1992). Exchanging data with the Clipboard is not necessarily an end in itself. Any application that can talk to the Clipboard can get the data your application exchanges with the Clipboard. Your application can, in turn, retrieve data from other applications through the Clipboard. The Clipboard enables you to handle almost any exchange you need in a combination of ways.

The Clipboard is built into Windows and is available, at little overhead, to any application that requests it. The Clipboard isn't the ClipBoard Viewer, which you use to view the contents of the Clipboard. When an application uses the Clipboard to exchange text or graphics data, it does not have to open the Clipboard Viewer. The Clipboard Viewer can be open, but that's irrelevant to how the application uses the Clipboard.

Several extensions to the Editor are added in this chapter, but remember that these extensions are general and are intended to show you how DDE operates. In any application, you use a control, or controls, to communicate with the Clipboard. The best way to exchange text is through a text box control. If you want to exchange graphics, use a form or picture box.

EDITOR3 can exchange text and pictures with the Clipboard. Thus, the application needs several command buttons or menu items for handling user requests. EDITOR3 uses menus to handle those commands for a couple of reasons. Menus take up little space (one bar for the menu names and pop-up and pop-back menus)—at the top of the form, not in the working area. Command buttons take up space on the form and cut into the limited space on the form. This application has the capacity to use the entire form for display (whether text or pictures). Therefore, the only controls put on the form are the ones capable of exchanging data.

Beginning with the Editor (EDITOR2) from the last chapter and using its current controls (a text box), go directly to step 3 and the menu items.

Step 1—Use the Editor form (from EDITOR2).

Step 2—No new controls (yet). Use the existing text box to exchange data with the Clipboard.

Step 3—Add menu items.

Open the Menu Design window and add a new menu called Edit. Also add menu items for cutting, copying, and pasting text (see Figure 19.1).

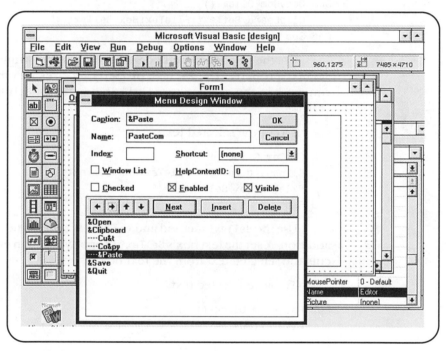

Figure 19.1. Menu Design for EDITOR3.

Step 4—The picture box in the Editor is PictureBox1. Any name is acceptable, as long as you use it consistently throughout the application.

Step 5—Write the event and general procedure code.

Select text in the text box to copy to the Clipboard.

> A text box in *Multiline* mode is a featured word processor and includes select and unselect text capability. You select text by pressing Ctrl+Shift while moving the arrow keys (left, right, and so on).

Because you want to copy, cut, and paste in response to menu selection, write event code for those menu items.

First, to copy the selected text:

```
Sub CopyCom_Click ()
    Clipboard.SetText FileTextBox.SelText
End Sub
```

Use the Clipboard method `SetText` to put the string contained in the `SelText` property. The `SelText` property receives its value from the text you mark in the text box (use Ctrl+Shift+arrow*)*. `FileTextBox` text box `CtlName`.

To cut the selected text:

```
Sub CutCom_Click ()
    Clipboard.SetText FileTextBox.SelText
    FileTextBox.SelText = ""
End Sub
```

Use the `SetText` method and the `SelText` properties as before, but, in addition, reset the text box's `SelText` property to `""` (an empty string). This cuts the selected text from the text box.

To paste selected text:

```
Sub PasteCom_Click ()
    FileTextBox.SelText = Clipboard.GetText()
End Sub
```

Set the `SelText` property in the text box to the string in the Clipboard. To get that string, use the Clipboard method `GetText()`.

That's all there is to it. During a copy, the text selected in the text box copies to the Clipboard. (Note that a copy of the selected text remains in the text box.) During a cut, the selected text in the text box copies to the Clipboard, but it is removed from the text box. During a paste, the text currently in the Clipboard copies to the text box.

You can also clear the Clipboard from your application using the `Clear` method:

```
Clipboard.Clear
```

You don't have to use the `Clear` method to clear the Clipboard before using it. It automatically clears before new text is added. For example, you might first paste the contents of the Clipboard to your application and clear the Clipboard:

```
TextBox1.SelText = Clipboard.GetText()
Clipboard.Clear
```

Figure 19.2 shows the Clipboard Viewer open (to show the contents of the Clipboard) before anything is copied or cut to it.

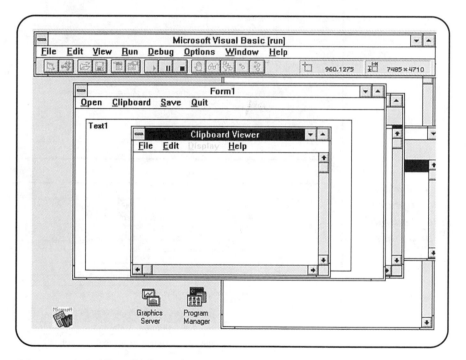

Figure 19.2. *The Clipboard Viewer.*

Figure 19.3 shows the EDITOR3 application with selected text.

Figure 19.4 shows the state of the Clipboard and the Editor applications after a copy.

Figure 19.5 shows the state of the Clipboard and the Editor applications after a cut.

Figure 19.6 shows the state of the Editor and Clipboard applications after a paste.

Figure 19.3.
Selected text
in EDITOR3.

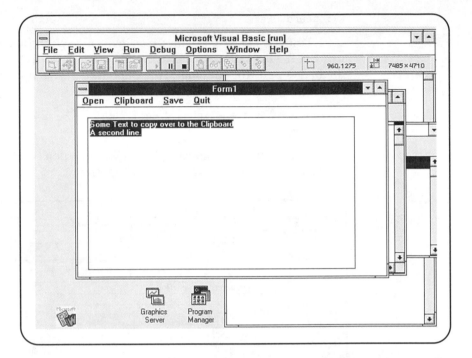

Figure 19.4.
The Clipboard
and the Editor
after a copy.

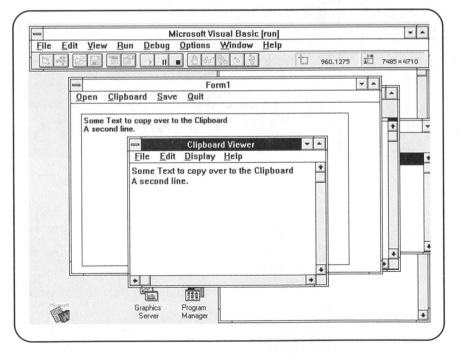

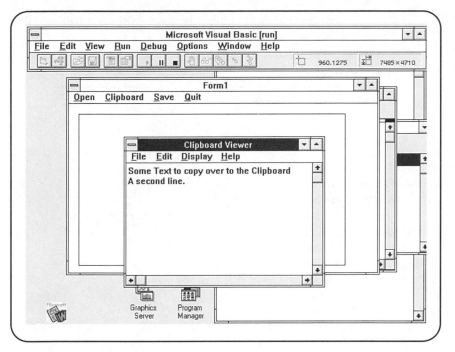

Figure 19.5.
The Clipboard and the Editor after a cut.

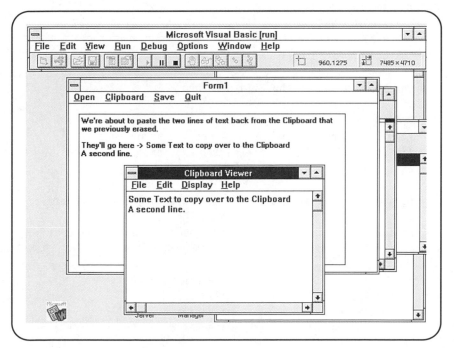

Figure 19.6.
The Clipboard and the Editor after a paste.

The complete code for this version of the application is contained in Listing 19.1.

Listing 19.1. EDITOR3.

```
' general declarations in module1


Global TheFileName As String
Global TheNewPath As String
Global FileInfoTitle As String
Global WorkingFileName As String

Global Const SAVEFILE = 1
Global Const LOADFILE = 2
Global Const REPLACEFILE = 1
Global Const READFILE = 2
Global Const ADDTOFILE = 3
Global Const RANDOMFILE = 4
Global Const BINARYFILE = 5

Const FileFormCLICK = 0
Const TEXTBOXCHANGE = 1
Const DIRSBOXCLICK = 2
Dim LastChange As Integer


' event procedures for the FileInFo form

Sub Drive1_Change ()
On Error GoTo ErrorHandler        ' Set the error trap
    If Err Then                    ' If Err, exit Sub
    Exit Sub
    End If
    Dir1.Path = Drive1.Drive       ' If no error, allow the drive '
                                   ' change
    Exit Sub      ' Make sure the error handler isn't called at the
                                   ' wrong time

ErrorHandler:                      ' Error Handler
    If Err Then                    ' If Err
     MsgBox Error$                 ' Report error
     Drive1.Drive = Dir1.Path      ' Reset drive to previous state
```

542

```
before error
    End If
    Resume                          ' Resume application at error
End Sub


Sub Dir1_Change ()
    File1.Path = Dir1.Path
    File1.SetFocus
    If File1.ListCount Then
     File1.ListIndex = 0
    End If
End Sub

Sub Dir1_Click ()
    LastChange = DIRSBOXCLICK
End Sub

Sub File1_Click ()
    LastChange = FileFormCLICK
End Sub

Sub File1_DblClick ()
    Command1_Click
End Sub

Sub Command1_Click ()
    TheNewPath = Dir1.Path
    If Right$(TheNewPath, 1) <> "\" Then
     TheNewPath = TheNewPath + "\"
    End If
    TheFileName = File1.FileName
    FileInfo.Hide
End Sub

Sub Command2_Click ()
    FileInfo.Hide
End Sub


' Editor form
```

19

continues

Listing 19.1. continued

```
' new copy/cut/paste events

Sub CopyCom_Click ()                    ' copy to clipboard
    Clipboard.SetText FileTextBox.SelText
End Sub

Sub CutCom_Click ()                      ' copy to clipboard & erase
                                         ' text
    Clipboard.SetText FileTextBox.SelText     ' that was copied
    FileTextBox.SelText = ""
End Sub

Sub PasteCom_Click ()                    ' copy from the clipboard
    FileTextBox.SelText = Clipboard.GetText() ' to the text box
End Sub



Function OpenAFile (NameToUse$, Mode%, RecordLen%) As Integer
    FileNum% = FreeFile
    On Error GoTo OpenFileError

    Select Case Mode
        Case ReplaceFile
            Open NameToUse For Output As FileNum%
        Case READFILE
            Open NameToUse For Input As FileNum%
        Case ADDTOFILE
            Open NameToUse For Append As FileNum%
        Case RANDOMFILE
            Open NameToUse For Random As FileNum% Len = RecordLen%
        Case BINARYFILE
            Open NameToUse For Binary As FileNum%
        Case Else
            Exit Function
    End Select
    OpenAFile = FileNum%
    Exit Function
```

```
OpenFileError:
    Action% = FileErrors(Err)
    Select Case Action%
        Case 0
            Resume
        Case Else
            OpenAFile = 0          'Open failed
            Exit Function
        End Select
End Function


Sub FileForm ()
    FileInfoTitle = "Open A File"
    FileInfo.Show MODAL
    WorkingFileName = TheNewPath + TheFileName
End Sub


Sub SaveAFile (ThisTextBox As Control)
    If ConfirmFile((WorkingFileName), ReplaceFile) Then
        FileNum% = OpenAFile((WorkingFileName), ReplaceFile, 0)
        If FileNum% = 0 Then
        Exit Sub
        End If
        Print #FileNum%, ThisTextBox.Text
        Close FileNum%
    End If
End Sub


Function FileErrors (errVal As Integer) As Integer      ' Translate
                                         ' error values
    msgType% = MB_EXCLAIM              ' to English
    Select Case errVal
        Case Err_DeviceUnavailable    ' Error #68
            Msg$ = "Device unavailable"
            msgType% = MB_EXCLAIM + 4
        Case Err_DiskNotReady          ' Error #71
            Msg$ = "Drive not ready."
        Case Err_DeviceIO             ' Error #57
            Msg$ = "Internal disk error"
            msgType% = MB_EXCLAIM + 4
```

continues

545

Listing 19.1. continued

```
        Case Err_DiskFull               ' Error #61
            Msg$ = "Disk full."
            msgType% = 35
        Case Err_BadFileName            ' Error #64
            Msg$ = "File name is illegal"
        Case Err_BadFileNameOrNumber   'Error #52
            Msg$ = "File name is illegal"
        Case Err_PathDoesNotExist       ' Error #76
            Msg$ = "Path does not exist."
        Case Err_BadFileMode            ' Error #54
            Msg$ = "Can't open file in current mode."
        Case Err_FileAlreadyOpen        ' Error #55
            Msg$ = "File already open"
        Case Err_InputPastEndOfFile     ' Error #62
            Msg$ = "Attempting to read past EOF"
        Case Else
            FileErrors = 3
            Exit Function
    End Select

    Response% = MsgBox(Msg$, msgType%, "Disk Error")      ' Tell
the user what's                                               '
happening.
    Select Case Response%                       ' User responds.
        Case 1, 4    ' OK, Retry buttons        ' Interpret the user's
                                                ' response.

            FileErrors = 0
        Case 5          ' Ignore buttons
            FileErrors = 1
        Case 2, 3    ' Cancel, abort buttons
            FileErrors = 2
        Case Else
            FileErrors = 3
    End Select
End Function

Function ConfirmFile (TheName As String, Operation As Integer) As
Integer
    On Error GoTo ConfirmFileError      'Turn on Error Trap
    TheFile$ = Dir$(TheName)            'Does file exist?
```

```
        On Error GoTo 0                      'Turn Error Trap off

        If TheFile$ <> "" And Operation = ReplaceFile Then
            Msg$ = "File exists. Do you want to overwrite?"
            Confirmation% = MsgBox(Msg$, 65, "File Message")
        ElseIf TheFile$ = "" And Operation = READFILE Then
            Msg$ = "File doesn't exist. Create it?"
            Confirmation% = MsgBox(Msg$, 65, "File Message")
        ElseIf TheFile$ = "" Then
            If Operation = RANDOMFILE Or Operation = BINARYFILE Then
                Confirmation% = 2
            End If
        End If

        If Confirmation% > 1 Then
            ConfirmFile = 0
        Else ConfirmFile = 1
        End If

        If Confirmation% = 1 Then
            If Operation = LOADFILE Then
                Operation = ReplaceFile
            End If
        End If
        Exit Function                    ' Don't fall into error handler.

ConfirmFileError:                        ' Error handler for the
                                         ' ConfirmFileError

        Action% = FileErrors(Err)
        Select Case Action%
            Case 0
                Resume
            Case 1
                Resume Next
            Case 2
                Exit Function
            Case Else
                Error Err
        End Select
End Function
```

continues

Listing 19.1. continued

```
Sub OpenCom_Click ()

    FileForm                    'Load FileInfo (Form & Controls)

    If WorkingFileName <> "" Then
        OpenMode% = LOADFILE
        FileNum% = OpenAFile(WorkingFileName, OpenMode%, 0)
    End If
    If FileNum% = 0 Then
        Exit Sub
    End If


    If LOF(FileNum%) > 32000 Then
        Msg$ = "File too large."
        Exit Sub
    End If

    Do Until EOF(FileNum%)
        Line Input #FileNum%, NextLine$
        LineFromFile$ = LineFromFile$ + NextLine$ + Chr$(13) +
Chr$(10)
    Loop

    FileTextBox.Text = LineFromFile$
    Editor.Caption = "Editing: " + WorkingFileName
    Close FileNum%
End Sub


Sub SaveCom_Click ()
    SaveAFile FileTextBox
End Sub

Sub ExitCom_Click ()
    End
End Sub
```

Working with Pictures

You can also exchange graphics data (pictures) with other applications through the Clipboard, using either the form or a picture box.

One possibility, developed here, is to add a picture option to an Editor. You can display text and graphics on a single form and manipulate each as distinct entities (a picture or text). You might move the picture box around the form, remove the picture box, clear it (to add new pictures), reshow it (after removing it), or save it to a file. The possibilities are extensive.

In EDITOR3, add a second control (a picture box called Picture1) to the form. Figure 19.7 shows the form (and controls) in design mode.

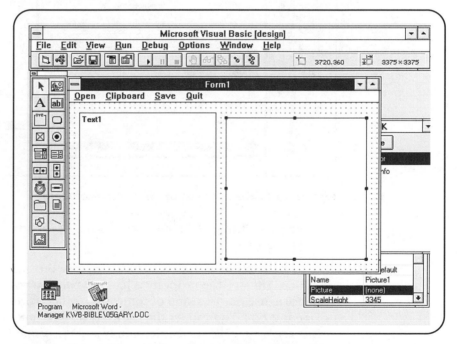

Figure 19.7. A form and its controls in design mode.

Step 1—Add the menu items: add a new menu called Picture and menu items for adding a picture, copying, pasting, deleting the picture, and saving the picture. In addition, add `AutoSize` and `Clip`, which are discussed shortly. Figure 19.8 shows the application in menu design mode.

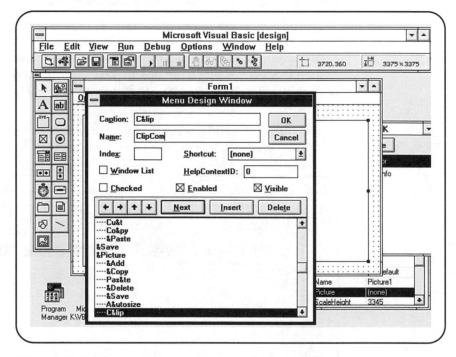

Figure 19.8. *The application in menu design mode.*

Step 2—Change the picture box `Visible` property to False (0) (see Figure 19.9).

In this way, the picture box doesn't appear on the form until the user asks for it. The `Visible` property is handy when you want to give the user a chance to use one of a kind of control—in other words, one picture box or one text box. You can let the user create, hide, and make the control visible at any time. For example, simply add the property change code to the application:

```
Picture1.Visible = -1   (make it visible)
```

```
Picture1.Visible = 0 (take it away)
```

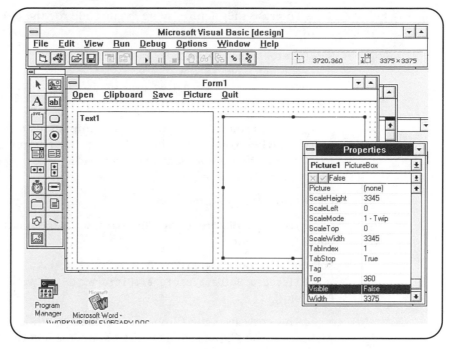

Figure 19.9. *Change the picture box* Visible *property to False.*

Step 3—Add the event and general procedure code.

Again, almost all the initial action begins with a menu item click, so add the following Click events.

Add a picture:

```
Sub AddPicCom_Click ()
    Picture1.Visible = -1
End Sub
```

To add a picture, simply show (make Visible) the picture box you created in design mode. The picture box isn't re-created when the user selects Add Picture—it's merely shown. Thus, it retains its contents from the last show. In the beginning, there will be an empty picture box if you don't put anything in the picture box at design time. (You didn't put a picture in it during design time in this application.) If a user copies a picture to the box (from the Clipboard in this application), that picture remains in the picture box unless the user erases it.

To erase the picture, write event code for the `DeletePicCom` menu event:

```
Sub DeletePicCom_Click ()
    Picture1.Visible = 0
    Picture1.Picture = LoadPicture()
End Sub
```

This code hides the picture box and empties, using the `LoadPicture()` function. When you use this function without a parameter, nothing loads to the picture box after it clears. You can load a file to the picture box, using `LoadPicture`, as follows:

```
LoadPicture("SomePicture.BMP")
```

To copy a picture to the Clipboard, write the following code for the `CopyPicCom` event:

```
Sub CopyPicCom_Click ()
    Clipboard.SetData Picture1.Picture, CF_BITMAP
End Sub
```

This code uses the Clipboard's `SetData` method to actually put the picture on the Clipboard. The last parameter lets the Clipboard know which kind of data it's receiving—it must know this because it handles various kinds of data (such as the text you copied to it earlier).

`CF_BITMAP` indicates a bitmap.

> `CF_BITMAP` is a symbolic constant (which the Clipboard recognizes). It and the other symbolic constants for the Clipboard are contained in CONSTANT.TXT. If you use the symbolic constants, you must either define them in code or copy the CONSTANT.TXT file to a module for the project.

To paste, reverse the copy. Send the Clipboard data back to the picture box:

```
Sub PastePicCom_Click ()
    Picture1.Picture = Clipboard.GetData(CF_BITMAP)
End Sub
```

Again, the Clipboard must know the kind of data you want. If the data in the Clipboard isn't the type you request, the data does not transfer. Thus, it's usually the responsibility of the application to know which kind of data it's receiving from the Clipboard.

If you use GetData and don't specify a data type, Visual Basic assumes you want a bitmap. If you use GetText (as earlier), Visual Basic only gets text.

To save a picture:

```
Sub SavePicCom_Click ()
    SavePicture Image, "Pix.bmp"
End Sub
```

Use the SavePicture statement to save the bitmap that's present on the form. The bitmap is the picture (in this example) that's in the picture box. Image represents a handle to the bitmap. This handle is automatically provided for you, and it is used by the operating system to locate and manipulate the bitmap.

SavePicture always saves an image (or picture) as a bitmap.

Two other events extend the picture's capability: AutoSizing and Clipping.

AutoSizeCom looks like this:

```
Sub AutoSizeCom_Click ()
    Picture1.AutoSize = -1
End Sub
```

This event changes the picture box from its current size to a size that holds the complete image you want to paste to the box. If AutoSize is True (-1), the picture box can expand. If AutoSize is False (0), the picture box does not expand. Instead, it clips the picture to the picture so it fits.

ClipPicCom looks like this:

```
Sub ClipPicCom_Click ()
    Picture1.AutoSize = 0
End Sub
```

Figures 19.10 and 19.11 show the EDITOR3 application running with the picture box added and in Clip (Figure 19.10) and AutoSize (Figure 19.11) modes.

Figure 19.10.
Picture box added and in Clip mode.

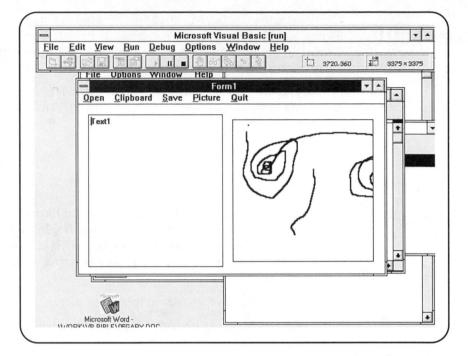

Figure 19.11.
Picture box added and in AutoSize mode.

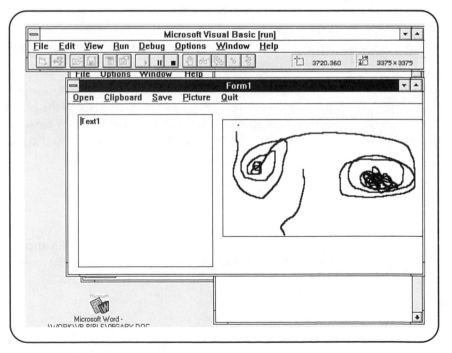

Return to Dragging

This application (and other similar applications that enable the user to control "controls") can benefit by making the picture box dynamic. That is, you can allow a user, operating a MouseMove event, to drag the picture box to a new location.

To accomplish this picture box movement, begin with a MouseDown event:

```
Sub Picture1_MouseDown (Button As Integer, Shift As Integer, X As
Single, Y As Single)
    Picture1.Drag 1
End Sub
```

This code activates (as an event) when the user presses a picture box with a mouse button. Picture1_MouseDown uses a Drag method to initiate a drag. The argument (1) indicates you're beginning to drag.

When the user releases the mouse, a MouseUp event generates:

```
Sub Picture1_MouseUp (Button As Integer, Shift As Integer, X As
Single, Y As Single)
    Picture1.Drag 2
End Sub
```

Use another message to the Drag method to indicate that the drag is done. The argument (2) signals the end of a drag.

Notice, however, at this point nothing has happened to the control. If you try this code as is, an outline of the picture box moves across the form, but after you release the mouse, the picture box returns to its original place.

To actually move the picture box, write a DragDrop event for the form:

```
Sub Form_DragDrop (Source As Control, X As Single, Y As Single)
    Picture1.Move X, Y
End Sub
```

This code indicates you want the control (called Source) to move to the new coordinates. The mouse events occur as the user clicks on the picture box. The DragDrop occurs as a form-level event (Figures 19.12 and 19.13 demonstrate this code).

19

Figure 19.12.
Moving the picture box.

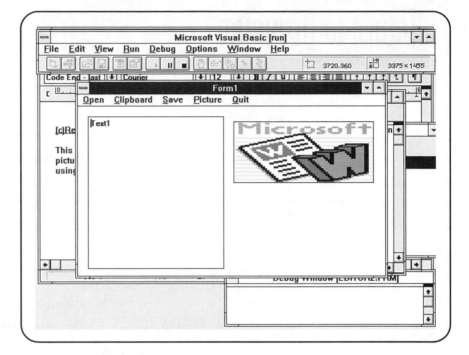

Figure 19.13.
Moving the picture box to another location.

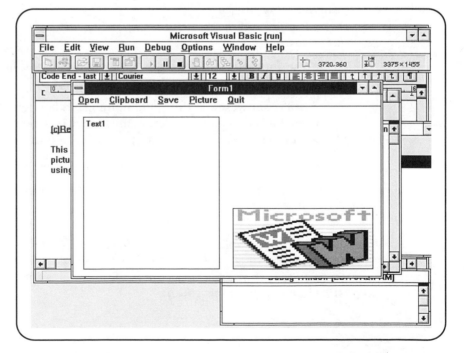

Listing 19.2 shows the complete code for EDITOR4.

Listing 19.2. EDITOR4.

```
Global TheFileName As String
Global TheNewPath As String
Global FileInfoTitle As String
Global WorkingFileName As String

Global Const SAVEFILE = 1
Global Const LOADFILE = 2
Global Const REPLACEFILE = 1
Global Const READFILE = 2
Global Const ADDTOFILE = 3
Global Const RANDOMFILE = 4
Global Const BINARYFILE = 5

Const FileFormCLICK = 0
Const TEXTBOXCHANGE = 1
Const DIRSBOXCLICK = 2
Dim LastChange As Integer

' event procedures for the FileInFo form

Sub Drive1_Change ()
On Error GoTo ErrorHandler        ' Set the error trap
    If Err Then                   ' If Err, exit Sub
    Exit Sub
    End If
    Dir1.Path = Drive1.Drive      ' If no error, allow the drive
                                  ' change
    Exit Sub      ' Make sure the error handler isn't called at the
                  ' wrong time

ErrorHandler:                     ' Error Handler
    If Err Then                   ' If Err
     MsgBox Error$                ' Report error
     Drive1.Drive = Dir1.Path     ' Reset drive to previous state
                                  ' before error
    End If
    Resume                        ' Resume application at error
End Sub
```

continues

Listing 19.2. continued

```
Sub Dir1_Change ()
    File1.Path = Dir1.Path
    File1.SetFocus
    If File1.ListCount Then
     File1.ListIndex = 0
    End If
End Sub


Sub Dir1_Click ()
    LastChange = DIRSBOXCLICK
End Sub


Sub File1_Click ()
    LastChange = FileFormCLICK
End Sub


Sub File1_DblClick ()
    Command1_Click
End Sub


Sub Command1_Click ()
    TheNewPath = Dir1.Path
    If Right$(TheNewPath, 1) <> "\" Then
     TheNewPath = TheNewPath + "\"
    End If
    TheFileName = File1.FileName
    FileInfo.Hide
End Sub


Sub Command2_Click ()
    FileInfo.Hide
End Sub



' Editor form

    ' form level variables if you want to base new
    ' picture position on Drag coordinates (optional)
Dim DragX As Single      ' for dragging the picture
Dim DragY As Single
```

```
Sub CopyCom_Click ()                      ' copy to clipboard
    Clipboard.SetText FileTextBox.SelText
End Sub

Sub CutCom_Click ()                       ' copy to clipboard & erase
                                          ' text
    Clipboard.SetText FileTextBox.SelText     ' that was copied
    FileTextBox.SelText = ""
End Sub

Sub PasteCom_Click ()                     ' copy from the clipboard
    FileTextBox.SelText = Clipboard.GetText() ' to the text box
End Sub



Function OpenAFile (NameToUse$, Mode%, RecordLen%) As Integer
    FileNum% = FreeFile
    On Error GoTo OpenFileError

    Select Case Mode
        Case ReplaceFile
            Open NameToUse For Output As FileNum%
        Case READFILE
            Open NameToUse For Input As FileNum%
        Case ADDTOFILE
            Open NameToUse For Append As FileNum%
        Case RANDOMFILE
            Open NameToUse For Random As FileNum% Len = RecordLen%
        Case BINARYFILE
            Open NameToUse For Binary As FileNum%
        Case Else
            Exit Function
    End Select
    OpenAFile = FileNum%
    Exit Function

OpenFileError:
    Action% = FileErrors(Err)
    Select Case Action%
        Case 0
            Resume
```

Listing 19.2. continued

```
        Case Else
            OpenAFile = 0          'Open failed
            Exit Function
        End Select
End Function

Sub FileForm ()
    FileInfoTitle = "Open A File"
    FileInfo.Show MODAL
    WorkingFileName = TheNewPath + TheFileName
End Sub

Sub SaveAFile (ThisTextBox As Control)
    If ConfirmFile((WorkingFileName), ReplaceFile) Then
        FileNum% = OpenAFile((WorkingFileName), ReplaceFile, 0)
        If FileNum% = 0 Then
        Exit Sub
        End If
        Print #FileNum%, ThisTextBox.Text
        Close FileNum%
    End If
End Sub

Function FileErrors (errVal As Integer) As Integer   ' Translate
                                                     ' error values
    msgType% = MB_EXCLAIM                ' to English
    Select Case errVal
        Case Err_DeviceUnavailable     ' Error #68
            Msg$ = "Device unavailable"
            msgType% = MB_EXCLAIM + 4
        Case Err_DiskNotReady          ' Error #71
            Msg$ = "Drive not ready."
        Case Err_DeviceIO              ' Error #57
            Msg$ = "Internal disk error"
            msgType% = MB_EXCLAIM + 4
        Case Err_DiskFull              ' Error #61
            Msg$ = "Disk full."
            msgType% = 35
        Case Err_BadFileName           ' Error #64
            Msg$ = "File name is illegal"
```

```
            Case Err_BadFileNameOrNumber   'Error #52
                Msg$ = "File name is illegal"
            Case Err_PathDoesNotExist       ' Error #76
                Msg$ = "Path does not exist."
            Case Err_BadFileMode            ' Error #54
                Msg$ = "Can't open file in current mode."
            Case Err_FileAlreadyOpen        ' Error #55
                Msg$ = "File already open"
            Case Err_InputPastEndOfFile     ' Error #62
                Msg$ = "Attempting to read past EOF"
            Case Else
                FileErrors = 3
                Exit Function
        End Select

        Response% = MsgBox(Msg$, msgType%, "Disk Error")      ' Tell
the user what's                                               '
happening.
        Select Case Response%                    ' User responds.
            Case 1, 4    ' OK, Retry buttons     ' Interpret the user's
                                                 ' response.

                FileErrors = 0
            Case 5        ' Ignore buttons
                FileErrors = 1
            Case 2, 3    ' Cancel, abort buttons
                FileErrors = 2
            Case Else
                FileErrors = 3
        End Select
End Function


Function ConfirmFile (TheName As String, Operation As Integer) As
Integer
        On Error GoTo ConfirmFileError       'Turn on Error Trap
        TheFile$ = Dir$(TheName)             'Does file exist?
        On Error GoTo 0                      'Turn Error Trap off

        If TheFile$ <> "" And Operation = ReplaceFile Then
            Msg$ = "File exists. Do you want to overwrite?"
            Confirmation% = MsgBox(Msg$, 65, "File Message")
```

continues

561

Listing 19.2. continued

```
    ElseIf TheFile$ = "" And Operation = READFILE Then
        Msg$ = "File doesn't exist. Create it?"
        Confirmation% = MsgBox(Msg$, 65, "File Message")
    ElseIf TheFile$ = "" Then
        If Operation = RANDOMFILE Or Operation = BINARYFILE Then
            Confirmation% = 2
        End If
    End If


    If Confirmation% > 1 Then
        ConfirmFile = 0
    Else ConfirmFile = 1
    End If


    If Confirmation% = 1 Then
        If Operation = LOADFILE Then
            Operation = ReplaceFile
        End If
    End If
    Exit Function                    ' Don't fall into error handler.

ConfirmFileError:                    ' Error handler for the
ConfirmFileError
    Action% = FileErrors(Err)
    Select Case Action%
        Case 0
            Resume
        Case 1
            Resume Next
        Case 2
            Exit Function
        Case Else
            Error Err
    End Select
End Function



Sub OpenCom_Click ()

    FileForm                    'Load FileInfo (Form & Controls)
```

```
    If WorkingFileName <> "" Then
        OpenMode% = LOADFILE
        FileNum% = OpenAFile(WorkingFileName, OpenMode%, 0)
    End If
    If FileNum% = 0 Then
        Exit Sub
    End If


    If LOF(FileNum%) > 32000 Then
        Msg$ = "File too large."
        Exit Sub
    End If

    Do Until EOF(FileNum%)
        Line Input #FileNum%, NextLine$
        LineFromFile$ = LineFromFile$ + NextLine$ + Chr$(13) +
Chr$(10)
    Loop

    FileTextBox.Text = LineFromFile$
    Editor.Caption = "Editing: " + WorkingFileName
    Close FileNum%
End Sub


Sub SaveCom_Click ()
    SaveAFile FileTextBox
End Sub

Sub ExitCom_Click ()
    End
End Sub

Sub AddPicCom_Click ()
    Picture1.Visible = -1
End Sub


Sub Picture1_MouseDown (Button As Integer, Shift As Integer, X As
Single, Y As Single)
```

continues

Listing 19.2. continued

```
    Picture1.Drag 1
    DragX = X        ' Save these, if you want to use current X
                     ' and Y
    DragY = Y        ' to base drag on (optional)
End Sub

Sub Picture1_MouseUp (Button As Integer, Shift As Integer, X As
Single, Y As Single)
    Picture1.Drag 2
End Sub

Sub Form_DragDrop (Source As Control, X As Single, Y As Single)
    Picture1.Move X, Y
End Sub


Sub AutoSizeCom_Click ()
    Picture1.AutoSize = -1
End Sub


Sub ClipPicCom_Click ()
    Picture1.AutoSize = 0
End Sub


Sub PastePicCom_Click ()
    Picture1.Picture = Clipboard.GetData(CF_BITMAP)
End Sub


Sub DeletePicCom_Click ()
    Picture1.Visible = 0
    Picture1.Picture = LoadPicture()
End Sub


Sub CopyPicCom_Click ()
    Clipboard.SetData Picture1.Picture, CF_BITMAP
End Sub
```

```
Sub SavePicCom_Click ()
    SavePicture Image, "Pix.bmp"
End Sub
```

Summary

The simplest way to exchange data with another application is by using the Clipboard. Figure 19.14 gives a visual version of how DDE works. The Editor created in this chapter sends data to the Clipboard. Microsoft Word then plucks that data from the Clipboard into this chapter.

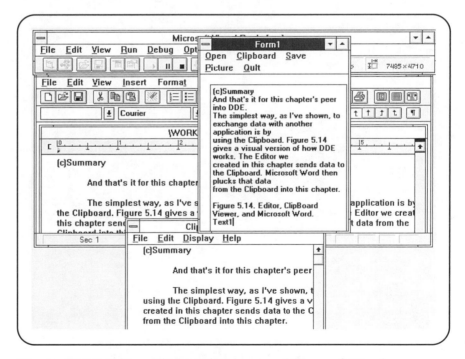

Figure 19.14. Editor, Clipboard Viewer, and Microsoft Word.

Part IV

Appendixes

ASCII/ANSI Code Chart

This is the Windows/Visual Basic version of the ANSI chart. All character information in BASIC applications is stored as strings of codes. The most commonly used characters are the ASCII codes (American Standard Code for Information Interchange), which comprise the first 128 codes in this table. Windows applications actually support most of the 256 character ANSI (American National Standards Institute) code set, of which the ASCII codes are a subset. The following table contains the ANSI characters, and their ASCII/ANSI codes in both hexadecimal and decimal format. Missing codes are unsupported by Windows.

Character	Hex code	Decimal code
Backspace	&H08	8
Tab	&H09	9
Line feed	&H0A	10
Carriage return	&H0D	13
Space	&H20	32
!	&H21	33

Character	Hex code	Decimal code
”	&H22	34
#	&H23	35
$	&H24	36
%	&H25	37
&	&H26	38
'	&H27	39
(	&H28	40
)	&H29	41
*	&H2A	42
+	&H2B	43
,	&H2C	44
-	&H2D	45
.	&H2E	46
/	&H2F	47
0	&H30	48
1	&H31	49
2	&H32	50
3	&H33	51
4	&H34	52
5	&H35	53
6	&H36	54
7	&H37	55
8	&H38	56
9	&H39	57
:	&H3A	58
;	&H3B	59
<	&H3C	60

Character	Hex code	Decimal code
=	&H3D	61
>	&H3E	62
?	&H3F	63
@	&H40	64
A	&H41	65
B	&H42	66
C	&H43	67
D	&H44	68
E	&H45	69
F	&H46	70
G	&H47	71
H	&H48	72
I	&H49	73
J	&H4A	74
K	&H4B	75
L	&H4C	76
M	&H4D	77
N	&H4E	78
O	&H4F	79
P	&H50	80
Q	&H51	81
R	&H52	82
S	&H53	83
T	&H54	84
U	&H55	85
V	&H56	86
W	&H57	87

A

Character	Hex code	Decimal code
X	&H58	88
Y	&H59	89
Z	&H5A	90
[	&H5B	91
\	&H5C	92
]	&H5D	93
^	&H5E	94
_	&H5F	95
`	&H60	96
a	&H61	97
b	&H62	98
c	&H63	99
d	&H64	100
e	&H65	101
f	&H66	102
g	&H67	103
h	&H68	104
i	&H69	105
j	&H6A	106
k	&H6B	107
l	&H6C	108
m	&H6D	109
n	&H6E	110
o	&H6F	111
p	&H70	112
q	&H71	113
r	&H72	114

Character	Hex code	Decimal code
s	&H73	115
t	&H74	116
u	&H75	117
v	&H76	118
w	&H77	119
x	&H78	120
y	&H79	121
z	&H7A	122
{	&H7B	123
¦	&H7C	124
}	&H7D	125
~	&H7E	126
.	&H91	145
.	&H92	146
..	&H93	147
..	&H94	148
O	&H95	149
–	&H96	150
–	&H97	151
	&HA0	160
¡	&HA1	161
¢	&HA2	162
£	&HA3	163
⊗	&HA4	164
¥	&HA5	165
¦	&HA6	166
§	&HA7	167

A

573

Character	Hex code	Decimal code
"	&HA8	168
·	&HA9	169
ª	&HAA	170
«	&HAB	171
¬	&HAC	172
–	&HAD	173
·	&HAE	174
–	&HAF	175
°	&HB0	176
±	&HB1	177
²	&HB2	178
·	&HB3	179
,	&HB4	180
µ	&HB5	181
·	&HB6	182
■	&HB7	183
,	&HB8	184
·	&HB9	185
º	&HBA	186
»	&HBB	187
¼	&HBC	188
½	&HBD	189
·	&HBE	190
¿	&HBF	191
À	&HC0	192
Á	&HC1	193
Â	&HC2	194

Character	Hex code	Decimal code
Ã	&HC3	195
Ä	&HC4	196
Å	&HC5	197
Æ	&HC6	198
Ç	&HC7	199
È	&HC8	200
É	&HC9	201
Ê	&HCA	202
Ë	&HCB	203
Ì	&HCC	204
Í	&HCD	205
Î	&HCE	206
'I	&HCF	207
Đ	&HD0	208
Ñ	&HD1	209
Ò	&HD2	210
Ó	&HD3	211
Ô	&HD4	212
Ǒ	&HD5	213
Ö	&HD6	214
.	&HD7	215
ø	&HD8	216
Ù	&HD9	217
Ú	&HDA	218
Û	&HDB	219
Ü	&HDC	220
Ÿ	&HDD	221

A

Character	Hex code	Decimal code
Þ	&HDE	222
ß	&HDF	223
à	&HE0	224
á	&HE1	225
â	&HE2	226
ã	&HE3	227
ä	&HE4	228
å	&HE5	229
æ	&HE6	230
ç	&HE7	231
è	&HE8	232
é	&HE9	233
ê	&HEA	234
ë	&HEB	235
ì	&HEC	236
í	&HED	237
î	&HEE	238
ï	&HEF	239
ð	&HF0	240
ñ	&HF1	241
ò	&HF2	242
ó	&HF3	243
ô	&HF4	244
õ	&HF5	245
ö	&HF6	246
·	&HF7	247
ø	&HF8	248

Character	Hex code	Decimal code
ù	&HF9	249
ú	&HFA	250
û	&HFB	251
ü	&HFC	252
ỳ	&HFD	253
b	&HFE	254
ÿ	&HFF	255

Key Code Chart

The key codes given in the following chart are needed by the KeyUp and KeyDown event procedures. These key codes identify particular keys on the keyboard that are being pressed, rather than the characters that the keys represent. Thus, they don't differentiate between shifted and unshifted keys, and keys on the keypad return different key codes from the same keys on the main keyboard. Not every keyboard supports all of these codes.

Key	Hex code	Decimal code
LeftMouseButton	&H1	1
RightMouseButton	&H2	2
Cancel	&H3	3
MiddleMouseButton	&H4	4
Backspace	&H8	8
Tab	&H9	9
Clear	&HC	12
Return	&HD	13
Shift	&H10	16
Control	&H11	17
Menu	&H12	18

Key	Hex code	Decimal code
Pause	&H13	19
CapsLock	&H14	20
Esc	&H1B	27
Spacebar	&H20	32
PageUp	&H21	33
PageDown	&H22	34
End	&H23	35
Home	&H24	36
LeftArrow	&H25	37
UpArrow	&H26	38
RightArrow	&H27	39
DownArrow	&H28	40
Select	&H29	41
Print	&H2A	42
Execute	&H2B	43
SnapShot	&H2C	44
Insert	&H2D	45
Delete	&H2E	46
Help	&H2F	47
0	&H30	48
1	&H31	49
2	&H32	50
3	&H33	51
4	&H34	52
5	&H35	53
6	&H36	54
7	&H37	55
8	&H38	56
9	&H39	57
A	&H41	59
B	&H42	60
C	&H43	61
D	&H44	62
E	&H45	63
F	&H46	64
G	&H47	65
H	&H48	66
I	&H49	67
J	&H4A	68
K	&H4B	69

Key	Hex code	Decimal code
L	&H4C	70
M	&H4D	71
N	&H4E	72
O	&H4F	73
P	&H50	74
Q	&H51	75
R	&H52	76
S	&H53	77
T	&H54	78
U	&H55	79
V	&H56	80
W	&H57	81
X	&H58	82
Y	&H59	83
Z	&H5A	84
0	&H60	90
1	&H61	91
2	&H62	92
3	&H63	93
4	&H64	94
5	&H65	95
6	&H66	96
7	&H67	97
8	&H68	98
9	&H69	99
;	&HBA	186
=	&HBB	187
,	&HBC	188
-	&HBD	189
.	&HBE	190
/	&HBF	191
`	&HC0	192
[	&HDB	219
\	&HDC	220
]	&HDD	221
`	&HDE	222
ScrollLock	&H91	145

B

581

Key	Hex code	Decimal code
Keypad Keys		
*	&H6A	106
+	&H6B	107
Separator	&H6C	108
-	&H6D	109
.	&H6E	110
/	&H6F	111
NumLock	&H90	144
Function Keys		
F1	&H70	112
F2	&H71	113
F3	&H72	114
F4	&H73	115
F5	&H74	116
F6	&H75	117
F7	&H76	118
F8	&H77	119
F9	&H78	120
F10	&H79	121
F11	&H7A	122
F12	&H7B	123
F13	&H7C	124
F14	&H7D	125
F15	&H7E	126
F16	&H7F	127

Index

Do It Yourself Visual Basic for Windows Examples Disk

If you want to use all the examples in this book, but don't want to type them yourself, you can obtain them on disk. Complete the following order form and return it to the address below with a check or money order for $20.00, US currency only. For countries outside of the United States and Canada, please add $1.00 for overseas shipping. For California orders, please add state sales tax (7.25%). The Visual Basic for Windows examples disk will be sent to you by first-class mail. Please specify the disk size.

William J. Orvis
226 Joyce St.
Livermore, CA 94550

Name: _____

Address: _____

City/State/Zip: _____

Disk Price $20.00

    Overseas shipping $1.00   _____
    (outside of the U.S. and Canada)

    State sales tax (7.25% = $1.45)   _____
    (California only)

Total   _____

Enclosed is my check or money order for $_____
(Make checks payable to William J. Orvis.) Please
send me the Visual Basic for Windows Examples Disk.

I prefer: ___5 1/4-inch disk

           ___3 1/2-inch disk

Sams Publishing is not affiliated with William J. Orvis
and assumes no responsibility for any defect in the disk programs.

Visual Basic for Windows Programs *Continued from inside front cover*

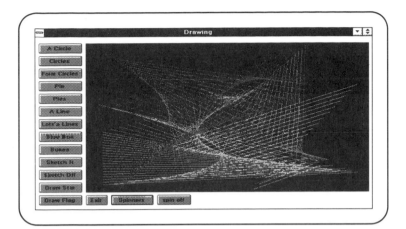

Plate III.
The Drawing Test program after the Spinners command.

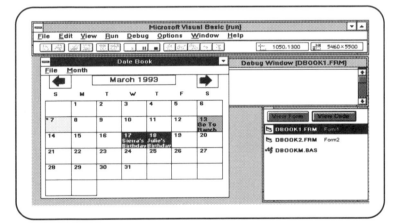

Plate IV.
The Datebook program.

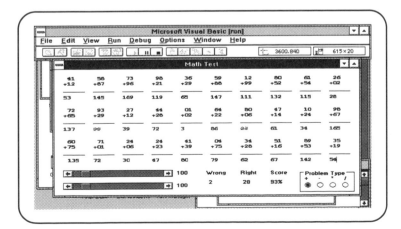

Plate V.
The Self-Paced Learning program, showing the result of correct and incorrect answers.

If you're just learning to program for the first time, or if you're making the switch to Windows™ programming, this is a great place to start. Packed with examples, this book shows you how to write feature-filled programs—complete with dialog boxes, buttons, and more.

The text is organized so that you build your programming knowledge in logical blocks. Now it's easy to adapt these skills to the new world of event-driven logic. Each topic is reinforced by exercises—while the step-by-step, hands-on approach leads you through the development of a complex application. You discover how to control the new Toolbar, the Object Browser, SQL server, and utilize keywords that increase the program's functionality. With the excellent sample programs included, you learn to build your own envelope addresser, self-paced learning program, check register, day planner, and drawing program. Plus, you learn more advanced topics, including how to program complex Windows events, how to assign properties to objects for your own personal programming touch, and how to implement Dynamic Data Exchange in your programs.

Do it yourself—and achieve programming success—with *Do-It-Yourself Visual Basic® for Windows*, Second Edition!

The Simplest Way to Learn Visual Basic Programming

- Detailed explanations help you work with the graphical user interface, objects, and menus

- Complete command reference documents all Visual Basic commands, properties, events, and objects

- Step-by-step demonstration of the most effective ways to design, create, develop, and enhance an application

- In-depth debugging and error-handling techniques

- Thorough coverage of Version 2.0 enhancements

GUARANTEED
TIMELY & ACCURATE

Approved for
Technical
Accuracy
by
Gary
Entsminger

INFORMATION CENTER

Beginning / Intermediate
How To
IBM Compatible
Programming
Visual Basic for Windows 2.0

SAMS
PUBLISHING

$24.95 US/$31.95 CAN

ISBN 0-672-30259-4

90000

9 780672 302596